Sacred Scripture

A Catholic Study of God's Word

DANAJ

Sacred Scripture

A Catholic Study of God's Word

Daniel Smith-Christopher
Rev. J. Patrick Mullen

ave maria press · notre dame, indiana

The Subcommittee on the Catechism, United States Conference of Catholic Bishops, has found that this catechetical text, copyright 2013, is in conformity with the *Catechism of the Catholic Church* and that it fulfills the requirements of Elective Course A of the *Doctrinal Elements of a Curriculum Framework for the Development of Catechetical Materials for Young People of High School Age.*

Nihil Obstat: Reverend Monsignor Michael Heintz, PhD
Censor Liborum

Imprimatur: Most Reverend Kevin C. Rhoades
Bishop of Fort Wayne-South Bend

Given at: Fort Wayne, Indiana, on 6 January 2012

Theological Consultant:
Rev. Thomas Jones, C.S.C.
Adjunct Professor of Theology
University of Notre Dame
Notre Dame, Indiana

www.avemariapress.com

Founded in 1865, Ave Maria Press is a ministry of the United States Province of Holy Cross.
Engaging Minds, Hearts, and Hands for Faith® is a trademark of Ave Maria Press, Inc.
ISBN-10 1-59471-171-2   ISBN-13 978-1-59471-171-8
Cover and text design by Andy Wagoner
Cover images © Thinkstock.
Printed and bound in the United States of America.

Engaging Minds, Hearts, and Hands for Faith

An education that is complete is the one
in which hands and heart are engaged
as much as the mind. We want to let our
students try their learning in the world and
so make prayers of their education.

—Bl. Basil Moreau, C.S.C.
Founder of the Congregation of Holy Cross

The Bible is a record of the divine plan of Salvation, of the presence of God in these holy words, and of his desire to share his merciful love with you. This text is a companion to the reading, studying, and praying with Sacred Scripture. The task is encouraged through

uncovering details of the composition of Sacred Scripture, including authorship and themes, to enhance a greater appreciation of the Bible as God's inspired Word.

engaging with the words of Scripture through reflection and prayer while continuing to ask how the Sacred Word is speaking to you.

taking up the message of essential Good News of the Bible and sharing it with others to the ends of the earth.

Contents

INTRODUCTION TO
SACRED SCRIPTURE

A Hunger for God
The Bible is a source of Divine Revelation that can help you to seek out God—who is also looking for you.

What Is the Bible?
For Catholics and most Christians, the Bible is a written record of God's Revelation.

Who Wrote the Bible? A Question of Inspiration
God inspired human authors to write the Bible and the Church to determine which books would be in its official canon.

How Can We Read the Bible?
The Bible must be read differently than any other book. It is primarily a prayer book reflecting on God's presence and inspiration.

A Hunger for God

As you move into adulthood, leaving childhood and adolescence behind, old relationships with parents mature and change, and new relationships with friends and potential spouses take on a new importance. At the same time, faced with opportunities at college and in employment, you may quite rightly find yourself asking new questions. And you may not be so readily accepting of old answers as you once were. This can be an exciting time, but also a time of inner turmoil and deep unfulfilled longing for meaning and companionship.

You were created by God for a purpose, part of which is to find happiness. So, foremost among your means of successfully negotiating life's new prospects at this time of change is to discover the plan that God has for you. New experiences, the struggle to be independent, being in love, having your heart broken, witnessing how much suffering there is in the world—and sometimes in your own life—all help you recognize how necessary it is to have a more *adult* relationship with God. In fact, you, along with many others your age, may experience a great *hunger* for the presence of God, who is the answer to so much of what we want out of life and each other. In that spirit, the ancient psalmist prayed, with anguish, fervor, and hope:

> O God, you are my God—
>   for you I long!
> For you my body yearns;
>   for you my soul thirsts,
> Like a land parched, lifeless,
>   and without water.
> So I look to you in the sanctuary
>   to see your power and glory.
> For your love is better than life;
>   my lips offer you worship! (Ps 63:2–4)

You have likely already recognized that you are not just an accident of the universe. You were fashioned by a Creator, and for a purpose. Inevitably, since God is *good*, fulfilling that end for which you were made will lead to your lasting joy and contentment. The psalmist understood this. The hunger you have to understand, fit in, express yourself, and be at peace are all intimately tied up with God's ultimate purposes and the way you cooperate with his plan—or not.

Thus, it is appropriate to hunger for more from this relationship, not simply because you are leaving the ways of a child behind, but because the pursuit of God's will is the only real way forward to a path of happiness and fulfillment. What you will discover once you begin the pursuit of understanding God and his will is that there will *always* be room for growth. At the same time, curiously, some of the most difficult struggles to be fully adult will also help you to gain the wisdom needed to enter into that relationship in a deeper, more satisfying way.

The Pursuit of God

Find a number of ways to develop a deeper understanding of God in your pursuit of that deeper relationship. You can find evidence of God in the beauty, complexity, wildness, and vast expanse of the created universe around us. St. Paul wrote in the Letter to the Romans, "Ever since the creation of the world, [God's] invisible attributes of eternal power and divinity have been able to be understood and perceived in what he has made" (Rom 1:20). The observant person celebrates the magnificence of both the easily experienced beauties of nature and the amazing complexities of living beings. We can also experience God in the best relationships we have with other people, who are made in God's image and likeness (Gn 1:26–28). In order to enter into real intimacy with God, we can only do so with the help of his grace. Through the natural light of human reason, we have the capacity to know God and to welcome him into our lives. Over the centuries, God gradually disclosed himself. The fullness of **Divine Revelation** is Jesus Christ, the Son of God made man, in whom God has established his covenant forever. The Son is the Father's definitive Word, and there is no further Revelation after Jesus. Hence, the richest experience of knowing God comes in the full participation in the sacramental life of the Church.

One of the most enriching aspects of the Church's experience of God comes from its reception of Divine Revelation

in the Bible. What you can discover in the Bible is that while you are seeking something more satisfying from God, he is seeking the same from you. In fact, the record of the Bible shows that God has been working throughout the entire course of human history to reach out to humanity and fashion a permanent bond with us, to last into eternity.

This book is intended to help you to consider how the Bible fits into your personal life, your life as a member of the Catholic Church, and to help you to understand God, hear his voice, and respond well.

Reflect

How do you imagine what it would be like to have an "adult relationship" with God?

Divine Revelation
The way God communicates knowledge of himself to humankind, a self-communication realized by his actions and words over time, most fully by his sending us his divine Son, Jesus Christ.

What Is the Bible?

If you ask several different people to define the Bible and explain why it matters, you would get several different answers. For Catholics and, in fact, for most Christians, the Bible is God's communication, God's *Word* in written form. From century to century, believers have found in the Bible comfort and challenge, support and guidance, teaching and correction that they have recognized, especially with deep study, as having come from God.

When respected people—such as presidents, priests, teachers, and parents—speak, wise people listen. Consider those individuals who are important and trustworthy to you in your own life and how carefully you pay attention to them. Being attentive is all the more important with God. It is astounding to consider even the possibility that God, who is infinite, all-powerful, and all-knowing, would make the effort to spend time communicating with us, his creation. In the Bible, God did precisely that.

Of all the materials and sources of information you might study, there is probably nothing more useful than the Bible—precisely because it speaks to questions that matter most: how you ought to treat parents or be treated by them; how you should respond to peer pressure; and why sex should be reserved for marriage. We might also ask, What does it mean to *really* love, or to be in love? Is it ever permissible to tell a lie? How should others treat us? The list of possible questions addressed by the Bible goes on and on, even addressing questions you might not have now, but will matter to you in the near future—when you have children or employees of your own, when you are sick or lonely, when your nation goes to war and asks you to serve in the military, or when you are trying to decide what matters most when voting.

The answers to these questions aren't always easy to find. The more you know about the Bible and consider its content, the clearer idea you will have on any given issue concerning God's perspective. With this assistance, you will be quicker at finding the answers you will be seeking. So, the Bible is key to understanding God and what matters to him, how God thinks, and how God is, in fact, speaking to *you* about your own life. For this very reason, it is easy to understand why the Bible is the best-selling book of all time, with over six billion copies sold in modern times.

As you will see, the Bible is filled with many rewards for those who pray with it. It can also be even more rewarding for those who study the Bible, which does have its challenges. Many parts of it require understanding other cultures, languages (Hebrew, Aramaic, or Greek), styles of writing (e.g., genealogies and epistles), or simply engaging in careful literature study that helps us to understand how things all fit together. A good place to start is to consider how the Bible came to be at all.

🔵 Review

What are some challenges of Bible study?

Who Wrote the Bible? A Question of Inspiration

Usually we know who wrote a book because the author's name is listed on the cover and title page. Most of the time, an author's biography is included as well. Sometimes, though, authors have been known to hide their identities with pseudonyms, such as Mark Twain, whose real name, as you know, was Samuel Clemens. It also happens that some authors have ghostwritten books for others. This often happens when the "author" of a biography, perhaps an actor, politician, or sports figure, is not really a proficient writer. He or she might use the services of a professional writer to make sure that his or her life is interesting and the biography well written.

The question "Who is the author?" should be an important one regarding the Bible. Curiously, many people, Catholics included, have never spent time considering the authorship of different Bible books, not to mention how they were written, how they were recognized as the Word of God, and how they were collected into one book. It's not enough to say, simply, that "God is the author," since the clouds did *not* open up and angels did *not* descend on powerful wings, presenting the believers of the Church with a completed text of the Sacred Scriptures, handwritten by God himself. God inspired human authors to compose the Bible.

The Bible's complex formation begins with each of its two sections, the Old Testament and the New Testament. Each have very different histories. *Sacred Scripture: A Catholic Study of God's Word* discusses how the two Testaments came to be and resulted in their current forms. For now, we will simply state that the ancient Israelites (called "Jews" after the Babylonian exile) and the earliest Christians believed that certain writings so clearly indicated that God's Spirit had guided the writers. The writings themselves were understood to be *inspired.* In other words, the Bible was a team effort where various people willingly cooperated with God's promptings while writing. Medieval artists painted portraits of biblical authors. The Holy Spirit, in the form of a dove, sat on the authors' shoulders and whispered into their ears—in essence, giving dictation. More likely, though, the authors wrote to the best of their abilities, responding to circumstances of their own time and place while using their God-given gifts. As you can see, this is not precisely like ghostwriting. Some authors were provoked by the evils they saw; others, like the psalmists, were moved to create expressions of their happiness, worry, fear, anguish, or triumph. Others, seeing a need for greater understanding, wrote Gospels and letters to teach, challenge, support, and comfort.

Some works, like the Book of Isaiah, took more than one generation of writing and more than one writer to reach the form we have now. Others, such as the very short Letter to Philemon, were probably composed in a single sitting. Many Old Testament books were written by very sophisticated people who had the best educations that their world offered. The Gospel of Mark, though, seems to have been composed by someone who, though clearly brilliant, was not particularly well educated, and may not even have been literate. If this is true, the author of Mark's Gospel would have had to dictate his entire book to a scribe. If so, he wouldn't have been the only one to get such help. For an example of how St. Paul used scribes, check out the end of his Letter to the Romans, 16:21–22, where the scribe, Tertius, while taking dictation from St. Paul, added a small greeting to Paul's letter.

Many Old Testament books were written for the great and powerful people who led the Israelites; others were written about those leaders, or even to challenge them; yet others, some of the most rich—and yet confusing—books of the Old Testament, were written to instruct priests in their care of the Temple and its rituals. Some New Testament books, such as the writings of St. Paul, were very practical responses to questions the early Christians posed, as in his two Letters to the Corinthians. These questions came to him through messengers, such as Timothy (1 Thes 3:6–3:7), or by letters, like the one from Chloe and her people (1 Cor 1:11). The Gospels, written to proclaim the life and teachings of Jesus, serve as the most important books of the Bible for Christians.

Some people today would be more comfortable with understanding the Bible if they knew that God simply took control of the writer, dictating word for word all of its content. But if you consider how God has been at work in your own life, then you will admit that God has never forced or manipulated you, or anyone else you know, to do or say anything. God has certainly encouraged you through your conscience and guidance from the good people around you. But *force* you? That is just not God's way. So it makes no sense to suggest that God would operate any differently with the people who assisted in the writing of Scripture.

As a result, some ideas, and even documents, had to pass through a number of editions and writers before they reached the final form that pleased God and communicated the fullness of what God wanted to convey. The guarantee, though, is that since God was so intimately involved in the authoring of the books of the Bible, we can depend on the Scriptures to accurately inform us of messages and teachings that God wants us to hear and know. This leads us to consider the Bible's primary message . A careful review of both the Old Testament and New Testament reveals that a primary message of the Bible is that God desires to save humanity from the terrible consequences of sin. We can also recognize that this Salvation extends beyond the events in this world to an eternal life to be shared with God forever. Being all-knowing and all-powerful, God always succeeds in his plans. Since the Bible is God's work, it only makes sense that we can depend on God to successfully communicate in its pages what we need to understand about our Salvation. As the Second Letter to Timothy states, "All scripture is inspired by God and is useful for teaching, for refutation, for correction, and for training in righteousness, so that one who belongs to God may be competent, equipped for every good work" (2 Tm 3:16–17).

Another important lesson to consider is that God's inspiration only *starts* with individual authors writing the books of the Bible. Once a book was written, it had to be recognized as God's inspired word. Many other religious writings from the Jews and early Christians were not accepted as inspired Scripture. For Catholics, deciding which books to include in the Old Testament meant recognizing that the Jews were God's Chosen People, and that their inspired books set the stage for the coming of the Messiah, Jesus Christ. (The title "Christ" means "Anointed One" or "Messiah.") Early Church leaders, who received their position through the inspiration of the Holy Spirit and **apostolic succession**, determined which writings were suitable to include in a *canon*, or official collection of biblical books.

Some books of the New Testament were chosen because they were associated very early on with eyewitnesses to Jesus' life and ministry. The Gospel of John is described as the eyewitness testimony of the "Beloved Disciple" (Jn 21:24). Other Gospels and books of the New Testament were accepted because their authors were understood to be the companions of the actual eyewitnesses. This may have been the case for Mark's Gospel. Eusebius, an early Church historian writing around AD 300, quoted Bishop Papias of Heirapolis (ca. AD 125?) who claimed that an unnamed "elder" had reported the following:

> Mark, who was Peter's interpreter, accurately wrote as much as he remembered of what the Lord did and said, although it was not in an orderly sequence, for Mark neither heard nor followed the Lord.

It was Peter who fashioned the teachings as necessary. When doing so, though, Peter did not give an orderly account of the Lord's words. So Mark did not err when writing the things he could remember, since his one intention was neither to omit nor to falsify them.

In fact, it took a few centuries before the early Church was able to determine with certainty which of the many books written after the time of Jesus should be considered suitable for proclamation and, hence, part of the New Testament. In the first centuries of the Church's history, some people were as motivated by non-Christian thoughts and ideas as they were by the teachings and life of Jesus. Because of these outside influences, the beliefs of some, who came to be known as Gnostics, were not acceptable to the Church. The disagreements between them, though, led the early Church to carefully examine what was truly necessary for belief, and what was erroneous. The majority of Gnostic writings simply were not faithful to the tradition handed down by Jesus and his eyewitnesses and shared with early Church members. As a result, they were not accepted into the New Testament canon. St. Athanasius, writing in AD 367, is the earliest Father of the Church to provide us with a complete list of all twenty-seven books of the New Testament that survive to this day.

apostolic succession
The handing on of the preaching and authority of the Apostles to their successors, the bishops, through the laying on of hands, as a permanent office in the Church.

In summary, "inspiration" implies more than simply a writer cooperating with God to produce a text. It also involves the guidance of the Holy Spirit to determine which books are inspired, and those that are not. The Church-approved canon of the Bible finally included forty-six Old Testament books—along with the twenty-seven books of the New Testament.

Reflect

- In what ways have you experienced God's inspiration in your life?
- Tell about a time that you have used (or can imagine using) the Bible for prayer or inspiration.

Why We Study the Bible

The Bible has passages that are both beautiful and inspiring, and others that are heartrending and shocking. The entire Bible is suitable for study as good literature. The primary purpose for Catholics to study the Bible is to help them to understand what God is saying in the texts. On the other hand, because human authors of the Bible wrote in ancient times, their understanding of things like history, physics, biology, the geography of distant lands, and the like, are much different from what is accepted as fact today. For example, people who had no concept of modern historical writing actually wrote many biblical texts that resemble what today might be considered historical accounts.

More importantly, the Bible tells us that the Sacred Scriptures "are capable of giving [us] wisdom for salvation through faith in Christ Jesus" (2 Tm 3:15–17) and the assurance that since God inspired the Scriptures, they are useful for teaching, rebuking, and correcting. This makes sense, since we recognize that God's primary purpose, while respecting our free will, is to bring us close in this life and to share eternal life with us in death. We have every reason to trust that God is all-powerful and all-knowing, and he accomplishes everything he sets out to do. If God *wants* to communicate with us, it's going to happen. If the Holy Spirit inspires a person to write, and the Church to recognize that writing as inspired by God, the writing will faithfully convey as much as God desires from it. For this reason, the Bible is *inerrant*—meaning that all the *religious* truths that God desires us to understand for the

sake of our Salvation are dependable, without error, and thus, trustworthy.

As you read the Bible, know that it is not intended to serve as a historical account. History, by and large, is not critical for Salvation. Also, while the sciences reveal the splendor of God's handiwork, knowledge of the sciences is not critical for Salvation, either. Nor are the details of geography essential to our relationship with God. Not all Christians read the Bible that way. Some take a literal or fundamentalist view, and hold that the entire Bible is inerrant in historical, scientific, and geographical detail because God, literally, is the author. Catholics carefully recognize that inerrancy extends to those things essential for our Salvation, and with spiritual maturity, ask whether it is necessary to extend inerrancy over every written detail in the Bible.

Review

1. What does it mean to say that God inspired the human authors of the Bible?

2. What is a primary message of the Bible?

3. Explain why God's inspiration of Scripture only starts with the writing of the books of the Bible by the individual authors.

4. Why did it take until the fourth century before the Church determined with certainty which books made up the New Testament?

5. How many books were approved by the Church in the final canon of the Bible?

6. What does it mean to say that the Bible is inerrant?

Reflect

Share an example that points out how historical facts differ from religious truth.

How Can We Read the Bible?

Because the uniqueness of the Bible is God's inspired word, it must be read differently than any other type of book. Above all, the Bible must be read as a prayer book, reflecting God's presence and inspiration. To enhance further Bible study, use the guidelines listed below, which are explained in the following sections. For reading biblical passages:

• Consider how the Church understands the passage.

• Realize that the Bible was written by multiple authors.

• Consider the intentions of the original author.

• Recognize the genre.

• Put the passage in context, both within its own text and within the Bible as a whole.

• Use a commentary, and read the notes.

• Remember that Sacred Scripture and Sacred Tradition are "bound closely together, and communicate one with the other" (*CCC*, 80).

Know What the Church Teaches

Sacred Tradition
The living transmission of the Church's Gospel message found in the Church's teaching, life, and worship. It is faithfully preserved, handed on, and interpreted by the Church's Magisterium.

First and foremost, it is important to remember that the Bible is the Book of the Church. Catholics believe that Sacred Scripture is the "speech of God as it is put down in writing under the breath of the Holy Spirit" (*Dei Verbum*, 9). The inspired texts of the Bible contain the fullness of God's Revelation. The task of interpreting God's Word (both in Sacred Scripture and **Sacred Tradition**) is entrusted to the Church alone.

That the Bible is the "Book of the Church" is significant, because for many Christians the opposite is true: they belong to a "church of the Book." Several Christian denominations do not assign equal weight to Scripture and Tradition. For some Christians, the Bible is God's *final* Revelation to the world. Answers to every human concern and modern issue can be answered according to this view. This is not the way that Catholics understand the Bible.

Remember that the Holy Spirit inspired the biblical authors to write, and then assisted the early Church in recognizing which writings were authentic. Even then, the Holy Spirit's work is not complete regarding the Bible. It is every bit as important that the Church understands God's Word. With this in mind, the Spirit has, from the beginning, assisted the Church to interpret, teach, and proclaim God's Word to the world, and especially to those who believe.

The Psalms insist that "[t]he generation to come will be told of the Lord, that they may proclaim to a people yet unborn the deliverance you have brought" (Ps 22:32). The Church, from its first days, has taken this mission seriously, studying all of the passages of the Bible. This project required drawing connections between the words of the prophets and Jesus' life. It also used Jesus' life and teaching as the primary lens for understanding all the beliefs of those who came before him. In fact, in the words of Sacred Scripture, God "speaks only one single Word, his one Utterance in whom he expresses himself completely" (*CCC*, 102). That word is Christ. The Church quite rightly reexamines how it applies Jesus' teaching in this or that particular time and place. The Spirit guides this process so that the Word can take root in the lives of those who read it and bear fruit. As the Book of Isaiah prophesied:

> For just as from the heavens
> the rain and snow come down
> And do not return there

till they have watered the earth,
	making it fertile and fruitful,
Giving seed to him who sows
	and bread to him who eats,
So shall my word be
	that goes forth from my mouth;
It shall not return to me void,
	but shall do my will,
	achieving the end for which I sent it.
(Is 55:10–11)

According to an ancient tradition, Scripture can be distinguished between two *senses*: the literal and the spiritual. The spiritual sense can be subdivided into the allegorical, moral, and anagogical senses.

The *literal sense* is what the words mean at the surface level and, as it was understood at the time, how things actually happened. The *spiritual sense* or mystical sense refers to not the words themselves, but rather what is *signified by* the words. The further divisions explain the spiritual sense more. The *allegorical sense* reasons out doctrine, those things we are supposed to believe, from the details of the biblical narratives and recognizes the significance of Christ in scriptural events. The *moral sense* seeks instruction for living and behaving; that is, what we are to do. The *anagogical sense* derives heavenly matters from the earthly matters described in the narrative; that is, what is being awaited—eternal life. For example, the Church on earth is a sign of our destiny in Heaven.

Two medieval examples help us to understand more about these terms (though the senses of Scripture are found not only in the medieval period, but also in antiquity and in Sacred Scripture itself). First, look at different ways to think about the city of Jerusalem. It was literally a city in the mountainous regions of Judea; allegorically, it represented the Church; morally, it symbolized the upright, moral soul; anagogically it epitomized the coming heavenly Jerusalem.

Next, consider the Exodus of the Chosen People from Egypt in the Old Testament. The Exodus, literally, was a historical fact; allegorically, it represented Jesus' Salvation of the world; morally, it symbolized the individual's conversion to God; anagogically, it embodied, in death, our departure from this life to the eternal life of Heaven.

It is possible to take these interpretive lenses too far. For example, using this often free and expressive kind of interpretation, St. Augustine, while preaching on the second multiplication of the loaves (Mk 8:1–9), concluded that the seven loaves represented the sevenfold work of the Holy Spirit, the four thousand men were all people from the four corners of the earth, and the seven baskets of fragments were the perfection of the Church. These interpretations are not part of the Church's official teaching.

But we can see, in other circumstances, that these interpretive approaches can help us frame some key questions that we might ask, particularly of narrative portions of Scripture (as opposed to letters or

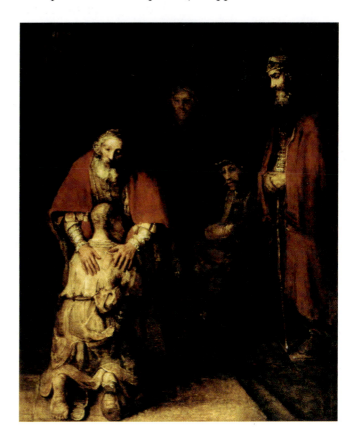

sermons). For example, when we read the parable of the prodigal son (Lk 15:11–32) we have to ask ourselves: did the story actually happen, or is it just a parable, a story from Jesus? What should we believe as a result of this story? Who do the characters represent? Is the father meant to represent the future of God, or people at their best? Are we the younger son or the older? Does the story imply any moral implications of greed and self-indulgence, intolerance, and judgmental behavior? Does it suggest that we should be quick to ask forgiveness, give pardon, or both? Is the banquet just a family celebration, or does it represent the heavenly banquet?

If a fool never learns, and an average person only learns from his or her own experiences, the real strength is to be like the wise men and women able to learn from the knowledge and understanding of others. By understanding the four senses of Scripture, your Bible reading will be transformed. By using this Catholic approach to the Word of God, you can more easily overcome the distance of time and discover the intimate solidarity that exists between the People of God in the Bible and your life in the Catholic Church today. In that spirit, every Catholic who reads the Bible needs to examine and take seriously the wisdom of the Church in every age. It makes sense, then, for you to spend time studying the Bible and its teachings with others, especially guided by Catholic religious education programs, high school religion classes, parish youth groups, college courses, and campus ministry programs.

Review

What do you think is the meaning of the parable of the prodigal son (Luke 15:11-32)?

Consider Multiple Authorship

If a single author had witnessed to all of the events portrayed in Scripture and wrote the books of the Bible, we would read the Bible differently. Actually, an ancient tradition says that Moses was the sole human author of the *Pentateuch*, the first five books of the Bible (Genesis, Exodus, Leviticus, Numbers, and Deuteronomy). This viewpoint obviously overlooked some important details. For example, Moses's death, burial, and subsequent mourning for him are recorded in Deuteronomy 34:5–8. It is an extraordinary author who can describe his own death and burial! Today, the Church accepts that several different people were actually responsible for authoring the texts of the Pentateuch, while not denying the role of Moses in its development. For one thing, Moses was lawgiver *par excellence*.

Within several Bible books, readers can detect a complete change in literary style and vocabulary from one passage to another, indicating more evidence of multiple authorship. Consider Genesis 15:5,

for example, where God takes Abram outside and asks him to count the number of the stars in the sky. Only a few verses later, in Genesis 15:12, though, the sun is only *then* beginning to set! Apparently two completely distinct stories, one about God's agreement to provide Abram with a son (verses 1–6), and another where God promises to give Abram land (verses 7–12), were combined into a new, joint account of God's covenant with Abram.

Many of the Old Testament books have very complex histories, were written by several authors, are from vastly different time periods, and were often refashioned by later editors/authors to address entirely new problems and questions. Wherever this is the case, it is good for us to know who was writing or editing, to whom they were writing, and the current political, social, and religious issues they were addressing before we begin the study process. The kind of Bible study based on looking at its sources and history, in both the Old and New Testaments, is called the **historical-critical method**. Some believers may be uncomfortable because they would like the Bible to be historically accurate in every detail, and the historical-critical method is often very suspicious of historical details in the Bible. The starting point for Catholics, though, is that God is speaking to us—whether the text is historical writing or not. If the historical-critical method can help us to identify the real author and time of writing, then we can better know the real context the stories and teachings addressed, helping us to interpret them correctly. The Pontifical Biblical Commission wrote that

> the historical-critical method is the indispensable method for the scientific study of the meaning of ancient texts. Holy Scripture, inasmuch as it is the "word of God in human language," has been composed by human authors in all its various parts and in all the sources that lie behind them. Because of this, its proper understanding not only admits the use of this method but actually requires it. ("The Interpretation of the Bible in the Church")

The Pontifical Biblical Commission also stated in the same report an even more crucial point that "no scientific method for the study of the Bible is fully adequate to comprehend the biblical texts in all their richness. For all its overall validity, the historical-critical method cannot claim to be totally sufficient in this respect." For that reason, the Church utilizes the method among others for studying the biblical texts.

Several passages help to engage the historical-critical method. For example, knowing that the story of Noah and the Great Flood (Gn 7) was borrowed from much earlier sources can help us to understand the point of the story. When the Chosen People were exiled in Babylon, the story was written in the

historical-critical method

A method the Church uses for understanding biblical texts in their original setting and for discovering the intention of the original author.

Epic of Gilgamesh
Part of a well-circulated Mesopotamian poem discovered to have been in circulation in the ancient world as early as 2000 BC. While there are similarities to this Epic and the Noah flood story, the biblical story is unique because it shows how God reveals himself to humans and hints to humans' eventual destiny.

form we have today. The Jews in Babylon were caught in a situation similar to Noah's. Their homes, towns, cities, and Temple had all been destroyed. While in Babylon, they also learned that they weren't as special as they thought. Jerusalem wasn't really the center of the world—Babylon was much more impressive. Even the great Temple of Solomon wasn't as imposing as the Babylonian ziggurats. Their whole understanding of who they were and how they fit into the world had crumbled. They were like Noah on that ark, surrounded by a sea of utter destruction.

Centric to the Noah story, though, is a key verse: "And God remembered Noah" (Gn 8:1). At that point, the floodwater receded, Noah and the animals were rescued from the ark, Noah built an altar, and God made a covenant with him. For the Babylonian exiles, the Noah story's purpose was *not* to teach ancient history, but to promise the exiles that if they could be as faithful to God in their time of trial as Noah had been in his, then God would remember *them.* The floodwater would recede in their own lives. They would return and rebuild their homes, towns, and cities, and God would renew a covenant with them.

Reading the story from the perspective of the actual time it was written offers new insights. Acknowledging that it is likely not historically based doesn't damage the meaning. Rather, we recognize that the story of Noah and the Great Flood was an instruction from God for the Jews to remain faithful in

hard times. It is an offer of hope for future generations. Understanding this, we can then apply the *real* point of the passage to our own lives. We, too, are challenged to remain faithful to God when it seems as though our own lives have crumbled around us. God, still using this story to talk with the present age, promises to remember *us*, too.

Scholars recognized that the Noah story was actually borrowed from more ancient stories, such as the flood hero Utnapishtim from the **Epic of Gilgamesh**. They determined that the monotheistic Israelite ancestors of the Babylonian exiles completely reworked the story's pagan roots to make it relevant to them. Scholars also realized that a couple of different versions were combined to create the form we have today—altering the story so that at its very heart, everyone could hear and appreciate the message that God remembers Noah (and us) in distress.

Consider the Intentions of the Original Author

The historical-critical method helps us to view biblical passages and books in the context of the inspired author and the original audience. It is one of the most important first steps in listening to God's voice in the Scriptures.

The people who wrote the Bible had no glass windows, polyester clothing, plastic bottles, machine-milled cloth, prescription lenses, pharmaceutical pain relievers, electricity—or *any*

of the things that electricity makes possible: hair dryers, televisions, computers, telephones, MP3 players, electric lights—the list of things from our world they didn't have or even think of goes on and on. The original human authors of the Bible could not have possibly imagined what our lives would be like today. We, too, can easily forget (or, perhaps, have never learned) what life was like in the Middle East two to three thousand years ago. It's hard for us to imagine their world, in which most people were illiterate, where people lived on the edge of hunger most of their lives, and where approximately 75 percent of those who didn't die as infants were dead by their mid-twenties. In fact, archeological evidence suggests that 60 percent of those who survived infancy were already dead by age sixteen. *That* statistic is bound to make us think about how different life was back then.

Ancient people also had very different ideas about human behavior. Slavery was *normal*. Fathers often had power of life and death over their children. Husbands had legal control of their wives. A very small percentage of people, less than 5 percent, owned almost everything and controlled the government. Religion and government (church and state) were *not* separate, as the state often interfered in and controlled religion.

When we consider the differences in the way of life between then and now, it's surprising how much of the Bible actually makes profound sense to us. Many things, though, if we are not careful, can confuse and mislead us. For example, if we don't know why almost all women covered their hair when they went out in public in biblical times, we cannot hope to understand why Paul would ask them to keep their heads covered when they prayed or prophesied (1 Cor 11:3–16). Only when we understand what an uncovered woman's head means in St. Paul's world can we think to apply the actual sense of such passages to our own lives, where covered and uncovered heads don't have the same significance.

Because of cultural differences in education, technology, and the like, the Church encourages us to begin our Bible reading by investigating what the Scriptures meant to the original writers and readers. Only after we understand the context can we hope to understand how to best apply God's communication to them to *our own* lives. This means that you will need some helps in order to do very thorough Bible study. You will need some kind of commentary or other good set of notes, such as those on the bottom of the study editions of the *New American Bible*. See also "How to Read and Pray with the Bible" (pages 305–13) for more ideas for biblical commentaries.

Recognize the Genre

When we see the sports page headline "Padres Beat Giants," most of us would be able to recognize that what will follow is a story about how a San Diego baseball team defeated another team from San Francisco. We recognize the *kind* of writing as a sports article, not a book or poem or political news report. Someone from the Middle Ages, though, knowing nothing about baseball or our team names, would almost certainly have misunderstood the title, picturing in their minds a story about priests beating up on tall people, and would have no way to understand the article itself.

Something similar happens when modern people look at ancient stories in the Bible. We often fail to recognize that they usually are *not* history texts, at least not as we understand the word "history." Rather, these stories intend to communicate *religious truth*, demonstrating the many ways that God has broken into human lives to save us. It is important to note that religious truth, and truth itself, is not the same thing as "historical fact."

For example, it is a *fact* that tortoises and hares do not actually race each other, as in Aesop's fable about the tortoise and the hare. It is *true*, though, that dogged perseverance will sometime win when erratic brilliance fails. This fable teaches a truth, not facts. The Scriptures are *not* fables, and often have very real historical events behind and underlying their record. At the same time, though, we have to ask ourselves what it is that we are really after when we read (and

pray with) the Bible: facts or truth? In doing so, admittedly, we open ourselves up to being disappointed if it's the "facts" that appeal the most to us.

Facts are good and valuable in their own place. They help us to order our understanding of the world around us. When we ask questions about how we are to live, and what God wants from us, though, truth may actually be more important. The point here is that, again, we need to consider what the ancient writers, who were neither historians nor scientists, intended when writing. History and science were much less popular writing forms for them, and had much less rigid standards than our own, leaving much more room for inventiveness and artistry than is typical in reporting today.

The important point is to recognize that the original human authors' understanding of what kind of writing was produced is the one that counts, and not necessarily how the biblical literature resembles writings that meet our standards. This points out again that we need resources like biblical commentaries, Bible study courses, and books like this to be able to read the Bible stories without getting confused. Ultimately, we need the help of the Church, "which exercises the divinely conferred commission and ministry of watching over and interpreting the Word of God" (*CCC*, 119).

Put the Passage in Context

Any phrase taken out of context can appear to mean something different from what was originally intended. For example, let's imagine that a governor said in her speech, "Some people say 'taxes are too low' but I say they should be even lower," and a newspaper was to quote her, word for word. The story might come out like this: "The governor said in her speech yesterday, 'taxes are too low.'" The newspaper, in this case, could say, "We quoted her exactly; those were her very words!" In a deceptive way the newspaper would be right, but the reporter made it appear, by leaving out eleven key words, that her position was the opposite of what she meant. This practice may actually be more common in the TV and film industries. In deciphering what you read and hear, it is important to look at the full context of someone's words.

Similar things happen when Scripture passages are taken out of context. For example, think about the passage from Jeremiah 29:11: "For I know well the plans I have in mind for you, says the LORD, plans for your welfare, not for woe! plans to give you a future full of hope." This sounds like a nice message, right? The only problem is that it wasn't addressed to a general audience or to us as individuals. If we look at the verses before and after this passage, we can see the Lord spoke that passage, through Jeremiah, specifically to the Babylonian exiles, promising to bring them back to Jerusalem at the appropriate time. We need to ask ourselves whether it is correct to take this pointedly direct statement and make more general applications of it.

In a similar way, in Luke 8:19–21, when Jesus heard that his mother and brothers were looking for him, he responded, "My mother and my brothers are those who hear the word of God and act on it." It would be possible to suggest from this passage that Jesus rejected his mother along with the rest of his relatives. (Another point to consider: the translation for "brothers" may actually refer to "cousins.") Earlier in Luke's Gospel, however, in 1:26–38, when the angel Gabriel told Mary that she would give birth to the Savior by the power of the Holy Spirit, Mary was in fact the very *first* person in the Gospel to hear the Word of God and act on it, when she responded, "May it be done to me according to your word" (Lk 1:38). Jesus' phrase does not exclude Mary; rather, it suggests that we have to be like her to be in the family of Jesus. The first passage (Lk 1:26–38) helps to better understand the fullest meaning of the second passage (Lk 8:19–21).

Context refers to more than a passage's immediate conditions, or even how it is shaped by the book or letter that contains it. It is fair to say that we can expect God to be consistent. In a unique way, the Bible can be seen as *one* unit, since God is the uniting and singular author, inspiring all of its books. Therefore, we can expect consistency and a principle of unity between any particular passage and all other passages in all the other books of the Bible on that subject. While Bible study can lead us to a deeper understanding of each passage, taken in isolation, a deeper and fuller understanding of the given topic of each passage requires further theological exploration. *Theology* means, in essence, the study of God. In this case, it would mean the study of God's fuller meaning of any given text.

As an example of this point, review this passage from the Second Letter to Timothy:

> He saved us and called us to a holy life, not according to our works but according to his own design and the grace bestowed on us in Christ Jesus before time began. (2 Tm 1:9)

Taken in isolation, it would seem to say that God saved us by "grace" and not by our "works." However, Romans 2:6–10 makes it clear that eternal life is only available to those who do good works. It is possible to take either passage alone and make the position, in the first, that good works don't matter (though the passage is almost certainly talking about observing the practices of the Jewish law and not good works at all), or in the second that *only* good works matter. The truth is really a more complex combination of both passages, that Salvation is always an undeserved gift from the mercy and grace of God. There is always an immeasurable inequality between God and us, for everything comes from him. Any merit that we receive is only because of God's free plan to associate us with the work of his grace. But, we demonstrate our openness to God's gift by using his grace to be and do good, which is, in itself obedience to Jesus' teachings.

To arrive at a better understanding of any passage, we have to know how it accurately fits in with the words and sentences around it, with the historical situation and cultural understandings of the writer, and with the rest of the Bible. The next section points out how we must also consider what the Church understands about the Scriptures as well.

Use a Biblical Commentary and Notes

Modern Catholic biblical commentaries and notes are helpful for making sense of the unusual passages, as well as those that are hard to translate. They also provide background on the outline of biblical books, comments on authorship, date of composition, and formation of the content of each book. Excellent commentaries can be drawn from the introductions in the *New American Bible* or from the *Catholic Study Bible for the New American Bible.* Other catechetical references like the *Catechism of the Catholic Church*, the *Compendium of the Catechism of the Catholic Church*, and the *United States Catholic Catechism for Adults* each provide various explanations of Scripture. For more discussion on this topic, note the Appendix section, "How to Read and Pray with the Bible," pages 305–13.

Biblical commentaries can help to explain the various translations of the text from the original languages. The Old Testament was written in Hebrew before being translated to Greek. Understanding the translation of the words and their meanings is important. Anyone who speaks two languages learns quickly that jokes that are hilarious in English usually fall completely flat in Spanish, French, or Vietnamese. Many ideas and expressions simply don't translate well.

For example, the prophet Isaiah described a vision in which seraphim, the angels in God's heavenly throne room, had two wings with which they "hovered aloft," and another two wings covering their faces, implying that the glory of God was too bright, even for angels. The peculiar thing is that they have still two more wings with which they cover their *feet* (Is 6:1–3). Why would they be covering their feet? The casual reader will almost certainly not stumble upon the right understanding of this curious detail without help. This passage only makes sense when we learn that in Hebrew "feet" is sometime used as code language that native speakers of the prophet's time understood for "nakedness." They were too prudish, at least by our standards, to say what they really meant. A good study text wants to be as close to the original as possible, but it will have to include notes at the bottom of the page to make curious passages like this one make sense for us. Check your own Bible and its commentary to see how or if it offers this passage any explanation.

Reflect

How does your Bible's commentary section interpret the passage in Isaiah 6:1-3 concerning two wings that cover the feet of the angels?

Remember That Sacred Scripture and Sacred Tradition Make Up Catholic Beliefs

Catholics have always recognized that some of Jesus' teachings were recorded in the New Testament—but many were not, as the Scriptures themselves indicate in John 20:30–31. We refer to the entire collection of Catholic beliefs as the Sacred Scripture and Sacred Tradition of the Church. To be clear, these beliefs begin in the teachings of Jesus Christ, which were preached by the Apostles after his Death, and have been preserved and interpreted from that time by the Church's **Magisterium**. Sacred Tradition and Sacred Scripture have the same source; they make up the single deposit of the Word of God. For example, some transmissions of the Gospel were recorded in the specific written form of the Bible; others are included in that body of beliefs shared by all Catholics that were not written in a scriptural way. In fact, both kinds of beliefs—Sacred Scripture and Sacred Tradition—have the same divine source and have always been accepted as true and necessary, precisely because they were handed down from the Apostles since the beginning. They were taught, and, where necessary, defended by the pope, bishops, and teachers of the Church in every age.

The Apostles' same preaching is also the basis of the New Testament.

A careful student of history will note that the very early Church existed for at least fifteen years before the first of the New Testament books was written, and long before they were collected into one "testament." The earliest letters of St. Paul, the first of the inspired authors to write after Jesus' Death, weren't written until AD 50 at the earliest, a good decade and a half *after* Jesus' Death, Resurrection, and Ascension. These first scriptural writings were a continuation of Paul's preaching ministry. Some were letters written to people he knew personally and had brought to faith and conversion, like the community of believers at Corinth. Other, later writings were to individuals and communities he had heard of but not yet visited, like the Church of Rome.

The material that eventually formed the four Gospels was also preached for four to six decades before they were put in the written form, as we have them today. The Gospel writers clearly did *not* put down everything that Jesus did or taught. The Church's faith has always accompanied the written Scriptures and has helped us to understand the Bible's teachings. For example, Christians have always believed in the Holy Trinity; that is, the belief that there is only one God, made up of the Father, the Son, and the Holy Spirit. We find some references in the New Testament that indicate this belief.

We can see that Paul believed that Jesus is God in Philippians 2:6 where, writing about Jesus, he says, "though

Magisterium
The official teaching office of the Church. The Lord bestowed the right and the power to teach in his name to Peter, the other Apostles, and their successors. The Magisterium is the bishops in communion with the successor of Peter, the Bishop of Rome (Pope).

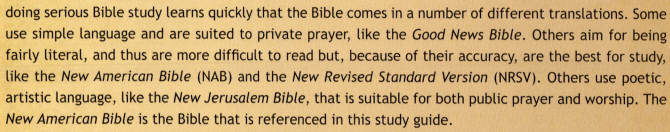

BIBLICAL TRANSLATIONS TODAY

Not all Bibles are translated the same way, even into the same language. Anyone who has spent time doing serious Bible study learns quickly that the Bible comes in a number of different translations. Some use simple language and are suited to private prayer, like the *Good News Bible*. Others aim for being fairly literal, and thus are more difficult to read but, because of their accuracy, are the best for study, like the *New American Bible* (NAB) and the *New Revised Standard Version* (NRSV). Others use poetic, artistic language, like the *New Jerusalem Bible*, that is suitable for both public prayer and worship. The *New American Bible* is the Bible that is referenced in this study guide.

Among the greatest differences between Catholic and Protestant Bible translations are the numbers of books listed in them. The differences between the lists spring from a historical problem. In the first century AD, Jews had more than one edition of their Hebrew scriptures, the core of the Old Testament. Most Jews at that time spoke Greek, and required a translation of the Hebrew scriptures into Greek. That translation was referred to as the *Septuagint*, which means "seventy," in Greek. This name sprang from a mythological story in which seventy-two Jewish scholars translated the books from the original Hebrew into Greek for the pharaoh of Egypt.

A problem arises, though, since the Hebrew version of the Bible seems to have contained only thirty-nine books, while the Greek edition of the text was longer! The Septuagint had a number of texts that the Hebrew version did not include, among them Tobit, Judith, 1 and 2 Maccabees, Wisdom of Solomon, Sirach (sometimes called Ecclesiasticus), and Baruch (including the Letter of Jeremiah), along with some additional material in Esther and Daniel (Susanna, Bel and the Dragon).

The inspired writers of the New Testament, as a general rule, preferred the longer Greek Septuagint version, probably because most of them spoke Greek themselves. The early Catholic Church leadership, as a result, followed their example and used the fuller version of the Septuagint. Sometime after the Death of Jesus and well after the establishment of Christianity, most Jews began to restrict themselves to the Hebrew texts. As the Church already existed independently of Judaism by this point, it was neither consulted in nor persuaded by that decision, and continued to use the longer Greek Septuagint as its Old Testament. As a result, the Catholic Church has had forty-six books in its Old Testament from the earliest days.

Much later, at the time of the Protestant Reformation in the sixteenth and seventeenth centuries, Protestant reformers decided to use the shorter list found in the Hebrew scriptures for their Old Testament. They relegated the additional books and additions to an extra section of the Bible called the "Apocrypha," a word that means "hidden." More recently, Protestant scholarship has shown a great interest in these books.

In contrast to the controversy on the length of the Old Testament, the number of books in the New Testament of the Bible is undisputed by both Catholics and Protestants. Both contain the identical canon, or list, of twenty-seven books.

he was in the form of God, he did not regard equality with God something to be grasped." Paul also wrote of God being one (Rom 3:30) and of God as Father (Phil 2:11), and made references to God's Spirit (1 Cor 2:11, 14). In John's Gospel, Jesus says, "The Father and I are one" (Jn 10:30). The very end of the Gospel of Matthew tells of Jesus' commission to his eleven disciples to baptize disciples of every nation "in the name of the Father, and of the Son, and of the Holy Spirit" (Mt 28:16–20).

There are other passages that name the Trinity all together (1 Pt 1:2). Unfortunately, none of the inspired writers gave a clear and concise written definition of the Trinity anywhere in the New Testament. This central mystery of the Church, the Holy Trinity, is found much more clearly expressed in the Sacred Tradition of the Church than it is in Scripture. In this way, the Tradition and the Scripture work together to help believers understand everything that God wanted to communicate to us.

Not all Christians accept the nonbiblical Tradition of the Catholic Church. Beginning with Martin Luther, most Protestants have believed that the Bible is the only authority for belief. Their phrase for this belief in Latin, *sola scriptura*, means literally "by scripture alone." Technically, in this Protestant understanding of Scripture, if a teaching cannot be demonstrated in the Bible, it may not be required for belief by a particular Protestant denomination.

This explains some of the most important differences between Catholic and Protestant biblical scholarship. Catholics can find assurance in the Bible itself, which never requires all beliefs to be contained in the Bible, and also points out that not everything Jesus said or did was contained in the Bible. In fact, the Bible itself says as much: "There are also many other things that Jesus did, but if these were to be described individually, I do not think the whole world would contain the books that would be written" (Jn 21:25).

The Sacred Scripture and the Sacred Tradition from which it sprang comes from the preaching of the Apostles. The Apostles trusted the Deposit of Faith, contained in the Sacred Scripture and Sacred Tradition, to the whole Church. In doctrine, life, and worship, the bishops who have been appointed in apostolic succession continue to preach and teach to every generation all that the Church believes. This teaching responsibility continues in the life of the Church to this very day, guided and protected like everything else in the process of inspiration, by the Holy Spirit. The Magisterium is the teaching authority of the bishops, in union with the pope, and safeguarded by the Holy Spirit. This is the very same Spirit-filled teaching authority used by the early Church when it wrote and selected the twenty-seven books of the New Testament.

Review

1. Why is it more likely that several authors composed the Pentateuch?

2. How does applying the historical-critical method to the story of Noah and the Great Flood help us to understand the point of the story?

3. What is the fullest way to understand a biblical passage in context?

4. Explain two traditional ways that Catholics have interpreted Scripture: the literal sense and the spiritual sense.

5. Why is it fair to say that the Church preceded the formation of Sacred Scripture?

6. What is the most important difference between Catholic and Protestant biblical scholarship?

Reflect

Share the history of a bible that is in your home or part of your family's tradition.

Research and Report

Use the *Catechism of the Catholic Church* (101–133) and its accompanying references to research the meaning of the following statements. Choose three statements and write two or three sentences explaining their meaning. Or, choose one statement and write a one-page essay that explains its meaning in more depth, citing other sources to back up your explanation.

- Christ is the one single Word of Sacred Scripture.
- God is the author of Sacred Scripture.
- Christianity is a religion of the "Word" of God, not a "religion of the book."
- Sacred Scripture must be read and interpreted in light of the same Spirit by whom it was written.
- Christians venerate the Old Testament as the true Word of God.
- The Gospels are at the heart of all the Scriptures.
- "Ignorance of the Scriptures is ignorance of Christ."

SCRIPTURE PRAYER *(from Psalm 63)*

I will bless you as long as I live;
  I will lift up my hands, calling on your
    name.

Lord, help me to know you, love you, and serve you.
In Christ's name.
Amen.

PART 1

THE
OLD TESTAMENT

Why Do We Read the Old Testament?
The Old Testament prepares us for the coming of Christ and is an indispensable part of Sacred Scripture.

Classifying and Arranging the Old Testament Books
The *New American Bible* arranges the Old Testament in four main categories: Pentateuch, Historical Books, Prophetic Books, and Wisdom Books.

Why Do We Read the Old Testament?

Catholics know the Old Testament to be several important things. It forms the longest part of the most important book of all time, the Bible. In contains laws and lessons for living that have been applied and lived by people throughout the generations. It is also a written record of the social structures, legal systems, and ordinary religious life that have shaped, and continue to form, most every aspect of our Western civilization.

All of these facts about the Old Testament are important and true. However, the most essential reason for reading, studying, and praying with the Old Testament is that it contains God's Revelation. The *Catechism of the Catholic Church* teaches that the "Old Testament is an indispensable part of Sacred Scripture" (*CCC*, 121). It is the true Word of God that is "to prepare for the coming of Christ, the redeemer of all and of the messianic kingdom, to announce this coming by prophecy (*Dei Verbum*, 15). The Old Law, or Law of Moses, contained in the Old Testament is a preparation for the Gospel. St. Irenaeus wrote, "The Law is a pedagogy and a prophecy of things to come." The Old Testament is important in several other ways:

- It contains the truth of God's promises to the Chosen People, and through them, to all people.

- It reveals our true identity as God's special creatures. Our own personal stories as individuals and as human communities are reflected in the many Old Testament stories.

- It records the experiences of our ancestors in faith. In fact, Jews, Christians, and Muslims acknowledge Abraham as a significant person in their faiths.

- It reveals a living God, who meets us when we read and pray with these words of Sacred Scripture.

The Second Vatican Council further taught that "God, the inspirer and author of both Testaments, wisely arranged that the New Testament should be hidden in the Old and the Old should be made manifest in the New" (*Dei Verbum*, 16).

This part of *Sacred Scripture* is intended as an overview of the part of the Bible that Christians refer to as the "Old Testament." Catholics include forty-six books of the Old Testament (forty-five if Jeremiah and Lamentations are counted as one book). Added to the twenty-seven books of the New Testament, these form the canon of Scripture.

The Old Testament is really a *collection* of books written over the course of a millennium, approximately between 1000 BC and 150 BC. The books were written predominantly in Hebrew. The early Church, however, differed with early Judaism in the decision of the Old Testament canon ("Biblical Translations Today," page 20). The Church included seven books

(1 and 2 Maccabees, Judith, Tobit, Baruch, Sirach, and Wisdom) not included in the Hebrew scriptures that were mostly written in Greek after 300 BC. These seven books are known as **deuterocanonical** to show that they are not accepted in the Jewish canon. Some deuterocanonical books include chapters added to older Hebrew books, such as Daniel and Esther.

At the time of the Protestant Reformation, the reformers adopted a canon created by Jewish rabbis around AD 90. They dropped the seven books written in Greek. Many Protestant Bibles today print these books in a separate section at the back of the Bible and refer to them as the *Apocrypha*, which means "hidden."

 Review

1. Why is the Old Testament important for Catholics?
2. In what language was the Old Testament composed?

Reflect

What are two of your favorite stories or people from the Old Testament? Explain why they are your favorites.

Classifying and Arranging the Old Testament Books

The way the Old Testament is classified and arranged varies slightly. Jews traditionally divide the books of the Hebrew scriptures into three distinct sections:

1. Law (in Hebrew, "Torah")
2. Prophets (in Hebrew, "Neviim")
3. Writings (in Hebrew, "Ktuvim")

If you put together the first letter of the three words of the Hebrew names for the sections you get the acronym TaNaK, which is the term often used as a shorthand by modern Jews to refer to the Hebrew scriptures.

The Old Testament in the *New American Bible* is arranged slightly differently, under these classifications:

- Pentateuch (in Greek, "five books")
- Historical Books
- Prophetic Books
- Wisdom Books

Part 1 of this text will survey the books in each of these classifications, with slight adaptations. The books of Joshua, Judges, and Ruth will be examined as a historical era that precedes the time of Israel's monarchy and featuring especially the books of 1 and 2 Samuel and 1 and 2 Kings. Discussion of the Wisdom books will precede the prophetic books, as the latter form an explicit and clear bridge to the latter part

deuterocanonical
A term meaning "second canon." Books included in the Catholic Old Testament but not in Hebrew scriptures. These additions are 1 and 2 Maccabees, Judith, Tobit, Baruch, Sirach, Wisdom, and parts of Esther and Daniel.

of the Bible—the New Testament and the full Revelation of God in the coming of his Son, Jesus Christ.

 **Review**

Explain the difference between how Jews divide the books of Hebrew scripture and how Catholics divide the books of the Old Testament.

THE
PENTATEUCH

Understanding the First Five Books of the Bible

The first five books of the Bible are called the "Book of Moses" or "The Pentateuch," a Greek term deriving from "five" combined with "books."

Narrative and Development of the Pentateuch

At least four major sources may have gone into the composition of the Pentateuch.

How We Read the Pentateuch

The Pentateuch contains mainly two kinds of writing: narrative stories and collections of Mosaic Laws.

Ancestor Stories in the Book of Genesis

The ancestor stories in the Book of Genesis are divided into two main sections: primeval stories and the stories of the patriarchs and matriarchs.

The Beginning of God's Revelation

God's Revelation to humans came about when he made himself known to our first parents.

The Great Flood

The covenant God made with Noah, centering on the story of the Great Flood, is part of the next stage of Revelation.

Abraham and the Patriarchs

Abraham was the "father of a multitude," God's Chosen People, who led his people to a new land.

The Blessing of Jacob

The patriarch Jacob tricks his brother into receiving a blessing, and then later humbles himself to seek reconciliation.

Joseph and His Brothers

Genesis 37, 39-50 is a literary masterpiece that revolves around Jacob's twelve sons, especially his favorite son, Joseph.

The Book of Exodus

The Book of Exodus focuses on the call and life of Moses, Israel's liberation, the Passover event, and the Sinai Covenant.

The Wandering of the People in the Wilderness

Exodus 15-18 details a story cycle of traditional stories—including the establishment of the Sinai Covenant—while God's People were wandering in the wilderness.

The Mosaic Law Codes

The Covenant Code, Deuteronomic Code, and Levitical Code are three different collections of the Law in the Pentateuch.

Understanding the First Five Books of the Bible

Reading the Bible begins with the opening books. A traditional way that Catholics understand the first part of the Old Testament is as "The Book of Moses" or "The Pentateuch" (a word constructed from two Greek terms meaning "five" combined with "books"). This latter term is rooted in the traditional idea that the first section of the Bible consists of five books: Genesis, Exodus, Leviticus, Numbers, and Deuteronomy.

The other description—"The Book of Moses"—is based on the idea that Moses was the author of this material. As mentioned before, passages such as that in Deuteronomy 34, describing the death of Moses, indicate that Moses was not the author of the books in the modern sense, but there is no reason to doubt

the events named in the Pentateuch. Even later laws added to the parts of these books are presented in the tradition of Moses. He is the unique figure of the Old Testament, one who had a central role, especially as lawgiver. Moses's influence on these books should not be diminished.

However, more recent study has attempted to name how several historical traditions or sources have come together in the first five books of the Bible. Each brings to these books its own language, theological viewpoints, and various interpretations of God's Revelation. Traditionally, four of these sources have been named as so-called Yahwist, Elohist, priestly, and Deuteronomic strands. They are abbreviated as J, E, P, and D. Each of these collections bring with them some differences in language and theological viewpoints. Though a speculative approach at studying the Pentateuch, it does offer an interesting theory for explaining the formation of these books.

As you proceed with studying the backgrounds and sources of human authorship of the Pentateuch, never forget that God himself is the author of Sacred Scripture, and that the Church reminds us that Scripture is to be read from both a literal and spiritual sense. These meanings will also be addressed in this section.

 Review

Name the books of the Pentateuch.

Reflect

Rate your level of familiarity with the first five books of the Bible.

Narrative and Development of the Pentateuch

The theory of four strands coming together to form the Pentateuch brings out some unique details of each strand. These details are often noticeable in examples of *doublets*, that is, stories told twice, but with slight differences. For example, two creation stories are included in the Book of Genesis. (These will be briefly analyzed in the following sections.) The differences are noticeable by the fact that some parts of the Pentateuch use different names for God.

In your Bible translation, it should be easy to spot that some stories use "God" as the name for God, while others use "Lord God" or "Lord." The English "God" translates to the Hebrew word "Elohim." "Lord" translates to a different name for God: "YHWH" (pronounced "Yah-way"). Two of the "sources" of the Pentateuch have been named according to the sections that use those terms for God: Yahwist (called the "J" source for the German translation of YHWH, "Jahweh.") and Elohist (called the "E" source for the name Elohim).

Because the Book of Deuteronomy is written in a very different style than the other four books of the Pentateuch, a third strand was identified and named "D" for Deuteronomist. Some biblical scholars also identified a fourth strand that occasionally is present in Genesis. This strand seems particularly concerned with ritual times of blessing and uses the same phrases when these events occur. Note that in key parts of the Book of Genesis—the creation of humanity (Gn 1:27–28), the re-creation after the Great Flood (Gn 9:1), the promises made to Abraham (Gn 17:5–7), Isaac's blessing of Jacob (Gn 28:3–4), and Jacob's name change to Israel (Gn 35:10–12)—God's blessings are accompanied in each case by a phrase directing the parties to "be fertile and multiply."

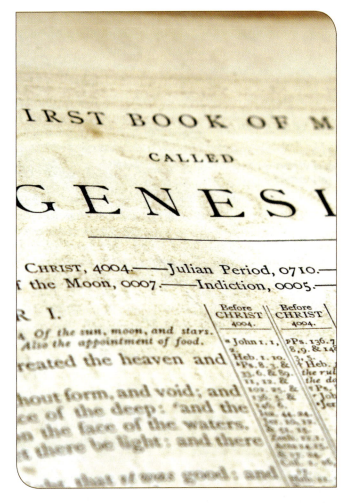

Consider that Genesis is filled with genealogical lists that always begin with the introduction, "these are the descendants of . . ." (see, for example, Gn 10:1, 11:10, and 25:12). These passages focus on, among other things, "being fruitful" and tracing descendants. Similarities were noted between these lists and the detailed concerns of the Book of Leviticus, which consists largely of priestly laws about ritual, sacrifice, and purity (note, for example, the detailed list of animals in Leviticus 11). Thus, the fourth strand was identified as "P," the priestly strand or source.

With this hypothesis identifying four strands of writing in the Pentateuch, another issue is to attempt to date the particular writings. It is commonly held that the Yahwist ("J") strand came first because the material is the most "primitive" in its theology (e.g., a humanlike image of God who "walked" in the garden

anthropomorphic
The attribution of human motivation, characteristics, or behavior to inanimate objects, animals, or natural phenomena.

of Eden, etc.). The material may have been gathered together during King Solomon's reign; that is, before 922 BC. This time was chosen because of the belief that Solomon ruled over a "cultural flowering" of ancient Israel—a time of wealth and prosperity in which scribes could have been commissioned to collect and record these materials.

The Elohim, or "E" portions, of the Pentateuch are often associated with the northern kingdom of Israel after its break from the southern kingdom, Judah, meaning that these sources would be dated sometime between 922 and 722 BC, the later date being the time when the Assyrian Empire conquered the northern kingdom. Sometime after this, it was thought that both versions were joined together. Others believe that it made much more sense that the "E" strands simply supplemented the older "J" account with a few insertions edited in that highlighted northern concerns, rather than drafting a completely separate document.

The Deuteronomist ("D") material is associated with King Josiah's scroll, discovered when he started to clean up the Temple (2 Kgs 22:8). The unique actions that Josiah instituted in his reforms (described in 2 Kings 23) are only specifically demanded in Deuteronomy (rather than Exodus or Leviticus). Where this scroll came from is an open debate. The traditional view is that it was an older scroll of the Law, perhaps from the north, and deposited by refugees from the Assyrian conquest of the north for safekeeping in the Temple until Josiah's helpers accidentally found it. Another group of scholars argue that Josiah intentionally drafted Deuteronomy as a reform of Moses's Law for his times, and as a basis for his reforms. Either way, the material in the Book of Deuteronomy became part of the traditional group of writings sometime after 640 BC.

Finally, it is noted that the only leadership left to the Hebrew people after the conquest of Jerusalem in 587 BC were the priests. So, it is possible that the priests edited the entire Pentateuch, added some relevant material for their times, and the work was completed. Thus, the assumption is that when Ezra brought "the scrolls of the law" (Neh 8:1–2) then the "Pentateuch" ("Torah") was complete.

To refer to the Pentateuch as a combination of "strands" identified by the letters "J," "E," "D," and "P" can be charted in graphic form:

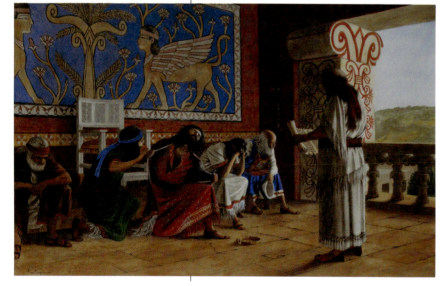

Source	Style	Where/ When	Examples	Themes	Comment
Yahwist ("J")	Uses the personal name YHWH for God; vivid, earthy style; anthropomorphic view of God: "YHWH walks and talks with us"; refers to Mount Sinai as place of the Mosaic covenant; refers to natives of Israel as "Canaanites."	Origin in the southern kingdom (Judah) prior to 922 BC during King Solomon's monarchy when pride was high.	Second creation account (Gn 2:4b-25) Egyptian plagues (Ex 7:14-10:29)	God's promises to the patriarchs: 1. The blessing of Israel as a people 2. The promise of land	The "J" tradition provides the basic outline of the Pentateuch: human origins, patriarchs, slavery in Egypt, the Exodus, the desert wandering, Mount Sinai covenant, and entrance to the Promised Land
Elohist ("E")	Uses the term Elohim for God; God is more abstract; refers to Mount Horeb as the place of the Mosaic covenant; refers to natives of Israel as "Amorites."	Origin in Ephraim in the northern kingdom between 922 and 722 BC.	Abraham and Sarah (Gn 20:1-18)	Marked by the emphasis of Elijah and Elisha; great emphasis on prophecy; covenant is central: God's relationship to Israel is understood by covenant promises.	E retold J's stories from a northern point of view. The south emphasized the role of the monarchy while the north (E) was more concerned with the covenant. Abraham is a central figure in the Elohist accounts. Perhaps around 750 BC an editor combined J and E into one narrative without bothering to drop repetitions or contradictions.
Deuteronomist ("D")	God is YHWH; emphasis on morals and the law; central role of several long speeches by Moses; meant to be spoken aloud to remind people of the demands of the covenant.	Possibly composed and/or edited after 640 BC by a priest in the northern kingdom at the shrine at Shechem. It may have been completed in Jerusalem.	The speeches of Moses (Dt 1:1-30:20)	Interprets Israel's history in a cycle of reward for fidelity and punishment for sin; Israel should respond to the covenant and the Law in worship; "Listen, Israel" is a constant refrain: the covenant is *now*.	Israel's fidelity to God's law is the uppermost concern of the Deuteronomist; obedience to God's law brings rewards and disobedience brings certain adversity.
Priestly ("P")	God is Elohim; formal style; interested in census lists and genealogies; concern for numbers, dates, ways of worship, Temple ceremonies, clean and unclean animals.	Composition often dated to the Babylonian exile (587-538 BC) to strengthen the faith and hope of the people; may have been completed as late as 400 BC.	First creation account (Gn 1:1-2:4a) Priestly laws (Lv 1:1-27:34)	Great emphasis on worship; sees life and God's action in the history of Israel as a liturgy.	Because it may have been the last source written, P gives a coherent framework to the Pentateuch. Priestly editors under Ezra gave the first five books of the Bible their final form.

Literary criticism of the Pentateuch provides a hypothetical tool for appreciating the origins, arrangement, and sources of the first five books of the Bible. Recognizing these strands is especially useful in helping us to understand the scriptural texts about creation that occupy the first four chapters of the Book of Genesis. The *Catechism of the Catholic Church* teaches that

> from a literary standpoint these texts may have had diverse sources. The inspired authors have placed them at the beginning of Scripture to express in their solemn language the truths of creation—its origin and its end in God, its order and goodness, the vocation of man, and finally the drama of sin and the hope of salvation. Read in the light of Christ, within the unity of Sacred Scripture and in the living Tradition of the Church, these texts remain the principal source for catechesis on the mysteries of the "beginning": creation, fall, and promise of salvation. (*CCC*, 289)

The next subsections unpack the two creation stories in Genesis and some other *doublets* found in the Pentateuch.

Two Creation Stories (Genesis 1:1-4:26) and Other Doublets

Everyone has a desire to know how life began. So did the ancient peoples, including the Hebrews. Their ideas about creation are in the Book of Genesis. The word *genesis* means "beginning." But an examination of the first four chapters of Genesis reveals something very interesting: there are two creation stories, not one! The first story in Genesis 1:1–2:4a is the familiar "seven days of creation" in which creation progresses for six "days" before God "rests" on the seventh day. Note that the setting for the beginning of the story is

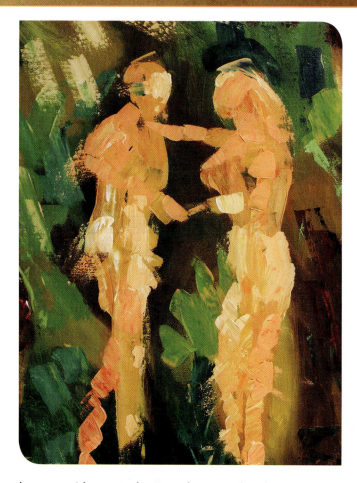

in water. Also note that man is created at the same moment and *both* male and female are said to be in the "image of God":

> In the beginning, when God created the heavens and the earth, the earth was a formless wasteland, and darkness covered the abyss, while a mighty wind swept over the *waters*. (Gn 1:1–2)

> Then God said, "Let us make man in our image, after our likeness. Let them have dominion over the fish of the sea, the birds of the air, and the cattle, and over all the wild animals and all the creatures that crawl on the ground." God created man in his image; in the divine image he created him; *male and female he created them*. (Gn 1:26–27)

In the second creation story (Gn 2:4b–25), the setting is not water, but rather barren land:

At the time when the Lord God made the earth and the heavens—while as yet there was no field shrub on earth and no grass of the field had sprouted, for the Lord God had sent no rain upon the earth and there was no man to till the soil. (Gn 2:4b–5)

Also, in this version, the order of creation is different: humans, then plants, and finally animals. (In the first creation story, the order is plants, then animals, and finally humans.) The second story reveals God as a crafter of humans. He makes man out of the mud, and actually "breathes life" into man. This is also the creation version where the names Adam and Eve are given, the Original Sin and its effects are described, and the promise of Redemption is offered. More information on these elements will be covered in "Ancestor Stories in the Book of Genesis" on pages 41–43. For now, note these important religious truths revealed in the stories of creation:

1. *There is only one God.* Differing from other creation myths of the time, the biblical author emphatically insists that there is only one God and that he created everything in existence.
2. *God planned creation.* Creation is not the result of chaotic forces or warring gods. Our God created the world in an orderly way to share his life and goodness with us.
3. *Everything God made is good.* Other ancient peoples believed that much of material reality was evil and constantly at war with the spiritual elements in the universe. In the Jewish and Christian understanding, Genesis presents a positive view of created reality, telling us that God was pleased with everything, especially human beings made in God's image and likeness, and trusted with responsible development of the rest of creation.
4. *The Sabbath is a special day of rest and worship.* The priestly writer reveals that God rested on the seventh day. Obviously, God does not need to rest. But we need to take time to be renewed by stopping our ordinary activities one day out of the week. Also, we need to recognize a kind and loving God as the source of our existence and worship him in prayer and thanksgiving.

Together, the two creation stories are an example of a *doublet*—stories told twice, but with slight differences. There are also two different narratives of the Great Flood (Gn 6:1–23). However, rather than standing back-to-back, as with the creation stories, the Great Flood narratives have been woven together so that it is more difficult to see that there are two separate stories. The evidence for two Great Flood stories includes:

1. Humanity is described as corrupt in both Genesis 6:5 and 6:11–12.
2. Noah's family enters the ark in Genesis 7:7, yet seems to enter it again in 7:13.
3. Genesis 6:19–20 says that Noah should bring two of every creature into the ark; Genesis 7:2 is different: "Of every clean animal, take with you seven pairs . . . ."
4. In Genesis 7:10–12, 17, and 8:6–7, the flood is described as lasting "forty days," but in Genesis 7:24 and 8:3, the duration is one hundred and fifty days.

These differences are also noticeable by looking at the way the different sources or strands name God; in this case, the "J" and "E" sources.

Review

1. What are some differences between the first and second creation stories?

Reflect

What is an example of a family story that has been told to you to teach a lesson?

2. How was it determined that the third author, "D," was involved in the composition of the Pentateuch?

3. How do we recognize a fourth voice of authorship that occasionally turns up in Genesis? How is the fourth author identified?

4. Explain how the four authors of the Pentateuch are dated.

5. What names for God are used by each of the four sources: "J," "E," "D," and "P"?

GOD IS THE AUTHOR OF SACRED SCRIPTURE

The text of the Bible has been written down under the inspiration of the Holy Spirit. How so? God *inspired* the authors of Scripture. The authors had the freedom to choose the words they wrote, including the stories and incidents they chose to share. As the Second Vatican Council explained, God chose the authors of the Bible:

and while employed by Him (2) they made use of their powers and abilities, so that with Him acting in them and through them, (3) they, as true authors, consigned to writing everything and only those things which He wanted. (*Dei Verbum*, 11)

Related to this understanding of inspiration is another fact: the Jews of biblical times, up to and including Jesus, were great storytellers. In reading the Old Testament, we must understand the difference between a story intended to teach a lesson and the description of a historical event, all the while remembering that the text is inspired. God intended for us to read it—both history *and* stories.

For example, the proper response to the fall of humankind and the flood narrative of the Book of Genesis is to appreciate the religious lessons of moral responsibility, God's care for humankind, and humankind's stubborn resistance. Joining an expedition to find pieces of the "authentic" ark of Noah on Mount Ararat in modern Turkey (to cite one popular example of people who supposedly take the Bible "seriously" by insisting on a literal flood) is not the most appropriate response to the biblical texts, because it misses their central message and attempts to make these texts into something that they are not—literal history. Rather, it is more important to learn from God's response to the Great Flood that he continues to love humanity despite its sinful nature, which demands correction and punishment. Sometimes we must use our best judgment to determine the differences between history and story, while some passages are more obvious.

Much of this religion textbook is devoted to looking at the religious meaning of the Old Testament, while providing some brief background on the context of a particular book.

How We Read the Pentateuch

One of the criteria for reading and interpreting Scripture taught at the Second Vatican Council is that the reader should be especially attentive "to the content and unity of the whole Scripture" (*Dei Verbum,* quoted in *CCC,* 112). This important lesson provides a format for how we should read the Pentateuch specifically. No matter the various sources and human authors of the Pentateuch, Scripture must be read as "a unity by reason of God's plan, of which Jesus is the center and heart, open since his Passover" (*CCC,* 112). Any and all parts of Scripture must be read and interpreted in relation to the whole.

Primarily because of the different sources involved in the Pentateuch's composition, the first five books of the Bible have been understood in various ways. Consider whether or not the first five books of the Bible were intentionally arranged in some kind of set. Certainly that is the tradition of the Jewish and Christian understanding, and that is the primary way that Catholics explore the meaning God intends and the Church teaches about the content of the Pentateuch.

But before proceeding, consider this question: Why would this first great "section" of the Old Testament end at the fifth book (Deuteronomy) when the people of Israel have still not arrived in the Promised Land, and Moses has just died? A possible answer is that the priest-editors intended the first section of the Bible to end after five books because the end of the Pentateuch paralleled their own story. As the Hebrews in the Torah were exiles first in Egypt and then in the desert, so too were the people at the time of its final composition in exile in Babylon. But, on the other hand, this seems to be an odd place to end the first major section—almost as if the reader is not privy to the final scene of a movie! It may be an interesting study to read the history of the Chosen People beyond the perspective of the Pentateuch to include the other historical books of the Old Testament that also speak of the rise and fall of Israel and the creation of a **Diaspora** people throughout the world.

However, let's return to the traditional Judeo-Christian understanding of the Pentateuch as the "Book of Moses"—a way to read and understand what God wants revealed in these books. We do this so that we can survey some interesting and important issues regarding its study. Before we proceed further, let's recall that the writings of the Bible are foremost valuable and powerful helps in our learning

Diaspora

A group migration or flight away from the homeland into one or more other countries. The word can also refer to people who have maintained their separate identity (often religious, but occasionally ethnic, racial, or cultural) while living in those other countries after migration.

about God, and learning about how God builds up his Kingdom. The judgment that these writings are inspired by God comes from the experience of the Church with these writings. The Magisterium read and studied them and realized that they were inspired. The Pontifical Biblical Commission wrote: "What characterizes Catholic **exegesis** is that it deliberately places itself within the living Tradition of the Church. . . ." All Catholics can join in the process of understanding the meaning of Scripture. It is ongoing prayerful dialogue and study. With this understanding of the Church's primary role in arbitrating the meaning of Scripture, we proceed in our study of the Pentateuch and the rest of the Old Testament.

Appreciating Story and Law in the Pentateuch

One of the most important tools of a journey through the Bible is an appreciation of stories. All ancient travelers collected stories. The Greek historian Herodotus is sometimes called "the founder of history writing"—but even his great history source is loaded with *stories* that he heard during his travels. Why are stories so important? For many reasons. Sometimes stories are based on real events, and we can reproduce historical events by listening carefully to stories.

But even if they are not based on historical events, they can often accurately reflect a culture and its values—what a people think to be important, valuable, and good. To understand a people, we need to learn to listen carefully to their stories. The most important question to ask from the stories is *not* "Did that really happen?" but rather, "What can we learn from this story?"

The ancient Hebrews loved to tell stories. They not only simply enjoyed the telling and retelling, but they also appreciated the fact that stories often teach religious lessons more powerfully than any other way of teaching. Jesus himself was a master storyteller, and many of his stories have become so widely known in the world that people can refer to them easily. Sometimes people don't even realize that they are quoting Jesus. For example, in everyday conversation, someone might say about a good person that he or she is a real "Good Samaritan" or describe a person who has returned home after a long time as a "prodigal son." Gospel stories and other stories from the Bible have become a part of our day-to-day culture. Stories are powerful and lasting!

So, one reason that Jesus told stories was that Jesus was a Jew—and the Jews were (and many modern Jews still are) brilliant storytellers. But the Hebrews began telling stories far back into their history. The creation stories were among the most powerful stories that they told. The creation stories helped them to think about where they came from, and

exegesis
A word that means "leading out." Exegesis involves critical explanation or analysis, especially of written text.

how God was involved in their lives. Did they take it seriously? Certainly they did. But that is not the same thing as believing that the creation stories were a literal report of history.

So, to begin to suggest ways to read the stories of Genesis, let's recognize that the Pentateuch contains mainly two kinds of writing:

1. Narrative stories collected in two main groups—the "Ancestor Stories" of Genesis, and the Moses/Exodus Story.
2. The Collections of Mosiac Laws.

Let us consider each of these two kinds of writing—story and law—as we proceed.

Review

1. What is a possible reason that the priest-editors decided to end the first section of the Bible after five books?
2. What are two main kinds of writing contained in the Pentateuch?

Reflect

Think about your day. What experience from today could translate into a story with a religious lesson?

Ancestor Stories in the Book of Genesis

The ancestor stories in the Book of Genesis are divided into two main sections: the so-called primeval stories that pertain to all of humanity (creation, the fall, Redemption) in Genesis 1–11, and then the stories of the patriarchs and matriarchs of Israel collected together in Genesis 12–50. In these collections of stories about famous biblical ancestors like Adam and Eve; Abraham and Sarah; Jacob, Rachel, and Leah; and Joseph, the writers of the Bible discuss how certain traditions, groups, and even places were organized, named, and involved with God. What are ways that we can read and understand the importance of these stories? This section looks first at ways these ancestor stories are related to one another; second, it examines in more detail some of the meanings of these stories.

God's Relationship with Humanity

The ancestor stories of Genesis—including the creation narratives—outline the stages of God's relationship with the Israelites. These stages include a series

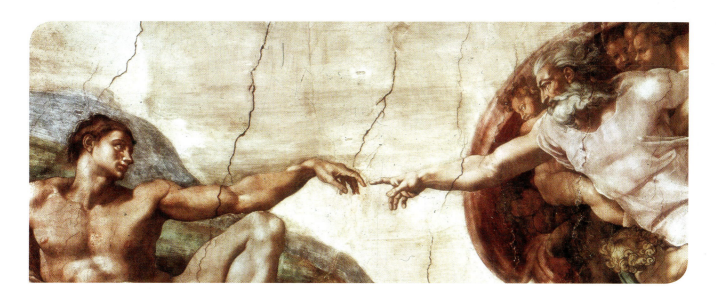

covenants

Binding and solemn agreements between human beings or between God and people, holding each to a particular course of action.

of **covenants** made between human beings and God. The various covenants are easy to chart in the Book of Genesis. Recall the priestly author's use of the descriptive phrase "be fertile and multiply" to mark the creation of humanity (Gn 1:28), the re-creation of humanity after the Great Flood (Gn 9:1), the covenant with Abraham (Gn 17:6–7), the continuation of the Abraham covenant when Isaac speaks to Jacob (Gn 28:3–3), and Jacob's taking on the name Israel (Gn 35:10–12). This phrase is a milepost to help the reader recognize the making of a covenant.

Consider also that the theme of the phrase—"be fertile and multiply"—continues well beyond the covenants of primeval history and is also used to prefigure the necessity of God's great covenant with Moses, the giving of the Law. Note the description of the Israelites when they were enslaved in Egypt:

> But the Israelites were fruitful and prolific. They became so numerous and strong that the land was filled with them. Then a new king, who knew nothing of Joseph, came to power in Egypt. He said to his subjects, "Look how numerous and powerful the Israelite people are growing, more so than we ourselves! Come, let us deal shrewdly with them to stop their increase; otherwise, in time of war they too may join our enemies to fight against us, and so leave our country." (Ex 1:7–10)

Viewing the Old Testament as a series of covenants in history allows us to come to a clearer understanding of the final and New Covenant established in the life, Death, and Resurrection of Jesus Christ. In the final covenant, Jesus commands his disciples to be fruitful in another way:

> Then Jesus approached and said to them, "All power in heaven and on earth has been given to me. Go, therefore, and make disciples of all nations, baptizing them in the name of the Father, and of the Son, and of the holy Spirit, teaching them to observe all that I have commanded you. And behold, I am with you always, until the end of the age." (Mt 28:18–20)

The Old Testament serves as a prelude to the New Testament and God's full Revelation in Christ. Though God's Revelation is complete, it is not explicit. It remains the task of the Church, and our own task, to understand its significance over the course of centuries.

 **Reflect**

Why is it important for you to understand the significance of God's Revelation for your own life?

The Truths of Creation

The creation of the world and the creation of man and woman was YHWH's first step at forging a covenant with

Israel. It is easy to understand why the Hebrew biblical authors addressed creation with two stories, and why these stories come first in the Bible. As the *Catechism* teaches:

> The inspired authors have placed them at the beginning of Scripture to express in their solemn language the truths of creation—its origin and its end in God, its order and goodness, the vocation of man, and finally the drama of sin and the hope of salvation. (*CCC*, 289)

God's creative actions also reveal several other important truths about him, including:

1. God alone created the universe freely, directly, and without any help. He began everything that exists outside of himself, he alone is the Creator, and everything that exists in the world depends on God, who gives it being (Gn 1:1).
2. God created everything through the eternal Word, his begotten Son, Jesus (Col 1:16–17).
3. Creation is the common work of the Holy Trinity. God the Father made all things "by the Son and the Spirit" (*CCC*, 292, quoting St. Irenaeus). The prologue to the Gospel of John likewise teaches that the Father created everything by his eternal Word, his beloved Son (Jn 1:1–5, see "Christology in John's Gospel, page 228). The Church also professes the Spirit's role as the "giver of life" (*CCC*, 291). The image of wind ("a mighty wind swept over the waters") in Genesis 1:2 attests to the presence of the Holy Spirit at creation.

God created the world to show his glory and to communicate it. God's perfection is shown through the gifts he offers us, his creations. Human beings are unique because we are made in the image and likeness of God. We are called to share "by knowledge and love" (*CCC*, 356) in God's own life. God, as a means for us to reach our eternal destiny, created everything for us. In turn, we are to offer all creation back to him by reproducing in our lives the image of God's Son made man, the "image of the invisible God" (Col 1:15).

The first story of creation also reveals a great deal about the human person. We have been created by God with both a body and a soul. The "soul" refers to the entire human person. It also refers to the innermost, spiritual aspect of man. God creates the soul immediately at the time of human conception. The soul is also immortal. It does not perish with the body when it separates at death, and it will be reunited with the body at the final resurrection. The human body, too, shares in the image of God because it is intended to be the temple of the Holy Spirit. Also, we are to regard the human body as good and to honor it, since God has created it and will raise it on the last day.

Review

1. What descriptive phrase helps to mark the covenants in the Book of Genesis?
2. In the New Covenant, how does Jesus command his disciples to be fruitful?
3. Name two truths about God revealed in creation stories.

Reflect

Tell three ways that God has made you unique.

The Beginning of God's Revelation

In the person and mission of Jesus Christ, God has fully been revealed. But this Revelation was a gradual one through history. The beginning of God's Revelation to humans came when he made himself known to our first parents.

God invited Adam and Eve to an "intimate communion with himself and clothed them with resplendent grace and justice" (*CCC*, 54). When Adam and Eve sinned ("Sin Interrupts the Story of Salvation," pages 44–45), God did not withdraw the Revelation of himself. Rather, he encouraged humankind with the hope of Salvation and the promise of Redemption.

Sin Interrupts the Story of Salvation

The second creation story in Genesis describes another reality: the sin of Adam and Eve. With their sin, the harmony of original holiness and original justice intended for humankind would be lost.

As with other events in primeval history, the fall of man described in Genesis 3 uses figurative language but describes an actual "deed that took place *at the beginning of the history of man*" (*CCC*, 390) that reveals with the certainty of faith that all human history is marred by an original, voluntary sin committed by our first parents.

The basic root of sin is man's rejection of God and opposition to his will. The second creation story describes how this first happened. Adam and Eve were tempted to sin by a serpent, a fallen angel who was "Satan" or the "devil."

What was the Original Sin? Essentially, it was an abuse of man's freedom. Tempted by the devil, Adam disobeyed God and lacked trust in God's goodness. The Book of Genesis describes the sin as Adam and Eve eating fruit from the forbidden "tree of the knowledge of good and bad" (Gn 2:17, 3:6). All sin, including this

Original Sin, is rooted in disobedience of God. The Original Sin, in essence, is that man *preferred* himself to God. Man was created to be like God in all his glory, but instead, he chose to be like God, but "without God, before God, and not in accordance with God" (*CCC*, 398, quoting St. Maximus the Confessor).

St. Thomas Aquinas taught that sin of Adam is shared by all of his descendants because the whole human race is in Adam "as one body of one man." The Original Sin has consequences for all of humanity. Adam and Eve immediately lost the graces of original holiness. The harmony of original justice is destroyed: human nature is weakened and inclined to sin, our spiritual control over our bodies are lost, tensions between men and women are introduced, and the rest of creation (e.g., animals, climate) becomes hostile to humankind. Moreover, "death makes its entrance into human history" (*CCC*, 400).

Yet it is important to note that even after the sin of Adam and Eve, God immediately offered his mercy and the first promise of a Redeemer for fallen humankind. God said to the serpent:

> I will put enmity between you and the woman
> > and between your offspring and hers;
> He will strike at your head,
> > while you strike at his heel. (Gn 3:15)

The woman's offspring is Jesus Christ. The First Letter of John teaches: "Indeed, the Son of God was revealed to destroy the works of the devil" (1 Jn 3:8).

Still, sin spread quickly after Adam and Eve. Cain's murder of his brother Abel is a personal sin, which arose from the shared Original Sin of humanity. After the incident (Gn 4:1–16), God asks Cain to explain himself and tell where his brother is. Cain responds by saying, "I do not know. Am I my brother's keeper?" Sin has caused him to abdicate his responsibility for others, a practice that continues on through each generation. Interestingly, notice that God allows Cain to live, a different punishment than is demanded for murder in the Mosaic Law (Ex 21:12). The story, in other words, tells us something about humans and law, but something even more about God and his compassion.

The doctrine of Original Sin is an essential truth of the faith. Without the doctrine of Original Sin, the mystery of Christ is undermined. We come into the world as sinners and need God's compassion and the Salvation that is offered to all through Christ. As the exultant at the Easter vigil proclaims:

O happy, fault, O necessary sin of
    Adam,
     which gained for us so great a
      Redeemer!

 Review

1. What is the basic root of sin?
2. What are the consequences of Original Sin?

Reflect

Why is the Original Sin a "happy fault"?

The Great Flood

The last story cycle in Genesis 1–11 is centered on the Great Flood. The covenant that God made with Noah is part of the next stage of his Revelation. Noah became the new ancestor for humankind. God blessed him and his sons and said to them: "Be fertile and multiply and fill the earth" (Gn 9:1). The covenant with Noah revealed the basic precepts of the law and combated paganism, a combination of idol worship (**idolatry**) and worship of many gods (polytheism). This covenant also called all people—including Gentiles—to relationship with God and remains in force "until the universal proclamation of the Gospel" (*CCC,* 58).

The ancient peoples surrounding the Hebrews also had flood legends. One of the most famous is part of the great myth cycle of a Mesopotamian poem known as the *Epic of Gilgamesh*. Many copies of *Gilgamesh* have been found by archaeologists, from as early as 2000 BC in some places and as early as the sixth century BC in other locations. It was obviously an ancient story that was widely known and very popular throughout the region. The Hebrews, too, would have known the story.

While there are similarities between the flood story of the *Epic of Gilgamesh* and the inspired text of Scripture, the Hebrew story shares how God reveals himself to man and a hint to man's

idolatry
Worshipping something or someone other than the true God. It is a sin against the First Commandment.

eventual destiny. Here are some of the unique teachings of the Hebrew version:

- Humanity is to be destroyed because they are evil and constantly doing violence to each other.

- Noah is saved because he is a righteous man.

- The Gilgamesh hero takes money on the ark. Noah only takes animals.

- The Hebrew version represents a "second creation story." Noah takes the place of a new "Adam."

Now we understand the wisdom of the Church's interpretation and understanding of elements of this story. The story says that God made an everlasting covenant with Noah and humankind. God intervenes in history and offers his Salvation. This will be an ongoing occurrence through the Old Testament, leading to God's ultimate intervention in history, the Incarnation of his Son, Jesus Christ, who offers Salvation to all.

 **Reflect**

How does God intervene in your life in a positive way?

WHY SO MANY FLOOD STORIES?

The *Epic of Gilgamesh* is one of many flood stories from the ancient world. There are some biblical scholars who believe that the reason for the many flood stories (including the Genesis story of the Great Flood) relates specifically to an ancient *historic* event.

One theory of the preponderance of flood legends, according to Columbia University geologists, is that as the Ice Age ended, glaciers melted, and a wall of seawater surged from the Mediterranean into the Black Sea. During the Ice Age, the geologists argue, the Black Sea was an isolated freshwater lake surrounded by farmland.

Then, according to the theory, about twelve thousand years ago, toward the end of the Ice Age, the Earth began growing warmer. Vast sheets of ice that sprawled over the Northern Hemisphere began to melt. Oceans and seas grew deeper as a result. About seven thousand years ago, even the Mediterranean Sea swelled. Seawater pushed northward, slicing through what is now Turkey. Funneled through the narrow Bosporus, the water hit the Black Sea with two hundred times the force of Niagara Falls. Each day the Black Sea rose about six inches and coastal farms were flooded. Settlements were discovered in what is today submerged former shorelines of the Black Sea.

Seared into the memories of terrified survivors, the story of the flood was passed down through the generations and eventually became the basis for some of the ancient flood stories.

This is a relatively recent theory, and lots of materials are available online and in recent books to assemble more information. Ruins of civilizations are being explored along what is supposed to be the ancient shoreline of the Black Sea to find out if these were the original villages and cities of the flood victims.

Cuneiform tablet describing Gilgamesh Flood Epic

The Tower of Babel: More Hope for the World

The last of the primeval history events of Genesis 1–11 details how the sin of pride brought into the world by the sin of Adam increased to the point that an entire city tried to make itself God. The short nine-verse story (Gn 11:1–9) also has a secondary motive: to show in an imaginative way how the many different languages of the world came to be. This of itself is a hopeful gesture to humankind (below).

Notice *where* this is taking place. The place is called "Shinar" (verse 2). This is an ancient term that the Bible often uses for "Babylon" (and thus the play on the name "Babel"). Why is Babylon important? Remember that Babylon was the great empire that conquered Jerusalem and destroyed Solomon's Temple in 587 BC. This powerful memory of the Hebrews

development. The Church teaches that God willed the diversity of his creatures and their own particular goodness, their interdependence, and their order. This diversity is deeply celebrated by God's liberation of the people that follows through a genealogy that begins with Noah's son, Shem, and ends with the patriarch Abraham.

The primeval history stories of Genesis tell us much about the Hebrew people—including what they value about life and their beliefs about YHWH. Here is a summary of some of the things these stories teach us about God and his will:

- God's will is to create a people in his image—both male and female.

- God's will is peace, not violence. Violence is considered sinful in these stories. God creates in peace—it is humans that bring on violence. The flood story suggests that God was so sickened by human violence that God regretted making humanity.

- God's will is trust and truthfulness—not the lies and deceptions of human beings in their society.

- God's will is care for creation—not destruction and exploitation.

- God's will is joyful diversity—not forced unification.

- God is not impressed with how great our human material accomplishments are, but with how we care for each other and also how we care for the created environment.

was so great that "Babylon" passed into history as a symbol for *any* oppressive empire or state. The New Testament uses Babylon to refer to the Roman Empire (e.g., 1 Pt 5:13; Rv 16:19; 18:2, 10, 21).

Next, consider the second part of the story. One interpretation of the diversity of languages is that God is punishing the people for their sins. However, the unification of all humanity under one language, and putting them all to work to build a great city and tower, would have been good only for the rulers. The scattering of the peoples into different languages would really have been God's *liberation* for most of the people of "Shinar."

Therefore, dividing into different peoples and languages was not punishment, but freedom. Consider the parallel story in Acts 2:5–13. We now can appreciate that each person gathered in Jerusalem at the Pentecost feast heard Peter *in his or her own language*, also a positive

Review

1. What are two unique teachings of the Hebrew version of the Great Flood?

2. How was the scattering of people into different languages really a source of liberation for most people of "Shinar"?

Reflect

Which teaching from the Genesis primeval history stories speaks most clearly to your life? Explain.

Abraham and the Patriarchs

Genesis 1–11 is markedly different from Genesis 12–50. As mentioned, the first eleven chapters of the Book of Genesis poetically describe primeval history, the world as God intended it to be and what human sinfulness made of it. In chapter 12, the focus changes to God's Revelation to a shepherd living in Ur, an ancient city in Mesopotamia. Abram was later renamed Abraham, the "father of a multitude," and called by God to travel to a new land. Abraham, and the account of the other **patriarchs**, Isaac and Jacob, and the narrative surrounding Jacob's son, Joseph, are not counted as history in the strict sense, though people from Abraham onward can be placed in the historical and social setting of the Near East from 2000 to 1700 BC.

The first thing to notice about Genesis 12–50, besides that it covers a great deal of material, is that this really reads like a collection of short stories. Each of these sections has a clear beginning and a clear ending. When the Bible was divided into chapters and verses (much later than the original manuscripts, of course, which have no such numbers) it was easy to divide Genesis into chapters because the stories easily divide into units.

This is the reason stories about the main characters in Genesis are often referred to as "cycles" of stories: they read very much like a series of short stories all based on prominent central characters which were gathered together into one cycle. When Genesis is read and studied this way, one aspect of the book becomes surprisingly clear. Look at the chapters in which the main characters of Genesis appear. The total chapters are in parentheses:

- Abraham—chapters 12–23, 25 (13)
- Isaac—chapters 24, 26–27 (3)
- Jacob—chapters 28–35, 49 (9)
- Joseph—chapters 37–48, 50 (12)

Who are the dominant people in the Book of Genesis? Abraham, certainly, but second to him are Joseph, followed by Jacob. Isaac is more like a transitional figure, without a great deal of tradition surrounding his life and adventure. This section of the text focuses the most attention on the patriarchs that the authors of Genesis wrote the most about. Also, it is worth noting that the stories of these ancestors describe both positive and negative experiences. The reason for this: the authors intended for the readers to learn both from what worked from their ancestors and from their mistakes. A prime religious lesson of these chapters is that God used these very human personalities to accomplish the divine will: the creation and preservation of a special People who would reveal God to all the nations.

🌐 Reflect

Do you learn better from the successes of those who have lived before you or their failures? Explain.

patriarchs
Male rulers, elders, or leaders. The patriarchs of the faith of Israel are Abraham, Isaac, and Jacob.

Covenant with Abraham

The Genesis account seems intent on showing that Abraham wandered throughout all of the known world. His journey foreshadows the one that the Hebrew people will later make in various stages of their history. For example, his return from Egypt is a preview of the Hebrews' journey out of Egypt following the Exodus that will form the people of Israel in the stories of Moses.

Abraham's descendants also eventually journeyed far and wide in the Jewish Diaspora. And, St. Paul, another spiritual descendant of Abraham, traveled all over his known world—the Roman Empire—to share the Good News of Jesus Christ, who was himself a traveling preacher teaching *all* people. God's message always "travels."

One of the most important elements of the Abraham tradition is the covenant God establishes with Abraham. God entered into a covenant with Abraham, assuring him that the Divine Word would come about and be maintained through his posterity, an early sign of the People's faith in the resurrection. The most important covenant in the Old Testament is God's covenant with Moses that includes the giving of the Law. There is also the covenant with Noah, as mentioned in "The Great Flood" on pages 45–46. God also established a covenant with King David. The *terms* of God's covenant with Abraham are laid out in Genesis 12:1–3. First, God tells what he requires of Abraham:

> Go forth from the land of your kinsfolk and from your father's house to a land that I will show you. (Gn 12:1)

God's part of the agreement comes next:

> I will make of you a great nation,
> and I will bless you;
> I will make your name great,
> so that you will be a blessing.
> I will bless those who bless you
> and curse those who curse you.
> All the communities of the earth
> shall find blessing in you. (Gn 12:2–3)

Besides the terms, there is typically a *sign* or *symbol* of biblical covenants. With Moses, for example, the sign is the giving of the laws themselves. With Abraham, there are two such signs. First, his name is changed from Abram to Abraham. His wife's name

is changed from Sarai to Sarah. More importantly, there is the sign of **circumcision**. The tradition of practicing circumcision on all Hebrew is attributed to Abraham himself. Since Abraham's heirs were to come from Abraham's own natural child (and not an adopted child, as Abraham apparently thought at first. See Genesis 15), then it seems obvious that this sign would somehow be connected to the idea of descendants or offspring. Thus, the sign was circumcision—a physical symbol on the male genitals—since God's part of the covenant deals with offspring and descendants (Gn 17:1–10).

Understanding the promise made to Abraham is a crucial element for gaining a modern Catholic understanding of the Bible. The Church teaches, for example, that God chose Abraham and made a covenant with him and his descendants, and that by the covenant God formed his people. Abraham's faith in God's promises is considered an act of righteousness; that is, the "right" attitude a person should have toward God. As St. Paul pointed out, "For what does the scripture say? Abraham believed in God, and it was credited to him as righteousness" (Rom 4:3). The Church is an extension of the covenant with Abraham, part of God's People. As the *Catechism of the Catholic Church* explains:

> The people descended from Abraham would be the trustees of the promise made to the patriarchs, the chosen people, called to prepare for that day when God would gather all his children into the unity of the Church. They would be the root onto which the Gentiles would be grafted, once they came to believe. (*CCC*, 60)

Blessing and Threats

Another important theme in the early ancestor stories of Abraham is "blessings," which have been promised to him and his descendants by God. It is God who is the source of the blessings. But in conjunction with the blessings are related "threats" which are not of God's doing but attributed to human weakness and doubt.

In other words, in many of these stories, even though God has blessed and made a promise, there are also threats to that promise—possibilities that the promise will not be kept. For example, Abraham is promised heirs through his wife Sarah, but she doubts that she will be able to have children because of her age. Later, Abraham himself feels threatened. Will he have to sacrifice his child? These twists in the plot and drama also serve to make the lessons learned even more memorable. The subsections below look at a few more of these.

External Threats to Sarah (Genesis 12:10-20 and Genesis 20:1-18)

Already in Genesis 12:10–20, the future of Abraham is threatened. Sarah

circumcision
The surgical removal of the male foreskin; it was the physical sign of the covenant between God and Abraham.

is taken into the household of Pharaoh. The details of this brief story are so minimal that it does not answer many questions that we have, but the fact that Sarah experiences the "captivity" of Pharaoh, and thus anticipates the later oppression of the Hebrews is surely a central idea in this brief story. But the threat is also very clear. How can Sarah bear the promised descendants of Abraham if she is in the harem of the Pharaoh? In 12:17, "the LORD struck Pharaoh and his household with severe plagues" (another reference to the later Exodus story?) so that he releases Sarah, and they are both asked to leave Egypt.

There is another example of this "external threat" in Genesis 20. There, the story is repeated with a ruler who is local in Palestine, and not from Egypt. Some of the other details are different. For example, the ruler in this version is warned by God (Gn 20:3) and therefore is able to avoid the sin of marrying a woman who is already married. Both versions of this story, however, represent "external" threats to God's promise.

Internal Threats to Sarah (Genesis 16 and 21:1-21)

Unlike external threats from the Egyptian Pharaoh or a local ruler, Abimelech, two stories in Genesis 16, and again in Genesis 21:1–21, Sarah has doubts that she really is going to be the bearer of the promised descendents of Israel. The internal threat is her own lack of faith.

In Genesis 16, she is so doubtful that she will be able to become pregnant that she asks Abraham to have a son through Hagar, an Egyptian servant of Sarah. (Hagar's son Ishmael is honored as the father of another great people, the later "Ishmaelites," who are often thought to be the Arab peoples in popular tradition.) Then, in Genesis 21:1–21, Sarah does herself produce a son—Isaac—who is the answer to God's promise.

But the image of Sarah's character is called into question in both stories. First, because of her doubts of

God's promise (Gn 16), and secondly because of her jealousy of Hagar and her son even though he is also an heir to Abraham. When Sarah notices Isaac playing with Ishmael, she demands that Abraham "drive out that slave and her son" (Gn 21:10). This seems very unfair. After all, Hagar had Ishmael only because Sarah suggested the plan.

What lessons could God have intended with these inspired writings? A key lesson involves Hagar herself. Hagar is a woman, a servant girl, and a foreigner, and yet the Bible shows how God's compassion extends beyond the central character of Abraham and his wife Sarah. In both Genesis 16 and Genesis 21, she is seriously mistreated, and yet God "hears her cries" and takes care of both her and Ishmael. The later Mosaic Laws, and the prophet Jeremiah, teach that God demands care for "the widow, the orphan, and the foreigner" (e.g., Dt 27:19; Jer 7:6; 22:3). The story of Hagar clearly illustrates this "justice of God." She and Ishmael *are* a "widow, orphan, and foreigner" when they are sent away by Abraham.

Threat to the Heir (Genesis 22:1-19)

Another incident that clearly follows the theme of promised blessing and threat is one of the most troubling in the entire Bible. It is the recounting of Abraham's near sacrifice of Isaac, Genesis 22:1–19. What a horrible threat this story seems to be! Could God actually have asked for a *human* sacrifice? Notably, there was human sacrifice in Canaanite religious practice, and in many other religious traditions surrounding the Israelites. That an Ancient Near Eastern deity asks for a human sacrifice would not have been unprecedented. It is possible that Abraham would have been sad, but not shocked, with this request, so common in other religions all around him.

However, the author of Genesis represents this challenge as a "test "of human character (much in the same way Job's character is tested in the Book of Job).

The climax of the incident is that God provides another sacrifice—the ram dies in place of Isaac—and thus saves the child. Child sacrifice is, in the story, finally not accepted. This is one of the lessons of the story: Hebrews do not sacrifice humans to their God. Others believe that the story is about Abraham's trust that God would somehow provide a way through this test.

Christians can read the passage in yet another way. It is a profound anticipation of another "Father" who is anguished at the *human* demand that he "sacrifice a son" on the Cross. God was faithful in affirming the promise—both at the mountain of Moriah in Genesis 22, and the mountain of Golgotha (see, for example, Mk 15:22). When God demanded sacrifice in Genesis 22, he provided an alternative to the loss of Abraham's son. When crowds gathered before Jesus, crying, "Crucify him!"—crowds that represent all human rejections of God's plan for our lives—we were not so generous.

There are several possible explanations for the contrast between blessings and threats in these incidents. Part of this interplay is probably the inspired author's art. All good stories involve a plot twist—a danger that the hero must overcome—in order for the story to be dramatic. We must consider another, more important, message as we try to understand God's intentions. These stories of the patriarchs teach us to trust God as the giver of all blessings—and to continue to trust him even when things seem difficult. A good story should surprise, upset, teach, and comfort. Genesis certainly does all of these things and more.

Review

1. Why are the stories of the main characters in Genesis 12-50 often referred to as "cycles" of stories?

2. What are the terms of God's covenant with Abraham?

3. Why is it important that the sign of circumcision in God's covenant with Abraham is connected with the male genitals?

4. Why is the covenant with Abraham crucial for Catholics in understanding the Bible?

5. Name an external and internal threat to Sarah from the Book of Genesis.

6. What is the lesson of the story of Abraham's near sacrifice of Isaac?

The Blessing of Jacob

Isaac's role in the Book of Genesis is smaller than that of Abraham, Jacob, and Joseph. Isaac is a transitional character between the Abraham and Jacob stories.

Rebekah loves her younger son, Jacob, while Isaac seems to prefer his firstborn, Esau. In order to secure Isaac's blessing on Jacob, Rebekah instructs him to deceive his father and take his older brother's place. Isaac is fooled and Jacob gets his blessing, but then he must flee.

An interesting point of consideration about the trickery involved concerns the possibility that the story was produced at a time when the Hebrews were in exile. In that case, Jacob's trickery becomes more meaningful to a people forced to use tricks and quick thinking as survival skills to deal with authority figures and domineering conquerors. Also, the story may have had an additional political message. The Hebrews had many local enemies, including the Edomites, a group that lived across the Jordan and south of the Dead Sea. In the story, Jacob tricked his brother Esau out of his birthright by cooking a *red* stew (Gn 25:29–30). The Hebrew word for "red" is also "edom." In fact, Genesis 36:8 makes the equation clear: "Esau is Edom."

Those points aside, the familiar story of Genesis 27 begins the stories of Jacob, all of which involve one form of trickery or another. In a sense, then, the figure of Rebekah and the deception she introduces really sets up the incidents involving Jacob. It could be argued that these stories represent the hope that Israel can at times live in peace with its neighbors, especially the Edomites. In this case, Jacob is able to humble himself, ask for forgiveness, and even offer compensation for past injustices, all in the name of making peace. Part of the power of this story is to suggest that if Jacob and Esau can reconcile, even peace between nations is possible.

⬤ Review

What does the story of Jacob and Esau teach about reconciliation?

Joseph and His Brothers

Some of the most dramatic stories in the Old Testament revolve around Jacob's twelve sons, especially his favorite son, Joseph (Gn 37, 39–50). The "J" author was the first to put these stories in writing, taking various stories about Joseph, Israel's earliest days in Egypt, and certain traditions about some of the brothers and tribes and weaving them into one story, a literary masterpiece. The story has elements of adventure, intrigue, romance, and suspense.

A good deal of the Joseph narrative is based on historical events and Egyptian culture.

Throughout most of ancient history—from about 3000 BC through the Roman era at the time of Jesus—Egypt had a massive, centralized economy served by thousands of slaves and poor agricultural farmers. The massive architecture of Egypt, so impressive today to modern tourists, was built on the backs of massive amounts of human labor (often foreign slaves like the Canaanites and Hebrews) working to serve Pharaoh.

The administration of Egypt famously hoarded impressive amounts of wealth, collected on the basis of rich agricultural produce from the Nile River and the widespread trade that Egypt engaged in with its agricultural surplus. Groups of people from the northern lands of Canaan would often take refuge in Egypt in times of severe famine, because the Nile River was considerably less susceptible to weather changes than the more fragile agricultural economy of Palestine.

Furthermore, there is little indication of much concern for the general well-being of the wider population, beyond the Pharaoh's religious responsibility to maintain good relations with the Egyptian gods, thereby "guaranteeing" the productivity of the land. It is hard to know, frankly, whether the Joseph narrative is based on an ancient Hebrew admiration for the achievements of Egypt, or resentment of Egyptian dominance (and frequent interference) in the affairs of the Palestine economy. One question to consider is whether we are meant to admire Joseph's role in Egyptian dominance or, like Jacob's trickery, question his judgment.

Finally, however, the Joseph stories set the stage for the main event of the Old Testament—the formation of the people of Israel by their Exodus experience and their efforts to carve out a life for themselves in Canaan. The Book of Genesis concludes with these words and a request made by Joseph to his brothers:

"I am about to die. God will surely take care of you and lead you out of this land to the land that he promised on oath to Abraham, Isaac and Jacob." Then, putting the sons of Israel under oath, he continued, "When God thus takes care of you, you must bring my bones up with you from this place." (Gn 50:24–25)

These verses and words of Joseph lead the journey to the study of the Book of Exodus. A point to move forward with from the Book of Genesis themes is the revelation of God's relationship to the world, and to Israel. God is a loving Creator, but also a just judge. YHWH, the God of the covenant, accepts human weakness and continues to love as a redeemer who is faithful to his Word. God works through human events, making good come out of apparent evil and molding people according to the divine will. These themes apply to our own lives as well. The Lord accepts and loves us, even in our sinfulness, and works in our lives in unexpected ways.

⊙ Review

What event marked the beginning of Israel as a separate nation?

Hyksos
A group of non-Egyptians who came to power in Egypt between 1650 and 1500 BC.

The Book of Exodus

At the end of the story of Joseph in the Book of Genesis, the setting is Egypt. As time passes, according to the introduction in the Book of Exodus, the Egyptians forget the positive accomplishments of Joseph and there is growing anxiety in Egypt about the increase in the number of Hebrews. In fact, the Joseph stories may have been situated in a brief period of foreign rule in Egypt that occurred between 1650 and 1500 BC. Egyptian records from that time do make reference to the rule of a people called the "Hyksos"—an Egyptian term for "foreigner." The **Hyksos** were probably not people of a distinct race but the rulers among the non-Egyptian population of the time. It would have been possible for a Hebrew like Joseph to rise to a high position among the Hyksos, and perhaps that explains the enslavement of the Hebrews. All those who served and benefited from the Hyksos's rule may have been punished once the Egyptian rulers regained power.

As with the other books of the Torah, the stories of Exodus were likely collected and edited at the time of the Babylonian exile, about seven hundred years after the events took place. The people exiled in Babylon would certainly have understood what it was like to be held in slavery, and they would have been comforted and encouraged by stories that celebrated the liberation of slaves.

Exodus is just such a recounting of events, telling of the miraculous release of the Israelites from Egypt, their journey across the Red Sea to Mount Sinai, where they entered into a special covenant with God. At Mount Sinai, through Moses, God gave the Israelites the Law—the moral, civil, and worship regulations which allowed them to become a holy people. Before the Exodus, the stories of the Bible focused on individual patriarchs and matriarchs and their families. But when God delivered the Israelites from slavery in Egypt, it marked the beginning of their history as a separate nation. God uniquely singled out Israel to witness to the one, true Lord.

This section focuses on four main elements of the Book of Exodus:

- The call of Moses and the prominence of his life.
- The Israelites' liberation from slavery to freedom.
- The Passover event.
- The Sinai Covenant.

The Call of Moses (Exodus 2:1-22)

Exodus 2 begins by telling the story of Moses's birth, the threat to his life from the edict of the Pharaoh, and his mother's attempts to protect him. The story of the infant Moses floating down the Nile River in a basket most likely had a long oral tradition. It is the only story that survives from his youth, but its existence in Scripture is enough to inform us that Moses's role will be an important one.

The Hebrew authors claim that Moses's name derived from the Hebrew verb *masha*—"to draw out" (Ex 2:10), though it is also strongly related to the names of Egyptian pharaohs "Thut<u>mosis</u>" or "Ah<u>mose</u>," meaning simply "son of" or "progeny of." The special attention paid in Exodus 2:10 to the Hebrew root of the name Moses has important significance. This was the only point made in verse 10. It serves to establish Moses's Hebrew identity despite his Egyptian upbringing, and refers both to his own being "drawn out" of

the River Nile and to his efforts to draw the Hebrew people out of Egypt. At that point, the story abruptly ends, and an entirely different time in the life of Moses begins at Exodus 2:11.

Beginning with Exodus 2:11–22, Moses is an adult, confronting for the first time one of the main themes of the entire Mosaic tradition—the slavery of the Hebrew people. While there are doubts about the exact historical details of the Mosaic stories, the slave economy of Egypt is quite clearly historically accurate, and is often referred to in Egyptian documents from that time. There are even ancient Egyptian writings that refer to the escape of slaves, although not in great numbers.

When Moses intervenes in two fights between Hebrew slaves and Egyptian slave masters, he immediately gets into trouble. In the first fight, Moses kills an Egyptian slave master to prevent him from beating a Hebrew slave. In the second, he is blamed by two Hebrews (who are fighting amongst themselves) for assuming that he has anything to teach them, and it becomes obvious that he has been recognized as the one who killed the Egyptian in the first fight. After these episodes, he lives for years among a desert-dwelling people called the Midianites, where he marries and learns to shepherd his father-in-law's flock. It is while he is living in the desert that he receives his amazing call to be the liberator of God's People.

This short introduction to Moses suggests that violence is not going to be the way of success for him. He will not defeat the Pharaoh in a great battle, nor free the slaves by force of arms. The inspired message of these early chapters of Exodus is that a power much greater than Moses's own human attempts is necessary to settle the issue of the Hebrews' slavery. God himself must liberate his people, though Moses will be the instrument he chooses to bring this about.

Tetragrammaton
Greek for "four letters," the term refers to the sacred term YHWH as it appeared in the sacred writings of the Jews.

 **Reflect**

How do you understand yourself to be an instrument of God's will?

"I Am the One Who Is" (Exodus 2:23-3:23)

In Exodus 3, God calls Moses to his mission. Moses meets God in a fiery bush in the desert, a bush that at first attracts Moses's attention because it does not burn though it is engulfed in flames. In Exodus 3:14, God shares his name with Moses. It is a mysterious name, translated into English as "I am who I am"—but actually built on the basic Hebrew verb "is" from which the biblical name "YHWH" derives. "It is a mysterious name because God is mystery" (*CCC*, 206). Orthodox Jews do not pronounce this name (believing it to be so sacred that they must not speak it). In 2008, Pope Benedict XVI reminded the Church of this practice of the Jews, and taught that the **Tetragrammaton** is not to be pronounced in Catholic liturgy or music ("What Is God's Name?" below).

WHAT IS GOD'S NAME?

In Hebrew, after the tradition arose among the Jews that one should not speak YHWH, the holy name of God, the Jewish scribes came up with a little trick to remind readers not to pronounce it by accident—especially in *public* reading of the Scriptures.

In order to understand this trick, remember that Hebrew is written with consonants only, and not vowels (which are indicated, instead, by little signs above and below the consonants). What the scribes did was to take the vowel signs from the word Adonai ("Lord") and artificially put them on the consonants of "YHWH." It was not really supposed to be pronounced. Rather, it was supposed to remind the reader to say "Adonai" not "YHWH."

At some point, the tradition was forgotten among Christians, and the word was misread, taking the consonants *and* the added vowels. This new word came out "Jehovah." This means that, contrary to what some Christians believe, "Jehovah" is *not* the "true" name of God. In fact, the opposite is true; it is a historically mistaken reading.

The traditional name for God is "YHWH" (usually pronounced "Yah-way," but even this is partly an assumed pronunciation). Parts of this name are heard in Hebrew personal names like "YAH-shua"= Joshua/Jesus, or "Jer-em-e -YAH"= Jeremiah. Also, "Elohim" is a name for God that was widely used, depending on the geographic region. Elohim was often thought to be more typical of the northern Israelites, and YHWH more common in southern Israel. Elohim appears in Hebrew names like "Mich-EL," "Dan-i-EL," and "Ari-EL."

What is important in the Moses tradition is not necessarily the *name* of God, but rather *how* God is known and *what* God has done and will do: "God, who reveals himself as 'I AM,' reveals himself as the God who is always there, present to his people in order to save them" (*CCC*, 207).

Exodus 3:15–17 presents an interesting summary of who God is by mentioning the ancestors of Israel (Abraham, Isaac, and Jacob) as well as the events that will take place—liberation from Egypt and entry into the Promised Land. This is what is really important to the Hebrews—God is known by what he does, not by special names or words.

Interestingly, the name of Jesus communicates this fact. The name "Jesus" literally means "YHWH Saves." Even the name of the Messiah communicates that God is known by what he *does*, not primarily by what he is *called*.

Slavery to Freedom

There are many elements to the great story of God's conflict with Pharaoh, and the horrific events that lead up to the final release of the Hebrews from Egyptian bondage. There are also a number of interesting understandings about how these stories—which include the ten plagues—are to be read.

One common understanding of the ten plagues is that each is directed against a specific Egyptian god. But trying to match up all the plagues with known deities and their images presents problems. Consider the following:

Plague	Egyptian God
1. Nile turned to blood	Khnum or Hapi (god of water or the River Nile)
2. Frogs	Heket (goddess of childbirth portrayed as frog)
3. Lice/gnats	?
4. Flies	?
5. Pestilence	Hathor (god portrayed as a bull)
6. Boils	?
7. Hail	Seth (god of wind and storms)
8. Locusts	Min (goddess of fertility and vegetation)
9. Darkness	Amon-Re (sun god)
10. Death of Firstborn	Osiris (god of judgment or death)

Not only does this theory fail to account for the three plagues that *cannot* be associated with any known gods, but some of the gods are associated with the plague by their image (i.e., Heket and Hathor), others by the area over which they were understood to have influence (i.e., Seth, Min, Amon-Re, and Osiris), and some of these gods were never "worshipped" by the Egyptians at all (i.e., Khnum or Hapi). The idea that each plague was directed against a specific Egyptian deity is a clever argument, but ultimately must be set aside as contrary to what we know, both of biblical texts and Egyptian history and culture. In fact, the biblical portrayal presents these plagues as directed against Pharaoh himself. He was, after all, considered a divine figure in Egypt whose responsibilities included the well-being of Egypt itself.

Similar questions must be raised about another popular theory that these plagues were actually naturally occurring circumstances. Perhaps, for example, red algae of some kind turned the Nile red and made the water undrinkable (the first plague). Perhaps excessive flooding of the Nile River Valley left pools of standing water for mosquitoes (the third plague). Perhaps there was an outbreak of anthrax among the livestock of Egypt, infecting cattle and even making the people sick (the fifth and tenth plagues). Hailstorms and locusts are obviously both naturally occurring phenomena (the seventh and eighth plagues). And so on.

Such an explanation starts out to prove that the story of the Israelites' escape from the Pharaoh is possible, that it can be believed because the plagues can be explained rationally. But others take that explanation one step further and argue that if that the plagues are not miraculous at all, if they are merely "natural events," then Moses, Pharaoh, and all the people were entirely fooled into thinking that some "God" was behind these merely freakish events of nature. In truth, no matter what way the story is examined, God was the initiator of these events. It was in the Exodus that "God formed Israel as his people by freeing them from slavery in Egypt" (*CCC*, 62).

The first nine plagues follow an arrangement of three sets of plagues, which are indicated by the special way that each set is introduced. Each set includes three different plagues:

Set A (plagues 1, 4, and 7)
- Introduced with a phrase instructing Moses to go to the pharaoh in the morning.

Set B (plagues 2, 5, and 8)
- Introduced with the phrase "The LORD said to Moses, 'Go to Pharaoh. . . .'"

Set C (plagues 3, 6, and 9)
- Introduced by instruction from God to Moses or Aaron to perform an act.

Plague	Introductory Phrase	Set
Nile turned to blood	Exodus 7:15	A
Frogs	Exodus 8:1	B
Gnats	Exodus 8:12	C
Flies	Exodus 8:20	A
Pestilence (cattle dying)	Exodus 9:1	B
Boils	Exodus 9:8	C
Hail	Exodus 9:13	A
Locusts	Exodus 10:1	B
Darkness	Exodus 10:21	C

The arrangement of the plagues into three sets by introductory phrases was an interesting literary technique. The purpose of the plague stories is not to show God's power over Pharaoh or even that he can work miracles, but that God's will is for liberation of slaves and the creation of a people out of the enslaved and oppressed. What is important is that God revealed his will to the Israelites, and they understood their history as a people in light of that Revelation. These stories teach us about God and the formation of his people, the Israelites. They teach that God chooses slaves—that he liberates the oppressed. They teach that earthly powers, such as Pharaoh, cannot maintain oppression when God wills liberation. They also teach that with liberation comes responsibility.

 ## Reflect

How do you find the statement "with liberation comes responsibility" to be true?

The Release from Egypt

It appears most likely that, once again, two different oral traditions have been woven together in the Book of Exodus to tell the story of how the Israelites left Egypt. In the conclusion of the nine plagues in Exodus 10:28, Pharaoh and Moses have the following exchange:

> "Leave my presence," Pharaoh said to him, "and see to it that you do not appear before me again! The day you appear before me you shall die!" Moses replied, "Well said! I will never appear before you again."

But look at the words of the Lord to Moses that begin chapter 11:

> Then the LORD told Moses, "One more plague will I bring upon Pharaoh and upon Egypt. After that he will let you depart. In fact, he will not merely let you go; he will drive you away." (Ex 11:1)

Exodus 10 ended with Moses saying that the Israelites were leaving, yet Exodus 11 opens with God calling for another plague. A discriminating reader will wonder why.

The usual answer is that the end of Exodus 10 and the beginning of Exodus 11 is a rather awkward transition between *two originally different traditions about how the people of Israel left Egypt*. Chapters 7 to 10 of Exodus represent the "nine plagues" tradition, and chapter 11 is the story of the Israelites leaving Egypt following the first Passover. By weaving in the beginning of the Passover tradition at the end of Exodus 10, it becomes the "tenth" plague. But, perhaps it was once an entirely unique story about how the people left Egypt after one horrendous event—the death of the firstborn of Egypt.

Furthermore, by adding the Passover tradition to the tradition of the nine plagues, the text obscures a connection that would otherwise be more obvious—that the "Passover" event is directly related to the *beginning* of the story of Moses. Without the intervening chapters that relate the nine plagues, it is possible to connect the killing of the firstborn Egyptian children (Ex 12:29–30) to the edict of the Egyptian pharaoh to kill the Hebrew boys at the time of Moses's birth (Ex 1:15–16). Rather than being merely horrendous or even cruel, the Passover event can be understood as punishment on the Egyptian people for the Pharaoh's original decree. Violence leads to violence.

The two traditions of the release of the Hebrews from Egypt may blur an exact understanding of how the Exodus actually took place in history. But there was a distinct religious purpose to editing these materials together to form the story as it is now included in the Old Testament, mainly that

* God keeps his promises to his people, and

- God is a God of liberation and not enslavement.

Another important teaching to keep in mind is that as Jews celebrate Passover today, they commemorate the saving actions of God and give thanks for them. The "Exodus events are made present to the memory of believers so that they may conform their lives to them" (*CCC*, 1363). In the Church's liturgy, the memorial takes on a new, deeper meaning and the saving events actually become present: "When the Church celebrates the Eucharist, she commemorates Christ's Passover, and it is made present: the sacrifice Christ offered once for all on the cross remains ever present" (*CCC*, 1364).

◉ Review

1. How does the meaning of Moses's name relate to his mission later in life?

2. Why do Orthodox Jews refrain from speaking the Tetragrammaton?

3. Who are the ten plagues directed against? Who initiated the plagues?

4. What are the lessons of the ten plagues?

5. How does the Eucharist give deeper meaning to the Passover events?

"murmurings"
The stories in the Book of Exodus about the complaints against Moses and against God.

elders
Mature, usually male, members of the Israelite community who met regularly to rule on specific disputes within the community.

The Wandering of the People in the Wilderness

After a canticle sung by Moses and the Israelites celebrating God's saving power (Ex 15:1–17), Exodus continues with another story cycle containing traditional stories about the life of the Israelites during the time they were wandering in the wilderness (Ex 15:18–Ex 18). Sometimes these episodes are referred to as **"murmurings"** as they are primarily a series of complaints from the people against the leadership of Moses, and eventually, against God himself.

These chapters depict an unruly and restive people who have left Egypt, unsure of their future. They complain about food (Ex 16:1–4) and water (Ex 17:1–3), and they face serious dangers from desert peoples who are considerably less than hospitable (Ex 17:8–16). Finally, Moses's father-in-law, Jethro, suggests that Moses select some helpers from among the people to assist in organizing the group (Ex 18). This story provides a plausible explanation of the leadership of **elders** among the Hebrews, although this is not a particularly unusual social system for agrarian societies.

How many people wandered in the wilderness with Moses? The traditional number, 600,000 (Ex 12:37), seems unacceptably high. Not only is this number quite likely larger than the

entire population of whole sections of Palestine, but also it would represent a massive number of people trying to survive in the Sinai desert. The problem is typically solved by pointing out that the Hebrew term usually translated "thousands" can also be translated "family group" or "village group." So, if there were six hundred "family groups" that left Egypt, a more reasonable number would be no more than six thousand (and perhaps much less)—certainly not over half a million people! We should also keep in mind that the Bible mentions that some Egyptians and possibly other foreigners left with the Hebrews (Ex 12:38)—so it was a group of mixed ancestry long before Israel was formed as a nation in the Promised Land.

 **Reflect**

What are some ways that contemporary people respond when they are unsure about their futures?

The Sinai Covenant

A very wise old Bible teacher once said: "There is no 'Exodus' without 'Sinai!'" The meaning of this, of course, is that freedom always comes with responsibility—a life lesson that most successful people eventually heed! For example, young people given more freedom by their parents to become their own persons simultaneously must learn to take on more responsibilities in order to use those freedoms wisely. The Bible teacher's important statement helps us to understand better that the events surrounding the Israelites' release from slavery are only one part of a *two-part* saga about the creation of the people of Israel. The Israelites did not become a "Chosen People" simply because they were released from Egypt. Their new freedom leads to the convocation at the foot of Mount Sinai and the reception of God's direction—his Law—on what it means and how to behave as his people. In other words, it is only when the Israelites make an agreement with God at Mount Sinai that they actually become a People. This central event—known as the Sinai Covenant—is the heart of the religion of the Israelites. Among its results:

- It bound God and the Chosen People in a practical, loving union.

- It revealed God's special love and mercy for them.

- It stipulated how God's People were to respond to his love and uphold their part of the covenant; that is, first, they must follow the commandments; second, they must be faithful to God through obedience and worship.

Essentially, the Sinai Covenant was a two-way agreement, with obligations for *both* parties involved. God agrees to be the God of this people ("I am the Lord your God . . ."), but this is immediately followed by the "stipulations" of the agreement for the people—highlighted by the famous "Ten Commandments." (Note that these commandments are made special in the Book of Exodus because *all* the people heard God speak these commandments, whereas only Moses heard the remainder of the laws after Exodus 20:18, and then passed them on to the people.)

In order to understand the central essence of Hebrew religion, we must understand this central point: the basic covenant between God and the people obligates them to obedience to laws or ethics. Therefore, at the very center of the relationship between God and the people in the Hebrew tradition are *both* **ethics** and a **doctrine** of God that acknowledges that the moral law is the work of Divine Wisdom. In the Hebrew tradition, both belief *about* God and *how you live your life* are equally important. The importance of ethics in

ethics
A set of principles of right conduct.

doctrine
The revealed teachings of Christ which are proclaimed by the Church's Magisterium and which Catholics are obliged to believe.

the Israelites' covenant with God is of great help in understanding the entire Old Testament, especially in the tradition of the Prophets, which will be discussed in Chapter 1E.

 Review

1. How does translating "thousands" as "family groups" help to determine a more reasonable number of people who left Egypt in the Exodus?
2. Name some results of the Sinai Covenant.

Reflect

"Freedom always comes with responsibility." Share an example from your life when you found this to be true.

The Mosaic Law Codes

For centuries, differences between the two similar "versions" of the Law of Moses have been noted—namely, the laws in the Book of Exodus and the laws in the Book of Deuteronomy. For example, although the Ten Commandments occur in both Exodus 20:1–17 and Deuteronomy 5:6–21, they are not identical in the two books. Although the laws themselves are almost the same, the reasons given for some of these laws differ. Finally, a third source of laws from the Book of Leviticus represents quite a different collection of laws altogether. So, it is generally held that there are *three different collections* of the Law in the "books of Moses." They are:

1. The Covenant Code (contained in Exodus 20–23).
2. The Deuteronomic Code (contained in Deuteronomy 5–28).
3. The Levitical ("Priestly") Code (contained in the Book of Leviticus).

All three of these collections, or codes, contain **civil laws** (dealing with day-to-day issues of living in an agricultural society) and **religious laws** (especially Leviticus). A survey of these laws provides further insight into what was valued in the early life of Israel: family integrity, property, and animals.

The emphasis of biblical laws is not on guilt and punishment, but on restoration of the community and the maintenance of social life. There is no mention of law enforcement (police) or prisons. In a small-scale agricultural society such as early Israel, laws and traditions were maintained by everybody together, but especially by the elders of the villages and towns. The elders met on a regular basis to determine specific cases based on traditional laws and values. When compensation was involved, it was not **punitive justice**, but rather **restorative justice** as much as possible. The idea was to *restore* the life of the community, because these people had to continue to live together after each case was settled. It was partly the pressure of *personal honor* and the shame of violating themselves and their families that kept the Israelite society functioning.

The practice of laws in ancient agrarian Israel seems dramatically different from the way law functions in modern urban life. Today, we hardly know our immediate neighbors, much less the

civil laws
Laws dealing with the day-to-day issues that arise between people living, in the case of the Israelites, in an agrarian community, such as the consequences when one person's animal injures another person, or when borders between properties are disputed.

religious laws
For the Israelites, laws that govern the actions of the priests, the regulations for sacrifice, and the building and maintenance of the Temple.

punitive justice
Laws which rely on punishment as a deterrent to criminal activity.

restorative justice
Laws which are concerned primarily with restoring community after an offense has occurred. The goal is to keep the community together, as the survival of the society depended on everyone fulfilling his or her role.

entire town or city. In our legal system, "restoring community" is not considered as important as punishing the guilty. The punishment is intended to be a deterrent for those who might break the law in the future. Also, the person who "wins" a case in a modern court will probably never see the other party again. Hardly a thought is given to what will happen to either party after a legal decision is rendered. In ancient Israel, this was not the case, so law had to restore honor and society. Two parties facing off in a legal case would most likely continue to be involved with one another for the rest of their lives. Hopefully, you can begin to understand how it is different for ancient Hebrews and modern Christians to follow the Law of Moses.

Catholics today are not obliged to follow too many of the specific laws (e.g., laws regarding clean and unclean food) of the three collections in Exodus, Deuteronomy, or Leviticus. It is the Ten Commandments that contain a "privileged expression of the natural law" (*CCC*, 2070). We can and do capture the spirit of justice expressed in the Mosaic Law—especially as that spirit is strengthened with the coming of Jesus Christ and the preaching of the Gospel. "The Old Law is a preparation for the Gospel" (*CCC*, 1964). For example, it is precisely the spirit of *justice* and *community* in the Mosaic Law that are embraced in the New Law, or Law of the Gospel. The New Law is a law of love. Love is the fulfillment of the Old Law. The New Law doesn't offer any new precepts to follow. Rather, it focuses on the attitudes and the motivations we have when we act. It finds expression above all in the Beatitudes preached in the Sermon on the Mount (Mt 5: 3–12) and uses the sacraments to communicate this grace to us. In fulfilling the Law of Moses, the New Law focuses on bettering relationships in the community, especially with the poor. The *Catechism of the Catholic Church* explains:

> The Lord's Sermon on the Mount, far from abolishing or devaluing the moral prescriptions of the Old Law, releases their hidden potential and has new demands arise from them: it reveals their entire divine and human truth. It does not add new external precepts, but proceeds to reform the heart, the root of human acts, where man chooses between the pure and the impure, where faith, hope, and charity are formed and with them the other virtues. (*CCC*, 1968)

Comparing the Collections of Laws

An interesting way to compare the Covenant Code, considered to be much older, with the Deuteronomic Code is to contrast the two versions of the same legal issue. Consider, for example, the issue of what the Hebrews most frequently called *slavery,* but was actually *indentured servitude.*

 **Reflect**

In the Covenant Code, read Exodus 21:1-11. Compare this to passages from Deuteronomic Code (Dt 15:12-18; 23:16-17) on the same subject.

The point is not to debate the issue of slavery per se. We know that the slaveholders of pre–Civil War America tried to justify slavery on the basis of the Bible. (Of course, they hoped that people would not read too carefully, because what the Bible calls "slavery" is clearly not the same thing that African Americans sadly suffered in American history.) But there is more to be seen in these two laws, from different time periods, on the subject of indentured servitude. What do we notice in our comparison between the two? It is often suggested that Deuteronomy represents further moral development from the older Covenant Code, a humanizing of the laws of slavery.

Whether or not the Covenant Code is older than Deuteronomy, there is clearly a difference in the approach. Deuteronomy seems to reflect the time of the prophets (Dt 24) during which interests in social justice were prevalent. Even the language of Deuteronomy seems similar to the language of the prophets—for example, Deuteronomy's famous interest in the poor and weak of society, especially the widow, the orphan, and often including the foreigner or stranger.

Reflect

Read and compare the Deuteronomy passages (10:11-18, 24:19-21, and 27:19) with those of the prophets (Is 1:17, Jer 7:6-7, Jer 22:3, Ez 22:7, Zec 7:10, and Mal 3:5) on the subject of widows and orphans. How are they alike? How are they different?

The most unusual law code of the three, of course, is the Levitical Code. This code covers mainly priestly laws and traditions—for example, what the priests should wear, what the high priest is to do, how the tabernacle is to be built and maintained, and how sacrifices are to be classified and performed. The Book of Leviticus also includes laws dealing with concerns about purity and maintaining a sense of "being clean" which applied to the entire community. Purity laws are very interesting, although they may seem, again, a bit unusual for those outside the modern traditions who still practice forms of purity laws (both Orthodox and Conservative Judaism and Islam practice forms of purity laws, but most forms of Christianity do not). Highlighted below are three areas of laws from the Levitical Code that are of most interest to modern Christians: laws of sacrifice, purity, and **Jubilee**.

Laws of Sacrifice (Leviticus 1-6:7)

The ancient Hebrews made many different kinds of sacrifices, depending on the reasons for the sacrifice. For example, there were *whole offerings*, that is, "wholly burned" sacrifices in which an entire animal except its hide was consumed in fire on the altar. Its purpose was to give glory and praise to God. There were *cereal offerings*, consisting of grains, such as barley. Also, there were *peace offerings* in which the meat of the sacrificed animal was partially eaten by priests and those who offered the sacrifice. Also, in some temples of other ancient peoples, and perhaps also in the Hebrew Temple, some of the leftover meat not consumed by the priests was actually sold. Thus, ancient temples often doubled as the local butcher shop.

Jubilee

Every seventh sabbatical year (every forty-ninth year). In a year of Jubilee, all debts were to be forgiven, and land that had been sold to pay a debt was to be returned to the original family. In this way, the wealth of the entire community was to be redistributed among the poor, preventing unrelieved poverty and large gaps between the rich and poor.

There is debate, however, about what the sacrifices mentioned in Leviticus were actually intended to accomplish. One explanation is that the person who brought a sacrifice offered the animal as a replacement for himself—he identified with the sacrificial victim, and thus expressed his repentance. Another interpretation is that the sacrifice was intended to remove the sin from the holy Temple and its altar.

In other words, the Hebrews believed that *two* things happened when people sinned. First, they were guilty themselves, and must be forgiven. This personal guilt was taken care of by the act of bringing the animals to the priests at the Temple. The gift represented repentance and sorrow, and served as the symbolic act of asking God for forgiveness. The acts of sacrificing the animals and sprinkling their blood on the altar took care of the *second issue*—the "pollution" of the Temple itself from the sins of the people. The actual killing of the animals, and then the handling of blood, therefore, seemed to be a kind of religious "cleansing agent" used mainly for the *purification of the Temple*, and not for "forgiving" the person who offered the animal.

Clearly, coming to an understanding of what was intended in the sacrificial system has interesting implications for our Christian understanding of the Death of Jesus—since it is often compared to the sacrifices made by the ancient Hebrews.

 Reflect

Describe a way that your personal sin can affect the entire community.

Purity Laws (Leviticus 11)

One of the most interesting chapters of the "purity laws" in Leviticus is the section dealing with laws of clean and unclean animals. Consider Leviticus 11. The first section of the chapter is rather neatly divided into "classes" of animals—some of which are used for food:

- Leviticus 11:2–8—land animals
- Leviticus 11:9–12—sea animals (fish)
- Leviticus 11:13–19—air animals (birds)
- Leviticus 11:20–23—winged insects

It has often been suggested that these "food laws" are based on some primitive form of hygiene; that is, the laws were given to protect the people from foods that are frequently dangerous (especially in an era before bacterial infection was understood), such as shellfish (which are easily infected), or pork (which contains parasites if not properly cooked).

The explanation that these laws are based mainly on hygiene does not explain all of Leviticus 11, nor many other purity regulations in the rest of Leviticus. Another suggestion was that purity laws, and laws that reflect a fear of contamination from various things, represented the Israelites' social fears of contamination from the "outside." The point is strengthened because many of the purity laws in Leviticus were particularly significant during the exilic period, after the destruction of Jerusalem in 587 BC. In other words, the purity laws reflected a minority society concerned about threats of assimilation with foreign cultures. This would parallel concerns about mixed marriages, for example, which one biblical priest called "pollution" (Ezr 9).

"Clean" animals in this theory are animals that *stay in their categories*, rather than violate "borders" between certain traits (e.g., fish that do not have both scales and fins, like shellfish or amphibians) or animals that do not chew cud and have cloven hoofs (like camels and pigs). Purity laws that reflected concerns of animals staying in their categories could be carried over to encourage people to stay in *their* categories in a multireligious society like the Babylonian, Persian, and Hellenistic Empires which ruled over the Hebrew people. In short, "purity" can be one way of ensuring that people maintain a unique identity.

Laws of Jubilee (Leviticus 25)

The laws of Jubilee are the last of the Levitical laws highlighted here. The name Jubilee comes from the Hebrew name for "horn" as the beginning of each year was proclaimed by the blast of a horn. According to the laws of Jubilee, after forty-nine years each man was free to return to his own homeland.

How did this understanding of a Jubilee Year develop? The priests were obviously fascinated with the number seven. There are seven days to the week, and every seventh year was proclaimed a "sabbatical year." This is when all the slaves (i.e., indentured servants) were released from their debts, and various parcels of land were allowed to "rest," along with farm animals. But the most impressive of these cycles of seven was the seventh sabbatical year—a kind of "super sabbatical" that was called the "Jubilee Year."

During the Jubilee Year, all the tribal land that had been leased, lost to debt, or bought up by unscrupulous landlords (e.g., Is 5:8) was to be returned to the original tribal families. It was to be one massive redistribution of land! It was similar to the prophet Ezekiel's plan to equally redistribute land, which was probably a version of the Jubilee distribution (Ez 45).

The laws of Jubilee show a radical concern for social justice. They also reflect a concern not only to deal with fair distribution of resources once, but also to revisit the issue of fair distribution on a regular basis. While we have little evidence that the laws of Jubilee were ever actually practiced on a regular basis, they at least offer a laudable ambition on the part of the Hebrew priests to reorient a society on the basis of a socially and economically just distribution.

Before addressing the books of the Old Testament that describe the Israelites' return to the

Promised Land—especially Joshua, Judges, and Ruth—it is also worth considering the Book of Numbers at this point in the study. It gets its name from the many lists it contains—lists of tribes, leaders, march formations, offerings, and two censuses as the Israelites approached the Promised Land after Mount Sinai—and hence, parallels the reception and practice of the Mosaic Law. We can apply the truth taught in the Book of Numbers to our own lives: We may sin; we may misuse and even fear our freedom; we may doubt God's presence with us; our sins may deserve punishment. However, the Book of Numbers teaches that God is faithful to us throughout our earthly journey.

 Review

1. Explain why the focus of biblical laws was on restorative justice, not punitive justice.

2. How do the Covenant Code, Deuteronomic Code, and Levitical Code differ?

3. What are two things that Hebrew people believed would happen when people sinned?

4. Where does the Book of Numbers get its name?

Reflect

What does the Israelites' practice of the Jubilee Year teach you about justice and fairness?

Research and Report

Do a careful reading of the two creation accounts in the Book of Genesis. Answer the questions related to each story and recreate them in a chart like the one below:

	Priestly Account (Gn 1:1–2:4a)	Yahwist Account (Gn 2:4b-25)
What name does the author give the Creator?		
From what does God make the world?	(Gn 1:2)	(Gn 2:5-7)
List the order of creation.	Day: 1. 2. 3. 4. 5. 6.	a. b. c. d. e.
Describe the creation of humanity.	(Gn 1:27)	(Gn 2:7, 21-22)
What are humans to do?	(Gn 1:26-30)	(Gn 2:15-20)
The Hebrew word *ruah* means spirit, breath, wind. How is it used in each story?	(Gn 1:2)	(Gn 2:7)
What is the relationship between man and woman in each story?	(Gn 1:27)	(Gn 2:18-25)

SCRIPTURE PRAYER *(from Deuteronomy 30:15-16; 19-20)*

"Here, then, I have today set before you life and prosperity, death and doom. If you obey the commandments of the LORD, your God, which I enjoin on you today, loving him, and walking in his ways, and keeping his commandments, statutes and decrees, you will live and grow numerous, and the LORD, your God, will bless you in the land you are entering to occupy. . . . I have set before you life and death, the blessing and the curse. Choose life, then, that you and your descendants may live by loving the LORD, your God, heeding his voice, and holding fast to him."

Lord, help us to live in your promise of love and compassion and keep your ways.
Though we do not deserve your abundant graces, we thank you daily for the gift of our lives in you.
In the name of your Son, and through the Holy Spirit.
Amen.

1B

HISTORICAL
TRANSITIONS

Charting the Course of God's People

The Book of Deuteronomy, the final book of the Torah, provides a historical transition to the Books of Joshua, Judges, 1 and 2 Samuel, and 1 and 2 Kings.

Joshua and the Era of Judges: The Rise of Ancient Israel

The Books of Joshua and Judges cover the time before the monarchy of Israel and offer two different accounts of how the Chosen People conquered the Promised Land.

Exploits of the Judges

The function of the judges—"temporary military leaders"—also included settling political disputes and continually reminding the people to turn back to God.

Israel at Home in Palestine

Palestine became the homeland for the people of Israel, and Israelite social formation began to emerge at the Iron Age (1200–1000 BC).

Charting the Course of God's People

The books of the Pentateuch in total remind us of God's love and the covenant he made with the Israelites. God completed this covenant with us through Jesus. We, like Israel, are undeserving of God's love. We, like Israel, have experienced an exodus—a rescue from sin and death by Jesus' Passion, Death, and Resurrection. And we, like Israel, are still on our journey to the Promised Land of Salvation. The Lord has provided food for the journey—the Eucharist—and given us a glimpse of what is in store for us.

The final book of the Torah, the Book of Deuteronomy, famously concludes with the Chosen People still wandering in the wilderness. We are not presented with the traditions of the conquest of the "Promised Land" until we begin the sequence of books that lead to more detailed coverage of the progression of Israel's history beginning with the Books of Joshua, Judges, 1 and 2 Samuel, and 1 and 2 Kings. There are similarities between the Book of Deuteronomy and these next six books.

"Deuteronomy" means "second law," though it actually does not contain a new law; rather it completes and offers explanation for the Mosaic Law founded at Mount Sinai. The historical events of the book are situated in the plains of Moab between the Chosen People's wanderings in the desert and the crossing of the Jordan River into the Promised Land, actually a period of no more than forty days.

The structure of the Book of Deuteronomy resembles that of the Book of Exodus. Note the following similarities:

Exodus	Deuteronomy
From Egypt to Sinai (Ex 1-18)	From Sinai to Moab (Dt 1-4:43)
Covenant and Ten Commandments (Ex 19-20:21)	Covenant and Ten Commandments (Dt 4:44-5:22)
Concluding Ceremony (Ex 24)	Concluding Ceremony (Dt 27-28)
Apostasy of Aaron, Intercession of Moses, Renewal of Alliances (Ex 32-34)	Apostasy of Aaron, Intercession of Moses, Tablets Rewritten (Dt 9:7-10:5)

The Book of Deuteronomy was written centuries after the Israelites had inhabited the Promised Land. At the time of the life of Christ, the Book of Deuteronomy and the Book of Psalms each had a significant religious influence for Jews. Jesus quoted the Book of Deuteronomy during the temptations he faced in the desert (see Matthew 4) and in explaining to the lawyer which commandment was the first and greatest (see Matthew 22:35–39).

While grouped with the Torah, the Book of Deuteronomy also shares literary and religious themes with the six historical books that follow it in the Old Testament canon. (One theory suggests that these six books are actually six parts of one long work in the same way that the Gospel of Luke and the Acts of the Apostles from the New Testament were originally part of one written volume, though this remains only speculation.)

Common Phrases

There are some phrases from the Book of Deuteronomy that are repeated in the other six historical books. Consider this literary comparison by looking at the the classic phrase from Deuteronomy about loving or following God with all your "heart and soul," which Jesus quotes as the greatest commandment:

> Therefore, you shall love the LORD, your God, *with all your heart, and with all your soul*, and with all your strength. (Dt 6:5)

Though the phrase is never found in any other book of the Torah, it is heavily used throughout the Book of Deuteronomy—for example, 4:29, 10:12, 11:13, 11:18, 13:4, 26:16, 30:2, 6, 10. The phrase turns up again in several places outside the Book of Deuteronomy. For example,

In the Book of Joshua:

> But be very careful to observe the precept and law which Moses, the servant of the LORD, enjoined upon you: love the LORD, your God; follow him faithfully; keep his commandments; remain loyal to him; and serve him *with your whole heart and soul*." (Jos 22:5)

In 1 Kings:

> . . . and the LORD may fulfill the promise he made on my behalf when he said, "If your sons so conduct themselves that they remain faithful to me *with their whole heart and with their whole soul*, you shall always have someone of your line on the throne of Israel." (1 Kgs 2:4)

The phrase is also used in 1 Kings 8:48 and in 2 Kings 23:3 and 23:25. From these examples it is possible that the history books seemed to have borrowed language, style, and even moral themes from the Book of Deuteronomy.

Some Common Religious Themes

There are several religious or theological themes that the Book of Deuteronomy and the other historical books have in common—such as the central importance of the city of Jerusalem, especially the Jerusalem Temple.

In Deuteronomy, there are three regulations that are found only there:

- The Temple is the *only* acceptable location for sacrifice on the face of the earth;
- astrology, the worship of stars, is forbidden; and
- celebrating Passover is legally required among *all* the Israelites.

These three regulations in Deuteronomy do not appear in the older collections of the Law (in Exodus or in the older parts of Leviticus). Furthermore, they are not actually put into practice until the time of King Josiah (640–609 BC), a very late king of Judah (2 Kgs 22–24). It is King Josiah who actually legislates these regulations among the Israelite people. He allows sacrifice *only* in Jerusalem at the famous Temple. He forbids star worship and he states that the Passover celebration is to take place each year.

It is reported in 2 Kings 22:8 that the high priest in King Josiah's reign "found the book of the law in the temple of the LORD." If it is not until 2 Kings 22–24 that we actually have an Israelite king who enacts the unique laws of Deuteronomy (laws not found in the Books of Exodus or Leviticus), then it seems likely that the book found in the Temple during Josiah's reign was the Book of Deuteronomy—the only part of the Law of Moses that specifically requires the same laws that Josiah passed. This also helps to date the composition of the Book of Deuteronomy as an addition to the Torah very late in history. How so? Think of it this way: If you are reading an American history book that claims to be comprehensive, and you do not know when that book was published, how might you decide roughly when the book was written? You would probably look at the *last* event described in the work. If the last event described in the book occurred when President George W. Bush was in office, you would likely conclude that the book was published during or shortly after the year 2008, when President Bush left office.

The last event described at the end of 2 Kings is the beginning of the Babylonian exile. Thus using this evidence it seems that this long historical sequence of books (which begins with Joshua and ends with 2 Kings) must have been written sometime after 587 BC.

To summarize:

- The Book of Deuteronomy was "found" during the reign of King Josiah (2 Kgs 2:26).

- Josiah reigned from 640 to 609 BC.

- The sequence of the six historical books beginning with Joshua was written after 587 BC.

The theology of the Book of Deuteronomy centers on God's love of Israel and unhappiness with the people for worshipping false gods and not responding wholeheartedly to his love. The book also teaches that discipline is a sign of God's love, and it exhorts Israel to make a choice between the way of obedience to God and the Law (life) and the way of disobedience (death). The Book of Deuteronomy reminds us that

we, like Israel, travel as a people. We journey not by ourselves but in community with others. We must look out for our fellow pilgrims along the way, especially those who are helpless, poor, and hurting. If we ignore them, we show ingratitude to a God who loves us and saves us.

As we pick up the story of God's People from where the Book of Exodus left off—the Israelites' foray into Palestine—it is important to keep two things in mind. First, it is likely that all of the records of this experience were finally written during the same historical period. And second, they were probably written many years after the incidents they describe actually occurred. The next sections sketch some of this history of God's People from these books of the Bible.

◉ Review

1. How is the Book of Deuteronomy patterned after the Book of Exodus?

2. What does the Book of Deuteronomy have in common with the next six historical books of the Bible, from literary and religious perspectives?

3. What evidence is there that the Book of Deuteronomy was written later in history than the other books of the Torah?

◉ Reflect

What are three steps you might take in order to trace your own family's history?

Joshua and the Era of Judges: The Rise of Ancient Israel

The setting and time frame for the Books of Joshua and Judges is from the death of Moses to the beginning of the monarchy, roughly from 1250 to 1010 BC. They describe the Israelites' move into the settlement of the Promised Land and their relationship to various Canaanite tribes living there. As mentioned, the theological concerns are the same as those found in the Book of Deuteronomy.

These books give two different accounts of how the Chosen People conquered the Promised Land. The Book of Joshua gives the impression that the conquest was swift and sure. Composed several centuries after the conquest, Joshua gives an idealized picture in order to convey its major theological theme: YHWH fought for Israel; Israel did not act on its own—without the Lord's help, the miracle of settling in the "land flowing with milk and honey" (Jos 5:6) would have never taken place.

The Book of Judges, on the other hand, reports a series of bitter struggles against the Canaanites and

other peoples, contests that spanned a period of around two hundred years.

Was it, in fact, a military invasion that drove out or killed most of the people who were in that land before? Was it a slow immigration of people into the land, living with other cultures and races while occasionally engaging them in arguments and small wars? Or, was it something else entirely different that helped the Israelites settle the Promised Land? These questions make up an interesting part of biblical study of that era.

Conquest of the Land: Immigration or Revolution?

Before discussing any of the details of the "conquest," as described in the Book of Joshua, it is important to place these events in larger context. In fact, the twelfth century BC was an incredibly turbulent time through the entire region from Greece to Egypt, and even into parts of Syria and Mesopotamia. There was evidence of widespread destruction that included the abandonment of living areas, economic collapse, and the appearance of new power structures and new population groupings. What caused such turbulence? Was it the sudden invasion of peoples from the north? Was it the sudden change of weather patterns that forced massive migrations? Was it, rather, the collapse of old regimes whose economic structures simply gave out under the strains of social change? There is so little actual information that historians can only venture opinions.

What is clear, however, is that the appearance of ancient Israel as a nation in a particular region on the coast of Palestine was only a small part of this general turbulence throughout the area. Could this explain why, for example, the area of Palestine was open for development into unique socio-political formations, including the Philistines and, eventually, another rival group called "Israel"? Did these smaller political groups form because the former great powers of the

Hittites (north into what is modern Turkey) and the Egyptians were both in decline in the twelfth century BC?

In fact, the earliest reference to the word "Israel" comes from an Egyptian inscription by Pharaoh Merneptah (1213–1203), who brags about a military campaign that he conducted throughout the region of Palestine, north of Egypt. The military expedition itself is more evidence of turbulence of the period. In this famous written record, called "The Merneptah Stele," the Pharaoh's scribes record the Pharaoh bragging that he conquered all kinds of people in this area, including his boast that "Israel is laid waste, and his seed is not. . . ." It is the earliest reference to Israel outside of the Bible, and is an important source for dating the formation of Israel, because it tells us that there was, in fact, a people in Canaan called "Israel" by around 1208 BC. Allowing for some time for the conclusion of the "wilderness wandering," it is believed that that the majority of the Israelites settled in Canaan by the mid-thirteenth century BC. But the more intriguing question is "How was early Israel formed?" The answers again center on whether Israel was formed by conquest or by gradual settlement of the Promised Land.

 **Reflect**

Prior to reading the section above, which image of Israel's settlement of the Promised Land did you have: by conquest or by gradual settlement?

Formation by Conquest: The Story in the Book of Joshua

The Book of Joshua famously describes a series of battles that resulted in the formation of the people of Israel. After the death of Moses, Joshua becomes a type of general and leads the initial conflicts in the land. The description of the siege of Jericho (Jos 5:13–6:27) is well known, especially as a popular subject

for children's books and songs. The very lengthy description of this battle at the beginning of the Book of Joshua alerts us to the fact that it was considered important as the opening battle for the land. (The entire record of the conquest battles is told in the first twelve chapters of Joshua, nearly half of which is devoted to the battle of Jericho alone.) According to Scripture, Jericho was conquered by means of a miracle of God, and the people only participated in the "cleanup operation" that followed the actual fall of the city. Chapters 12 to 21 of the Book of Joshua mainly explain how the land was divided among Israel's tribes, though "a very large part of the land still remains to be conquered" (Jos 12:1).

The descriptions of the battles in the Book of Joshua are interesting and include various kinds of writing. Some battles are described very briefly, while other descriptions not only are more detailed, but also include descriptions of strange tactics, such as the circling of Jericho seven times, and lifting torches and blowing horns (Jos 6:15–21). The first series of descriptions of battles is summarized at the end of Joshua 11:

> Thus Joshua captured the whole country, just as the Lord had foretold to Moses. Joshua gave it to Israel as their heritage, apportioning it among the tribes. And the land enjoyed peace. (Jos 11:23)

Even after Joshua 11, more battles are described as the land is distributed among the traditional twelve tribes. But a revealing and climactic speech by Joshua near the end of the book offers clues that the Promised Land was not settled—at least completely—by force. It begins as if God is addressing the people through Joshua, and then quotes Joshua directly addressing the people:

> I gave you a land which you had not tilled and cities which you had not built, to dwell in; you have eaten of vineyards and olive groves which you did not plant.
>
> Now, therefore, fear the Lord and serve him faithfully and sincerely. Cast out the gods your fathers served beyond the River and in Egypt, and serve the Lord. If it does not please you to serve the Lord, decide today whom you will serve, the gods your fathers served beyond the River or the gods of the Amorites in whose country you are dwelling. As for me and my household, we will serve the Lord. (Jos 24:13–15)

There is something unusual about this speech. Who are these peoples who would have worshiped the gods "beyond the River" (read: Mesopotamia), or "the gods of Egypt," or "the gods of the Amorites" (local tribal peoples)? If Joshua were in fact addressing only Israelites who left Egypt with Moses, then this was a strange way to do so. It sounds, rather, that Joshua's audience was a mixed group from many different backgrounds and traditions who have joined together to form Israel: some were from Egypt, some local, and some were even from Mesopotamian background.

Joshua's speech to the diverse audience supports the idea that the Promised Land was gradually assimilated by the Israelites and is more in line with the events described in the Book of Judges that follows. Judges describes a land that is filled with all kinds of people—not just Israelite tribal groups. If they were really all conquered and driven out in the Book of Joshua, where did all these people of other races and cultures come from in the Book of Judges immediately following the Book of Joshua and seemingly continuing the same story? Could Judges be describing a different kind of story?

Also, the Book of Joshua names some cities as conquered in Joshua's time that do not quite fit the historical record in other parts of the Bible. For example, Joshua 10 describes battles that included conquering Jerusalem. Yet Joshua 15:63 reports that the Israelites could not drive the Jebusites from Jerusalem so they allowed them to stay. Later, when David conquers Jerusalem in 2 Samuel 5:6, the Jebusites not only are in full control, but also clearly don't believe that David is able to conquer them! So, the textual descriptions of the various battles in Joshua seem, at times, to be difficult to reconcile with other parts of the historical books of the Bible.

Archaeological questions are raised as well. Perhaps the most famous battle described in the Book of Joshua is the famous conquest of Jericho (Jos 6). But important archaeological work at the site of ancient Jericho (Tel el-Sultan in the West Bank today) reveals a striking historical problem—the city of Jericho was not an occupied site when the invasion is likely to have taken place. Also, Ai, another conquered city described in the Book of Joshua (Jos 8:1–29) appears not even to have existed yet by the time Joshua and his people would have been in the area. Certainly, in

looking for answers to these questions, the Book of Judges reveals a different picture of the settlement of the Israelites in Canaan from those in the Book of Joshua.

 ## Reflect

What experience do you have in moving to a new place? What are some ways you felt welcomed in a new area (or welcome another who was new to your area)?

Settlement Perspective from the Book of Judges

The Book of Judges includes an element of peaceful settlement of the land, in contrast with the more exclusive use of military campaigns detailed in Joshua. The following differences can be found in the two accounts:

- The Book of Joshua finishes with the end of the conquest before settlement takes place (Jos 23 ff.). But the Book of Judges suggests that some settlement preceded the battles of conquest.

- An encounter with Jabin, king of Hazor, is described in Joshua 11:1–11, where it is finally said that Hazor was "burned with fire." But in Judges 4:1–5:31, Jabin is mentioned again, Hazor is still in existence, and the city is being fought over once more. It is unclear why the battle is mentioned in both books. Judges may simply be a second, more detailed version of the same battle. Or it may be that the two books have two different accounts of what happened.

- Joshua describes a complete campaign of conquest: "And so the LORD gave Israel all the land he had sworn to their fathers he would give them. Once they had conquered and occupied it, the LORD gave them peace on every side, just as he had promised their fathers" (Jos 21:43–44). The Book of Judges suggests a much more mixed population of peoples throughout the land, with various pagan peoples existing alongside the Israelites "to this very day."

- There are even differences within the Book of Judges. In Judges 4, two tribes engage in the battle of Kishon. In Judges 5, the text says that six tribes were involved.

What is clear is that the Books of Joshua and Judges both contain accounts of battles, biographies of soldiers, and details of the conquest of the land of Palestine (particularly the settlement of the twelve tribes). Both books describe God as being actively involved in the military campaigns, although often in highly unconventional battles. When the Israelites are faithful to God and to the covenant, he rewards them with victory. More information on this "literature and theology of warfare" is detailed in the next section.

Israelite Warfare Traditions

War was most certainly a major part of the experience of the Hebrew people. Recall that Palestine was in the middle of the main roads that linked Egypt with Mesopotamia. Israel was very familiar with the armies of each civilization, as they marched through Palestine on their way to engage each other. In short, given the location of Palestine, it seems hardly surprising that war is a major subject of the Old Testament.

But location alone does not account for all the warfare described in the Old Testament. The early Israelites were involved in many conflicts with ancient societies that had gods of war. These people believed that their gods went to war with their armies to help in the conflict. Consider the carving of the Assyrian monarch Assurbanipal. Flying over the head of the mighty Assyrian ruler is an image of the god, Assur, the national god of the empire, with his bow drawn. This carving illustrates the belief that the gods fought *with* the armies of the ancient world. The Israelites had a rather different notion about the connection of YHWH with warfare. Recall how Moses reassured the people as they prepared to cross the Red Sea:

Fear not! Stand your ground, and you will see the victory the LORD will win for you today. These Egyptians whom you see today you will never see again. The LORD himself will fight for you; you have only to keep still. (Ex 14:13–14)

The unique idea in this passage is that the Lord will actually fight *for* Israel, not merely *with* Israel's warriors. The idea of warfare in earliest Israel was very unusual. It was fought miraculously by God alone, with minimal involvement of the people and sometimes, as with the case with the Egyptian defeat in the Red Sea, no involvement at all!

In Judges 7, this idea is illustrated again in a very powerful (and somewhat humorous) way. The judge Gideon thinks that he needs a huge army to defeat the Midianites. He starts with nearly 30,000 soldiers. But God tells him to *reduce* his armies. In the end, Gideon is told to go to war against the Midianites with an army composed of just three hundred men carrying horns in one hand and jars and torches in the other (Jgs 7:20).

They don't have a hand free to draw a sword or any other weapon! The point of this unusual story for the Israelites was that wars were won through the power of God, not men.

Also interesting to note are all the exemptions listed in Deuteronomy 20, allowing men to avoid fighting in a war. A man who had just planted a garden, built a house, or become engaged to marry was to refrain from fighting. Also, those who were afraid were supposed to go home (Ex 20:8–9). The reason the exemptions are so liberal is again to show that it is only God's power that matters in war. As Moses told the soldiers:

> Hear, O Israel! Today you are going into battle against your enemies. Be not weak-hearted or afraid; be neither alarmed nor frightened by them. For it is the LORD, your God, who goes with you to fight for you against your enemies and give you victory. (Dt 20:3–4)

This practice of God fighting miraculously alone for Israel did not continue. Why not? The reason is explained in 1 Samuel 7–8, when Israel chose a human king.

In 1 Samuel 8, the people ask for a king, and Samuel the prophet is disappointed. God is also disappointed, so it seems, because he tells Samuel, "They are rejecting me as their king" (1 Sm 8:7). This passage infers that God is King! An ancient king was mainly a warrior. By rejecting God as their warrior and king, that meant the Israelites no longer trusted God to protect them by means of miracles. To make matters worse, the rejection of God as king and the request to "be like the other nations" (1 Sm 8:5) occur right after 1 Samuel 7, which tells of yet another miraculous deliverance of the Israelites from the Philistines by God. The request for a king in chapter 8 is doubly ungrateful, given what just happened.

Another intriguing point from 1 Samuel 8 is all the things that the people will have to face when they get a human king instead of honoring God as their king—mainly taxation and the military draft. The theological point is clear: in the past, the Israelites trusted God for deliverance from enemies. Now they want to do it themselves. God tells the Israelites that they will suffer all the financial and social strains of maintaining a military just as the other nations do (1 Sm 8:10–18).

From this time on, the warfare of the Israelites becomes much more conventional in focus. There are only occasional reminders of the days of Miraculous Warfare—typically associated with prophets, especially Elijah and Elisha (2 Kgs 6).

In summary, there is a major change in the practice of warfare in ancient Israel—from the early period of God fighting miraculously for his people to the later period, during the monarchy, of conventional warfare. There is an impression that some of the authors treated that earlier period as a kind of "golden age" when Israel trusted God more deeply and God responded with miraculous protection. Perhaps the story of the fall of Jericho reflects this same tendency to describe events as if they were "better then because of our greater trust in God." Whatever the case, the Old Testament authors associated conventional warfare with a time when the Israelites rejected God and failed to remember the universal lesson of Scripture, "that the solicitude of divine providence is *concrete* and *immediate*; God cares for all, from the least things to the great events of the world and its history" (*CCC*, 303).

Review

1. How was the first written reference of the word "Israel" recorded?
2. How does Joshua's speech in Joshua 24 support the idea that the Promised Land was gradually assimilated by Israel?
3. How do the accounts of the Chosen People's settlement of the Promised Land differ in the Books of Joshua and Judges?

4. In the battles described both in the Books of Joshua and Judges, what happens to the Israelites when they are faithful to God?

5. How does the location of Palestine contribute to the occurrence of warfare described in the Old Testament?

6. How did the Israelites' understanding of YHWH's connection with war differ from how other societies understood their deities' participation in war?

7. Name an example of how God fought miraculously for his people.

8. Why didn't the practice of God fighting miraculously for his people continue?

 **Reflect**

When you imagine a "golden age" for your own life, is it from the past, present, or the future? Explain.

Exploits of the Judges

The Hebrew word *shofet* was traditionally translated by the English word "**judge**," although the actual meaning of a "shofet" may be closer to "temporary military leader." The function of the judges as described in the Book of Judges included other responsibilities besides military leadership. For example, judges also settled political disputes within their own tribe and between tribes and continually reminded the people to turn to God.

The judges filled the gap in leadership between the time of Joshua (ca. 1200 BC) and the beginning of the monarchy (ca. 1010 BC). The judges were leaders who were spiritually selected by God to lead the tribal peoples—though they rarely led *all* of the tribes at the same time. Three of the most well-known judges are the following:

- *Deborah*, a woman who successfully called a war in which Israel was victorious, and is heralded in the famous "Song of Deborah" (Judges 5);

- *Gideon*, a man who had serious doubts about God's ability to lead his people; and

- *Samson*, who was considered wise, yet allowed his love for the

judge

In ancient Israel, one who acted as a temporary military leader, as well as arbiter of disputes within and between tribes. Judges were also expected to remind the people of their responsibility to God.

wrong woman (a Philistine woman named Delilah) to lead him to foolish decisions.

While it is difficult to place dates on the exact time of the judges, a major theme of the judge stories seems to be that there *was* a time when the Israelites were led by God. Whenever God needed assistance, he would spiritually "deputize" a judge for a brief period. Also, when any of these judges was asked to be "king," he or she very dutifully reminded the people that *YHWH alone was their king*. The concluding chapters of the Book of Judges note some of the disintegration of the unity within and among the tribes of Israel, leading to the call for a new form of leadership. The final verse of Judges expresses this: "In those days there was no king in Israel; everyone did what he thought best" (Jgs 21:25).

The following sections briefly detail the stories of the three most famous judges.

Deborah (Judges 4-5)

Deborah is called both a prophetess and a judge. Her story is a second version of the defeat of the king of Hazor.

After another incident of Israel offending YHWH, the Israelites found themselves under the reign of the Canaanite Jabin, who reigned in Hazor. The general of his army was Sisera. Deborah summoned the Israelite general Barak and asked him to march on the troops of Sisera. Barak responded to Deborah, "If you come with me I will go; if you do not come with me, I will not go" (Jgs 4:8). Deborah consented and also pointed out that God would eventually have Sisera fall under the power of a woman.

The fall occurred when Sisera was retreating from Barak's forces. When he sought to hide in the tent of a friend's wife, Jael, he expected her to help him avoid capture. Instead, she murdered him while he was asleep, driving a peg through his temple down into the ground.

Sisera's cowardice in deserting his army and hiding behind a woman was seen as even worse than Jael's disregard for the customs of hospitality, which would ordinarily prohibit the murder of a guest.

The story is accompanied by a poem—the Canticle of Deborah—in which Sisera's fate is further ridiculed and Jael is redeemed:

> Blessed among women be Jael,
> blessed among tent-dwelling women.
> He asked for water, she gave him milk;
> in a princely bowl she offered curds.
> With her left hand she reached for a peg,
> with her right, for the workman's mallet.
> She hammered Sisera, crushed his head;
> she smashed, stove in his temple. (Jgs 5:24–26)

The poem itself is considered to be among the oldest passages in the entire Bible, perhaps written before the time of the Israelite monarchy.

Gideon (Judges 6-8:35)

Following the time of Deborah, the Israelites again offended the Lord and faced the rule of the Midianites. God raised a young man, Gideon, to lead the people as judge. Gideon protested to the Lord: "How can I save Israel? My family is the meanest [poorest] in Manasseh, and I am the most insignificant in my

father's house" (Jgs 6:15). The Lord responded, "I shall be with you, and you will cut Midian down to the last man" (Jgs 6:16).

After Gideon led victory over the Midianites, the people wanted him to be king. He told them: "I will not rule over you, nor shall my son rule over you. The LORD must rule over you" (Jgs 8:23).

However, the story immediately reports that Gideon next asked the people for their gold taken as booty from the latest battle. From the gold, Gideon fashioned an *ephod*, which was likely a golden idol. The story shows how easily even a leader of Israel could be swayed away from God. Later, God brought a curse on Gideon's sons because of Gideon's idolatry.

Samson (Judges 13-16)

Samson's story begins with the legend of his birth, announced by an angel to his mother, who was thought to be barren. (Remember, birth stories occur in the Bible when the person is to play a significant role in the history of Israel.) The woman had her son take the Nazorite vow, described in Numbers 6:5, to set himself apart for the Lord and let his hair grow freely. The Lord said to her:

> As for the son you will conceive and bear, no razor shall touch his head, for this boy is to be consecrated to God from the womb. It is he who will begin the deliverance of Israel from the power of the Philistines. (Jgs 13:5)

The legend about Samson was that his strength came from his long hair. Actually, his reliance on God was the source of his strength. Among his legendary feats were these:

- He killed a lion with his bare hands, tearing it "in pieces as one tears a kid (goat)" (Jgs 14:6).
- He fixed torches on the tails of three hundred foxes and set them loose in the grain fields of the Philistines (Jgs 15:5).

- He killed a thousand men with the "jawbone of an ass" (Jgs 15:15).
- He pushed on two columns of the temple of Dagon, killing himself along with "more than those he had killed during his lifetime" (Jgs 16:30).

Earlier, Samson's fiancé betrayed him to the Philistines at their wedding feast and then married his best man. The men of Gaza laid an ambush for Samson while he was with a harlot in their city. And then there was Delilah. Samson's weakness was his foolish love for Delilah. His infidelities caused the loss of his personal strength in the same way Israel's infidelities to the Lord caused a loss of its independence and power as a nation.

The Book of Judges provides more evidence of the need for Israel's reliance on YHWH. When the Israelites are faithful to the covenant, they are supported by the Lord. When they are not, they fall under the rule of oppressors. What the Book of Judges does not do, however, is provide much additional detail on the formation of Israel as a people and the development of their religious codes.

Reflect

What are some things that you do to help you to remember that God is the source of all of your strength?

The Book of Ruth

A glance at the table of contents of the Old Testament will show that the Book of Ruth comes immediately after the Book of Judges and just prior to 1 and 2 Samuel. This placement was made in later Greek and Latin canons of the Bible, probably because the book contains a genealogy that connects Ruth, a Moabite woman, with the family of King David. The book was most likely written sometime after the Babylonian exile. But the book itself also claims to come from the time of the judges (Ru 1:1).

The story of Ruth involves a foreign woman's fidelity to the Jewish family of her widowed husband. Ruth follows her mother-in-law, Naomi, back to the land of Judah after the death of her husband, despite Naomi's protests that she ought to return to her father's house and be married

again. Once back in Judah, Ruth *is* married again, observing a law detailed in the Book of Leviticus that required her to marry her nearest male relative. This was a called a **levirate marriage**; it would allow her to bear a son who would be considered her first husband's heir. This law was intended to keep property within the same clan or family by ensuring that there was an heir even if a man died before he had a son. By eventually marrying Boaz, her relative by marriage, Ruth was sealed by covenant to the Israelite family, becoming an ancestor of King David (and of Jesus). Although Ruth was a foreigner, she accepted the God of her Jewish husband, and today is honored for her choice.

A lesson of the Book of Ruth is God's loving concern for those who suffer in the midst of tragedy. It shows that good comes from family devotion and faithfulness. It also reveals how God's plan of Salvation takes place in unexpected ways. Finally, Ruth symbolizes God's utter faithfulness and care for the Chosen People. Her fidelity and devotion mirror God's covenant love for his people.

Review

1. What were the functions of the judges?

2. How did Deborah kill the enemy general Sisera?

3. How did Gideon fall prey to idolatry?

4. What was the real source of Samson's strength?

levirate marriage
The marriage of a widow to a near relative of her deceased husband. The first male child of a levirate marriage would be considered the first legal son of the widow's first husband.

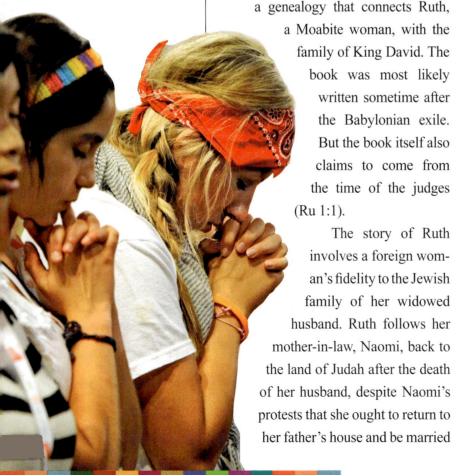

5. How did Ruth become an ancestor of King David (and Jesus)?

Israel at Home in Palestine

Returning to the larger question of how Palestine was settled by the Israelites, the answers to two related questions can help shed more light on the issue:

- Did most of the people who formed the twelve tribes of Israel come to Palestine from Egypt with Moses?

- Or, were most of these people native to the land, simply changing their religious and political identities upon the arrival of some returning slaves from Egypt?

From archaeological evidence it can be determined that the central hill country of Palestine suddenly grew in population in the early Iron Age, that is, between 1200 and 1000 BC. In previously uninhabited land, where only about twenty-three villages once existed, archaeologists have identified some 114 new villages from that period. Furthermore, judging from the material remains of many of these villages, their pottery styles are virtually the same as Canaanite cities on the coastal plains.

Everyone agrees that new villages suddenly appeared in the hill country. But where did the people who formed these villages originate? Were they all former slaves from Egypt? Consider for a moment if they were not all former slaves from Egypt.

This position is supported by the Book of Judges, which seems to describe slow settlement among other peoples rather than the organized military campaign as described in the Book of Joshua. The stories of a slow settlement and the similar pottery and architecture suggest that some of the new villages in the hill country were established by people who had never left Canaan and who had never been slaves in Egypt. Instead, they simply left the larger coastal towns and the Transjordan (land across the Jordan River from Palestine) and settled in the new villages in the hills.

There are a number of reasons why people from the lowlands of Canaan might have relocated to the hillsides. There was general unrest throughout the Ancient Near East in this time. Egyptian authority was weakened, and there were small warring city-states in the area that is now Syria and Lebanon. Perhaps the people wanted to escape the upheaval in the cities caused by invaders. Also, the groups of "sea peoples"

(some of whom were the famous Philistines) arrived from what are today Greek territories, and their arrival may have pushed some of the peasants further into the hills to escape these new warriors.

There is some evidence to indicate that the Philistines and other sea peoples may have come to Canaan because of climatic changes that made their own homelands uninhabitable. Perhaps the radical climate changes and political pressures in these centuries forced major population shifts, which might have caused many peoples to abandon the Canaanite cities on the coast for an independent existence in the hills. After all, the Bible not only records conflict with the Philistines but also points out that they were fearsome warriors. Perhaps the many battles of the Books of Joshua and Judges were generally correct memories of conflict, retold much later in simplified and well-ordered terms.

It is also possible that people left the Canaanite city-states because life there was oppressive—especially for the poor. Their movement may have been a revolutionary response to their poverty, a deliberate escape to a place where land did not end up in the hands of the few wealthy landowners and kings of the Canaanite cities. The Law of Moses contrasts dramatically with what we know about the older Canaanite religious views. Certainly the stories of the prophets emphasize a great contrast between the injustice and violence of the Canaanites and the more just and equal sharing of the Mosaic Law. This new society would have been appealing to people who were poor and oppressed.

According to the stories that fit more typically under the Book of Judges than the Book of Joshua, the settlement process was much slower than Joshua's "lightning campaign" and likely took between 200 and 300 years or longer. Certainly there may have been some violence in the lives of the Israelites (raiding parties, trouble with Canaanite cities, conflict with the Philistines) as described in both Joshua and Judges, but these battles may not have been part of a large organized conquest of one people by another. Instead, the formation of a people in the hillsides of Palestine may have been the result of a combination of the common interests of the arriving former slaves from Egypt and the rural peoples caught between the competing interests of major empires (Egypt and Mesopotamia) and affected by the lesser political ambitions of smaller states and cities. Although almost all scholarship rejects the idea of a huge migration of former slaves

from Egypt—certainly not 600,000 as the traditional biblical number would have it—there is also little doubt that some Hebrew slaves came from Egypt and that Moses was most certainly a historical figure who led and taught them during their wilderness sojourn between Egypt and Palestine. With some people already living in Canaan (e.g., Rahab from Joshua 2–6), these groups organized into a coherent identity—the tribes of Israel.

The entire process resulting in the formation of a people of Israel settled in Palestine may not have been complete until the start of the monarchy (ca. 1010 BC). Under this view, it was only when the Israelites looked back while in exile in Babylon that they were able to write and edit the version of the experience that appears in the books of Joshua and Judges. But why do the books of Joshua and Judges represent the foundation of Israel as a military conquest by people exclusively outside of Canaanite society when evidence suggests that in reality people from Canaan joined in the formation of the Israelite people during the course of a slow settlement of the region?

The Books of Joshua and Judges were written after the fall and destruction of Jerusalem in 587 BC. One of the central questions the authors faced was why God allowed this to happen. Was it because the people lacked faith? Remembering the settlement stories as part of an organized conquest may well have been motivated by the religious lessons the authors wished to teach a later generation. Perhaps the laying out of the events in Joshua and Judges was meant to exaggerate the contrast between the loss of faith in the present time (the time of exile), which resulted in catastrophe, and the trust of the people in the earlier era, which resulted in great feats of conquest and glory. It is as if God inspired the authors to say, "Look what we accomplished when we truly trusted YHWH, rather than our own resources."

The Israelites: People of the Hills

However the Israelites actually settled Palestine, it is clear that

- the hill country of Palestine was the area that became the homeland for the people of Israel.
- Israelite social formation began to emerge at the Iron Age (1200–1000 BC) and continued to evolve to a monarchy system after 1000 BC.

Other elements of an Israelite government and social structure can be gleaned from both the Bible and other historical and archaeological sources.

The basic social unit of a village in Israel was the *Bet Av* ("House of the Father"). This was a patriarchal household of extended family members. There is even strong evidence that the famous "four pillar house" that archaeologists have identified in many early Israelite villages was the basic physical unit of residence for these "Bet Av" units.

The Bet Avs were themselves gathered into associations that became known as "clans" (a *Mishpachah* in Hebrew). These clans probably arose from two natural needs—agricultural needs for families to help each other with planting and harvest, and military needs for families to help defend each other.

Finally, as the Israelites emerged as a people, so did the traditional "tribes." These tribes were probably originally identified by the geographical regions they occupied, though some of the tribal names may even predate their association with the Israelites. Of course, the biblical authors wrote from a later perspective suggesting that these "tribes" had their origins in the twelve sons of Jacob.

The village-based tribes were governed by councils of elders—the heads of the various "Houses of the Father." Many biblical texts explain that day-to-day judgments and general order were maintained by appealing to these elders. The elders made decisions based on traditional laws that were supplemented by the formal religious traditions associated with Moses (whose laws may well have included much of these traditional village laws in the first place). Some anthropologists compare early Israel to villages in developing societies today, some of which have elders who preside over village life.

Early Israelite Religious Practices

The biblical texts tell us that the early Israelites were influenced by the Canaanites, even in religion. They turned to **Baal** to help ensure abundant crops and livestock in defiance of the covenant, though they did not entirely abandon YHWH. While there are clear signs of Canaanite influence throughout the Bible, the Israelites' religion

Bet Av

The basic social unit of Israelite society, a patriarchal household of immediate and extended family members.

Baal

The Canaanite god of fertility, associated with storms and rain. He was the most prominent of the Canaanite gods and the one most often worshipped by the Israelites.

He reared up an Altar for Baal, in th Houfe of Baal, in Samaria
1 King ch.xVI.v.3

Pub by H gg & C. Paternoster row

eventually became a distinct tradition, radically different from all the surrounding religious options.

The Israelite religion was revolutionary in its expectations of the people. The life of the people in the hills of Palestine was to be a place to model this new social existence. But more temptations followed, and the worshippers of YHWH eventually had their strength and moral convictions tested. The time of the kings was one of even greater betrayal of the covenant, until eventually the people were removed from the land and sent into exile.

Review

1. What archaeological evidence exists that the central hill country of Palestine grew in population between 1200 and 1000 BC.

2. Why might the Israelites set the Books of Joshua and Judges around a conquest?

3. Define *Bet Av*.

4. Who governed the Israelites' village-based tribes?

Reflect

The Israelite religion was revolutionary in its expectations of the people. How does your own religion require revolutionary expectations of you?

Research and Report

Choose and complete at least one of the following assignments:

1. Read about the death of Joshua in Joshua 24:29-33. Then briefly summarize the behavior of the Israelites after Joshua's death and God's response to it (Jgs 2). Research background information about Baal, the name for the chief Canaanite god.

2. Research the following topics: (1) How Leviticus 11 compares to present-day Jewish dietary laws. (2) How the Jubilee Year was implemented during Old Testament times and its results.

3. Read the Book of Ruth in its entirety. List three qualities that describe Ruth's character. Cite verses that support your descriptions.

SCRIPTURE PRAYER *(from Judges 5:31)*

May all your enemies perish thus, O Lord!
    but your friends be as the sun rising in its
        might!

Heavenly Father, keep us company in your company.
Preserve us from temptation.
Bring us to our eternal home.
We ask this in the name of your Son, Jesus Christ.
Amen.

1c

THE HISTORICAL BOOKS

Rise and Fall
The historical books detail the prosperity of Israel's monarchy contrasted in the later historical books with the breakup of the kingdom.

Foundations of the Monarchy
The story of Israel's kings led to some negative occurrences but also positive aspects, including the foundation of a family line that eventually led to the birth of Christ.

The "United" Monarchy: Saul, David, and Solomon
Saul, David, and Solomon ruled Israel at a time when the social dynamics included interesting and complex interactions with their Canaanite and Philistine neighbors.

The Divided Monarchy
After King Solomon, Israel divided into two separate kingdoms, Judah in the south and Israel in the north.

The Last Days of the Independent Monarchy
The ambitions of foreign regional powers and the idolatry practiced by God's People spelled the end of the independent monarchy.

Exile and Return
The challenges faced by God's People during the Babylonian exile were countered by the inspiring messages of several important biblical texts that inspired the people to be faithful and brave.

Tracing Jewish History to the Roman Rule
The final historical books of the Old Testament are the First and Second Books of Maccabees, written about 100 BC.

Rise and Fall

The historical books tell how the Hebrews lived out the covenant in the Promised Land. They begin by describing Israel's desire for a monarchy, the stories of kings such as Saul, David, and Solomon, and the declining monarchy up to the time of the Babylonian captivity and the destruction of Jerusalem in 587 BC.

The Books of 1 and 2 Samuel detail a century of history during the end of the period of the Judges to the rise of the monarchy. Most important during this period of history was the Lord's promise to David in 2 Samuel 7 of a lasting dynasty from which the understanding of the kingly messiahship was born.

Four centuries of history beyond the Second Book of Samuel are told in 1 and 2 Kings. The traditions surrounding the prophets Elijah and Elisha are also interspersed in the historical narrative of that time.

The two Books of Chronicles form a unified historical work that represents a fascinating "rethinking" of Israelite history that was written a few hundred years later than the Books of Samuel and Kings. The Books of Chronicles cover the time span between the reign of Saul and the exile, roughly the same period as covered in the Books of Samuel and the Books of Kings. However, the Chronicles omit certain themes from other historical sources and write a report that stresses two religious themes: true worship of YHWH and the importance of the Temple and the priests to God's People. This history emphasizes issues of interest to the community well into the period of Persian Rule (539–333 BC).

The Books of Tobit, Judith, and 1 and 2 Maccabees, as well as part of Esther, are deuterocanonical. Recall that they are not contained in the Hebrew canon but are accepted by the Church as divinely inspired and canonical. Tobit, Judith, and Esther are written in the style of a religious novel, with historical dates and descriptions of events interspersed. For example, Judith offers a reflection on the annual Passover observance, and Esther tells of the origins, significance, and date of the **Feast of Purim**.

Later historical books tell of the breakup of the kingdom—the disobedience of the kings, the disasters preceding the exiles, and the exiles themselves. The First and Second Books of Maccabees were written in approximately 100 BC and provide two different views of the Jewish revolt against the Seleucid ruler Antiochus IV and the Hellenistic Greek culture that was imposed during his reign.

The theological perspectives of the historical books, especially the earlier books that involve the establishment of the monarchy, include these themes:

1. God remains with the Israelites when they most need his help.
2. Israel's leaders, including King David, reflect Israel's pattern of infidelity in their own lives.
3. God's mercy preserves Israel from it enemies.

Review

Name the books classified as historical books in the Old Testament.

Reflect

If you were to choose one topic to focus on as a historian, what would it be? Why is this an important topic for you?

Feast of Purim
Also called the "Feast of Lots," it celebrates the victory of the Jews over the Persian "prime minister," Haman, in the fifth century BC. "Lots" refers to the lots Haman randomly drew to determine the day on which he would slaughter the Jews.

Foundations of the Monarchy

Late in the eleventh century BC, tribal Israel took a decisive step in its organizational structure by appointing a monarch to rule them. What is curious about this step, however, is the fact that the historical books of the Old Testament take a decidedly mixed attitude toward this development. The prophet Samuel issued several warnings about a king, concluding:

> He will tithe your flocks and you yourselves will become his slaves. When this takes place, you will complain against the king whom you have chosen, but on that day the LORD will not answer you. (1 Sm 8:17–18)

Still, the people did not drop their request: "Not so! There must be a king over us. We too must be like the other nations, with a king to rule us and to lead us in warfare and fight our battles" (1 Sm 8:19–20).

Many biblical scholars believe that 1 Samuel 8 was not written *before* there were kings, but rather, long *after* the fall of monarchy, as a commentary on what happened. The monarchy was placed in this context in order to send a message to the Jews reading the text many years later: "We should have known better than to do this," and perhaps even, "We are not meant to have any king but YHWH. We are better off with no king." Perhaps this was meant to comfort and even guide them during the time of exile.

Also, in reading 1 Samuel 8, note the incident that precedes Israel's request for a king: the routing of the Philistines in 1 Samuel 7. For twenty years, the Israelites had "turned to the LORD," giving up their foreign gods and the sin of idolatry and worshipping God alone. Once again, God had miraculously delivered the Israelites from the powerful Philistine army. The request for a king was probably precipitated by Israel's fear of the Philistine armies, yet there is irony in the timing: just after a twenty-year period of faithfulness and a mighty display of God's power to defeat their enemies, the Israelites suddenly didn't trust God's

power to protect them. They wanted a king, such as other nations had, to fight their battles. This incident serves only to highlight the religious significance of the stories, that Israel prospers when the people honor the covenant, yet time and again, they turn their backs on YHWH.

The Monarchy: Positives and Negatives

It is important to read the story of Israel's kings with balance. There were also many positive aspects of the monarchy in Israel's history. For example, Israel became a nation with a strong central leadership, as opposed to a fragmented cluster of clans as during the time of the judges. A holy city was built in Jerusalem. And from the family of King David, a dynasty was formed with an ancestral line that eventually led to the birth of a messiah, or one anointed by God. Jesus Christ is connected in Scripture to the Davidic line (Mt 1:6 and Lk 23:31).

While many positive aspects of the monarchy are explicitly tied to King David, it is equally true that the Scriptures also detail his failings—including his ill-fated affair with a married woman, Bathsheba, when he abused his powers and killed her husband to cover his sin (2 Sm 11–12). David's son, Solomon, too, ended his life having compromised his faith in God for the sake of political alliances with nations all around him.

The Old Testament (especially 1 and 2 Kings) is critical of Israel's other kings as well. For example, the kings are criticized for an economic system that favored the rich while hurting the poor. In fact, only two of Israel's forty-two kings, Hezekiah and Josiah, received unmitigated praise:

> [Hezekiah] pleased the LORD, just as his fore-father David had done. It was he who removed the high places, shattered the pillars, and cut down the sacred poles. He smashed the bronze serpent called Nehushtan which Moses had

made, because up to that time the Israelites were burning incense to it. He put his trust in the LORD, the God of Israel; and neither before him nor after him was there anyone like him among all the kings of Judah. (2 Kgs 18:3–5)

> Before [Josiah] there had been no king who turned to the LORD as he did, with his whole heart, his whole soul, and his whole strength, in accord with the entire law of Moses; nor could any after him compare with him. (2 Kgs 23:25)

When these Scripture references of praise for Hezekiah and Josiah are measured with failings of Israel's kings (including at its very origin in 1 Samuel 8), the influence of the prophets who called the people (including the kings) back to a proper observance of the Law stands out in a prominent way. The prophetic books are the subject of Chapter 1E.

Review

1. What lesson could Jews glean from the story of the routing of the Philistines in 1 Samuel 7?

2. Name some positive aspects of Israel's monarchy.

3. Explain why the prophets were more authentic as heroes than the kings.

The "United" Monarchy: Saul, David, and Solomon

The monarchy began under the conditions of both internal and external crisis. At the same time that the tribes of Israel were consolidating, or at least loosely bringing themselves into an often stormy union, the legendary Philistines were coming together to take their share of Palestine.

The social dynamics of 1200–1000 BC Palestine included interesting and complex interactions between traditional Canaanite settlements, newly emerging Israelite settlements, and Philistine settlements. The conflicts between the Israelites and Philistines became most severe at times. In the midst of these conflicts, the Israelite tribes determined to organize themselves more effectively against the Philistine threat.

The Philistines threatened in two significant ways. First, they had the ability to fashion weapons with iron, which tribal Israel was not yet capable of doing. Iron was a decided advantage over bronze, not only in weaponry but in agriculture as well. Iron plows, for example, were much sturdier and more effective for farming. Agricultural advantage meant economic advantage. Second, the Philistines' military strength was partly based on their effective self-organization. Tribal Israel, on the other hand, was rather poorly organized. There were clearly times when the Philistines dominated over tribal Israel.

Saul and the Philistines (1 Samuel 9-10)

Saul, from the family of Benjamin, was selected the first king of Israel. When the prophet Samuel first caught sight of Saul, the Lord told him: "This is the man of whom I told you; he is to govern my people" (1 Sm 9:17). However, Saul was a deeply troubled leader, and the texts even suggest he had a fragile mental state. He failed to establish a centralized government.

During Saul's rule, Israel was probably not an organized entity at all, much less an actual state. He was as much the last of the judges as he was the first king. He "reigned" over a loose-knit organization of tribes and people who were mostly farmers. It has been estimated that the largest settlement in his "kingdom" probably amounted to no more than one hundred people. There was no capital city or administrative center.

Saul was essentially a warrior with limited success against the Philistines—especially in the southern Israel hill country where his heartland was located and where the emerging state of Judah would be located. The following description of a battle led by Saul and his son Jonathan provides a clue to the difficulties the Israelites faced in battling the Philistines during the time of Saul:

> Not a single smith was to be found in the whole land of Israel, for the Philistines had said, "Otherwise the Hebrews will make swords or spears." All Israel, therefore, had to go down to the Philistines to sharpen their plowshares, mattocks, axes, and sickles. . . . And so on the

day of battle neither sword nor spear could be found in the possession of any of the soldiers with Saul or Jonathan. Only Saul and his son Jonathan had them. (1 Sm 13:19–20, 22)

Eventually, Saul's unfaithfulness to YHWH and the charismatic rise of one of Saul's assistants, David, led to the anointing of Israel's greatest and most well-known king.

 ## Reflect

What are some characteristics of effective leadership?

David's Rise to Power (1 Samuel 16-17)

David was king from approximately 1009 to 969 BC. His rise to power is described in differing biblical accounts. David is first introduced when the prophet Samuel is impressed with one of the older sons of Jesse, though he does not have a clear sense from God that this young man is really the future king. As the story continues, God scolds Samuel for trusting in only outward appearances of the older sons, all of whom God rejects. When Samuel asks Jesse if he has any other sons, Jesse replies,

> "There is still the youngest, who is tending the sheep." Samuel said to Jesse, "Send for him; we will not begin the sacrificial banquet until he arrives here." Jesse sent and had the young man brought to them. He was ruddy, a youth handsome to behold and making a splendid appearance. The LORD said, "There—anoint him, for this is he!" Then Samuel, with the horn of oil in hand, anointed him in the midst of his brothers; and from that day on, the spirit of the LORD rushed upon David. (1 Sm 16:11–13)

David goes on to succeed Saul eventually as the chosen king of Israel, though the story of how it happens varies. Part of the difficulty is that David's reign as king has to be clearly justified, since he is not of the family of Saul. The First Book of Samuel represents Saul as having been rejected for his sin (1 Sm 15:1–35), but there are two different traditions about how David came into Saul's employ:

- In the first, David becomes Saul's "armor-bearer" (1 Sm 16:14–23).
- In the second version, David comes to Saul after the famous incident when he kills the Philistine warrior, Goliath, in a single battle (1 Sm 17). David is then presented to Saul as a conquering hero.

After a series of wars between the relatives of Saul and David and his associates, David finally consolidates his reign. But the path to the throne for David is clearly paved in blood. He systematically eliminates rivals to the throne from the family of Saul; he also engages in military conquests that include not only successful raids against the Philistines, but also successful military campaigns against the political communities across the Jordan River—the peoples of Ammon, Moab, and Edom.

The significance of conquering these Transjordanian states cannot be overemphasized, since this was the path of most of the major trade routes through Palestine, linking Egypt, Phoenicia, and the Mesopotamian Empires. Controlling these trade routes meant David's regime would also control taxes and payment of passage fees. David's regime seems to have become wealthy on precisely these terms.

Ironically, there is very little archaeological evidence of David's kingdom or mention of its existence outside the Bible. There are occasional hints, however. An inscription from a later time period, from the kingdom of Moab, refers to the royalty in Israel as the "House of David." This is the oldest nonbiblical reference to the time of David.

At the very least, David was probably a mobile warrior who enforced his control over a wide range of territory by means of a well-trained private (and probably relatively small) army. It is more accurate to think of David less as a king over a vast kingdom and more as a military leader who enforced submission in a large territory. There was no vast administration or central bureaucracy in Israel—yet.

Most importantly for Christians, the Second Book of Samuel records a central promise made to David by the Lord:

> It was I who took you from the pasture and from the care of the flock to be commander of my people Israel. I have been with you wherever you went, and I have destroyed all your enemies before you. And I will make you famous like the great ones of the earth. I will fix a place for my people Israel; I will plant them so that they may dwell in their place without further disturbance. Neither shall the wicked continue to afflict them as they did of old, since the time I first appointed judges over my people Israel. I will give you rest from all your enemies. The LORD also reveals to you that he will establish a house for you. And when your time comes and you rest with your ancestors, I will raise up your heir after you, sprung from your loins, and I will make his kingdom firm. . . . Your house and your kingdom shall endure forever before me; your throne shall stand firm forever. (2 Sm 7:8–12; 16)

The prophecy is the basis for the Jewish expectation of a Messiah, a son of David, which Jesus would eventually fulfill. The Gospels of Matthew and Luke provide genealogies of Jesus that trace his ancestry through David.

Solomon: A Mixed Portrait

More than with his father, David, there is considerable archaeological evidence of King Solomon's role as an administrator of a united kingdom. This makes sense, because Solomon was reputed to be the great builder in the Bible. Solomon not only built up Jerusalem, including an actual palace and the Temple itself, but also built many other walled cities as military fortresses. Many of these walled fortresses—dated to nearly the exact period of Solomon's rule—have been excavated by archaeologists to lend nonbiblical evidence to his rule.

THE TEMPLE OF SOLOMON

King David had great concern for the **Ark of the Covenant**, which had been housed in a tent through Israel's wanderings in the wilderness. His desire was to build a Temple for the ark. However, the Lord, through the prophet Nathan, said that such a place was unnecessary. "In all my wanderings everywhere among the Israelites, did I ever utter a word to any one of the judges whom I charged to tend my people Israel to ask: Why have you not built me a house of cedar?" (2 Sm 7:7). Nevertheless, David's son, Solomon, proceeded with the plans for a Temple. Chapters 6 to 8 of the First Book of Kings describe in detail the building, furnishing, and dedication of the Temple.

Many details of the Temple reflected Canaanite-Phoenician patterns. Its basic floor plan consisted of three parts. Approaching from the east, one walked between two free-standing, bronze-covered pillars into a small vestibule. This opened into the largest of the three rooms, the Holy Place. It was about sixty feet long and contained an incense altar, a table of **Showbread**, and ten candlesticks. Canaanite-style art of pomegranates, lilies, and palms decorated the walls. The third room, the Holy of Holies, was thirty square feet in measurement. There were no windows. This room housed the ark of the covenant. On both sides of the ark were cherubim. This was the place where YHWH was believed to be present, enthroned over the ark. Other rooms along the back and side walls were used for storage. The Temple's small size was due in great part to the fact that only priests could enter the building. Worshippers stood in the courtyard *near* the Temple.

Throughout the years of the monarchy, a close connection was maintained between the Temple and the kings. The Temple was destroyed in the Babylonian capture of Jerusalem in 587 BC. It was rebuilt after the exile (520-515 BC). This "second Temple" was destroyed in AD 70 by the Romans.

The biblical portrait of Solomon is a mixture of positive and negative impressions. Among the positive impressions is the famous story of a king who wisely settles a dispute between two women who both claim an infant as her own (1 Kgs 3:16–28).

Another is the story of Solomon's response when God tells him to ask for anything he wants and God will grant it to him. Solomon asks God only for the gifts of "an understanding heart to judge your people and to distinguish right from wrong" (1 Kgs 3:9).

God is so impressed with this request that he promises Solomon both wisdom and the wealth that comes with human success. But it is clear that the bright portrait of Solomon dims as he grows older. He apparently engages in a number of political marriages, and the biblical historians portray this as the

Ark of the Covenant
The portable shrine built to hold the tablets on which Moses wrote the Law. It was a sign of God's presence to the Israelites. Solomon built the Temple in Jerusalem to house the ark.

Showbread
The twelve loaves of bread presented on the altar every Sabbath as an offering to God. The priests consumed the bread at the end of every week. (This is also sometimes spelled "shewbread" but the pronunciation does not change.)

Judah
The name of the southern kingdom after the splitting of the monarchy. It included the territory originally belonging to just two of the twelve tribes, Judah and Benjamin.

source of his downfall—not because civil law did not permit many wives (ancient treaties were often sealed by exchanging royal children in marriage), but because many of these were pagan women whom Solomon allowed to foster polytheistic religious practices among the Israelites.

But there is an even more serious issue blotting Solomon's record—namely, how he treated his own people. Even his great building accomplishments are called into question: How could Solomon afford such extravagant projects? An older section from 1 Kings claims that Solomon enslaved foreigners and maintains that he would never enslave or overburden his own people with the tasks of his great building campaigns:

> All the non-Israelite people who remained in the land, descendants of the Amorites, Hittites, Perizzites, Hivites, and Jebusites whose doom the Israelites had been unable to accomplish, Solomon conscripted as forced laborers, as they are to this day. But Solomon enslaved none of the Israelites, for they were his fighting force, his ministers, commanders, adjutants, chariot officers, and charioteers. (1 Kgs 9:20–22)

But in another part of the record of Solomon, it states clearly that he certainly *did* force his own people into labor: "King Solomon conscripted thirty

thousand workmen from all Israel" (1 Kgs 5:27). From this passage, it is not completely clear if the workers were all actual Israelites. However, the proof that they were is most evident in the events that overtake Solomon's son and successor, Rehoboam.

When Rehoboam hears that the northern Israelite peoples are upset and angry over their years under Solomon, he goes to meet with the elders of the northern tribes to find out why they are so upset:

> They said to Rehoboam: "Your father put on us a heavy yoke. If you now lighten the harsh service and the heavy yoke your father imposed on us, we will serve you." "Come back to me in three days," he answered them. (1 Kgs 12:3–5)

When the people returned, Rehoboam showed little of his father's reputed wisdom. His answer to the people led directly to the split of the kingdom, into a northern kingdom and southern kingdom. Rehoboam told them:

> Whereas my father put a heavy yoke on you, I will make it heavier. My father beat you with whips, but I will beat you with scorpions. (1 Kgs 12:11)

These words of Rehoboam make the case against Solomon fairly tight. Solomon enslaved his own people and a large percentage of them resented it. Eventually, a group broke away from the southern kingdom and formed a separate state under a new king, Jeroboam. Usually, the final split between the two kingdoms is dated at the death of Solomon, approximately 922 BC.

 **Review**

1. What were two threats that the Philistines presented to Israel?
2. What were some of Saul's shortcomings as king?
3. What are two traditions concerning how David came into Saul's service?
4. Why was Israel's control of the Transjordanian states so significant?
5. Why is King David an important ancestor of faith for Christians?
6. Name a positive and negative characteristic of Solomon.

Reflect

Name and describe the most impressive church you have ever visited.

The Divided Monarchy

When Solomon died, Israel was divided into two separate kingdoms. The southern kingdom was called **Judah**. It consisted of the traditional territory of only two tribes: Benjamin and Judah. The northern kingdom was called "Israel" and was made up of the other ten tribes. The two kingdoms existed side by side for several centuries, ruled by a succession of kings. Both Judah and Israel engaged in several internal struggles during those years as well as fighting battles with outside nations, including the Arameans.

Judah's kings considered themselves the legitimate rulers because their ancestors could be traced to King David. However, the unequal division of the tribes strongly hints that the majority of the people from the former united Israel rejected the kings of Judah because of the abuse of Solomon and the threats of Rehoboam.

The Books of 1 and 2 Kings tell details of the divided monarchy. Some kings have several details provided about their reign. Others are mentioned very briefly indeed. The next sections report on some of the highlights of this historical period leading to the sieges of the northern kingdom by the Assyrians in 722–720 BC and of the southern kingdom by the Babylonians over a century later.

The Insurrection of Jeroboam

Jeroboam, son of Nebat, led the insurrection against King Rehoboam and founded the northern kingdom of Israel (1 Kgs 12:12–33; 2 Chr 11:1–4). There are a number of interesting elements to Jeroboam's story. As King Solomon's officer, he was in charge of forced labor (1 Kgs 11:28). Did he, like Moses, observe the suffering of "his people" and come to be a voice for liberation from the enslavement of Solomon's regime? It is certain that Jeroboam fled

Solomon's anger after speaking out against the people's mistreatment. He sought sanctuary in an unlikely place—in the land of Pharaoh Shishak of Egypt (1 Kgs 11:40).

Shishak may have accepted Jeroboam as a protected guest because Shishak entertained the thought of reasserting Egyptian dominance in the lands of Canaan lost during the rules of Saul, David, and Solomon. Egyptian records carved on the walls of the Temple of Karnak on the banks of the Nile River (still visible today) verify that Shishak most certainly did engage in military campaigns in Judah and Israel. Egypt probably did retake control of the region during Shishak's rule. As 1 Kings reports:

> In the fifth year of King Rehoboam, Shishak, the king of Egypt, attacked Jerusalem. He took everything, including the treasures of the temple of the LORD and those of the royal palace, as well as all the gold shields made under Solomon. (1 Kgs 14:25–26)

What the relationship of Jeroboam was to this campaign is not clear. According to 1 Kings 15:1, Jeroboam continued to rule in the north after the reign of Rehoboam in Judah ended.

Rivalry and Religion in the Northern Kingdom (1 Kings 12:26-33)

Jeroboam feared the reunification of Judah and Israel that might possibly arise through continued worship at a single Temple in Jerusalem. In the northern cities of Dan and Bethel, Jeroboam brought gold calves and built temples there. He also appointed priests from among the people living in those areas who were not Levites, the traditional tribe of priests.

Most people living in the north were already disillusioned by the burdens placed on them by Solomon and Rehoboam so that their loyalties to Jerusalem and

the Temple had waned before the establishment of temples in Dan and Bethel. The sacrificing to golden calves in these temples led to the sin of idolatry (1 Kgs 12:30).

The continued social, political, and religious relationship between Judah and Israel was one of constant conflict—conquest and counter-conquest. These battles with one another were complicated by the involvement of other local regimes and larger empires.

By 900–800 BC, the rise of the Neo-Assyrian Empire, based in the northern Mesopotamian city of Nineveh, caused difficulties for all the regimes in the area of Palestine, Syria, and the coastal port cities of what is today Lebanon. The Assyrian Empire used brute force to dominate the entire region. By 722 BC, the Assyrian Empire finally conquered all of the northern kingdom.

The First and Second Books of Kings (and 2 Chronicles) describe the period between 922 and 722 BC as a time of corruption of the kings of both Judah and Israel. Though there were many notable achievements of these various kings, the Bible focuses more on the survival and perpetuation of the form of YHWH worship that

1. was much more consistent with the messages of the prophets, and
2. was opposed to the official versions of the religious establishments supported by Israel's and Judah's rulers.

The rivalry between and often within Judah and Israel can be described as a conflict between a form of YHWH worship that also allowed the worship of other lesser deities in addition to YHWH, and a more prophetically inspired form of worship that was *exclusively* devoted to YHWH.

Each of these religious views had strong links to particular socioeconomic ideas about how society ought to be organized. Those who believed YHWH alone should be worshipped (represented strongly by the prophets) seem to have had a more radical orientation on the Law. They supported a community where the rich shared with the poor, where social balance was maintained, where justice was practiced, and where land was distributed fairly to all. The other perspective, identified in the Bible as a form of paganism, was more closely identified with the ancient polytheism of the Canaanites and with the kings and landowning classes. In short, this view might be called an **Establishment religion**. Recall that perhaps the most powerful expression of this difference is given in the famous story of Elijah and the prophets of Baal recorded in 1 Kings 18.

 Review

1. Why did Judah's kings consider themselves the legitimate rulers (and not the kings of the northern kingdom)?

2. What experience of Jeroboam was similar to an experience of Moses?

3. Why did Jeroboam build temples and anoint high priests in the northern kingdom?

Reflect

Read 1 Kings 18. What is the message of this story?

Establishment religion

A religion that tends to support the power of the ruling class over the common people. In the case of the Israelite monarchy, it joined YHWH worship with the worship of other Canaanite gods.

The Last Days of the Independent Monarchy

The first great outside threat to the northern kingdom of Israel was the **Neo-Assyrian Empire** in Mesopotamia. The preface "neo" means "new" and indicates that there were some older empires in this same location. This empire was located in what today is the northern portion of Iraq and parts of Syria.

Another threat to Israel came from a rising local power, based in the ancient city of Damascus in Syria. Damascus organized a group of "coalition states" that recognized Damascus as their head. The Assyrians directed a great deal of their fury at keeping the Damascus coalition subservient, though they were not always successful. When Damascus was powerful, the coalition frequently engaged in conflict with the northern kingdom of Israel.

The ongoing tensions between Damascus and Assyria weakened each state and distracted them from attacking Judah and Israel. The years between 785 and 730 BC were fairly prosperous for both Hebrew states, especially the northern kingdom of Israel. During this time, prophets condemned the fact that this prosperity benefited mainly elite landowners.

Neo-Assyrian Empire
A new empire in the Mesopotamian region that eventually conquered the northern kingdom, sending its ruling class into exile in 722 BC.

Assyrians Assert Power

The wealth and success of the northern kingdom leadership began to unravel with the accession of Tiglath-Pileser III (745–727 BC) as ruler of Assyria. He revived the military power of Assyria, and began to reassert that power in the west, including the northern kingdom of Israel. His successors, Shalmaneser and Sargon II, crushed a revolt that broke out in that region.

Finally, in 722 BC, the Assyrians completely obliterated the northern kingdom of Israel and carried it up into the Assyrian districts. As part of their dominance, the Assyrians practiced a military strategy of deportation. The Assyrian conquerors would remove the upper class and elite of the captured society and exile them elsewhere in their vast territories in order to quell any revolt before it even got started.

At the conquest of Israel, the Assyrians carried away a substantial number of the northern elite (most likely the royal family members, military leaders, landowners, and any others who might threaten a revolt) and dispersed them. These exiles are often referred to as the "Ten Lost Tribes of Israel." Although this group is never heard from again in history, the Assyrians certainly did not exile the entire population of the northern kingdom. After all, the Assyrians were interested in resources and taxes. They would certainly have left the majority of the population in place to work the land and provide wealth to the new Assyrian overlords.

The Assyrians and Judah

The Old Testament suggests that Hezekiah, the king of the southern kingdom of Judah, escaped Assyrian wrath and was allowed to stay on the throne by actually aligning with the Assyrians. In fact, Hezekiah maintained relations to Assyria as a vassal until a conflict broke out between 705 and 700 BC at the rise of Sargon II. Sargon attacked Jerusalem. In order to survive the long siege, Hezekiah dug the famous tunnel that still exists in Jerusalem. This tunnel allowed water from the Gihon Spring to flow within the walls of Jerusalem, so that the people in the walled city could have fresh water and a chance for survival.

The Assyrian siege of Jerusalem is worth mentioning, precisely because it is one of the rare occasions when an event is covered by more than one source that we can read even today: in this case Sargon's own Assyrian archives *and* the description in 2 Kings 18–20. Both sources agree that the siege was unsuccessful. In 2 Kings 19:35–36, an "angel" miraculously strikes down the Assyrian soldiers. Assyrian records say that Sargon simply determined that his point of strength had been made, and he broke the siege. In the end, Hezekiah's tribute to Sargon's successor, Sennacherib, the Assyrian king, guaranteed he would remain on the throne in Judah though the northern kingdom had been decimated.

Archaeologists have determined that there was some movement of population to the southern state of Judah from the north after Israel collapsed. The next century, the eighth century BC, brought even more changes to the region. Egypt reasserted its independence and the tribes south of Assyria (centered near the ancient city of Babylon) unified to rise and conquer Assyria itself, leaving only Egypt and Babylon with power in the region.

Babylonian Destruction of the Southern Kingdom (2 Kings 23:36-25:26 and 2 Chronicles 2-23)

After 722–720 BC, the northern kingdom of Israel no longer existed as an independent political state. The southern kingdom of Judah continued for another 135 years, although for part of this time, it was under the imperial control of Egypt or Babylon. Babylon had asserted independence from Assyria from the middle of this turbulent century onwards. When the Chaldean tribes of Babylon unified the southern peoples into an imperial power, their ambitions were finally realized. Their young prince Nebuchadnezar, who finally defeated the last of the Assyrian forces, also conquered the Egyptian forces in two great battles north of Palestine (609 BC and 605 BC). The way was clear for Nebuchadnezzar to control the land route to Egypt.

The final days of Judah were largely determined by the rivalry between the Egyptian and Babylonian Empires. From 609 to 597 BC, following the death of King Josiah in a battle with the Egyptians, the royal house in Judah (King Jehoiakim and his son, King Jehoiachin) were really Egyptian puppet rulers. Their

Ugarit

An ancient city of the Canaanites which was discovered in 1928. Many texts were found there, from which scholars have learned a great deal about the Canaanite religion.

government was established in Jerusalem by Pharaoh Necho in order to create a buffer between Egypt and Babylon.

When Nebuchadnezzar defeated Jerusalem in 597 (young King Jehoiachin surrendered), he chose one of the descendants of Josiah to be the figurehead of Babylonian rule in Jerusalem. King Josiah (640–609 BC) seems to have been predisposed to an alliance with Babylon. Perhaps that alliance explains Nebuchadnezzar's choice of Mattaniah, whom he renamed "Zedekiah," to rule Jerusalem.

Zedekiah was initially loyal to Babylon, but was eventually persuaded by Egyptian agents, including a false prophet, Hananiah (Jer 26–29), to attempt a revolt against Babylonian power and join a coalition with Egypt. The results were catastrophic. Nebuchadnezzar's forces returned to Jerusalem in 587 (or 586 BC) and devastated it. The catastrophe of the fall of Judah in 587 BC was a major event

in the history of God's People. The years that followed the exile were marked by a reorientation in the way the Jews kept their part of the covenant with God.

To summarize the events leading to the collapse of the kingdom and the captivity of God's People: It is clear that Hebrew fate was largely determined by the ambitions of regional powers in Egypt and Mesopotamia. The reigns of the various kings of the northern and southern kingdoms took place under the shadow of these larger conflicts. From a religious point of view, the stories chronicled in the time of the kings also pointed a finger at the Chosen People themselves for creating kings for themselves other than YHWH and for breaking the covenant by worshipping foreign gods. The feature "Religious Developments during the Monarchy", pages 108–110shares some reasons why this was so.

RELIGIOUS DEVELOPMENTS DURING THE MONARCHY

It is easy to see why Israel clashed so strongly with the societies who honored the ancient pagan and polytheistic religions. The central event of Israelite religion was the liberation of slaves away from the greatest known "king" of the ancient world—the Pharaoh of Egypt. Furthermore, the basis of the religion of Israel was a collection of "laws" that guaranteed that all people shared with one another, took care of one another, and made sure that nobody ruled oppressively over another. Israelites especially offered care for the "widow, the orphan, and the foreigner"—the weakest members of society. The Israelite religion was a revolutionary religion of changing circumstances (it started by ending slavery in Egypt) and maintaining community ties that were not oppressive.

So why were the kings of ancient Israel so deeply tempted to encourage pagan religion in their kingdom? A polytheistic religion with many gods supported the rule of the kings much more strongly than the questioning, radical religion of YHWH that placed even the highest king under judgment for his behavior. (It was for this reason that American slaveholders never wanted their African slaves to learn to read. Although they wanted their slaves to be "Christian," they feared the slaves might read the Bible and learn about Moses and the release of the Hebrews from slavery.)

What was the nature of the pagan religion of the Canaanites that is so often condemned in the Bible? Who were the false gods Baal and Asherah so often mentioned? In the past century a great deal more about Canaanite religion has been learned, largely because of one magnificent archaeological discovery—the ruins of **Ugarit**.

Ugarit was an ancient capital city at the center of a small territorial expanse that flourished in the second millennium (2000-1180 BC). Evidence suggests that the site was finally abandoned following a major destructive act in 1180 BC. What makes this archaeological site so very significant is the amount of texts found in it. Most of the texts were written in a local language now known as "Ugaritic." This language closely resembled Hebrew. (In fact, it is often suggested that Hebrew is a dialect of the same language family as Ugaritic.)

Among the many different kinds of texts discovered at Ugarit were a number of religious texts that told stories of some of the Canaanite gods and characters known to us from the Bible—most prominently the god Baal. Baal was considered the god of fertility and was often associated with images of storms and rain. (A rain god would have been very important to a largely agricultural society, particularly in the relatively arid climate of Palestine.) Many of the texts in Ugarit portrayed Baal as a god in battle.

The Ugaritic texts provide more insight into why pagan worship was tempting for the Israelites. First, it was the common religion of the area. Many of the people who lived near or even among the Israelites practiced some form of it. Second, it was associated with fertility, and agriculture was obviously the main basis of all ancient economies. What was good for the economy probably seemed absolute and true. Third, and perhaps most importantly, it was a religion that served the establishment. Kings and priests ruled the people according to these religious ideas, which provided stability and an explanation for why things were the way they were. But it was a stability that was often oppressive since these traditional fertility religions typically bolstered the authority of the kings and told the common people that their state in life was determined by the gods.

Prophets Preach against Pagan Religions

Consider how the great Israelite prophet, Elijah, battled against the paganism, and Baal in particular, in incidents involving him and the Canaanite princess Jezebel who married the northern Israelite king Ahab (1 Kgs 21). Hebrew law limited the power of the king so that even he could not seize whatever land he wanted, but Jezebel the Canaanite thought this was ridiculous and took matters into her own hands. Ahab wanted property that by right belonged to an Israelite peasant named Naboth. Jezebel had Naboth executed and took his land. She was acting as a Canaanite ruler might have. This story illustrates what pagan religion would mean in terms of its social consequences. It contrasts sharply with the stories of Elijah living with and saving the lives of a widow and her only son in the name of the one, true God, YHWH (1 Kgs 17-18).

Also, in 1 Kings 18, at Mount Carmel (near present-day Haifa on the northern coast of Israel), there is a dramatic contest between Jezebel's hired priests and priestesses of Baal and Elijah, the sole defender of worship of YHWH. By stopping the rain, YHWH proved that he alone was the provider of the rain. By feeding the woman and child (and Elijah himself), YHWH demonstrated that the God of Israel was, in fact, the provider of the produce of the fields. Finally, by healing the child, YHWH demonstrated that it was the God of Israel who provided human life, not Baal. In the great demonstration described in 1 Kings 18:21-46, Elijah proves that YHWH is the true God.

Unfortunately for Elijah, Jezebel was angry about the defeat. She threatened his life. So Elijah took refuge at Mount Horeb (Sinai)—the same place where Moses received the laws and encountered YHWH. This location was fitting, for it was Elijah's mission to restore God's covenant and the pure faith among the people. Elijah met the Lord at Horeb—not in a strong and heavy wind, not in an earthquake, and not in a fire. Rather, "after the fire there was a tiny whispering sound. When he heard this, Elijah hid his face in his cloak and went and stood at the entrance of the cave" (1 Kgs 19:13).

Elijah rightly holds a place among the great prophets of the Old Testament. Elijah, through it all, was a prophet who symbolized the struggle between the religion of YHWH and the religion of the Canaanites. At the Transfiguration of Jesus, Elijah appeared along with Moses. Future generations of Jews thought Elijah was the one who would announce the coming of peace to the world at the end of time. He was also believed to be the precursor to the Messiah. In fact, when Jesus came to the earth, many thought him to be Elijah, while the New Testament cast John the Baptist in the role of Elijah announcing Jesus as Messiah.

The biblical authors understood the importance of Elijah, which is why many chapters feature stories about both Elijah and Elisha. Though there is no typical miraculous birth story to introduce him (Chapter 1E), there is a uniquely miraculous story to mark his passing: He is described as being transported to Heaven in a whirlwind. Conversing with his successor, Elisha, "a flaming chariot and flaming horses came between them, and Elijah went up to Heaven in a whirlwind" (2 Kgs 2:11). Elisha's life paralleled Elijah's. Their lives and ministries set the stage for the prophetic books that make up a large section of the Old Testament.

Review

1. Why did the Assyrians deport the northern elite while allowing others to remain at home in the northern kingdom?

2. What are the differences between the Israelites' and the Assyrians' accounts of Sargon's failed siege of Jerusalem?

3. What was the costly decision made by Zedekiah, the figurehead ruler in Jerusalem?

4. Why is Elijah considered among the great prophets of the Old Testament?

Exile and Return

The Old Testament describes the conditions of exile in very dark terms. Several places mention the exiles being held with chains and bonds (e.g., Na 1:13, 3:10; Is 52:2; and Ps 107:14). The Second Book of Chronicles reports of the imprisonment of Jehoiakim: "Nebuchadnezzar, king of Babylon, came up against him and bound him with chains to take him to Babylon" (2 Chr 36:6). The Book of Lamentations also speaks of sieges and chains after the conquest of Jerusalem:

> He has hemmed me in with no escape
> and weighed me down with chains;
> Even when I cry out for help,
> he stops my prayer;
> He has blocked my ways with fitted stones,
> and turned my paths aside.
> (Lam 3:7–9)

There are frequent descriptions of the exiles as prisoners. The "release of prisoners" is mentioned often, indicating the kind of treatment they received (Ps 146:7–8; Zec 9:12; Is 42:7, 61:1).

It is difficult to estimate the human extent of the crisis. For example, if around 20,000 Jews were previously exiled in 597 BC, how many more residents of Jerusalem and the surrounding area were taken in 587 BC? Higher estimates reach as much as 50,000–60,000. Some estimate those numbers as being almost the entire population of the

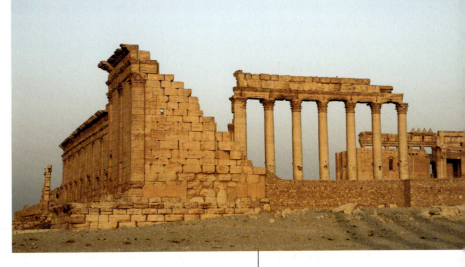

region. It is important to note, however, that the Bible does not even attempt to determine the numbers of those who fled or were killed, especially in the critical year of the invasion of Jerusalem in 587.

By combining the archaeological evidence of destruction and difficult times in exile with Scripture references that indicate the emotional response of the Jewish people, the horrific picture of what happened is very clear. The Babylonians destroyed the Temple of Solomon. They carried many of the religious implements of worship into exile with the people. The policy of Nebuchadnezzar was to place captured religious implements or statues in the temple of **Marduk**, the main state god, in the city of Babylon in order to symbolize the capture of the people and the defeat of their gods. In the case of the Jews, a capture of Temple vessels served the same purpose. (This practice may underlie the stories of Belshazzar's feast in Daniel 5 and the return of the Temple furnishings in Ezra 1–6.)

Marduk
The main state god of the Babylonians during the reign of Nebuchadnezzar. It was to his temple in the city of Babylon that the Temple furnishings and vessels from the Temple of Solomon were carried following the destruction of the Temple in 587 BC.

remnant
The exiles and former exiles who remained faithful to YHWH during the time of captivity and who are expected to restore Jerusalem.

There would have been a succession of crises for those Jews who remained in Jerusalem and Judah during the exile. The famous ancient Jewish historian, Josephus, suggested that Nebuchadnezzar was back in Palestine again in 582, probably in reprisal for the murder of Gedaliah, the Jewish governor he left in charge after the siege of 587. The historical evidence, then, suggests a series of traumatic events were experienced by the Jews—whether in exile or back in the land, including the kidnapping of the prophet Jeremiah who was taken to Egypt.

What is known about the end of the Babylonian exile is that the Persians eventually invaded Babylon and allowed at least some of the exiled Jews to return to their homeland (see Ezra 1–6). The Persians even sponsored some of the caravans that returned to Judah, complete with some of the holy items from the Temple that were originally captured by the Babylonians. The condition of the land and community found in Judah upon the exiles' return is difficult to assess. It is often presumed that some form of religious life continued in the ruins of the Temple, but there is no direct evidence of it. Some conflict broke out between those who returned from exile and those who had been left behind in Judah (see Ezra 4). The exiles and former exiles who had remained faithful to YHWH during the time of captivity are known as God's **remnant**, the remnant spoken of by the prophets, including Isaiah:

A remnant will return, a remnant of Jacob,
to the mighty God. (Is 10:21)

This history  of this period—from exile to return—was detailed in the Bible by several important books. The First and Second Books of Chronicles, Ezra, and Nehemiah come from the time after the exile. They provide details about the challenges faced by the Jewish people as they resettled in Judah. They, along with the first six chapters of the Book of Daniel and the Books of Tobit, Judith, and Esther, all carry messages meant to inspire people to remain faithful and brave during troublesome times. The latter books tell more of different ways the Jews survived while under the rule of foreigners. More details of these biblical books is provided in the sections below.

🌀 Reflect

What are modern situations of people in exile that parallel the experience of the Jews in Babylonian captivity?

Chronicles, Ezra, and Nehemiah

Both Books of Chronicles once formed a single work with Ezra and Nehemiah. The author of Chronicles, a priest from Jerusalem, wrote sometime in the fourth century BC with the intent of writing a sacred history that focused on the Jews as a priestly people. Two of the main religious themes were true worship and true kingship in Israel.

The Books of 1 and 2 Chronicles instructed the post-exilic generation to learn from their history, especially that the people's happiness depends on its true fidelity to God. God does honor his covenants. However, he also punishes idolatry and disobedience of the Law, as the history of both the northern and southern kingdoms showed.

The present order of the Books of Ezra and Nehemiah assumes that Ezra came first, though historically Nehemiah probably did. Nehemiah describes the rebuilding of Jerusalem and introduces religious reforms, after which Ezra came to reestablish the faith of the people, based on the "scrolls of the Law."

The Book of Ezra begins with Cyrus of Persia's decree to let the Jews return home. Chapters 1–6 of Ezra detail the first two groups of exiles returning home, one led by Sheshbazzar (538 BC) and the other by Zerubbabel (around 520 BC). These chapters also tell some of the problems the returning exiles met in trying to rebuild the Temple (Ezr 4). The Temple was completed in 515 BC, helped by the urging of the prophets Haggai and Zechariah. However, the Temple lacked the splendor of Solomon's Temple.

Around 445 BC, Nehemiah persuaded the Persian king Artaxerxes I to make him the governor of Judah. Though opposed by the Samaritans, Nehemiah then proceeded to oversee the rebuilding of the walls of the Temple. This accomplishment reestablished the autonomy of the Jewish nation in the Promised Land. Nehemiah served two twelve-year terms as governor, concluding in 417 BC. Nehemiah 17 and 11–13 provide a biographical sketch of his rise to and time in leadership.

Ezra was a priest who came to Jerusalem either soon after Nehemiah or during the reign of the Persian king Artaxerxes II, probably around 398 BC. Ezra is credited with restoring the practice of the Torah and with vigorously reforming the Jewish faith. He is called the "second Moses." Among Ezra's reforms:

- First, he forbade mixed marriages, and even dissolved Jewish marriages with non-Jews.
- Second, he forbade unnecessary mingling with foreign nations.

His intent was to establish the purity of the Jews as God's People. He was concerned with the survival of the Jewish nation. He unified them and gave them a spiritual vision that helped preserve them as a distinct nation.

Chapters 8–10 of the Book of Nehemiah describe Ezra's greatest achievement: the promulgation of the Torah. Ezra read the Law. The people of Jerusalem confessed their failure to live the Law. Finally, the people rededicated themselves to the Law and promised to observe its precepts. Ezra established the Torah as the constitution of Judaism.

Daniel 1-6

The Book of Daniel is divided into two sections of stories and apocalyptic visions (see "Daniel," pages 165–66) and was finished between the years of 167 and 164 BC, though it is set in the royal household during

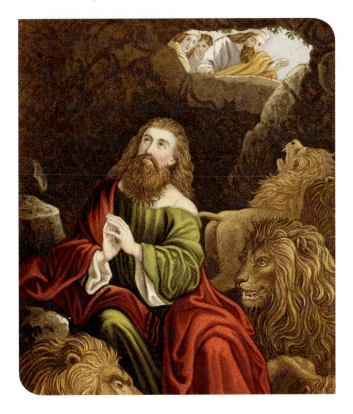

the Babylonian exile four hundred years earlier. Chapters 1 to 6 are built around Daniel, a young Hebrew taken into the Babylonian king's service where he distinguishes himself by his interpretation of dreams and prophecy. Daniel and his companions very carefully observe Jewish laws in spite of opposition from others in the royal court. For example, in chapter 1, rather than eating the king's food and wine (which has not been prepared according to the Law), Daniel and his friends eat only vegetables and water for ten days to prove that by obeying God's laws they will be even healthier than the others in the court.

In chapter 6, Daniel refuses to worship pagan idols and disobeys the petition of the king not to address petitions to God for thirty days. He continues to pray in his room three times a day until the men who have promoted the petition of the king (expressly to be able to punish Daniel) catch him in the act. Though the king hates to punish his faithful servant, he is bound by the law he has signed. Before casting Daniel into the lions' den, the king says to him: "May your God, whom you serve so constantly, save you" (Dn 6:17).

God sends an angel to keep the lions' mouths closed so that Daniel will not be hurt. The message of this story, as with the others in chapters 1 to 6, is that cooperation with civil authorities combined with faithful prayer and obedience to God's Law will protect the Jews and allow them to survive and even thrive under foreign rule. It is likely that the stories about Daniel are much older than the apocalyptic visions in chapters 7 to 12.

Tobit

The Book of Tobit is written as a religious novel. It is a deuterocanonical book from the second or third century BC. In 1948–1955, fragments of the book in Aramaic were found near the Dead Sea. As with the stories in Daniel 1–6, Tobit emphasizes the benefits of traditional forms of Jewish piety—prayer, fasting, and almsgiving. Its message is that God will never abandon his people as long as they remain faithful to him.

Tobit is set at the time of the fall of the northern kingdom to the Assyrians. It is actually two stories. The characters—Tobit, his wife, Anna, and their son, Tobiah—are deported to Nineveh. Their story takes place there. Tobit suffers several trials, including blindness from cataracts. But Tobit is persecuted as a kind and just man who cares deeply for his community in exile.

In another city some miles away, a young woman, Sarah, also experiences misfortune. All seven of the men she has married have died on her wedding night at the hands of a jealous demon. The stories come together when Tobiah marries Sarah, survives the wedding night under the protection of the angel Raphael, defeats the demon, and returns home with Sarah to help his father regain his sight. These tales contain some striking insights about living as a faithful minority in a foreign land.

In chapter 13, Tobit praises God in a joyful prayer. It, too, reminds the Jews of the need to remain faithful in spite of hardships:

> He scourged you for your iniquities,
>   but will again have mercy on you all.
> He will gather you from all the Gentiles
>   among whom you have been scattered.
> When you turn back to him with all your heart,
>   to do what is right before him,
> Then he will turn back to you,
>   and no longer hide his face from you. (Tb 13:5–6)

The religious message is that the virtue of God's People will triumph over the sinfulness of their oppressors and their own sinfulness.

Judith

The Book of Judith tells another story with a message about what the Jews must do to survive life in the Diaspora under foreign rule. The story introduces a fictional woman named Judith ("Jewish woman") in chapter 8, after King Nebuchadnezzar's general Holofernes has besieged the Jews for thirty-four days and cut off their water supply rather than attack them directly and risk the loss of his soldiers. As the people perish, the Jews are considering surrender. Judith chides the Jews for their inaction and promises that YHWH will save his people through her.

Faithfulness to YHWH, as in the other stories described above, was paramount in the protection of the Jews living in the Diaspora. But Judith does more than resist passively. After praying, she actively stands up for her faith on behalf of God's People. She disguises herself, enters the enemy camp, and beheads Holofernes (Jdt 13:4–10). This type of proactive response is interspersed in the historical events related to the Jews living under foreign rule in the centuries prior to the birth of Christ.

Esther

The Book of Esther is another example of a story whose message says it is better for the Jews to negotiate with foreign kings and function religiously under foreign rule than to oppose them with military force or other forms of extreme nationalism. The story is set in Persia during the reign of Ahasuerus (or Xerxes I). Esther, a beautiful Jewish maiden, is chosen to replace the former queen of Persia. Meanwhile, Ahasuerus, because of the influence of a power-hungry assistant named Haman, has decreed that all Jews should be obliterated. Haman targets the Jews for destruction because Mordecai, Esther's uncle, refuses to kneel in worship to him.

Esther persuades the king to reverse the decision (Est 6–8). The king—because of his love for Esther—spares the Jews, and Haman is hanged instead. The Jews celebrate this triumph with a great feast (Est 9). The feast is the origin of the Jewish spring festival Purim, which means "lots" (referring to the lot that Haman drew to determine the day to slaughter the Jews).

The message of Esther is much the same as the one in the Book of Daniel: cooperation with the civil rulers and refusal to compromise in religious matters, combined with the traditional elements of Jewish faith—prayer, fasting, and almsgiving—will ensure God's protection. There is another similarity between the two stories. In both stories, it is not the king whom the Jews have to fear; it is the unscrupulous, jealous, or power-hungry men who surround the king that threaten the Jews' survival.

Esther is also unique because it exists in two forms—a Hebrew edition and a longer Greek edition. The Greek text is not simply added to the end of the Hebrew text; it is interspersed within it. In the *New American Bible*, the added text appears in chapters A through F, which interrupt the numbered chapters of the Hebrew story.

Review

1. What is known about the end of the Babylonian exile?

2. Who are the *remnant*?

3. Identify Ezra, his reforms, and his greatest achievement.

4. How is the Book of Daniel divided?

5. Where is the Book of Tobit set?

6. What response did the fictional woman Judith take against God's enemies?

7. How is the message of the Book of Esther similar to the one in the Book of Daniel?

Tracing Jewish History to the Roman Rule

The final historical books of the Old Testament are the First and Second Books of Maccabees, written about 100 BC, which contain independent accounts of the attempted suppression of the Jewish people in the second century BC. The original version of 1 Maccabees was apparently written in Hebrew, though that edition was lost. The earliest translation was from pre-Christian times and written in Greek. The author, probably a Palestinian Jew, is unknown. The Books of Maccabees have always been accepted by the Catholic Church as inspired, but not by Jews and Protestants, as they were not included in the Jewish canon of books from the end of the first century AD.

As mentioned, the Books of Maccabees address a very particular time in Jewish history—the second century BC. The next sections surround the era of the Maccabees by detailing more of Jewish history from the end of the Persian rule through the rise of Alexander the Great and Hellenism to the coming of the Romans in 63 BC.

Under Persian Rule

The Persian Period lasted over two hundred years, from the time of Cyrus's conquest of Babylon in 539 until the conquests of Alexander the Great in 333 BC. Little is known about what daily life was like under the Persians. As mentioned before, the most significant sources are the biblical books of Ezra and Nehemiah, and these short works do not report the general conditions of living under the Persian Empire. At least part of the oral tradition that formed the stories of Daniel 1–6 may reflect conditions in the Persian Period, but it is difficult to be certain. Finally, 1 and 2 Chronicles were written in the Persian Period, but they are concerned with *earlier* history.

The Persians controlled vast amounts of land extending from Egypt in the West to the Indus River in the East. Palestine was part of a large Persian province known as "Beyond the River." The Jews did have a fair amount of religious and personal freedom, although they were without political rights. The official Persian religion was **Zoroastrianism**, a religion that held that the universe was caught in a constant struggle between light and darkness. The influence of this religion on the Jews can be seen in their growing belief in angels and in the larger role assigned to Satan, the fallen angel. By the second century BC, the Books of Daniel and 2 Maccabees clearly stated these beliefs.

Zoroastrianism

The official religion of the Persian Empire, which understood the universe to be caught in a constant struggle between light and darkness. Jewish belief in angels and in Satan's influence can be traced to the influence of this foreign religion.

Reflect

How do you think you would adapt if you lived under a government that did not allow you to practice your religion?

The Beginning of Hellenization

The famous conqueror Alexander the Great brought sweeping changes to the region. His time of campaigns was a short nine years (334–323 BC) but he conquered massive amounts of territory: Asia Minor in 334 BC; Phoenicia, Palestine, and Egypt by 333–332 BC; the crushing defeat of the Persian army and the ensuing capture of Babylon, Susa, and Persepolis by 331 BC. One ancient legend of Alexander tells that when he reached northern India and realized there were no more lands to conquer, he wept.

Alexander introduced Greek ideals, language, learning, dress, and customs to the people whose lands he controlled. Greek athletic contests became popular, and the common Greek language, *koine*, became the official language of the Near East. (The process of imposing Greek culture on conquered civilizations is called Hellenization.) Greek remained the common language of the Middle East until AD 500, when it was supplanted by Latin. The **Septuagint** translation of the Hebrew scriptures and the entire New Testament were written in Greek. As a result of the extent of Alexander's empire and the success of his policy of Hellenization, all of Western culture retains the influence of Greek thought, learning, values, and ideals to this day.

The principal biblical sources describing Hellenistic influence on the Jews are the First and Second Books of Maccabees and the Wisdom books of Solomon. The First Book of Maccabees was written to describe events from the Jewish revolt in 167 down to the period of John Hyrcanus (134–104 BC), the first ruler of the brief Jewish dynasty known as the Hasmoneans. The Second Book of Maccabees focuses mostly on the events of the revolt itself, but has a more pious tone than 1 Maccabees. The Jewish historian Josephus, who lived during the time of Christ, provides more information about this period. However, his sources are sometimes called into question, and like the New Testament as a whole, he comes from the later Roman Period.

Upon his death at the young age of thirty-three, Alexander's vast empire was divided among his generals. Although there were periods of

Septuagint

The oldest, complete edition of the Old Testament, it is a Greek translation of earlier Hebrew texts, probably written in Alexandria during the time of Ptolemaic rule over Palestine. The word itself, *Septuagint*, is Latin for "seventy," which refers to the traditional story that seventy scholars from the Promised Land were brought to Alexandria to accomplish this translation.

cooperation between them, there were many incidents in which one general would dispute with another to try to re-establish control of a larger territory.

The two generals that had the most effect on the Jews were Ptolemy, who ruled in Egypt, and Seleucus who ruled from Syria and controlled large parts of Alexander's eastern empire (Mesopotamia and the Northern Palestine/Lebanon territories). Once again, geography became destiny. The struggles between these two ruling dynasties over the little strip of land that was Palestine determined the fate of the Jews for the next few centuries.

The Rule of the Ptolemies

The **Ptolemies**, rulers in the dynasty that descended from Alexander's general Ptolemy, controlled Palestine from about 320–200 BC. The Ptolemies were known for retaining strong, centralized economic control of their territories and laying heavy taxes on the occupied people. However, the Ptolemies also allowed religious autonomy and apparently made no outright efforts to impose Hellenization on the Jews. However, whether forced or not, the Jews themselves divided into ruling factions over the issue of Greek influence. One group began to adopt Greek customs—games, plays, athletics, and philosophy. Another group was staunchly opposed to Greek assimilation and remained strictly loyal to Jewish practices and customs. Of course,

Greek culture inevitably had some influence even on the traditional factions, and other groups formed as well.

The Egyptian city of Alexandria also came under the rule of the Ptolemies. Alexandria was to become a great seaboard city—the "Jewel of the Mediterranean"—and an important cultural and economic center. One of the most important developments under the Ptolemies was the construction and maintenance of the great Library of Alexandria, but it was a cultural and economic center as well as a busy port.

The Jews in Palestine were free to immigrate to Alexandria. A Jewish community began to grow there as many Jews settled in Alexandria to take advantage of its cultural and economic opportunities. The Alexandrian Jewish community would remain an important center of Jewish culture in the Diaspora for centuries after this. It is likely that the Book of Wisdom originated in Alexandria around 100 BC. Most likely, the great task of translating the Hebrew scriptures into Greek was also undertaken in Alexandria. (See "The Septuagint," page 119).

Ptolemies
The dynasty descending from Ptolemy I, a general under Alexander the Great, that ruled Egypt and Palestine from 320 to 200 BC, when they lost control of the land to the Syrian Empire.

Dead Sea Scrolls
Ancient scrolls containing the oldest known manuscripts of the books of the Old Testament in Hebrew. They were discovered in caves near Qumran on the Dead Sea between 1947 and 1953.

THE SEPTUAGINT

The Septuagint (Latin for "seventy") is the term used to refer to the Greek translation of the Hebrew scriptures. It is often indicated by simply using the Roman numeral LXX. Until the discovery of the Dead Sea Scrolls, the Greek versions of the Old Testament were the oldest actual manuscripts available for doing textual analysis of the Bible in ancient languages. They are still the oldest *complete* editions of the Bible.

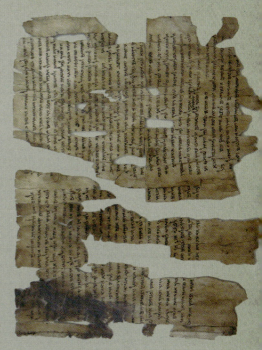

The legend of the Septuagint appears in a book known as the "Letter to Aristeas." This work says that the Ptolemies were deeply disturbed to find that the Library of Alexandria did not include the great writings of the Jews. So they brought seventy-two Hebrew elders (six from each tribe) to Egypt and commissioned them to translate the Bible into Greek. (These seventy-two translators are where the Septuagint gets its name.) The translators divided into teams, and when they were finished, a miracle had occurred. Each of their translations was exactly the same! Though a delightful story, the only probably historical basis to the tale was that the Septuagint was produced in Egypt in the time of the Ptolemaic rule over Palestine.

In actuality, the writing of the Septuagint does not appear to have been a well-organized effort. There are indications of many different translators at work on the various books. There were clearly multiple attempts to translate similar passages. The resulting earliest work—known as the "Old Greek"—was itself often criticized and re-translated by others.

There are some interesting curiosities about the Greek versions of the scriptures. For example, material that was written at a later period—closer to the time of the Septuagint translation—was added to a number of older books. The Book of Esther, for example, grew to almost twice the size of the Hebrew version. Daniel picked up a number of new chapters. Whole books, such as Sirach, Tobit, Judith, and the Maccabean literature, were all eventually made a part of this collection. This expanded collection of books became for Christians the "Old Testament."

These additional books and passages are what makes the "Catholic Bible" different from the "Protestant Bible." It is not that Catholics "added" these additional books; rather, Martin Luther and the Protestants removed them in the sixteenth century. Today these books that are unique to the Greek versions of the Old Testament are known as "apocryphal" books.

Seleucid Rule

The Seleucid rulers, who based their part of the old Alexandrian Empire in Babylon and the Eastern cities, also ruled over much of Syria. In approximately 200 BC, these rulers drove out the Egyptian-based Ptolemies and came into power in Palestine under the leadership of Antiochus III. While the Jews hailed the Seleucids as liberators at first, Jewish life under Seleucid rule deteriorated rapidly. The Roman Empire was also increasingly becoming a strong and forbidding

Antiochus III

presence in the region. It was during this time that historical events began to get complicated.

There was considerable internal turmoil among the Jewish community in Palestine early in the reign of the Seleucids over the issue of control of large sums of Temple funds. The Temple acted as the most secure "bank" for the Jews in this region, and thus considerable sums of money were accumulated in Temple treasuries. This made the Temple and its administrators prime targets of the Seleucid rulers. (Temples of most religions throughout the region also served as the local "bank" so they were nearly always prime targets for outside conquerors who often went to the temple, first, when they invaded a city.)

Inevitably, a struggle broke out among Jewish factions over who would be the high priest and thus earn the right to negotiate financial and trade deals with the Seleucids. There were other key administrative positions for Jews to seek as well—such as the right to collect taxes. A tax collector's reward was to keep whatever he collected beyond the obligations to the government. Obviously, the potential for abuse under such a system was very great.

These internal debates were made worse by the fact that a growing faction of Jews continued to be more Hellenized in attitude, practice, and outlook. Accompanying this, some of these Jews became less and less scrupulous about the observation of traditional Jewish practice and rites. Such Hellenistic attitudes inevitably drew a reaction from more traditional Jews. After all, the Jewish people had lived under pagan imperial control since 587 BC. They had no real ruler, and did not control their land, so their traditions and faith were the centerpieces of their existence. This placed the Temple at the center of the political and religious controversies of both groups of Jews.

Antiochus IV and the Impending Revolt

The Temple debates led to two opposing Jewish factions confronting each other: the Hellenized Jews and a more militant traditional group. The confrontation came to the forefront when a wealthy Jewish family (the house of Tobiah) who had created their financial dynasty from their business dealings with the Hellenistic administration attempted to remove Onias III as high priest. The more traditionalist Jewish families considered Onias to be the legitimate head of the Temple.

Both Jewish factions appealed to the Seleucids for support. But the Seleucid family at the time was also unstable. Antiochus III died and was followed by Seleucus IV. But Seleucus IV was soon killed, probably by the one who then assumed the throne, the infamous Antiochus IV who called himself "Epiphanes" ("God is with us").

In order to consolidate his power, Antiochus IV acted quickly in dealing with the Jews. When Onias came to Antioch to appeal for his rightful role as the high priest, Antiochus IV imprisoned him, and appointed Onias's brother Jason as the high priest, most likely because he had been bribed by Jason and his supporters. Jason was sympathetic to the Hellenized Jews. Three years later a powerful family called the Tobiads outbid Jason, and the disastrous Menelaus was made high priest. Menelaus further enraged the more traditional Jews by his support of Greek traditions. He even cooperated with Antiochus IV in the construction of Greek shrines in Jerusalem and the looting in the Temple.

Antiochus IV was as zealous about Hellenization as Alexander the Great had been. Believing that the Jews were the cause of many of his problems (including his unsuccessful efforts to take control of Egypt), he virtually banned the practice of traditional Jewish religion. He forbade study of the Law, observance of the Sabbath, circumcision of male children, and Temple sacrifice (unless it was pagan sacrifice).

It is likely that Antiochus IV was acting under the advice of some of his Hellenized Jewish supporters, who wanted to gain a permanent advantage over the traditionalist Jews. In fact, among the Jews who were attracted to Greek culture, Antiochus IV's policies met with little or no resistance. Among these "modernist" Jews, Greek dress and participation in the gymnasium were popular. (Some of these Jewish males even had surgery to reverse their circumcisions in order to avoid embarrassment when participating in athletics in the nude!) Those who participated in athletics at the gymnasium had to recognize the Greek gods who were the gymnasium's patrons. Worship of false gods was the greatest abomination to traditional Jews.

The policies instituted by Antiochus IV were certainly brutal in their own right. But it is important to understand that some of Antiochus IV's mandates were instituted in response to the internal conflict among the Jews that Antiochus was determined to use to his own advantage.

 **Reflect**

Give an example of how internal bickering damaged the unity of a group of people that you belonged to.

From the Maccabees to Roman Control

The conditions of internal conflict and resentment over the barbarous mandates of Antiochus IV were soon to reach their boiling points. Antiochus certainly did not understand the uncompromising nature of Jewish monotheism, the belief in YHWH alone. As Jewish resistance to his policies mounted, Antiochus enacted sterner measures. When Antiochus suffered the humiliating forced withdrawal of his troops from Egypt at the order of the Romans near 167 BC, he blamed the Jews. He then unleashed his army on the Jews in Jerusalem and issued an edict forbidding the practice of Judaism in all traditional forms. Jews were even forced to eat foods forbidden by the Law (2 Mc 6:18–7:42).

The final offense came when an altar to Zeus was erected in the Temple in Jerusalem and unclean swine's flesh was sacrificed on it. Jews considered

Antiochus IV

hasidim

A Hebrew word meaning "loyal ones." It refers to a group who supported the Maccabees in the military effort against Antiochus IV. They also were probably the core members of the later group known as the Essenes.

Pharisees

A group of Jews whose response to foreign rule was one of cultural and religious separatism. They valued adherence to the Law, and exhibited great respect for teachers and interpreters of the Torah. They were responsible for the introduction of rabbis and synagogues into the cultural life of the Jews.

Essenes

A group of Jews whose resistance to foreign influence took them to the extreme position of living in entirely separate communities in the desert around the Dead Sea. Probably, they were the ones who hid the Dead Sea Scrolls, which were not discovered until the middle of the twentieth century.

this act to be an "abomination of desolation" that defiled the entire Temple. The First Book of Maccabees describes some of the desperation of the traditional Jews' situation:

> . . . the king erected the horrible abomination upon the altar of holocausts, and in the surrounding cities of Judah they built pagan altars. They also burnt incense at the doors of houses and in the streets. Any scrolls of the law which they found they tore up and burnt. Whoever was found with a scroll of the covenant, and whoever observed the law, was condemned to death by royal decree. So they used their power against Israel, against those who were caught, each month, in the cities. . . . But many in Israel were determined and resolved in their hearts not to eat anything unclean; they preferred to die rather than to be defiled with unclean food or to profane the holy covenant; and they did die. Terrible affliction was upon Israel. (1 Mc 1:54–58; 62–63)

Judas Maccabeus

In the village of Modin, north of Jerusalem, a revolt against the Seleucid powers broke out, led by Mattathias and his sons. Mattathias, a local priest of the family later known as the Hasmoneans,

refused the order to sacrifice to Greek gods and killed the king's officer who came to his village to enforce it. Mattathias called all Jews who were loyal to their faith to resist and fight against Antiochus. Support also came from a group known as the **hasidim** ("loyal ones"). This group was probably the forerunners of both the **Pharisees** and **Essenes**, later Jewish sects with similarly resistant positions against Hellenistic influences, but tended to be less militant.

When Mattathias died shortly after the revolt began, leadership passed to one of his five sons, Judas, who turned out to be a brilliant military strategist. Judas was called "Maccabeus," which may be translated as "the Hammer." A series of victories by Maccabeus against local military forces led to revolutionary control of the Temple in Jerusalem in December 164 BC, three years to the month from the time that the Temple was profaned.

After the Temple's purification and rededication, the Jews offered sacrifices there again. This event is still commemorated by Jews in the celebration of "Hanukkah," the Festival of Lights. According to Jewish tradition, a miracle occurred at the rededication of the Temple. The lamp, which was supposed to burn in the Holy of Holies, was fueled with a special oil. But when the Maccabees had purified the Temple and were ready to rededicate it, they found only enough oil to fuel the lamp for one day. Despite this, the

Reverence and Respect for the Lord
A lesson of Wisdom literature in the Old Testament is that people should reverence God and respect his power.

Wisdom Literature: Themes and Styles
The Wisdom literature of the Old Testament—basically moral in character—is applicable to people of all generations.

Wisdom Books: A Unique Form of Spirituality
A surprising feature of the Wisdom books is that the central themes and people from other places in the Old Testament rarely appear.

Reverence and Respect for the Lord

After the exile, the Persians and later the Greeks ruled over the Israelites. Then came Roman domination, which lasted through the life of Christ. At this time, Wisdom literature, a unique literary response to faith, emerged and became refined in the Jewish communities living in the Diaspora. Wisdom literature focused on four main themes: God's creation, the natural laws, the future, and the meaning of life itself.

Wisdom literature was a part of many different cultures in the Middle East. These various cultures all had collections of wise sayings, proverbs, and short stories to help people deepen their faith and understand how to live. The Jewish Wisdom authors borrowed from the collections of nations such as Egypt and Greece, and those peoples likely borrowed from Jewish writings as well for additions to their own collections. In the Old Testament, Wisdom literature includes the books of Job, Psalms, Proverbs, Ecclesiastes, Sirach, Wisdom, and Song of Songs.

While Hebrew tradition borrowed and adapted a great deal from the writings of other cultures, it remained clear and unique about one thing:

The beginning of wisdom is the fear of the LORD, and knowledge of the Holy One is understanding. (Prv 9:10)

According to Hebrew Wisdom literature, people are to reverence God and respect his power. Humans should know that God is the Creator, and we are only the created. The first nine chapters of the Book of Wisdom express "fear of the LORD" as the moving force behind a wise person's way of life.

Review

What are four main themes of Wisdom literature?

Reflect

Describe life's moving force, the "fear of the LORD," in positive terms.

Wisdom Literature: Themes and Styles

The purpose of Wisdom literature is fairly clear. Wisdom literature has to do with gaining what is called, in Hebrew, *hokma* ("wisdom"). The wisdom described is basically moral in character, involving lessons in truth, moderation, prudence, and kindness.

Many people seek guidelines, proverbs, or general principles to help them determine the best way to live their lives. Some may ask an older or more experienced person for his or her opinion of a decision or an idea. Sometimes a favored teacher or coach will impart lasting wisdom through short sentences that are often repeated frequently enough that they are committed to memory.

The Book of Proverbs is precisely that—a collection of short, wise sayings—so it is a good place to begin looking at Wisdom literature. One characteristic of proverbs specifically, and Wisdom literature in general, is how universal they are. The message of any wise saying is usually applicable between cultures across different eras as well. Consider the following two "proverbs":

- The journey of folly must be traveled a second time.
- Don't be proud of your knowledge, but consult the ignorant and the wise. The limits of art are not reached; no artist's skills are perfect.

Both of these sayings strike us as quite true and wise even though the first saying is taken from a modern African culture, while the second comes from Ancient Egypt and is over four thousand years old. Both sayings communicate their message perfectly well for today's audience. This is the fascinating thing about wisdom—it seems to apply to anyone, anywhere. Perhaps this is because human nature does not change much from culture to culture or over the centuries. People everywhere seek answers to the meaning of life and want to live in the best way possible. People are still made happy or unhappy in the same ways.

They want to know why they are here, what the point of life is, what will bring them the most happiness, how best to get along with other people, and what will be the most meaningful work for them to do with their lives. Wisdom offers insights into just these sorts of perennial questions.

It should hardly come as a surprise then that some of the same Wisdom sayings from the Book of Proverbs appear in ancient Egyptian writings. Although the Hebrew authors needed to resist any encroachment of foreign religion in their worship of YHWH, they were more willing to exchange insights into less explicitly theological questions with their foreign neighbors. The early American statesman, Benjamin Franklin, followed similar principles. Franklin was fascinated with short, wise sayings and collected a number of them to pass on to his friends. Many of them are still familiar today, for example:

Early to bed, early to rise, makes a man healthy, wealthy and wise.

A penny saved is a penny earned.

These sayings, too, could apply to anyone, anywhere, at any time.

The Wisdom books—Job, Psalms, Proverbs, Ecclesiastes, Song of Songs, Wisdom, and Sirach (Ecclesiasticus)—share styles as well as the themes we have been discussing. One popular writing style contrasts the behaviors of a wise person with those of a foolish person. Here are some examples from the Book of Proverbs:

> A wise son makes his father glad,
>> but a foolish son is a grief to his
>> mother. (Prv 10:1)

> Wisdom builds her house,
>> but Folly tears hers down with
>> her own hands. (Prv 14:1)

> A wise son makes his father glad,
>> but a fool of a man despises his
>> mother. (Prv 15:20)

Jesus taught using this same formula:

> Everyone who listens to these words of mine and acts on them will be like a wise man who built his house on rock. . . . And everyone who listens to these words of mine but does not act on them will be like a fool who built his house on sand. (Mt 7:24, 26)

🌐 Reflect

Write some brief words of insight that describe what you believe about the meaning of life.

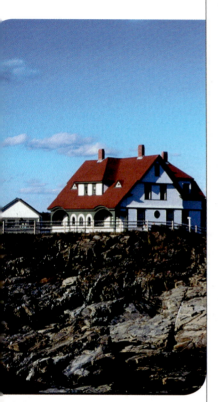

sage

A sage is a person venerated for his or her experience, judgment, and wisdom.

Wisdom in the Bible

The Wisdom movement originated outside of Israel in neighboring nations where it typically revolved around a **sage** who operated within the organized government and was supported by its leaders. The Second Book of Samuel describes a "gifted woman of Tekoa" who was sought out for her advice (2 Sm 14:2). However, most sages identified in the Old Testament seem to have been the "wise counselors" of other nations, and they are generally not well thought of by the Old Testament authors. For example:

> Utter fools are the princes of Zoan!
>> the wisest of Pharaoh's advisers
>> give stupid counsel. (Is 19:11)

> I will make [Babylon's] princes and her wise men drunk, her governors, her prefects, and her warriors, so that they sleep an eternal sleep, never to awaken, says the King whose name is the LORD of hosts. (Jer 51:57)

Sages are rarely mentioned in Israel itself, so it's uncertain who the authors of the biblical Wisdom sayings might have been. It may be that the authors of Wisdom literature in the Bible were men with experience and wealth in ancient Israel. Consider this example from Proverbs:

> He is in a bad way who becomes surety (takes on a loan) for another,
>> but he who hates giving pledges
>> is safe. (Prv 11:15)

Obviously, poor people would not have to worry about whether or not they should accept another person's debt. No one making such a loan would consider their pledge to be worth much in the first place.

Also, note this passage from the Book of Sirach:

Seek not from the LORD authority,
nor from the king a place of honor.

This passage advises people to remain humble before a powerful person who might be easily offended. Only the wealthy would be in a position to meet royalty on any regular basis. Passages such as these are the basis for the supposition that the upper class authored much of Wisdom literature.

Some Wisdom sayings, however, deal with issues and use images that come from the simpler life of the majority of the people—family concerns, reputation, and images taken from the experience of agriculture, farming, and herding. This makes it more likely that the Wisdom sayings in the Bible were collected from all levels of society.

Wisdom Books: A Unique Form of Spirituality

The inspired Wisdom literature in the Old Testament is a unique form of spirituality. Except in the later Book of Sirach, the central themes and characters of the Old Testament (the Exodus, the patriarchs, YHWH's presence in history, and the Law) scarcely appear in biblical Wisdom literature.

This is surprising. These teachings and people were essential to the religious identity of the Jews. It would seem logical, then, that these central teachings and characters—especially the Law of Moses—would find a prominent place in Wisdom literature with its teachings about the meaning of life and how to live. But for the most part, they do not. Instead, Hebrew Wisdom literature focuses more on God as Creator and on creation itself. Readers discover who God is by studying what he has made. The tough questions presented by God to Job are an example of this:

 ## Review

1. Describe wisdom.
2. How did the Wisdom movement originate?
3. Which class of people may have authored a portion of biblical Wisdom literature?

Reflect

Tell about a "sage" in your own life, that is, someone you have sought out for advice.

Where were you when I founded the earth?
    Tell me, if you have understanding.
Who determined its size; do you know?
    Who stretched out the measuring line for it?
Into what were its pedestals sunk,
    and who laid the cornerstone,
While the morning stars sang in chorus
    and all the sons of God shouted for joy?
    (Jb 38:4–7)

Everything about God's identity in this passage centers on God as Creator rather than as YHWH, the God of the patriarchs, the Chosen People, and the Mosaic covenant. Wisdom literature describes God by what he has made; it is descriptive, rational, and objective. This is a different form of spirituality than that found in the writings of the prophets, which tends to be more emotive and charismatic.

The spirituality of Wisdom literature—knowing God by what he has made—is actually very similar to the faith of those today who seek God through their scientific discoveries as physicists, astronomers, biologists, or mathematicians. Modern science carried out in a truly scientific manner without contradicting moral law is very compatible to the inspired Hebrew Wisdom literature in that both have elements of rationality and observation and both ultimately derive from the same God. The recognition of the scientific process in Wisdom literature also suggests the part that human reason plays in our faith. In fact, "though faith is above reason, there can never be any discrepancy between faith and reason" (*Dei Filius* 4, quoted in *CCC*, 159). Our faith is trustworthy because it is perfectly reasonable to believe what God has revealed. Both the Wisdom literature of the Old Testament and modern scientific discoveries give us a more profound sense of the work and accomplishments of God.

Is all Hebrew Wisdom literature from the post-exilic era of biblical history? This is likely so, although some part of the Proverbs may be from as early as the time of the kings. It is traditional to assign much of Wisdom literature to King Solomon, but this is mainly because Solomon was known as a wise king (1 Kgs 3). Solomon certainly did not write all of the Wisdom literature, or even all of the Book of Wisdom which is sometimes called the "Wisdom of Solomon."

Many suggestions have been made to explain why Wisdom literature became popular in the post-exilic Diaspora. They include:

- The Jews were impressed with the Wisdom teachings in other cultures and were inspired to collect their own texts of wise sayings and stories.

- Based in human realities, Wisdom literature could be shared with people of other cultures. It was an area of common ground between Jews and foreigners.

- Wisdom sayings were comforting to a minority people living under foreign rule. They reminded the Jews of how to live a good and prosperous life and of their status as God's Chosen People.

- The Diaspora was seen as a threat to the Jewish community. Parents were concerned about their children remaining grounded in their faith and staying out of trouble. It has been suggested that as urban areas formed after the time of Alexander the Great (323 BC), a delinquent element of teens was also present (see, for example, Prv 1:10–15). Wisdom literature was intended to train young people.

Wisdom literature was another response of the Jews to the challenges of living as a minority people in the ancient world. The next sections briefly examine the Wisdom books of the Old Testament. The Book of Psalms is covered in the most depth in a feature titled "The Book of Psalms," on pages 138–141.

Job

The author of Job is unknown, but the book itself was probably written between 500 and 400 BC. Though there are some similarities to the text of Job in both

Egyptian and Babylonian literature of the time, the work is highly unique, especially in the Bible.

The standard belief of the time was that a good person would be rewarded with good health, material wealth, and general good fortune (see, for example, Ps 37). But human experience then, as now, was sometimes contrary to this. Bad things did happen to good people. The Book of Job rejects the simplistic belief that good is rewarded and evil is punished. Job does not so much solve the problem of the suffering of the innocents as it ponders it, lives with it, and explores it.

The faithful Job, a wealthy man with a large, loving family and many possessions, loses everything: first his possessions, then his family, and finally his own health. He does not understand why any of this has happened, but rejects the conventional wisdom of his friends that he must have sinned in some way. He rejects as well the idea that God sends trials to those he loves, and he finally cries out to God for an explanation. Although God does not explain himself to Job, choosing instead to remind Job of his prerogative as the Creator of all, the face-to-face encounter is enough to console Job and restore his trust in God. His faith has been strengthened and deepened by his suffering and his experience of God. The story ends with Job being restored to health and prosperity and having more children, but it is, by this point, anti-climactic and to a large degree beside the point.

The Book of Job reveals much about the perplexing question of why God permits physical and moral evil. There is physical evil because God has willed that there be limitations in the world that he created. There exists physical evil as long as creation has not reached perfection. Moral evil is caused by a person's freely created will acting against God's will. God permits moral evil because he respects our freedom and mysteriously knows how to derive good from it. Ultimately, we only have to look to the greatest moral evil ever committed—the Passion and Death of God's only Son—and the subsequent good (Christ's Resurrection and our Redemption) that came from it.

 Reflect

How do you answer the question "Why do good people suffer?"

THE BOOK OF PSALMS

More than any other part of the Old Testament, the Psalms present an inward journey of worship and prayer that prepares Christians for the coming of Jesus and his proclamation of God's Kingdom.

Psalms is derived from a Greek word that comes from the name of a stringed instrument called a "psalter," a kind of harp. The Book of Psalms actually refers to "songs to be sung with a psalter." The Hebrew word for the Book of Psalms is *Tehillim*, which means, "praises."

Literary Styles of the Psalms

The overall literary style of the Psalms is poetry. Understanding Hebrew poetry requires understanding the poetic style called "**parallelism**" in the verses of the Psalms. There are many types of parallelism. One common form refers to the practice of restating the same thought. Another kind of parallelism alternates between commonly paired ideas (e.g. light and dark, night and day), while yet another contrasts opposite ideas.

Psalm 2 offers an example of a parallel verse form that simply repeats the same thought in different words:

> Why do the nations
>> protest
>
> and the peoples grumble in vain?
>> (Ps 2:1)

The parallel thoughts are easy to read. *Nations* equates with *peoples* and *protest* is parallel to *grumble in vain*.

An example of parallelism that contrasts opposing thoughts is Psalm 1:

> For the LORD watches over the way of
>> the just
>
> but the way of the wicked leads to
>> ruin. (Ps 1:6)

Note the difference. In the Bible, "the way" is a common term for "manner of living" or moral conduct. The "way of the just" is approved by the Lord, while the "way of the wicked" is not permitted to continue.

Finally, another literary style of the Psalms has the lines of a verse building up or advancing a thought, almost like a stair-step:

> They are like a tree
>> planted near streams of water,
>
> that yields its fruit in season;
>
> Its leaves never wither;
>
> whatever they do prospers. (Ps 1:3)

It is important in reading biblical poetry—including prophetic poetry, but especially the poetry of the Psalms—to pay attention to the relationship between the lines in different verses. Noting the different types of parallelism or the building of lines within a verse can assist a reader in determining the meaning of the verse and the entire Psalm.

Origins of the Psalms

The evolution of the Psalms over a long period of time is clear to anyone who reads the references to David in the first few dozen Psalms, but then reads the references to the Babylonian exile—hundreds of years after the time of David—in Psalm 137. In fact, many who have studied the

---

parallelism
A characteristic common to Hebrew poetry in which two lines express the same or opposite thoughts, one right after the other.

Psalms suggest that originally there were five "books" of the Psalms (that perhaps coincided with the five books of the Pentateuch). The five original books were:

- Book 1: Chapters 1–41
- Book 2: Chapters 42–72
- Book 3: Chapters 73–89
- Book 4: Chapters 90–106
- Book 5: Chapters 107–150

The evidence that these books were originally separate is twofold:

1. The final chapters of each book (i.e., 41, 72, 89, 106, and 150) each include a doxology that ends with "Amen. Amen." This may well have been a conclusion that appeared at the end of each separate book.
2. There is one "doublet" or repeated passage in the Book of Psalms. Psalm 14 and Psalm 53 are the same. In other biblical research, doublets are evidence that two different text versions have been brought together, creating some duplication of material.

As to actually dating the psalms, the evidence above provides several clues. Traditionally, it was thought that King David was the author of the Psalms, at least through Psalm 72, which states: "end of the Psalms of David, son of Jesse" (Ps 72:20). The historical books of the Old Testament mentioned that David, as a young boy, played a stringed instrument in the court of King Saul. The idea of David writing Psalms comes from the early report that David actually played a psalter, though the Greek name of the instrument is evidence enough that the period of the Psalms was much later than the time of David.

In fact, almost two-thirds of the entire Book of Psalms come from the period of the Second Temple, that is, after 520 BC, but before 333 BC. The correct dates for most psalms

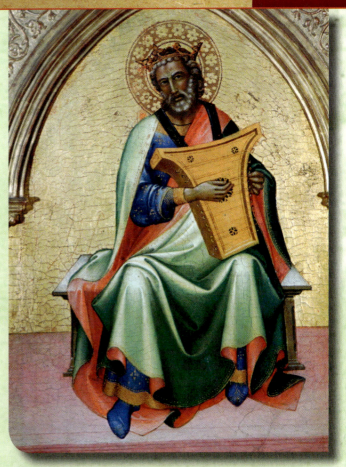

are hard to determine exactly. Those that mention historical events are easier to date. Again, Psalm 137 is the easiest example because it mentions a historical event—the Babylonian exile. It is certain that Psalm 137 can be no *older* than 587 BC. The historical Psalms 105 and 106 must have been written after the last events mentioned in their poetic lines. The historical survey of Psalms 105–106 also includes references to the destruction of Jerusalem and the Babylonian exile. For example:

So the LORD grew angry with his
      people,
    abhorred his own heritage;
He handed them over to the nations,
    and their adversaries ruled them.
Their enemies oppressed them,
    kept them under subjection.
(Ps 106:40–42)

Psalm 29 may be the oldest Psalm in the Bible because its poetry is considered very similar in style to ancient Canaanite poetry of an earlier era. In Psalm 29, YHWH is depicted as a storm God with thunder and lightning as his weapons. For example:

> The voice of the LORD strikes with
>> fiery flame;
>>> the voice of the Lord rocks the
>>>> desert,
>>> the LORD rocks the desert of
>>>> Kadesh. (Ps 29:7-9)

Psalms about the Temple (e.g., Ps 65:5, 68:30), obviously, cannot come from David, because the first Temple was built by his son, Solomon. Furthermore, it is not always clear which Temple is being talked about—Solomon's Temple or the Second Temple built around 520-515 BC.

Different Kinds of Psalms

However the Book of Psalms came together, there is agreement that many different kinds of Psalms make up the overall collection. Not all the psalms seem to have been written for the same occasion or purpose. Four main categories of Psalms are as follows:

1. Psalms of Lament (sorrow over tragedies)

The Psalms of lament come in two types, individual and communal. That is, the speaker in the Psalm is either a single person or the entire Hebrew community. They are Psalms requesting God's help and protection in dealing with a variety of needs. Many of these Psalms conclude with a few lines of thanksgiving and praise for God's response to the appeal for help.

- Psalm 3 (military threat)
- Psalm 10 (legal problems or grievances from fellow Israelites)
- Psalm 38 (personal illness)
- Psalm 44 (communal laments for groups to sing)

2. Psalms of Praise and Thanksgiving

Psalms in this category focus on praising God. They often begin with an invitation to join in the praise and continue with a list of reasons for praise and thanksgiving to God.

- Psalm 19
- Psalm 33

3. Psalms of Instruction

These Psalms can be divided into two types. The wisdom Psalms share the same themes as the Wisdom literature that has been discussed throughout this chapter ("Wisdom Literature: Themes and Styles," pages 132-134). The **historical Psalms** retell portions of the history of the Chosen People.

- Psalm 1 (wisdom Psalm)
- Psalm 104 (wisdom Psalm)
- Psalms 105-106 (historical Psalms)

4. Liturgical Psalms

Some Psalms were intended for use during Temple celebrations. They often reveal a dialogue structure and may have been written to be sung by two choirs or by a cantor with the congregation responding.

---

historical Psalms

A Psalm recounting events from the history of Israel such as the covenant with the patriarchs, the Exodus, or the settling of the Promised Land.

- Psalm 24 (perhaps to be sung while traveling to the Temple)

How were the Psalms used? Some, such as the liturgical Psalms, were used for worship in the Temple. Other Psalms were used for religious festivals outside of the Temple. There is no description in the Bible of exactly how the Psalms were used in Temple services, but it is presumed that choirs sang some of them (Ps 68:27). All but thirty-four of the Psalms have titles or musical directions. These addendums were added much later than the text of the Psalms themselves, so we know they became useful in worship at some point.

Obviously not all the Psalms were intended for Temple singing. It would be hard to imagine an occasion for singing the historical Psalms, such as Psalms 105–106, unless students sang them as a way to recall the history of Israel. In fact, that might be especially valuable for Hebrew children growing up in the Diaspora where songs would be an effective way to maintain identity and to provide a connection with their religious and spiritual traditions, but that is clearly different from worship.

Other Psalms seem to have been used for entirely different occasions. Read, for example, Psalm 35, a lament Psalm. The Psalm is an appeal to God for help. But help against whom? Verses 1-3 describes the threat of an enemy. However, verses 11-14 refer to "unjust witnesses" that have risen up and spoken against the Psalmist, repaying "evil for good." It may be that the help requested from God in Psalm 35 is to settle an argument between two groups of Israelites. In cases like this, where the argument is with fellow Israelites, the dispute would have been brought to the Temple where the two parties would have appealed to the priests. The priests in turn would instruct them to seek God's vindication to settle the dispute, which may have been over money, debts, business, or marriage contracts. It is not certain how the Psalm might have fit into the process of seeking a judgment from the priests, but it does seem to be connected to that process.

Part of the continuing appeal of the Book of Psalms is that these songs to the Lord help modern readers "hear the hearts" of the Israelites despite the great differences of time and culture that separate them. The Psalms help to engage readers and pray-ers of all generations in the most intimate moments of pain, praise, joy, and sorrow of the ancient Hebrews. Jesus, himself, turned to the comfort of one of the lament Psalms at the moment of his Death:

> My God, my God, why have you
> abandoned me?
> Why so far from my call for help,
> from my cries of anguish?

(Ps 22:2)

It important to note here that the Psalm Jesus chose ends in triumph just as Jesus' pain was ultimately vindicated in his Resurrection—the triumph over the Cross and over Death. The Psalms are expressions of the deepest human pain and highest human joys. When we are feeling such joy that we are speechless or such deep pain that we don't know what to say, the words of the Psalms can become our words, too.

Reflect

Peruse the Book of Psalms and list a Psalm that expresses an intimate connection between you and God.

Proverbs

The Book of Proverbs was collected as the best of the Israelite Wisdom tradition, probably in the fifth century BC. Some of the proverbs may well date back to the time of Solomon. Other proverbs come from unknown times and places.

The proverbs teach three types of wisdom: knowledge of God's created world, the skill of making right choices, and the art of living before God. Some proverbs are also secular, with little or no religious implications. As introduced in "Wisdom Literature: Themes and Styles" on page 133, most of the proverbs teach by comparison. "The fear of the LORD is the beginning of wisdom" (Prv 1:7) is the main teaching of the text. Wisdom is also known as the "firstborn" of God:

> The LORD begot me, the firstborn of
>   his ways,
>   the forerunner of his prodigies
>   of long ago. (Prv 8:22)

laments
Songs or poems that express grief or mourning.

Ecclesiastes

The title of the book is the Greek translation of the Hebrew word *Qohelet*, meaning "someone who calls an assembly." The title refers to someone like a preacher or teacher who presides over a meeting, but not to an actual historical person. Ecclesiastes is a loose collection of proverbs, **laments**, poems, and rhetorical questions. Qohelet may simply refer to "a gatherer," that is, a person who gathered or assembled all these sayings. It was written about the third century BC.

The book is concerned with the value of human life. Hard work does not guarantee happiness, for it is often marred by suffering. Riches and pleasures will not bring happiness nor guarantee long life. Talents and skills generally result in the stress of competition with others for praise and honor, which even if won is fleeting. A major theme of the book is the vanity of all things. People cannot find happiness and answers to the mysteries of life without God. The author eventually recognizes that

> there is nothing better than to be glad and to do well during life. For every man, moreover, to eat and drink and enjoy the fruit of all his labor is a gift of God. I recognized that whatever God does will endure forever; there is no adding to it, or taking from it. Thus has God done that he may be revered. (Eccl 3:12–14)

Song of Songs

Though the Song of Songs has been attributed to Solomon, its language and style reveal that it was written after the Babylonian exile. It is a collection of love poems. The title itself is a Hebrew way of saying "the greatest of songs."

The love poems express the alternating views of two lovers describing each other in very erotic language. From a Jewish point of view, the love poems were also said to refer to the love between YHWH and Israel. Catholics have interpreted the Song of Songs as an allegory describing Christ's love for the Church. Song of Songs is also a joyful celebration of the love between a husband and wife in a marriage blessed by God, and as such is read during the Liturgy of the Word at wedding Masses.

Wisdom

The complete title of this book is "Wisdom of Solomon," although the author actually was a Jew living in Alexandria in Egypt. The book was written in Greek and reveals a **Hellenistic** influence, though the author was also deeply versed in the Hebrew scriptures.

The Book of Wisdom was the last book of Old Testament to be written, sometime in the middle of the first century BC. It has been divided into three main sections:

- The Book of Eschatology (1:1–6:21). This section speaks of the reward of justice. While human destiny is in God's hands, the choices made by a person can make a difference.

- Praise of Wisdom (6:22–11:1). Wisdom is personified as the spirit of God. The author reviews Israel's history to show how God's wisdom was present through all times.

- God's Special Providence during the Exodus (11:2–19:22). This section focuses on two main ideas

related to the Exodus: (1) the sufferings of the Egyptians were due to their own sins and (2) the evils that affected all the enemies of Israel were a part of God's Salvation offered to his Chosen People.

Sirach (Ecclesiasticus)

The Book of Sirach is unique among Wisdom books because the author is identified: Jesus, son of Eleazar, son of Sirach. He was likely a sage who lived in Jerusalem and who had great love for the law, priesthood, Temple, and worship. The book, which contains numerous sayings, laments, Psalms of praise, and moral maxims, was written in Hebrew in the second century BC. The book has also been called *Liber Ecclesiasticus*, meaning "Church Book," because it was used extensively by the early Church in the formation of catechumens and in the instruction to the faithful. It is the longest, and most widely cited, of the writings

Hellenistic
Relating to the culture, history, or language of Greece after the death of Alexander the Great in 323 BC.

included in the Latin Christian Bible not found in Hebrew scriptures.

Sirach is similar to the Book of Proverbs in style but it is better organized, with proverbs addressing similar topics grouped together. In fact, it has been considered an updated Proverbs for the later challenges facing Israel.

In summary, Wisdom writings were based on tradition. Their subject matter was taken from looking back at the gleaned experience of the Hebrews and other peoples to answer current questions and problems of the day. The value of wisdom is best summarized at the opening of the Book of Proverbs:

That men may appreciate wisdom and discipline,
    may understand words of intelligence;
May receive training in wise conduct
    in what is right, just and honest;
That resourcefulness may be imparted to the simple,
    to the young man knowledge and discretion.
A wise man by hearing them will advance in
        learning,
    an intelligent man will gain sound guidance,
That he may comprehend proverb and parable,
    the words of the wise and their riddles.
The fear of the Lord is the beginning of knowledge;
    wisdom and instruction fools despise. (Prv 1:2–7)

 Review

1. Rather than central themes and characters of the Old Testament, what does Wisdom literature focus on?

2. What are similarities between the spirituality of inspired Wisdom literature and the modern scientific method?

3. When was the great majority of Wisdom literature written?

4. Why did Wisdom literature become popular in the post-exilic Diaspora?

5. What is the main teaching of the Book of Job?

6. What is the meaning of the word *Psalm*?

7. What are two types of parallelism in the Psalms?

8. What evidence is there that the Psalms were originally divided into five separate books?

9. When are most of the Psalms dated?

10. Why is Psalm 29 believed to be the oldest Psalm?

11. What are the four types of Psalms?

12. Describe the different ways the Psalms were originally used?

13. What three types of wisdom do the Proverbs teach?

14. How did Ecclesiastes get its title?

15. What is a major theme of Ecclesiastes?

16. What are three ways to interpret the Song of Songs?

17. What are the three main sections of the Book of Wisdom?

18. How is the Book of Sirach unique among Wisdom books?

19. Why has the Book of Sirach been called *Liber Ecclesiasticus*?

Reflect

What is your definition of wisdom?

Research and Report

Choose and complete at least one of the following assignments:

- Several Psalms follow a definite pattern. The first part is an invitation to praise God; the second part gives the reason for the Psalm; the third part is a repetition of the first part. Chart the following Psalms according to the threefold pattern: Psalms 32, 46, 95, and 102.
- Illustrate Ecclesiastes 3:1–9 using original artwork or photography. Or set the words of Scripture to original music.

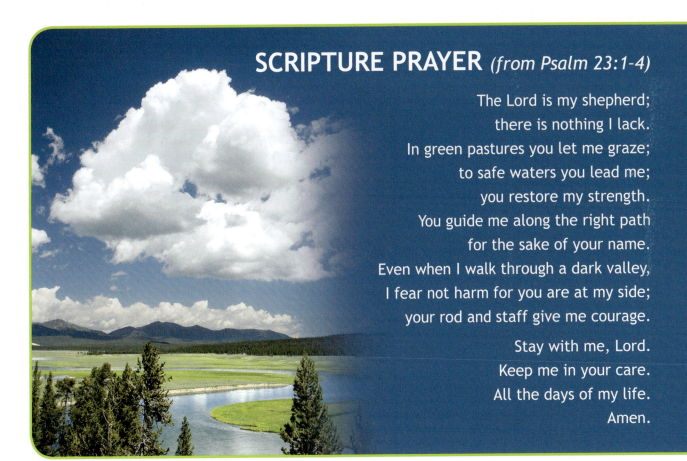

SCRIPTURE PRAYER *(from Psalm 23:1-4)*

The Lord is my shepherd;
there is nothing I lack.
In green pastures you let me graze;
to safe waters you lead me;
you restore my strength.
You guide me along the right path
for the sake of your name.
Even when I walk through a dark valley,
I fear not harm for you are at my side;
your rod and staff give me courage.

Stay with me, Lord.
Keep me in your care.
All the days of my life.
Amen.

1E

THE
PROPHETS

Origins of the Prophets and Prophecy
Besides the "former prophets," a group of "latter prophets" emerged who were also part of a literary movement among the prophets.

Marks of the Prophets
Prophets received a call from God, left their former way of life, and preached a message that was mostly unpopular with the ruling establishment.

Major Prophets
The "major prophets" Isaiah, Jeremiah, and Ezekiel—along with Lamentations, Baruch, and parts of the Book of Daniel—highlight messages calling God's People back to him.

Minor Prophets
The section of Old Testament beginning with Hosea, a prophet of the north, and ending with the Book of Malachi, is a survey of prophets who, because they wrote on a single scroll, are known as "minor prophets."

Origins of the Prophets and Prophecy

The prophet is a special kind of messenger from God. Prophets were present through the early and late stages of the Old Testament. In fact, the Hebrew word associated with prophet, *nabi,* is connected, first, with Moses. Moses was the prophet who heard God's message of liberation and shared it with the people while they were still enslaved in Egypt. Moses's brother, Aaron, was also called a prophet because he spoke for Moses before the Pharaoh.

The prophets are mentioned throughout this period of history. Samuel, the last of Israel's judges, was also called a prophet. Deborah, another judge, was a "prophetess" (Jgs 4:4). The second Book of Samuel mentions the prophet Nathan confronting David about his sinful behavior involving Bathsheba and Uriah, though no other biographical information is told of him. Also included among these "former prophets" are the prominent figures of Elijah and Elisha mentioned in Chapter 1C.

Prophecy became a literary movement too. The sayings of selected prophets were gathered up and kept, just as the sayings of Jesus were kept by the earliest Christians. Amos (approximately 740 BC) was the earliest prophet whose gathered sayings were written in book form. After Amos, other books were formed from the sayings of different prophets. And then, somewhat mysteriously, the books of prophetic messages ceased in the Old Testament, although it was revived in early Christianity because the early Christians also had prophets.

The group of "latter prophets" (as opposed to the former prophets who appear in earlier times) was made up of three **major prophets** (Isaiah, Jeremiah, and Ezekiel) along with a larger group of **minor prophets** (Hosea, Joel, Amos, Obadiah, Jonah, Micah, Nahum, Habakkuk, Zephaniah, Haggai, Zechariah, and Malachi). "Major" and "minor," incidentally, are terms that refer to the size of the book, not to the importance of the prophet or his message.

A main objective of this chapter is to introduce the origins of the Old Testament prophets in total. Several ideas will be explored, each one contributing

MAJOR PROPHETS	
Isaiah	
Jeremiah	
Ezekiel	
MINOR PROPHETS	
Hosea	Malachi
Joel	Zechariah
Amos	Haggai
Obadiah	Zephaniah
Jonah	Habakkuk
Micah	Nahum

to how the prophets took on a central role with God's People of the Old Testament. Next, the "writing prophets"

major prophets

Three of the latter prophets—Isaiah, Jeremiah, and Ezekiel—whose books in the Old Testament are quite lengthy.

minor prophets

The twelve prophets of the Old Testament whose recorded sayings are much briefer than those of the major prophets: Hosea, Joel, Amos, Obadiah, Jonah, Micah, Nahum, Habakkuk, Zephaniah, Haggai, Zechariah, and Malachi.

and the books of the Bible that are named after them will be introduced by their designation as major or minor.

Review

1. Who is the first person in the Old Testament associated with the term *prophet*?

2. What do the terms *major prophet* and *minor prophet* refer to?

Marks of the Prophets

Several common marks or roles of the prophets provide clues to their origins.

First, prophets received a call from God and felt compelled to leave their former way of life to follow it. Amos, for example, was a shepherd: "The LORD took me from following the flock, and said to me 'Go, prophesy to my people Israel'" (Am 7:15). A call from God came in different ways. Prophets heard voices, had dreams, saw visions, or received inspiration to share God's message. In some ways, they were like the oracles of other religious traditions (ancient Greek) to whom people went to ask questions about God. However, false prophets are also mentioned in many places throughout the Old Testament, sometimes making it difficult to determine who were the true prophets.

Second, the prophet often spoke messages that were unpopular with the ruling establishment. In response, the king sometimes tried to rid himself of the prophet in the belief that doing so would keep the prophet's dire message from coming true. Needless to say, "killing the messenger" did not, in any way, make the message less true. In general, the message of the prophets was

call narratives
Stories that describe a person's initial awareness that God wanted him or her to do something specific. The calls of the prophet have five common elements: (1) there is something mysterious and holy about the encounter; (2) God acts first; (3) the prophet resists; (4) God reassures; and (5) God sends the prophet on his or her mission.

meant to convert their listeners to God. They did so by warning the people to repent for their sins under the penalty of punishment if they failed to do so. More characteristics of the prophets follow.

🌐 Reflect

Classify a person(s) today who fits these marks of a prophet: someone called by God who leaves a former way of life to speak a message that is unpopular with the majority.

The Prophets Inherited the Role of Moses

The concept of a person being called by God or his angel to perform a particular task or to play a certain role in the life of the community of Israel is central to the understanding of prophets. The **call narratives** of Isaiah and Jeremiah (Is 6:1–9 and Jeremiah 1:4–10) each follow a similar pattern:

1. The setting is one of mystery or holiness.
2. God initiates the call.
3. The person resists.
4. God reassures the person.
5. God sends the person on a mission.

This pattern is the same as Moses's call to be God's deliverer of the Hebrews held in slavery by the Egyptians:

> Moses, however, said to the LORD, "If you please, LORD, I have never been eloquent, neither in the past, nor recently, nor now that you have spoken to your servant; but I am slow of speech and tongue." The LORD said to him, "Who gives one man speech and makes another deaf and dumb? Or who gives sight to the one and makes another blind? Is it not I, the LORD? Go, then! It is I who will assist you in speaking and will teach you what you are to say." (Ex 4:10–12)

Like Moses, the prophets Isaiah and Jeremiah protested that they were not good enough to speak for God. It seems that the similarity is intentional. The latter prophets were carrying on the work of Moses, interpreting the signs of the times in light of the covenant. Was Moses the first prophet? Consider this passage from the time of Moses's death:

> Since then no prophet has arisen in Israel like Moses, whom the LORD knew face to face. (Dt 34:10)

The prophets usually based their criticism of Israel on the statutes and commandments of Moses; these ethical guidelines were the basis for their denouncing Israelite behavior. All of this suggests a strong connection between Moses the "lawgiver" and the prophets as "law protectors" (insisting that the Law of Moses be obeyed). This was certainly the case in the examples of the prophets Elijah and Elisha. So, in determining the origins and development of the prophets, the connection with Moses is important. But it is still not the complete picture of the prophets.

The Prophets Were "Spiritual Warriors"

There is textual evidence throughout the Old Testament to support the identification of the judges as prophets also. As mentioned, the judge Deborah, who was a military leader, was directly called a prophet (Jgs 4:4). Other judges shared the experience of being called by God, or by an angel of God, to their position of leadership. Recall the story of the call of Gideon as he was selected for leadership:

> . . . the *angel of the* Lord *appeared to him* and said, "The Lord is with you, O champion!" (Jgs 6:12)

Or consider the call of Samson before his birth,

> *An angel of the* Lord *appeared to the woman* and said to her, "Though you are barren and have had no children, yet you will conceive and bear a son." (Jgs 13:3)

Compare these calls with the call of Moses at the burning bush:

> There *an angel of the* Lord *appeared to him* in fire flaming out of a bush. As he looked on, he was surprised to see that the bush, though on fire, was not consumed. (Ex 3:2)

The appearance of "an angel of the Lord" at the moment of the call of these judges indicates that, like Moses, the judges, too, were considered prophets. But, uniquely, they combined the vocations of prophet (a person summoned by God or his messenger and selected by God to guide his people) and king (someone chosen to be a warrior and to lead the people to military victory). A judge was a "warrior-prophet" in a sense, combining both roles in one vocation.

When the Israelites decided to choose kings of their own, they wanted warriors to fight their battles and lead them to victory over adversaries (recall 1 Samuel 8). The kings of Israel were more one-dimensional than the judges. They were warriors without the spiritual dimension that came from being called directly by God.

Did this mean that God stopped "calling on" men and women to speak to the people during the time of the kings? Indeed not. It was during the time of the kings that the prophetic movement became particularly influential and important. Remember, it was the prophet Samuel who identified the king the people had asked for. Although God chose Saul and then David to rule as king of Israel, he did not call them directly, nor did his angel appear to them. Instead, God communicated his choice to his prophet, Samuel, and Samuel anointed Saul and later David as a sign to the community of God's choice. One way to describe the prophets during the time of the kings is "demilitarized judges," since warfare became the business of the kings. The prophets then became the "spiritually selected messengers of God."

This idea suggests that prophecy was rooted in the early military leaders of Israel, before the rise of the monarchy under Saul, and later, the House of David. The Old Testament supports the idea that prophets once had a military role in early Israelite society. For example, when a servant of Elisha doubted the prophet's strength, Elisha prayed for the appearance of a "heavenly army":

> "O Lord, open his eyes, that he may see." And the Lord opened the eyes of the servant, so that he saw the mountainside filled with horses and fiery chariots around Elisha. (2 Kgs 6:17)

Passages like this strongly associate prophets with miraculous acts of warfare. This could be because of the prophets' earlier association with warfare from the time of the judges. In the time of the kings, the prophets retained their connection to the military activities of Israel since they were often consulted about the likelihood of victory prior to battles. Still, there is more to the prophets than this.

The Prophets Were Social Revolutionaries

The Old Testament prophets showed passionate concern for the poor whenever they suffered oppression by the rich. The prophets spoke to both groups of people and were known to "afflict the comfortable and comfort the afflicted." It is hardly accidental, then, that the strongest prophets (e.g., Amos, Micah, and Isaiah) appeared precisely during the time when there was the worst oppression and mistreatment of the poor. Their testimony on behalf of the poor was forthright, unflinching, and forceful. God would revoke his word from the Israelites:

> Because they sell the just man for silver,
>   and the poor man for a pair of sandals.
> They trample the heads of the weak
>   into the dust of the earth,
>   and force the lowly out of the way.
> Son and father go to the same prostitute,
>   profaning my holy name.
> Upon garments taken in pledge
>   they recline beside any altar;
> And the wine of those who have been fined
>   they drink in the house of their god. (Am 2:6–8)

Many of the prophets announced that God would judge Israel by a single "measuring stick" of their righteousness—that is, how they treated the weakest members of their society: the widow, the orphan, and the foreigner. The Law demanded that the people most "at risk" in society be cared for so that they could survive, and live reasonably stable lives, rather than being neglected or taken advantage of by the rich. Isaiah and Jeremiah made very clear what they considered the faults of Israel:

> Woe to those who enact unjust statues
>   and who write oppressive decrees,
> Depriving the needy of judgment
>   and robbing my people's poor of their rights,
> Making widows their plunder,
>   and orphans their prey!
> What will you do on the day of punishment,
>   when ruin comes from afar? (Is 10:1–3)

> Thus says the Lord: Do what is right and just. Rescue the victim from the hand of his oppressor. Do not wrong or oppress the resident alien, the orphan, or the widow, and do not shed innocent blood in this place. (Jer 22:3)

Also read Isaiah 1:17, Ezekiel 22:3, 7, Zechariah 7:10, and Malachi 3:5.

These passages make it clear that the prophets were concerned about the social and economic practices of their times, especially the oppressive behavior of the rich in both the kingdoms of Judah and Israel. The religious concern of the prophets—to serve YHWH and no other gods—was always accompanied by their social and political concerns.

When Jesus taught about compassion for the poor (e.g., Matthew 25:31–46) he was clearly standing in the prophetic tradition of ancient Israel. Thus, the element of justice is crucial to understanding the prophets. But it is still not the whole picture of the role of the prophets.

Reflect

Who are people most "at risk" today? In what ways are they cared for by others?

The Prophets Were Messengers of God

The common understanding that prophets were "messengers of God" gains credence from consistent textual evidence. First, the prophets almost always spoke in the first person, as if God were speaking. They often began their speeches with the famous words: "Thus says the LORD," which means quite literally, "Here is the message from God." This short little bit at the beginning of the speeches is often referred to as the "**messenger formula**." It may have been borrowed from other correspondences in the ancient world, particularly messages sent between kings. For example:

> [Ben-hadad] sent couriers to Ahab, king of Israel, within the city, and said to him, "This is Ben-hadad's message . . . (1 Kgs 20:2–3)

When the prophet says "Thus says God" (in one form or another), it certainly resembles the language of other messengers in the Old Testament. Though prophets began speeches using other formulas as well, the prevalence of the "messenger formula" makes a clear connection between the prophets and other messengers, thus enabling us to identify the prophets as "messengers of God."

In addition, the prophets are often classified as God's servants:

> And though the LORD warned Israel and Judah by every prophet and seer, "Give up your evil ways and keep my commandments and statutes, in accordance with the entire law which I enjoined on your fathers and which I sent you by my servants the prophets," they did not listen. (2 Kgs 17:13–14)

> From the day that your fathers left the land of Egypt even to this day, I have sent you untiringly all my servants the prophets. (Jer 7:25)

By now we have seen that there are reasons to identify the prophets with many different roles. How are we to know which is correct? Are the prophets messengers, law-protectors, advocates for the poor, servants? The answer is: all of the above!

All of these points tell something of the origins and development of the Old Testament prophets. They also make it clear that prophecy was a complex and

messenger formula
The opening words of a prophetic speech, attributing what follows to God, as in "Thus says the LORD . . ." or "The LORD said . . ."

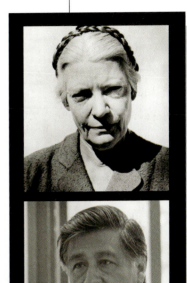
Dorothy Day

Cesar Chavez

Mother Teresa

Oscar Romero

multi-faceted phenomenon in ancient Israel. The central role of the prophets in the Old Testament is undeniable. While the historical books often condemned the kings of ancient Israel, the prophets were revered, at least by the time their stories were recorded. This brings us to an overview of some of the major and minor prophets and the biblical books that bear their names.

2. Why can the judges also be described as prophets?

3. What does it mean to say that the prophets were "spiritual warriors"?

4. How were the prophets "social revolutionaries"?

5. What text evidence from Scripture indicates that the prophets were "messengers of God"?

Review

1. What are similarities between Moses, the first prophet, and later prophets?

LITERARY STYLES OF HEBREW PROPHECY

The basic literary style of the written prophecies in the Old Testament is an oracle. An oracle, in its basic form, is a brief, poetic declaration following the formula establishing it as a message from God: "Thus says the Lord." Most of the books of the latter prophets are collections of oracles that resemble the poetic texts of the books of Psalms and Proverbs. However, only the prophetic books of Obadiah, Micah, Nahum, Habakkuk, and Zephaniah are entirely written in poetic form. The oracles in the Book of Ezekiel are contained within autobiographical narratives of the prophet. (Biographical information was not crucial in these works. However, there is usually a superscription that indicates the prophet's family connections and the kings who ruled during the time the oracles were given.)

oracle
A brief, poetic declaration preceded by the messenger formula, "Thus says the Lord," which establishes it reliably as a message from God.

While some of the autobiographical material of the prophets may have been recorded by the prophets themselves, the oracles were more likely collected over a long period of time by the prophet's disciples. It is important to remember that the prophecy of the writing prophets began as oral speech first delivered in meetings between the prophets and those who heard them. The settings varied between places such as the court of the Temple (Jer 7:1-2), a lesser shrine (Am 7:13), or a city gate (Jer 17:19). These speeches were only written down years later.

Major Prophets

The "major prophets" are Isaiah, Jeremiah, and Ezekiel. Note that two short prophetic books—Lamentations and Baruch—have traditionally been associated with Jeremiah and will be discussed briefly with the Book of Jeremiah. Also, the Book of Daniel is classified in the Catholic canon of the Old Testament with the prophetic books. The Hebrew scriptures lists Daniel with the Writings. Chapter 1C pointed out that the Book of Daniel contains history. It also includes apocalyptic literature and some prophecy. More explanation of how the Book of Daniel is organized is in the section "Daniel" on pages 165–166.

Isaiah

The New Testament quotes Isaiah more than any other prophetic book. However, the Book of Isaiah presents some interesting dilemmas for analysis.

Isaiah of Jerusalem, the prophet for whom the book is named, is said to have started his ministry in the reign of King Uzziah (Is 1:1). Uzziah died about 740 BC. The problem with accurate dating occurs with the mention of the Persian emperor Cyrus in Isaiah 45:1. Cyrus defeated Babylon in 539 BC. It is virtually certain that the same prophet did not begin his career before 740 and then live to see the rise of Cyrus the Persian two centuries later.

This issue along with others has led to the understanding that the Book of Isaiah actually contains the work of more than one writer, from more than one time. The Book of Isaiah is usually divided as follows:

1. *Isaiah 1–39.* These chapters are mostly stories about, and sayings of, the actual prophet Isaiah of Jerusalem for whom the book is named.
2. *Isaiah 40–55.* A second, unnamed prophet is generally credited with this portion of the book. He may have lived at the end of the Babylonian Period and the beginning of the Persian Period (545–535 BC) and likely witnessed the collapse of Babylon to the Persian empire.
3. *Isaiah 56–66.* The final chapters are thought to have been collected by disciples who inherited the spirit of the great prophet. They may have been writing from Jerusalem and the Diaspora after the exile. These chapters emphasize the importance of the Temple and invite all nations to join Israel as God's Chosen People.

The first thirty-nine chapters of the Book of Isaiah detail the ministry of the prophet in Jerusalem. At the Temple, Isaiah had a vision of the Lord in glory. Isaiah was humbled and proclaimed his unworthiness to be God's messenger. The story tells of a seraphim (an angel) touching Isaiah's mouth with an ember from the altar and thus removing his sinfulness.

> Then I heard the voice of the Lord saying, "Whom shall I send? Who will go for us?" "Here I am," I said; "send me!"

The prophet then foretold to the people their stubbornness, which would eventually lead to the fall of Judah. Isaiah asked the Lord how long this period would be:

> Until the cities are desolate,
>   without inhabitants,
> Houses, without a man,
>   and the earth is a desolate waste.
> Until the LORD removes men far
>   away,
>   and the land is abandoned more
>   and more. (Is 6:11–12)

The first thirty-nine chapters of the Book of Isaiah include several other notable passages, including the **Vineyard Song** (Is 5) that depicts the Chosen People as the vine of God. This image recurs in the New Testament in the words of Jesus (Mt 21:33–44) and the letters of Paul (Rom 11:23–24).

The anonymous prophet who authored Isaiah 40–55 lived at the time of the end of the Babylonian exile. The prophet understood that Persia was soon to be the new power of the region and that its more tolerant ruler, Cyrus, would be God's instrument to return the Jews to their homeland. Cyrus, indeed, was a key factor in the end of

Babylonian captivity for the Jewish exiles even though the Persians maintained rule over the lands of Palestine and the Jewish people.

The text of this portion of the Book of Isaiah includes four **Servant Songs** (Is 42:1–4; 49:1–6; 50:4–9; 52:13–53:12). A messianic figure, known as the "Servant of God," is described as having the mission to bring righteousness to the world. He is opposed, suffers, and is put to death. The Servant Songs were clearly connected with the qualities of the Messiah that would be well represented in the mission of Jesus. The fourth song was understood to describe the redeeming nature of Jesus' Death:

> But he was pierced for our offenses,
>   crushed for our sins;
> Upon him was the chastisement that
>   makes us whole,
>   by his stripes we were healed.
>   (Is 53:5)

It is important to remember that the prophet's words had comfort for the people at the time they were written as well as 500 years later with the coming of Jesus Christ. So, who might the prophet have been referring to as the Suffering Servant at the time these words were written?

The prophet clearly believes that at least one identity of the "Suffering Servant" is the Jewish people themselves, due to their experience in exile. They are collectively the "Servant of God." And if this is the case, then what is their new mission to be? Was it to forget

Vineyard Song
An important passage of the Book of Isaiah depicting the Chosen People as the vine of God. The image recurs in the New Testament in the words of Jesus and the writings of the Apostle Paul.

Servant Songs
Four songs in the Book of Isaiah that describe a messianic figure, known as the "Servant of God," who is described as bringing righteousness to the world. The Servant Songs are connected with the mission of Jesus.

what they have learned in their suffering and to punish the nations that hurt them so badly? Some passages seem to indicate this (Ps 137:1, 8–9), but Isaiah represents another tradition, one that recognizes that suffering has given the people a more peaceful and loving way to view and respond to the rest of the world:

> It is too little, he says, for you to be my servant,
>> to raise up the tribes of Jacob,
>> and restore the survivors of Israel;
> I will make you a light to the nations,
>> that my salvation may reach to the ends of the
>> earth. (Is 49:6)

In this passage, the prophet goes far beyond simply preaching the restoration of Israel. Now, the People of God will be a missionary people, with a "light" to take to all the nations.

While many other identifications of the Suffering Servant have been proposed (e.g., the prophet himself, or another prophet living at that time), the Church is clear in its pronouncement that the Suffering Servant prophecies are fulfilled in Jesus Christ. The *Catechism* teaches:

> The Scriptures had foretold this divine plan of Salvation through the putting to death of "the righteous one, my Servant" as a mystery of universal redemption, that is, as the ransom that would free men from the slavery of sin. Citing a confession of faith that he himself had "received," St. Paul professes that "Christ died for our sins in accordance with the scriptures." In particular, Jesus' redemptive death fulfills Isaiah's prophecy of the suffering Servant. (*CCC*, 601)

The final eleven chapters of the Book of Isaiah are a mixture of poetry and prose composed by the disciple(s) of Isaiah shortly after the return from exile. The message of these chapters is one of hope; it looks forward to a New Jerusalem and a day when God's light will attract all people to God. Some of these passages even prepare the way for Jesus' inclusive message of God's love for *all* people, Jews and Gentiles alike:

> I come to gather nations of every language; they shall come and see my glory. I will set a sign among them; from them I will send fugitives to the nations . . . that have never heard my fame, or seen my glory; and they shall proclaim my glory among the nations.

> From one new moon to another,
>> and from one sabbath to another,
> All mankind shall come to worship
>> before me, says the LORD. (Is 66:18–19, 23)

⊙ Reflect

How can a Christian emulate Jesus and be a "suffering servant"?

Jeremiah

The prophet Jeremiah began his ministry during the reign of King Josiah in approximately 626 BC. He finally disappeared from the pages of history sometime after 587 BC. He was chosen from the womb, born from a priestly family, and grew up just outside the walls of Jerusalem in the small town of Anathoth. Jeremiah remained in Jerusalem through all the events of the siege and the exile of the people. His prophecies were recorded by a secretary, Baruch.

According to the Book of Jeremiah, Judah was paying a price for its sins of infidelity and the best course of action would be to submit to Babylon so that Jerusalem could escape destruction. Jeremiah walked through the streets of Jerusalem with a wooden yoke on his shoulders preaching this message. This course of action was not popular among God's People, especially among those who wanted to forcibly resist Nebuchadnezzar.

But Jeremiah hoped to avoid the destruction of the Temple. He also understood the current political subjugation to Babylonian rule to be God's response to the people's sinfulness. As such, they should not resist it, but should submit to it and repent of their idolatry and their abuse of the poor in their midst, in the hope that God would relent and return them to their previous position. It is possible that if Jerusalem had not tried to revolt against Babylon in 587, the first Temple would have remained standing and thousands of people would not have been killed. As it was, however, the Temple was destroyed along with the whole city of Jerusalem in response to Zedekiah's revolt.

In his Temple Sermon (Jer 7), the prophet's full message is clear as he warns that those who oppress refugees, orphans, or widows will not be spared just because they come to the Temple. They must first reform their evil ways. Jeremiah stood in the very Temple area itself, and proclaimed his message. Here are the main points:

- The sacrificial system does not automatically take away the consequences of sin. The sacrifice is invalid if the person intends to sin again.

- Jerusalem is not immune to punishment just because the Temple stands there. God destroyed Shiloh, another famous Temple, and he can destroy Solomon's great Temple as well.

- The sins of pagan worship and oppression of the "alien, orphan, and widow" are severely condemned (verse 6).

Perhaps most famous point is Jeremiah's bitter attack on the Temple itself as a "den of thieves" in Jeremiah 7:11. These are the very words used by Jesus to condemn the corrupt Temple practices of his day (Mt 21:13). Anyone who heard Jesus' warnings would have instantly recognized the reference (other similarities found in the feature "Jeremiah and Jesus" on page 159). Jesus was quoting one of the most radical accusations made by *any* of the prophets, and in Jeremiah, the prophet went on to suggest that the Temple would in fact be destroyed for the sins of the people. Was Jesus implying this too? (The Temple Jesus knew was destroyed in AD 70, not long after his Ascension to Heaven around 33–34.)

Jeremiah had to struggle with the personal trauma of being a prophet with an unpopular message. A series of "confessions" in the Book of Jeremiah describe much of his personal agony: See Jeremiah 8:18–23; 15:10–21; 17:14–18; 18:18–23; 20:7–18.

In the final confession, Jeremiah reveals an intimate connection with God and his commitment to preaching his word in spite of derision he receives from those who oppose him:

Yes, I hear the whisperings of many:
 "Terror on every side!

Denounce! let us denounce him."
All those who were my friends
    are on the watch for any misstep of mine.
"Perhaps he will be trapped; then we can prevail
    and take our vengeance on him."
But the LORD is with me, like a mighty champion:
    my persecutors will stumble, they will not
       triumph." (Jer 20:10–11)

Eventually, Jeremiah's enemies did manage to silence him. Even though there was a substantial number of Judeans who agreed with Jeremiah, not all of them did. He was smuggled to Egypt by some Jews who supported Egyptian hopes to bring Judah into an alliance of nations opposed to Babylon. After Jeremiah was taken to Egypt, no further mention of him occurs in the Bible. Presumably he died there, a lonely and unpopular prisoner of those Judeans who did not agree with his theology or politics.

JEREMIAH AND JESUS

There are many similarities between the life of the prophet Jeremiah and the life of Jesus. God was active in the lives of each in similar ways at key times. Jeremiah prefigures Jesus in several ways, including:

- They are rejected by their family members and neighbors (Jer 12:6; Lk 4:24-29).
- Jeremiah and Jesus each weep over the city of Jerusalem (Jer 8:23; Lk 19:41).
- The authorities harass both Jeremiah and Jesus over the truth of their message.
- Jesus denounces the corruption of the Temple by quoting the famous phrase of Jeremiah that the Temple had become a "den of thieves" (e.g., Mk 11:17).
- Jeremiah, like Jesus, condemned a love of violence.

Lamentations

The canon of the Bible places this book of five poetic laments after the Book of Jeremiah. It is doubtful, however, that Jeremiah wrote them, since both the content and style differ from Jeremiah.

These poems mournfully lament the destruction of Jerusalem and the Temple, a symbol that God had abandoned his people. Today, Jews still read Lamentations aloud in the synagogues in mid-July to recall the destruction of the Temple in 587 BC and later destruction in AD 70. Also, a comparison of the poems in Lamentations with writings of the prophet Ezekiel (see "Ezekiel" and "What Do Ezekiel's Actions Mean?" on pages 160–164) reveal the deep pain the destruction of Jerusalem caused God's People.

Baruch

The opening verses of the Book of Baruch are attributed to Jeremiah's well-known secretary, though in actuality the book was composed nearly two centuries after the exile in order to encourage Jews to remain faithful in the midst of an increasingly oppressive Greek culture. The book itself contains five very different styles of writing—the first and last in prose and the others in poetic form.

The final chapter of Baruch is positioned as a separate work and patterned after an earlier letter of Jeremiah (Jer 29). It likewise reminds Jews living in far-off lands not to be tricked by the predominance of idols. It reminds them that "the better for the just man who has no idols: he shall be far from disgrace!" (Bar 6:72).

Ezekiel

Of the sparse information known about the prophet Ezekiel, his writings reveal that he was a priest. Although some of the other prophets (e.g., Jeremiah) may have been from priestly families, Ezekiel seems to have been the only prophet who served actively as a priest. Priests were in charge of maintaining the purity of individuals and all of Israel. Part of this task

was accomplished by conducting Temple sacrifices. He likely met with Jewish elders in others places outside the Temple, perhaps the first synagogues. Another part of the priest's ministry was to advise the people on issues of conduct and day-to-day living, especially maintaining ritual purity and eating properly.

Unlike Jeremiah who remained in Jerusalem, Ezekiel was deported with the first group of exiles in 597 and began his role as a prophet five years later in Babylon; he was the first prophet called to prophesy outside the Promised Land. Ezekiel's "call narrative" describes a vision of cherubim who gave him a scroll containing the word of God which he was to proclaim to the people. The words "Lamentation and wailing and woe!" were written on the scroll that he was instructed to eat. This event was the first in a series of bizarre visions and actions Ezekiel experienced through the course of his prophesying (Ez 3:1–4). For example, he shaved, burned, and divided his hair as a sign of the fate of the people of Jerusalem when they were defeated by Nebuchadnezzar for the second time (Ez 6:1–4), and he pantomimed the actions of the exiles (Ez 12:1–20).

The Book of Ezekiel is laid out with a clear division of parts:

- *Ezekiel 1–24.* This section—known as "Oracles of Judgment"—warns of Jerusalem's impending doom, sometimes reaching a rather severe level of rhetoric and anger.

- *Ezekiel 33–48.* These "Oracles of Hope" speak of the restoration of Jerusalem after the exile and culminate in a grand vision (Ez 40–48) in which Ezekiel "sees" a hopeful reestablishment of the Israelite state under equitable and just circumstances.

This division leaves a somewhat enigmatic section in Ezekiel 25–32. These chapters may have been added by an editor at a later time, because the subjects of chapters 24 and 33 are precisely the same: the fall of Jerusalem. It seems that these originally connected

chapters were split by the insertion of the passages that now make up chapters 25–32.

Ezekiel 25–32 is sometimes called the "Oracles against the Nations," because it contains speeches of judgment directed against foreign nations. Why were these chapters inserted in this part of the Book of Ezekiel? It is easy to figure out at least part of the answer. Look at the timing and placement of these speeches: they were placed in the text at the very moment of Jerusalem's destruction by a foreign nation (Babylon). Perhaps they were meant to assure the reader that the evil done to Jerusalem would have its consequences for the perpetrators.

The unique character of the Book of Ezekiel is best understood by the series of visions and actions of the prophet.

The Visions of Ezekiel

1. The Call (Ezekiel 1-3)

The first vision is really the "call narrative" of Ezekiel; he receives his "commission" as a prophet in the first two chapters. In this vision, Ezekiel sees the throne of God in Heaven, accompanied by a series of strange creatures and equipped with wheels and wings. The theme appears to be movement: the creatures are moving and the setting for the throne of God

is moving. Before his vision is complete, however, Ezekiel is called to be a prophet, even though he is told that the people may well reject his message:

> But speak my words to them, whether they heed or resist, for they are rebellious. (Ez 2:7)

It was at this point of his commissioning that Ezekiel was handed a scroll covered with writing on front and back. The Lord then makes an unusual request:

> Son of man, eat what is before you; eat this scroll, then go, speak to the house of Israel. (Ez 3:1)

Ezekiel ate the scroll "and it was as sweet as honey" (Ez 3:3). Then, God said:

> Son of man, go now to the house of Israel, and speak my words to them. (Ez 3:4)

Ezekiel was so overcome with this experience that he sat stunned for seven days.

2. The Transport to Jerusalem (Ezekiel 8-11)

In his second great vision, Ezekiel is transported to Jerusalem with other exiles from Babylon. They are stopped on four occasions, each time moving closer and closer to the Temple. At each stop, Ezekiel is appalled by what he sees—pagan worship and rituals being performed—right up to the steps of the Temple itself.

Keeping in mind that Ezekiel was a priest, this vision of the severity of pagan mixing with the religion of YHWH must have been particularly distasteful. At the end of his "tour of sin" around the Temple complex, Ezekiel is placed on a hillside overlooking Jerusalem, and he sees something that he wouldn't imagine in his worst nightmare. The Spirit of God actually leaves Jerusalem:

> And the glory of the LORD rose from the city and took a stand on the mountain which is to the east of the city. (Ez 11:23)

Ezekiel was shown two important things in this vision: (1) the extent of the pagan corruption in Jerusalem, and (2) the fact that God was not permanently "locked" to the Temple; his spirit could be found anywhere and everywhere. This second point was very important to exiles who might have believed that when they left Jerusalem, they also literally left God behind at the Temple.

3. The Valley of the Dry Bones (Ezekiel 37)

In the most well-known vision from the Book of Ezekiel, the prophet is set among a valley of bones, a horrific sight. One theory is that this valley was in the midst of a battlefield, and the dry bones represented the fallen of Israel who had died in the battles and destruction of the exilic events themselves. Before his eyes, Ezekiel sees the bones drawn together, filled out with flesh and skin, and restored to life.

Remember, this vision is recorded in the "Oracles of Hope" section. Ezekiel is seeing a vision of the restored Israel. The message from this vision is that restoration is possible. Even the devastation of the destruction brought down on Israel as a result of the conquests of Assyria and Babylon can be overcome in the plan of God.

4. The Restored Israel (Ezekiel 40-48)

The entire final section of the book contains a dramatic vision about the restoration of Israel. There are many details about the reconstructed Temple and some elements of the city. But what is particularly interesting is the fact that Ezekiel envisions a redistribution of land in this vision. Each of the tribes is to get equal shares of land in the restored Israel. The royal leader will only be given a set amount of land and will no longer oppress the people. This vision describes Ezekiel in the tradition of the earlier prophets, speaking for the rights of the people against the greed of the royal and aristocratic leaders:

. . . the princes of Israel will no longer oppress my people, but will leave the land to the house of Israel according to their tribes. Thus says the Lord GOD: Enough, you princes of Israel! Put away violence and oppression, and do what is right and just! Stop evicting my people says the Lord GOD. (Ez 45:8–9)

This vision let the people know that the restored Israel would not go back to its old ways. A new and just Israel was on the horizon.

 Reflect

If you were calling people to a new and restored order of living, what would your message entail?

WHAT DO EZEKIEL'S ACTIONS MEAN?

Some of the actions of Ezekiel give the impression that he was mentally unstable, because of the extreme variations of his personality. For example, examine these seven acts of Ezekiel:

- After his call from the Lord, Ezekiel sits in his own house; unlike many of the prophets who seek out the people to whom God wishes to speak, Ezekiel waits until people come to him. Even then, he speaks only when the Lord opens his mouth (Ez 3:24-27).

- Ezekiel builds a model of Jerusalem, complete with battering rams, siege walls, and other weapons of war. He then lies—first on his left side and then on his right side—facing the model. He eats impure food cooked in an impure manner—probably representing the sickness, death, and starvation of the people living under siege conditions (Ez 4).

- Ezekiel cuts off his hair, and then divides it into thirds, cutting one part, burning one part, and throwing one part to the wind. This likely represents the fate of the people of Jerusalem in the coming destruction—a third will die by the sword of the invaders, a third will burn in the fire of siege and conquest, and a third will flee as refugees or be taken as prisoners of war to the "far corners of the earth" (Ez 5).

- Ezekiel packs an exile's bag and is seen leaving the city again and again, re-enacting the events of being conquered and exiled by Babylon (Ez 12).

- Ezekiel returns to his model of the city of Jerusalem, adding a road approaching it from Babylon. This is likely meant to show that Nebuchadnezzar would return to Jerusalem to destroy it (Ez 21).

- When Ezekiel's wife dies suddenly, he does not mourn for her in the customary ways; instead, he puts on his sandals and turban and goes about as usual. When the people question him about it, he tells them that this will be their response, too; when Jerusalem falls—there will be no time for mourning (Ez 24:15-26).

- After the vision of dry bones, Ezekiel joins together two sticks marked "Israel" and "Judah" to represent the reunification of the old rival states of the Hebrews (Ez 37:15-22).

What do the symbolic actions of the prophet Ezekiel mean? Were these just theatrics meant to impress the importance of his message on the people? Was he, in fact, mentally unstable? A comparison with the poems of the Book of Lamentations suggests another idea:

Compare Ezekiel 3:22-27 and Lamentations 3:7-9.
Ezekiel sits confined in his home with hands tied by cords. Lamentations speaks of a prophet hemmed in and bound by chains.

Compare Ezekiel 4:1-3 and Lamentations 1:11; 2:12; 4:4; 9-10.
The siege of Jerusalem forces some people to eat impure foods, or foods prepared in an impure manner. Lamentations echoes the concern with the ability to feed one-self and family properly. (Also see Jer 52:6 and 2 Kgs 25:3.)

Compare Ezekiel 5:1-17 and Lamentations 1:1; 2:21.
Ezekiel acts out the tri-fold punishment of Jerusalem—a third of the people burnt in the city, a third dying by the sword, and a third exiled ("strewn to the wind"). Lamentations bemoans the lonely, once crowded city.

Compare Ezekiel 12 and Lamentations 1:3, 18.
Ezekiel prepares "an exile's baggage" and is led through a hole in a wall to exemplify being taken as a prisoner of war. He is reliving the events of the exile—first, his own exile to Babylon, and second, his image of events to come when Jerusalem will fall and be utterly destroyed. Lamentations mourns the fate of Judah, finding no place to rest as her people are led into exile.

Compare Ezekiel 21 and Lamentations 2:21; 5:9.
In Ezekiel, the image of the sword is used to refer to Babylonian forces. In Lamentations the image of the sword is a symbol for foreign rule.

The Book of Lamentations expresses in powerful, emotional terms the devastation of the city of Jerusalem, and the profound grief of the people of Judah and Israel. When the Book of Ezekiel is read with Lamentations, we realize how deeply Ezekiel suffered from the devastation of the siege he went through in 597 BC, and the destruction that he and others heard about while in Babylon in 587. His actions, therefore, must be understood, not as the ravings of one afflicted with mental illness, but as the outpouring of an almost overwhelming sense of grief, loss, and pain.

Today we know much more about the psychological impact of warfare and disaster. Ezekiel is as much a prophet for modern times as he was for the exiles in Babylon. He suffered the same fate as the millions of homeless and refugees fleeing warfare and hunger today who also must deal with the psychological and spiritual impact of a horrific situation. God chose a broken refugee to be a prophet of hope to all who find themselves in a similar situation.

Daniel

In the canon of the Hebrew scriptures, the Book of Daniel is classified with the Writings. These books include Wisdom literature and the Psalms. The Catholic Old Testament canon includes Daniel with the prophetic books though Daniel did not receive the traditional call by God to preach. In reality, the Book of Daniel has three main divisions and includes prophecy, history (see "Daniel 1–6" on pages 113–114), and **apocalyptic literature**:

- *Daniel 1–6.* This part includes six stories about a young Jewish boy, Daniel. Along with his friends, Daniel remains faithful to YHWH under the reigns of King Nebuchadnezzar II and the Persian kings. These stories probably originated in the Persian era, but were retold during the persecution of the Jews by Antiochus IV (Chapter 10).

- *Daniel 7–12.* This section contains four symbolic visions that center on the heavenly destruction of Israel's enemies, especially Antiochus IV (below).

- *Daniel 13–14.* Three other stories found only in the Septuagint (not considered inspired by Jews and Protestants) end the book. In one of the stories, Daniel saves a young maiden named Susanna, and in the other two reveals pagan idols to be false gods.

The middle section of Daniel was written in approximately 164 BC by an anonymous author. The story is told as if it had occurred four centuries earlier. This was done for one reason: doing so allowed the author to take on the role of the prophet and discuss the difficulties facing the people during the time of Antiochus IV without fear of persecution. By using symbols and giving the story a supposedly historical context, the author could speak more freely than the oppressive government would normally allow.

The visions of Daniel 7–12 repeat the dream of Nebuchadnezzar in Daniel 2. In Daniel 7:1–28, the prophet sees four beasts coming from the sea. The beasts signify the Babylonian empire, the kingdom of the Medes, the Persian empire, and the empire of Alexander. The message of these visions is that pagan kingdoms grow progressively worse, reaching their climax in the "little horn" that represents Antiochus (Dn 7:8). The people are destined to suffer under him for a period of apparently three and a half years. Relief will come only when God himself intervenes.

Why did apocalyptic writing appeal so much to Jews in the centuries prior to, during, and immediately after Jesus' life on earth? Most likely, the apocalyptic books arose in circumstances of oppression—when the social and political policies of the Persian, Greek, or even later Roman rulers became especially brutal. In such circumstances, the Jews literally cried out to God and had visions from God of hopeful reassurance that he was with them. The highly symbolic nature of the writing protected the authors—as well as the readers—from persecution since the language would

apocalyptic literature
A highly symbolic style of writing in which hidden truths are revealed within a narrative framework. The revelation is often delivered by an angelic or visionary being.

be difficult to decipher by those outside the cultural context of the author and his intended audience. The Book of Revelation in the New Testament employed the same symbolic and allegorical language found not only in the Book of Daniel, but also in the apocalyptic sections of Ezekiel and Zechariah.

Consider the mood and thinking surrounding apocalyptic literature. The times were bad and the Jews held on to the belief that God was going to bring about immediate change. This is one of the central messages of apocalyptic visions: God is in control. What seems awful and unpredictable is *not* outside of God's control.

🜂 Review

1. How is the Book of Isaiah typically divided?

2. What is the main subject of the first thirty-nine chapters of the Book of Isaiah?

3. Who might the prophet have been referring to when he wrote of the "Suffering Servant."

4. How does Jesus fulfill Isaiah's prophecy of the Suffering Servant?

5. When were the final eleven chapters of the Book of Isaiah composed?

6. Why did Jeremiah think the people of Judah should submit to Babylonian rule?

7. What were three main parts of Jeremiah's Temple Sermon?

8. What is the subject of the Book of Lamentations?

9. Who is the attributed author of the Book of Baruch?

10. What are two things about Ezekiel's personal history that are unique among Old Testament prophets?

11. How was the Book of Ezekiel divided?

12. What is the message of Ezekiel's vision in the valley of dry bones?

13. How does the Book of Lamentations help to shed light on the meaning of the actions of Ezekiel?

14. How does the classification of the Book of Daniel differ between the Old Testament and Hebrew scriptures?

15. Why was apocalyptic writing popular in the centuries surrounding the time of Jesus?

Minor Prophets

The section of prophets in the Old Testament canon beginning with Hosea, a prophet of the northern kingdom who lived in the eighth century BC and ending with the Book of Malachi, composed before Nehemiah's arrival in Jerusalem in the fifth century BC, is known as the "minor prophets." Again, this definition does not diminish the message of these prophets in any way; they are simply shorter writings. As with the other prophets of the Old Testament, they were men called by God who stress the interpretation of current events in light of God's plan of Salvation. Rather, this distinction is based on the length of their writings. While each of the major prophets took up one scroll in composition, the minor prophets together were written on the same single scroll. A brief overview of each prophet and their writings follows.

Hosea

The Book of Hosea offers some brief biographical information on the prophet. Hosea was born and prophesied in the northern kingdom. His ministry overlapped that of Amos (see "Amos," on pages 169–171) and probably began in the last years of Jeroboam II. Both prophets seemed to anticipate the fall of Israel to the Assyrian Empire in 722 BC.

Hosea lived a very interesting life! In the opening verses, it is explained that God called Hosea to marry a known prostitute, Gomer. The Lord said to Hosea:

> Go, take a harlot wife and harlot's children,
> for the land gives itself to **harlotry**,
> turning away from the LORD. (Hos 1:2)

This action was no doubt shocking to the people who knew and listened to Hosea. Yet it makes very clear the fact that Hosea was a prophet who must be both *watched* and *listened to*. In other words, Hosea acted out part of his message in his own life. His first audience—and readers of the Book of Hosea—must pay attention to what his strange actions may mean.

Hosea did marry Gomer, and then proceeded to have three children with her—each child named for one of Hosea's controversial ideas. The name of the first child, Jezreel, implied a criticism of the house of King Jehu for the murder of the entire house of Ahab in the valley of Jezreel. Even though Jehu thought he was doing God's will when he murdered all the members of the family of Ahab, Hosea hinted strongly that he went too far, and his bloodshed was an unnecessary brutality. The name would have been understood as a criticism of the royal house of Jehu. (Hosea was obviously unafraid of political comment.)

harlotry
In the Old Testament, this term refers not only to a woman's illicit sexual behavior, but perhaps even more commonly to the practice of worshipping Canaanite gods along with YHWH. Jezebel is referred to as a "harlot" in this sense, not because she was ever unfaithful to Ahab.

Hosea then named his second child Lo-ruhamah. This translates literally as "she is not pitied." Hosea's message connected with Lo-ruhamah was a dire warning:

The LORD said to him:
Give her the name Lo-ruhama;
I no longer feel pity for the house of Israel:
  rather, I abhor them utterly. (Hos 1:6)

Finally, Hosea's third child has the most ominous name of the three: Lo-ammi, which means "not my people." The warning attached to this name was most deeply threatening:

Then the LORD said:
Give him the name Lo-ammi,
  for you are not my people,
  and I will not be your God. (Hos 1:9)

This was the ultimate threat because it was a reversal of God's promise to Israel in the covenant promise made to Moses:

I will take you as my own people, and you shall have me as your God. You will know that I, the LORD, am your God when I free you from the labor of the Egyptians and bring you into the land which I swore to give to Abraham, Isaac and Jacob. (Ex 6:7–8)

In the following sections of the Book of Hosea (Hos 2–3), it is clear that the prophet is "acting out" the role of God, and that his controversial marriage symbolizes God's relationship with Israel. Gomer's unfaithfulness mirrors Israel's desertion of YHWH in favor of worshipping Baal.

In Hosea 2, it appears as if the prophet is angry with his own wife Gomer and makes many kinds of threats against her (presumably for adultery on her part). But as the chapter proceeds, the reader learns that it is *really* God's relationship with Israel that is threatened:

I will punish her for the days of the Baals,
  for whom she burnt incense
While she decked herself out with her rings and her
    jewels,
  and, in going after her lovers,
  forgot me, says the LORD. (Hos 2:15)

After these words one would expect the prophet to bring final condemnation and judgment. But here the Book of Hosea takes a fascinating turn. Just at the moment when one would most expect to hear a word of condemnation and judgment from the prophet, suddenly he assures the reader of God's forgiving compassion:

So I will allure her;
  I will lead her into the desert
  and speak to her heart. (Hos 2:16)

Not only does God speak words of forgiving compassion, but also the rest of the section reads like a wedding vow as God proposes marriage to his adulterous partner, Israel, as a way to reestablish their relationship:

I will make a covenant for them on that day,
  with the beasts of the field,
With the birds of the air,
  and with the things that crawl on the ground. . . .
I will espouse you to me forever:
  I will espouse you in right and in justice,
  in love and in mercy;
I will espouse you in fidelity
  and you shall know the LORD. (Hos 2:20a; 21–22)

In Hosea 3, God tells the prophet to take Gomer back as his wife. This is symbolic of God's everlasting love for his people: after a period of trial (the dissolution of the kingdom), the people will fully return to their relationship with the Lord. Human passion is compared favorably to God's love for humanity, and this is an important message. The prophet compared the love of God with the two most powerful passions in human existence: the love between a husband and a wife and the love between a parent and a child (Hos 11:1–4). This faithfulness and love of YHWH for his people is the lasting message of the Book of Hosea.

Joel

The Book of Joel is filled with apocalyptic images and addresses the last days. Likely finished in about 400 BC, its primary theme is the "day of the Lord." Joel was a Temple prophet who believed that a locust plague that ravished the country was a sign of God's judgment on his people. Joel's message was a call to repentance and fasting, after which he promised that God would bless the nation:

> Yet even now, says the LORD,
>> return to me with your whole heart,
>> with fasting, and weeping, and mourning.
> Rend your hearts, not your garments,
>> and return to the LORD, your God.
> For gracious and merciful is he,
>> slow to anger, rich in kindness,
>> and relenting in punishment. (Jl 2:12–13)

The prophet told of the "day of the Lord" when God would battle all evil forces (the pagan nations) at the Valley of Jehoshaphat near Jerusalem. This day would mark an entirely new beginning, a fresh creation of the world when God will pour out his spirit on all humanity.

Because Joel quotes or alludes to many other Old Testament prophets, scholars believe that it was one of the last prophetic books composed. It was an important book for the early Church. St. Peter, for example, quotes Joel 3 on Pentecost (Acts 2:17–21).

Amos

Amos is described as a shepherd and tree farmer from Tekoa, near Bethlehem, in the southern kingdom. His prophetic ministry takes place during the rule of Jeroboam II (786–746 BC). Thus Amos is considered the first prophet for whom there is a separate, recorded collection of sayings. As with the other books of the prophets, the Book of Amos was probably collected and recorded by the prophet's disciples. Like Elisha's relationship to Elijah, it seems clear that prophets almost always had disciples with whom they were close and who participated in their itinerate travels and ministry.

Because of his background as a shepherd, Amos is often depicted as one from working-class origins. However, that assumption depends on the interpretation of Amos 7:14–15, where Amos says to the priest of Bethel:

> I was no prophet, nor have I belonged to a company of prophets; I was a shepherd and dresser of sycamores. The LORD took me from the following flock, and said to me, Go, prophesy to my people Israel. (Am 7:14–15)

From the passage it is not clear whether Amos was a hired shepherd or the owner of the land and flocks. One idea is that the first two chapters of the Book of Amos indicate that Amos knew too much about international events to be a poor farm laborer. However, Amos could have been well informed and still have been a hired shepherd!

The prophet Amos was perhaps strongest on the issues of social justice. He spoke out against many of the sins of those living in the northern kingdom: genocide, cruelty, anger, dishonesty, greed, lawlessness, sexual excess, desecration of the dead, rejection of the prophets, robbery, violence, selfishness, deceit, injustice, and pride. He also condemned the abuses of the wealthy. He was particularly angry with an abusive lifestyle that extorted work from the poor for very low wages. At times this concern of Amos reaches a spectacular literary flourish. Speaking to the people of Samaria who had been living in luxury oblivious to their sins and the threat of the Assyrians, Amos said about them:

> Lying upon beds of ivory,
>> stretched comfortably on their couches,
> They eat lambs taken from the flock
>> and calves from the stall!
> Improvising to the music of the harp,
>> like David, they devise their own accompaniment.
> They drink wine from bowls
>> and anoint themselves with the best oils;
>> yet they are not made ill by the collapse of Joseph!
> Therefore, now they shall be the first to go into exile,
>> and their wanton revelry shall be done away with. (Am 6:4–7)

It is easy to imagine the indulgent parties described in this passage—people wealthy enough to have furniture with inlaid ivory (not native to Palestine, so it must have been imported), to feast on young animals (a luxury that would appall most of the poor), and to drink wine (according to Amos 2:8, this wine was bought with the taxes and fines they imposed on the poor) not from cups, but from *bowls*—abandoning any moderation at all.

Amos was particularly angry at the wealthy for pouring excess money into shows of Temple worship. The rich seemed to justify their oppressive lifestyles by purchasing many animals for Temple sacrifice, and

thus made great public shows of their "piety." Amos spoke strongly against this practice:

> I hate, I spurn your feasts,
>> I take no pleasure in your solemnities;
> Your cereal offerings I will not accept,
>> nor consider your stall-fed peace offerings.
> Away with your noisy songs!
>> I will not listen to the melodies of your harps.
> But if you would offer me holocausts,
>> then let justice surge like water,
>> and goodness like an unfailing stream.
> (Am 5:21–24)

As with other Old Testament prophets, Amos's message was often one of judgment. However, most of the time when prophets preached a warning, the warning itself was intended to keep the dire event from happening. There is some debate about whether or not the prophet Amos had any hope that the people of the northern kingdom would be able to adhere to his words and thus avoid the judgment he predicted. Some scholars are of the opinion that Amos did not believe Israel could possibly comply, hence making him a "prophet of doom":

> Then the LORD said to me:
> The time is ripe to have done with my people Israel;
>> I will forgive them no longer.
> The temple songs shall become wailings on that day,
>> says the Lord GOD.
> Many shall be the corpses,
>> strewn everywhere.—Silence! (Am 8:2b–3)

Amos did know that the destruction of the people by God was intended to be instructive, not destructive. Though people persisted in their sinfulness, Amos believed that such behavior could never completely frustrate the plan of God for the Salvation of humankind. The closing words of the Book of Amos reveal his hope in a future that would bring God's blessings again:

> But I will not destroy the house of
>   Jacob completely . . .
> I will bring about restoration of my
>   people Israel;
>   they shall rebuild and inhabit their
>   ruined cities,
> Plant vineyards and drink the wine,
>   set out gardens and eat the fruits. (Am 9:8b, 14)

 ## Reflect

In your own life, how do you practice moderation as opposed to living to excess?

Obadiah

The Book of Obadiah is the shortest book of the Old Testament at only twenty-one verses long. Written as an oracle, it also contains one of the harshest messages of any of the prophets. Nothing is known about the author of the prophecy. Because it directs its message against Edom, a longtime enemy of Israel, it is dated sometime in the fifth century BC.

The Edomites were descendants of Jacob's brother, Esau. They had moved into southern Judah and participated in the sack of Jerusalem. In addition, they were among those who resisted the resettlement of the returning exiles. Obadiah sharply denounces the actions of this enemy, predicts their destruction, and prophesies the restoration of Judah.

Jonah

The Book of Jonah likely comes from a late historical period, certainly after the destruction of Jerusalem in 587 BC. Thus, the book derives from the long period of occupation of the land of the Hebrews, but also a time when thousands of Hebrews lived as minorities throughout the Diaspora.

The city of Nineveh was, for a time, the capital of the Neo-Assyrian Empire. The Assyrians conquered the northern kingdom of Israel in 722 BC and deported a group of the upper class from that region. In this story, Jonah is called to deliver his prophetic message to the center of one of the most feared and hated regimes the Hebrews ever faced. (Also, Nineveh is a symbol of the non-Jewish population.) Any sane Jew feeling himself "called" to the center of the Assyrian Empire would also probably hop a boat heading in the opposite direction. And that is exactly what Jonah does. But Jonah soon realizes that there is no escape from the God of the Hebrews. Even the "sea monsters" are subservient to God (see Jonah 1:17).

The heart of the Book of Jonah is the Psalm of thanksgiving that appears in Jonah 2:3–10. Biblical scholarship has suggested that the Psalm is much older than the Book of Jonah and that the story of Jonah was modeled to fit around the Psalm, illustrating the

midrash
Commentaries compiled between AD 400 and 1200 by Jewish rabbis on the Hebrew scriptures.

meaning (a teaching method that Jewish rabbis came to call a **midrash**).

The references in the Psalm to missing the Temple (Jon 2:4) and being away from the land, and the allusions to prison (Jon 2:6) all suggest that it dates from the exile when the people in the Diaspora lamented their fate (cf. Psalm 107:10–16; 137; Isaiah 42:7; Lamentations 3:34). So it seems clear that the Book of Jonah derives much of its power and meaning by being read in the Diaspora. This is a major clue to the meaning of the text.

Jonah's news to the king and people of Nineveh has a most interesting result: The king descends from the throne, removes his robe, and all the people fast and mourn. The king also decreed:

> Every man shall turn from his evil way and from the violence he has in hand. (Jon 3:8)

In other words, the Assyrians repent of their ways and change their behavior. God recognizes the Assyrian's repentance, and Jonah is furious at God's compassion. It is, of course, the same compassion that earlier saved his own sea-soaked skin. But now that God is showing compassion to an *enemy*, it is too much.

There is no escaping the power of this story: The Book of Jonah is about God's compassion on *all* people, even those who are not Jews. God cares for the well-being and transformation of all. But there is more.

The Book of Jonah is often described as a parable with a double meaning. Jonah, we must remember:

1. is called by God.
2. rejects the call.
3. is sent into darkness.
4. is released to a mission.

Does this sound familiar? This pattern is the general historical theme of the Bible, preeminently represented in the books of Joshua, Judges, 1 and 2 Samuel, and 1 and 2 Kings. In fact, some believe that the prophet Jeremiah's famous comments may have originally inspired the Book of Jonah:

> He has consumed me, routed me,
>   [Nebuchadnezzar, king of
>   Babylon,]
>   he has left me as an empty
>   vessel;
> He has swallowed me like a dragon:
>   filled his belly with my delights,
>   and cast me out. (Jer 51:34)

In this tale, *Jonah is Israel*. The people of Israel were called by God, but sinfully rejected the call and listened to their own voices. As punishment, they were sent into exile. If Jonah does represent Israel, what have the people learned from the experience of the exile? The author of Jonah teaches that there is now a radical redefinition of what it means to be the People of God. If this is true, then Jonah is a symbol of Israel herself, missionary to the world and agent of God's Salvation. But Jonah is reluctant; sin and rejection of God's laws sent Israel into exile as Jonah was sent into the belly of the big fish.

With Jonah (and Isaiah 49:6), the point is made that *during* the exile some of the Jews finally came to understand the profound nature of their call from YHWH. It was the same call that was repeated and taken up so powerfully in the teaching and example of Jesus. Jesus, too, renewed God's call and initiated his Kingdom. Jesus told the people: "You are the light of the world" (Mt 5:14).

Micah

The prophet Micah was born in the lowly village of Moresheth in the Judean foothills. He preached at the same time as Isaiah of Jerusalem, during the reigns of Jotham, Ahaz, and Hezekiah in the eighth century BC. His images were drawn mostly from the rural life. Micah's warning was traditional: If the people did not return to the Lord and observe the Law of Moses, they would be destroyed, but Micah also had harsh warnings for the leaders and elite who lived privileged lives in Jerusalem.

The Propeht Micah

Micah witnessed the fall of Samaria and the advance of the Assyrians on Jerusalem in 701 BC. He was the first prophet who preached the eventual fall of Jerusalem:

Therefore, because of you,
Zion shall be plowed like a field,
and Jerusalem reduced to rubble,
And the mount of the temple
to a forest ridge. (Mi 3:12)

However, like Isaiah, Micah told of a time when God would bring a universal reign of peace:

They shall beat their swords into
plowshares,
and their spears into pruning hooks. (Mi 4:3)

The same passage appears in Isaiah and thus shows a consistency in the messages of the two prophets.

Micah also wrote of a messiah who would come to lead Israel to peace and justice. This anointed one will be from Bethlehem, a good shepherd who will rule by the strength of the Lord. He will gather God's remnant, a righteous group who would survive God's chastisement of the nation. This remnant will lead the nations to true worship of God. Micah's prophecy concerning the birth of the Messiah in Bethlehem (Mi 5:1) is cited in Matthew 2:6 and John 7:42.

Nahum

The prophet Nahum spoke of the fall of Nineveh (Na 2:2–14) shortly before the fall of the despised capital city of Assyria in 612 BC. Only after the conquest of Nineveh was the scope of the cruelty of the Assyrians realized: inscriptions of Assyria revealed mounds of decapitated heads, enslaved citizens, and scores of looters.

Nahum depicts God at first as an avenger who protects his people from their enemies:

The LORD is slow to anger, yet great in
    Power,
And the LORD never leaves the guilty
    Unpunished. (Na 1:3)

But YHWH is also merciful and orders the world in his moral goodness. The words of the prophet Nahum and the destiny of Nineveh also foreshadowed the fate of Jerusalem, which years later would experience the same type of judgment.

Habakkuk

Shortly after Nahum, the prophet Habakkuk warned that the Babylonian King Nebuchadnezzar II would not stop with Nineveh and Egypt (captured in 605 BC). Babylon would set its sights on Judah, he warned:

Look over the nations and see,
    and be utterly amazed!
For a work is being done in your days
    that you would not have believed, were it told.
For see, I am raising Chaldea,
    that bitter and unruly people,
That marches the breadth of the land
    to take dwellings not his own. (Hb 1:5–6)

The prophet was correct. Nebuchadnezzar's siege of Jerusalem began in 597 BC. From Nebuchadnezzar's own inscriptions, he appointed in Jerusalem "a king of his liking, took heavy booty from it, and brought it into Babylon." The Judean king Jehoiachin, only on the throne for three months, surrendered, was deposed, and was deported to Babylon.

Habakkuk was probably a prophet attached to the Temple who lived during Jehoiachin's reign. The first two chapters of the short book are a dialogue between the prophet and the Lord. The third chapter is a lyrical reminder of Israel's past that borrows from the poetry of ancient Canaan. The book ends with a song of faith in God, the Savior.

Zephaniah

The prophecy of Zephaniah comes immediately before the prophecy of Jeremiah during the early days of King Josiah's reign, perhaps between 640 and 625 BC. The language style and ideas in the Book of Jeremiah are similar to those in the Book of Zephaniah.

Idolatry was prevalent during Zephaniah's time. Zephaniah announced a "day of the Lord" that would bring doom:

Near is the great day of the LORD. . . .
    a day of anguish and distress,
A day of destruction and desolation
    a day of darkness and gloom,
A day of thick black clouds,
    a day of trumpet blasts and battle alarm
Against fortified cities,
    against battlements on high. (Zep 1:14–16)

Yet, in spite of the infidelities of God's People, the consistent message is that God in his mercy will spare a holy remnant. The Book of Zephaniah closes with a joyful hymn sung by the restored remnant (Zep 3:1–20).

Haggai

When the Babylonian exile ended and life under Persian rule was just beginning, the Jews had a chance to reflect on what directions their life would take as the People of God. Several questions persisted: Were they meant to return to Palestine and rebuild the Temple in Jerusalem? Or, given that there were still Jews living outside of Palestine even after the end of the exile, was there any reason the Jews should focus on reclaiming political rule? Should they be more concerned with re-dedicating themselves to interior spiritual life?

The prophet Haggai sought to encourage the Jews to complete the rebuilding of the Temple. The returning exiles laid the foundation for the Temple in 538 BC but enthusiasm quickly waned. In the next years, the people worked on rebuilding their own homes and businesses, and the Temple project remained incomplete. Haggai began a campaign in 520 BC to encourage the people to re-start the work. Within months, the project began.

The Book of Haggai is organized around five oracles:

- The call to rebuild the Temple
- The future glory of the new Temple
- The unworthiness of Samaritans to offer sacrifice at the restored altar
- A promise of immediate blessings which follows the promise to rebuild the Temple
- A pledge to Zerubbabel, a descendent of King David, that reemphasizes the promise and hope of a Messiah

Haggai exhorts the people to rebuild the Temple by linking the connection between the ills of the Jews (poverty, drought, and crop failure) to their thoughtless concern about rebuilding their own houses while neglecting God's house.

 **Reflect**

How have you experienced the human nature of putting your own needs ahead of the needs of others?

Zechariah

The prophet Zechariah's ministry began two months after Haggai's. The first eight chapters of the Book of Zechariah belonged to the prophet who preached from 520 to 518 BC, about two decades after the return of the exiles. In these chapters, he, too, encouraged the completion of the Temple. The Temple was, in fact, rebuilt about 520–515 BC. Zechariah also predicts a messianic age to come. As the son of a high priest, Zechariah emphasizes the role of the high priest, Joshua, more than in the Book of Haggai.

The last six chapters of Zechariah represent the work of one or more other authors and are sometimes called "Deutero-Zechariah." These chapters are divided into two sections—chapters 9–11 and chapter 12, each with its own introductory title. Zechariah 9:9 begins a vision of a Messiah who comes not as a conquering warrior, but in lowliness and peace:

> See, your king shall come to you; a just savior is he, meek, and riding on an ass, on a colt, the foal of an ass. (Zec 9:9)

This verse is taken up later in the four Gospels to describe the entrance of Jesus into Jerusalem on Palm Sunday.

Malachi

The prophet Malachi's name means "my messenger." Though the identify of the prophet is not known, he provides an accurate glimpse into life in the Jewish community between the period of Haggai and Nehemiah and Ezra's reforms. As a prophet attached to the Temple, Malachi's predominant theme is fidelity to God's covenant.

Malachi challenged the Jewish priests who were making a mockery of their worship of the Lord. They offered lame, blemished, blind animals for sacrifice instead of the clean ones required by the Law:

When you offer a blind animal for
    sacrifice,
is this not evil?
When you offer the lame or the sick
is it not evil? (Mal 1:8)

Malachi also denounced the Jewish men who divorced their wives to marry wealthy Gentile women. They rationalized their twisted logic, claiming that God is pleased with sinners:

You must then safeguard life that is your
    own,
And not break faith with the wife of your
    youth. (Mal 2:15)

The prophet also prophesies a coming messenger who will announce the day of the Lord. On this day of judgment God will purify the priests and the Temple, save the faithful, and usher in the reign of God. The Book of Malachi is fittingly the last book in the Old Testament canon. Its concluding verses serve as a bridge between the testaments. First, they remind the Jews to be faithful to Mosaic Law. Second, they look forward to the day of the Lord:

Lo, I will send you
    Elijah, the prophet,
Before the day of the LORD comes,
    the great and terrible day,
To turn the hearts of the fathers to their children,
    and the hearts of the children to their fathers,
Lest I come and strike

the land with doom.
Lo, I will send you
    Elijah, the prophet,
Before the day of the LORD comes,
    the great and terrible day. (Mal 3:23–24)

Review

1. What was significant about the names of Hosea's children?

2. What was symbolic about God's request of Hosea to take Gomer back as his wife?

3. What is the primary theme of the Book of Joel?

4. What was the prophet Amos's background?

5. Whom did Amos direct his anger against?

6. How was the Book of Obadiah dated?

7. How is Jonah representative of Israel?

8. How is the message of Micah similar to the one that appeared in the Book of Isaiah?

9. How did Nahum describe God?

10. What did the prophet Habakkuk warn of?

11. What positive message does the Book of Zephaniah end with?

12. What was Haggai concerned about when the returning exiles worked at rebuilding their own homes and businesses?

13. How is the Book of Zechariah divided?

14. Why is it fitting that the Book of Malachi is the last book of the Old Testament canon?

● Final Reflections

The Old Testament remains essential for seeing how the Old Covenant prefigured the work of Salvation that was accomplished in the fullness of time through Jesus Christ.

● Why Should Catholics Know the Old Testament?

Knowing and understanding Christ and the mysteries of our faith is more fully accomplished by a thorough reflection on the Old Testament.

Final Reflections

Needless to say, the development of the Old Testament canon took many years. None of the authors of the sacred books could have imagined that what they were writing at the time would be used by generation after generation for thousands of years to come. Recall, too, that though the prophets knew they were being used as "mouthpieces" for God, their written prophecies were not recorded until years later.

Around the time of King Josiah's reform following the Babylonian exile, books of the Law were found and used as the basis for reform. This was the first time the Jews considered their writings to be sacred and God's inspired Word. From 621 BC to about 400 BC, the writings surrounding the Law of Moses grew and eventually became the Torah. Some of the prophetic books also came on the scene. By 200 BC, these books of the prophets were considered part of Sacred Scripture. In the last stages of history prior to the birth of Christ, the Wisdom literature and other post-exilic books developed. The disputes over the canonicity of some of these books have been covered, but in any case the number of books in the Old Testament had filled out, as determined by the Church.

The early Church made constant use of the Old Testament, looking in its pages for how the Old Covenant prefigured the work of Salvation only accomplished in the fullness of time in the person of Jesus Christ, God's Incarnate Son.

The opening of the Letter to the Hebrews describes the climax of God's Revelation, which comes with the presence of Jesus Christ, who in the unity of his Divine Person is the one and only mediator between God and humanity:

> In times past, God spoke in partial and various ways to our ancestors through the prophets; in these last days, he spoke to us through a son, whom he made heir of all things and through whom he created the universe,
>
> who is the refulgence of his glory,
>   the very imprint of his being,
> and who sustains all things by his mighty word.
> When he had accomplished purification from sins,
> he took his seat at the right hand of the Majesty
>   on high
> as far superior to the angels
> as the name he has inherited is more
>   excellent than theirs. (Heb 1:1–4)

Review

How did the early Church make use of the Old Testament?

Why Should Catholics Know the Old Testament?

This question is important for reflection, although many Catholics today might answer: "We really *don't* need to know the Old Testament very well. After all, Jesus is the most important person in the Bible, and we learn about him in the *New* Testament, not the Old Testament."

The *Catechism of the Catholic Church* teaches that this answer is hardly accurate:

> Christians . . . read the Old Testament in the light of Christ crucified and risen. Such typological reading discloses the inexhaustible content of the Old Testament; but it must not make us forget that *the Old Testament retains its own intrinsic value as Revelation* reaffirmed by the Lord himself. Besides, the New Testament has to be read in the light of the

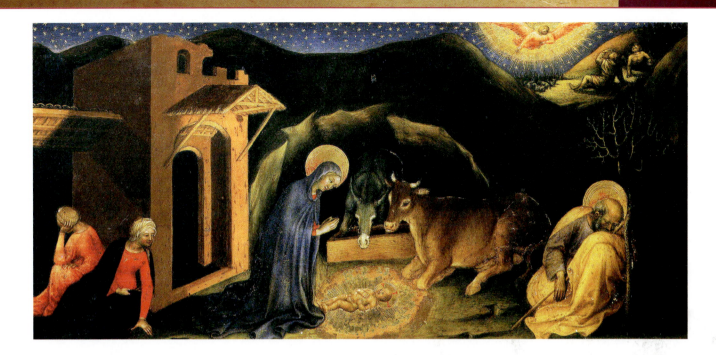

Old. Early Christian catechesis made constant use of the Old Testament. As an old saying put it, the New Testament lies hidden in the Old and the Old Testament is unveiled in the New. (*CCC*, 129; emphasis added)

In other words, fully understanding Christ and the mysteries of our faith can be more fully accomplished by understanding the text and nuances of the Old Testament's sacred pages.

Review

What does the Church teach about the importance of Catholics reading and knowing the Old Testament?

PART 2

THE NEW TESTAMENT

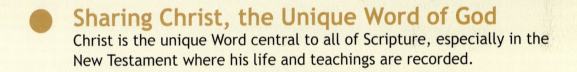

Sharing Christ, the Unique Word of God

Christ is the unique Word central to all of Scripture, especially in the New Testament where his life and teachings are recorded.

Classifying and Arranging the New Testament Books

The New Testament appears in five categories: Gospels, Acts of the Apostles, Letters, the Catholic Epistles, and the Book of Revelation.

How to Study the New Testament

It makes the most sense to begin a study of the New Testament with the four Gospels.

Sharing Christ, the Unique Word of God

The New Testament is a collection of twenty-seven books, all written within one hundred years of Jesus' Death. Most of the books were written before the beginning of the second century. In the entire Bible, Christ is the unique Word. The books of the New Testament all share a commitment to Jesus Christ, who is mentioned by name in twenty-six of them. Even the very short Third Letter of John, the only one not to explicitly *say* the name of Jesus, still refers to him (3 Jn 7). St. Augustine expounded on the centrality of Christ in Scripture:

> You recall that one and the same Word of God extends throughout Scripture, that is one and the same Utterance that resounds in the mouths of all the sacred writers, since he who was in the beginning God with God has no need of separate syllables; for he is not subject to time. (quoted in *CCC*, 102)

The books of the New Testament are very short by our standards. Take a quick look at the Third Letter of John, the Letter of Jude, or the Letter addressed to Philemon as examples of just how short these books can be. Their original form, when first written, would not have looked like books at all. Rather, the various pages of each text would have been joined, end to end, into a very long, single page. Small rods would have been attached at either end and the entire item would have been rolled up into a scroll. It wasn't until the fourth century that the New Testament books were bound together with writing appearing on only one side of a page.

Of course, infinitely more important than how the writings were reproduced, the singular distinction of all these books is that they were inspired by the Holy Spirit and recognized for that by the Church. The New Testament books reflect the true life and teaching of Jesus Christ that had been received and handed on by the Apostles.

 **Review**

Which is the only book of the New Testament to not explicitly mention Jesus?

Classifying and Arranging the New Testament Books

The New Testament books can be divided into five categories or kinds of literature that appear in this order (with the exception of the letters and epistles, which are mixed together):

- **The Gospels.** There are four narrative proclamations of the key events and teachings from the life of Jesus. Please note that even though historical and biographical information is contained in the Gospels, they are neither historical accounts nor biographies.

- **The Acts of the Apostles.** This is an account of the very early Church and of the missionary work of St. Paul. The same author of the Gospel of Luke wrote the Acts of the Apostles. A comparison of Luke 1:1–4 with Acts 1:1–2 is evidence of that point. It is correct to think of Acts as the second volume of Luke's Gospel.

- **Letters.** You can construe letters to be just as they are named. These messages were written to specific local churches, such as those at Corinth or Galatia, or to individuals, such as Philemon, Timothy, or Titus. Most of the letters were written or attributed to St. Paul.

- **The Catholic Epistles.** The word *epistle* originates from a Greek word meaning "to send a message." Epistles are extended homily-like writings addressed to the universal Church rather than to a local community. Two examples are the Epistles of James and Hebrews, which are not addressed to any particular locale or person. Epistles are also called "catholic letters" as a way to describe their universal audience. However, the terms "letter" and "epistle" are not always used carefully, and are often interchanged. Some books are disputed as to whether they are letters or epistles. Most, though, are clearly one or the other.

- **The Book of Revelation.** The final book of the Bible is a visionary teaching warning the Church not to be complacent. This book uses many symbols and metaphors that may have been well understood by the people of the time, but require proper study for later generations and people from other cultures. If you skim through this book briefly, reading almost anywhere at random, you will quickly recognize the text as highly symbolic and telling of visions of God, the risen Lord, and the future.

Review

1. How are the New Testament books divided into five categories or kinds of literature?

2. In the New Testament, what is the difference between a letter and an epistle?

Similarities in the Synoptic Gospels

Scholars early on noted that the Gospels of Matthew, Mark, and Luke contained a great deal of common material. For example, about 85 percent of the content in Mark, the shortest Gospel, very closely resembles about 50 percent of the Gospel of Matthew, which is considerably longer. In fact, of Mark's 660 verses, six hundred of them contain material also found in Matthew. A slightly smaller percentage of this material makes up Luke's Gospel. Besides the common subject matter, Matthew, Mark, and Luke also follow a very similar order. They also contain a common vocabulary.

When these three Gospels are laid out side by side, observant readers are actually able to "see with their eyes" the similarities between them. As a result, Matthew, Mark, and Luke have been called the **Synoptic Gospels**. In other words, they can be "looked at together"—another meaning of the term *synoptic*. For example, note the following comparison:

Synoptic Gospels
The Gospels of Matthew, Mark, and Luke, which because of their similarities, can be "seen together" in parallel columns and mutually compared.

Matthew 5:13	Mark 9:49-50	Luke 14:34-35
"You are the salt of the earth. But if salt loses its taste, with what can it be seasoned? It is no longer good for anything but to be thrown out and trampled underfoot."	"Everyone will be salted with fire. Salt is good, but if salt becomes insipid, with what will you restore its flavor? Keep salt in yourselves and you will have peace with one another."	"Salt is good, but if salt loses its taste, with what can its flavor be restored? It is fit neither for the soil nor for the manure pile; it is thrown out. Whoever has ears to hear ought to hear."

The simplest explanation for the similarities is that one of the three Gospels was used as a primary source when the other two were written. For a variety of reasons, early on, many biblical scholars thought that maybe Matthew's Gospel was the primary source for the other two, and the first one written. But a number of observations of the three Gospels together lead to a different conclusion.

If Matthew's Gospel was written first, it is difficult to explain why Mark, whose Gospel is considerably shorter, would have eliminated so much of Matthew. It is particularly puzzling, since many of those missing moments are when Jesus was actually teaching, like in the Sermon on the Mount (Mt 5:1–7:29). Why would

Mark leave out the Beatitudes or the Our Father? It makes more sense to suggest that Matthew added that material to Mark, than to conclude that Mark deleted it from Matthew.

An additional point to consider was first proposed by Greek experts who pointed out that Matthew and Luke's use of grammar is better than Mark's, which is very rough at best. The follow-up question is: why would Mark deliberately turn their good grammar into something less polished? The more likely conclusion is that Matthew and Luke corrected the grammar in Mark's Gospel.

Also, at times, the narrative sequence between Matthew and Mark are different. Whenever Matthew and Mark differ, Luke's sequence always agrees with the order in Mark's Gospel. When Luke does change the sequence, Matthew and Mark always agree. It makes the most sense to hold that Mark contained the original order that, on occasion, Matthew or Luke independently chose to alter.

Putting all the observations together, the hypothesis most likely to be accurate is that Mark's Gospel was written first. It was then copied and distributed, and made its way independently into the hands of the authors of the Gospels of Matthew and Luke. They were apparently attracted to what Mark had done and, in turn, used it as a foundation for writing expanded narratives of the life of Christ. Matthew and Luke also have in common another 220–235 verses (in whole or in part). Scholars also theorize that the authors of Matthew and Luke also drew on another common source known as "Q" (probably from the German *Quelle*, meaning "source"). This hypothetical document was not in the form of a Gospel, but was mostly a collection of sayings of Jesus that came down to the evangelists in either written or, perhaps, oral form. While it is one way to study the Synoptic Gospels, the so-called two-source theory of Mark and Q as sources common to the two other Synoptic Gospels remains just that, a theory.

It is also noted in this theory that in addition to Mark and Q, Matthew and Luke use materials that were unique to each of them, termed "M" and "L," respectively. The authors of Matthew and Luke fit in the additional material they had collected about Jesus as they saw fit, independently of one another.

The author of the Gospel of John, written later than the Synoptics, may have shared common written or oral traditions with Mark's Gospel, and was likely to have known certain traditions that also appear in Luke's Gospel. It is possible that the final editor of John's Gospel had contact with one or more of the Synoptic Gospels. However, the fourth Gospel does not rely heavily on any of them. Rather, its sources are independent traditions preserved in the churches from which it was created.

Review

1. Define Synoptic Gospels.
2. What are three similarities in the Gospels of Matthew, Mark, and Luke?
3. Why is it more likely that the Gospel of Mark was written before the Gospel of Matthew?

Dating the Gospels

There was more than one calendar in use in the Roman Empire during the time the Gospels were composed. One calendar was from the beginning of the empire. Another, the Julian calendar, was introduced by Julius Caesar in 45 BC. The dual calendars posed a problem for Gospel authors, who wanted to date some of the incidents. Frequently, the best they could do was to relate their narrative's events to other significant historical events or people that were concurrent to them. For example, Luke uses this method to help date the ministry of John the Baptist and the beginning of Jesus' public ministry:

> In the fifteenth year of the reign of Tiberius Caesar, when Pontius Pilate was governor of Judea, and Herod was tetrarch of Galilee, and his brother Philip tetrarch of the region of Ituraea and Trachonitis, and Lysanias was tetrarch of Abilene, during the high priesthood of Annas and Caiaphas, the word of God came to John the son of Zechariah in the desert. (Lk 3:1–2)

The difficulty with this type of dating is that the reader needs to be able to convert the dates to the current Gregorian calendar (between AD 27 and AD 29 in this case). Even then, the Gospel text may include confusing facts that would make accurate dating difficult. For example, in the above passage, Luke apparently did not know that Annas and Caiaphas were not high priests at the same time. Annas had been high priest AD 6–15 and Caiaphas AD 18–36, although Annas was apparently still alive during Caiaphas's reign.

Dating Jesus' life on earth poses another particular problem. It is hard to put concrete dates on a person who began his life as a humble son of a carpenter from an otherwise obscure town of Nazareth, and whose later activities were only briefly noticed by religious and political enemies at the end of his life. In the absence of any archeological evidence, dating his life is somewhat of a hypothetical effort, as is dating the Gospels that recount his story. A curious note in this regard is that both Matthew and Luke indicate that Jesus was born while Herod the Great was still alive (Mt 2:1; Lk 1:5). Historical records indicate that Herod died in 4 BC. So, if Jesus was born during Herod's reign, Jesus had to have been born not later than 4 BC.

There are more reliable ways to date the creation of the Gospels themselves. For example, when the Gospels mention known and dated events from history, it is accurate to be able to date the Gospel sometime *after* those events. Or, when the Gospel is quoted by other datable writings, it is accurate to be able to say that the Gospel was written *before* the document it was quoted in.

The easiest of the Gospels to date is Mark's Gospel, because of a detail in Jesus' description of the end of the world in Mark 13. The last days were important to the early Christians, since many of them believed the world was going to end during their lifetimes. In the midst of Jesus' words of warning, the narrator's voice adds a brief aside in parentheses: "When you see the desolating abomination standing where he should not (let the reader understand), then those in Judea must flee to the mountains" (Mk 13:4). This interruption suggests that there was something happening about the time that Mark's Gospel was being written that the author knew that his readers would be aware of. Historians went looking for something of great import that could explain this aside, all the while acknowledging that it could be something local that they might possibly never discover. As Jesus' teaching in this case was prompted by his comment that the stones of the Temple in Jerusalem would all be torn down (Mk 13:2–4), there was good reason to tie the aside into the destruction of the Temple itself.

What is the historical record of this event? Very long dissatisfied with incompetent Roman governance, the Jews of Judea rebelled against the Roman Empire in AD 68. The Roman army responded fiercely, and for two years, under General Vespasian and then his son, Titus, reconquered Judea by force of arms. The war was terrible, lengthy, and newsworthy, especially among Jews and Christians. Finally, in the year 70, Titus took the last standing fortress in Jerusalem, the Temple itself, entering it as a conqueror. It is reasonable to assume that he was the "desolating abomination standing where he should not." For this reason, many scholars date the composition of Mark's Gospel to sometime during these difficult events (AD 68–72). A more definite hypothesis is that the Gospel of Mark was written in AD 70, the year that the Temple was destroyed.

If Matthew and Luke, in fact, used Mark's Gospel as a starting point for their own writings, then their own Gospels must have been from sometime later than AD 70. Allowing time for the slow process of hand-copying Mark's text, and a similarly slow method of walking a completed version from one place to the next, there had to be a few years after Mark's composition before Matthew and Luke examined it and decided that it was a good source for their own narratives about Jesus.

Dating Matthew's Gospel is aided because it is quoted by a number of sources, including 1 Peter 2:12 and 3:14, as well as the *Didache*. St. Ignatius of Antioch also appears to refer to it repeatedly in his letters. Using the known dates of these documents, scholars are inclined to agree that Matthew's Gospel was written after AD 70 and before AD 100. A mediating date around AD 85–90 seems reasonable, if uncertain.

Luke's Gospel is also dated after Mark's in time, but as Luke does not seem to know of Paul's letters, it cannot have followed Mark by too late a date. Paul's letters were likely

Didache

A Greek word for "teaching," it refers to the teaching directed to Christians who have accepted the Gospel.

John Rylands Greek papyrus

A fragment of John's Gospel, found in Egypt and written on Greek papyrus that dates from around 130 BC. It is the earliest fragment from any New Testament book. It is preserved at the John Rylands University Library in Manchester, England.

distributed quite widely and early on. A common date for the authorship of Luke's Gospel is in the AD 80s.

John's Gospel is more difficult to locate in time. It was once quite common to date the Gospel to AD 120–130, and even later. There has been a tendency among scholars to push that date ever earlier, to around AD 90. Interestingly, a small fragment from John's Gospel is the earliest section of any New Testament book in existence. Found in Egypt, this **John Rylands Greek papyrus** dates from around AD 130. It shows that the Gospel of John had wide circulation throughout the Mediterranean world a mere thirty to forty years after its composition.

Review

1. What was a problem the authors of the Gospels had with dating narrative events?

2. Using evidence from Matthew and Luke's Gospels, why is it possible that Jesus was not born later than 4 BC?

3. How was the date of composition of Mark's Gospel connected to the destruction of the Temple?

4. What are some criteria used to date the Gospels of Matthew and Luke?

Reflect

What are three important historical events that occurred in the year that you were born?

Formation of the Gospels

Jesus Christ entrusted the preaching of the Gospel to the Apostles. In keeping this command of the Lord, the Gospel was handed down in two ways: orally in their preaching, and in writing "by those apostles and other men associated with the apostles, who under the inspiration of the same Holy Spirit, committed the message of salvation to writing" (*Dei Verbum* 7, quoted in *CCC*, 76).

If the dates for the creation of the four Gospels are correct (and they seem to be the best we can do in this matter), there was an extended period of time between the life and Death of Jesus in the first third of the first century and the writing of the Gospels in the last third of the first century. During the years in between, the Gospel was passed on orally in the preaching and teaching of the Apostles and other eyewitnesses. The Church teaches, and biblical scholars agree, that there were three stages in the formation of the Gospels: (1) the period of the public life and teaching of Jesus; (2) a period of oral tradition and preaching by the Apostles and early disciples of Jesus; and (3) the written Gospels themselves.

This time of the oral tradition and transmission inevitably had a profound effect on the Good News itself. Consider in your own life what happens to stories as they are told. Inevitably, they are shaped to fit both the given moments of their telling and the needs of the listeners. A certain amount of creativity is required to suit the story to the audience, whether they are parents, peers, younger siblings, or teachers.

Believe it or not, because the Gospel was transmitted in the presence of the Church and guided by the Holy Spirit, the greatest concerns about the effects of oral storytelling on the Gospels are not primarily about falsehoods or fabrications that could have surfaced when the Gospel was recounted orally. Consider that when some preachers took unfair advantage of their freedom to drastically alter the story they had received—and there were those who did precisely that—it was the early Church as a whole that witnessed to what was true and what was not. We know that the Church took this responsibility seriously, since, as a result of careful inspection, there were a number of documents produced in the first century that were not accepted into the biblical canon and others judged heretical.

Evidence for this process or inspection is alluded to at the beginning of Luke's Gospel:

> Since many have undertaken to compile a narrative of the events that have been fulfilled among us, just as those who were eyewitnesses from the beginning and ministers of the word have handed them down to us, I too have decided, after investigating everything accurately anew, to write it down in an orderly sequence for you. (Lk 1:1–3)

This opening passage points out that Luke is aware of a number of narratives that preceded his own work. Though he, himself, is not an eyewitness, he is concerned about rooting his own work in the words of those who are. Accuracy in everything is a value for him.

Toward the end of John's Gospel, similar concerns referring to the legitimacy of sources are raised by the testimony of the "beloved disciple," a companion of Jesus, about whom it was written: "It is this disciple who testifies to these things and has written them,

and we know that his testimony is true" (Jn 21:24). The authenticity of the Gospel was rooted in the words, written or spoken, of an eyewitness.

The second stage of Gospel formation—the oral tradition—took three key forms:

- *The **kerygma**, or preaching to unbelievers.* The Acts of the Apostles includes several sermons that Peter and Paul preached about Jesus. To help them in this preaching, they and the other Apostles and disciples would have followed a basic outline of Jesus' works, Death, Resurrection, and Ascension. (Think of it like an outline you might work from in giving an oral report in class.) They would also have used many passages from the Old Testament to show how the prophecies made about the Messiah were fulfilled in Jesus. During this period, the disciples began to assemble collections of material about Jesus—for example, miracle stories, parables, and the Passion narrative. Later evangelists would have drawn on these sources to help compose their Gospels.

- *The Didache, or teaching.* This teaching was really further catechetical instruction for those who accepted Jesus. *Catechesis* literally means to "sound down," that is, to repeat the message and explain it in more depth. Early converts needed further knowledge about how to live a more Christ-filled life. Lists of sayings of Jesus, for example, and the Sermon on the Mount were probably assembled to help in this instruction.

- *The liturgy, or worship, of the Christians.* The way people pray

kerygma
The core teachings about Jesus Christ as Savior and Lord.

reflects their beliefs. The celebration of the Eucharist helped the Church shape and preserve key events, teachings, and prayers of Jesus that were recalled in the early Eucharistic celebrations. Some examples include Jesus' words at the Last Supper, the Lord's Prayer, and the story of Jesus' Passion. In some cases, different communities slightly varied the wording of what was remembered. However, they all faithfully recounted what Jesus did and said.

The material proclaimed, taught, and celebrated during this period of oral tradition was shaped by the different local churches of the day. The early preachers' and teachers' primary interest was to interpret the meaning of the key events, deeds, and sayings of Jesus that the Father wanted revealed. They wanted to enliven the faith of Christians. As a result, they did not set out to give a detailed biography of Jesus. However, what they remembered, saved, and proclaimed was at the heart of Jesus' message—related to the Old Testament and adapted to the audiences who heard it.

It is important to note that although the four canonical Gospels were composed between AD 65 and 100, preaching about Jesus based on oral traditions carried on well into the second century.

⊕ Review

1. What are the three stages of Gospel formation?

2. Why is there little concern about falsehoods or fabrications creeping into the Gospels during the time of the oral tradition?

3. What are the three forms of the oral tradition?

4. What was of primary interest to those who shared the Gospel in the oral tradition?

⊕ Reflect

Do you prefer to learn new material orally or through the written word? Explain.

Authorship of the Gospels

Although none of the four Gospels actually name or identify their authors in the texts, there are ancient traditions (note the small "t") from as early as the second century AD of assigning names to them. The names chosen coincided with people who were otherwise mentioned in New Testament texts. For example, Matthew was identified as a tax collector called by Jesus (Mt 9:9); Mark was known to be a companion, first of Paul and Barnabas, and then apparently of Peter (Acts 12:25; 1 Pt 5:13); Luke was Paul's beloved physician (Col 4:14; 2 Tm 4:11; Phlm 24); John was the brother of James and the son of Zebedee (Mt 4:21). It should be pointed out, though, that the texts of the Gospels never actually state the names or identities of their authors. The Second Vatican Council reiterated that the "Church has always and everywhere maintained, and continues to maintain, the apostolic origins of the four Gospels" (*Dei Verbum*, 18). How

this apostolic connection takes place is an interesting element of study.

It *would* be helpful if the Gospels were actually written by verifiable eyewitnesses. Both Matthew and John were members of the Twelve Apostles, and thus would be among the best eyewitnesses, having journeyed with Jesus through most of his public ministry. Second in value would be the companions of eyewitnesses. A number of ancient traditions connect John Mark with the St. Peter in Rome ("Babylon" is coded language for Rome in 1 Peter 5:13). The Scriptures do not place Luke in the company of any of the Twelve Apostles. However, the Letter to Philemon (verse 24) places Luke in the company of Paul, suggesting that he was not an eyewitness, but may have lived fairly close to the time of Jesus' ministry.

Though a connection with the apostolic tradition cannot be disputed, the position that Apostles or companions of Jesus undertook the *actual* authorship of the Gospels is not as certain. One reason is because the most likely dates for the composition of the Gospels were from the very late 60s for Mark and through the end of the first century for John. It was rare for people in the first century, except for some of the affluent, to survive past their thirties. The best evidence suggests that Jesus died in his early to middle thirties, somewhere in the third decade of the first century. While it is not impossible for people about the same age as Jesus when he died to have lived well into the second half of the first century, it would have been rare for the time.

Attributing the Gospel of Matthew to the Apostle Matthew may have been because of his having something to do with some of its traditions. However, it is even less probable that the Apostle Matthew, an eyewitness to Jesus' life and ministry (Mt 9:9; 10:3), would have relied as heavily as the Gospel of Matthew does on the written testimony of Mark's Gospel when John Mark was not an eyewitness or an Apostle.

The author of Luke demonstrates in his use of Greek vocabulary and writing style that he had an elite classical education, reserved for only a very small percentage of the population. The differences between Luke and, say, Mark, whose writing style was very humble, would have been as striking as those between a college professor and a fourth-grade student today. However, physicians in the first century were not typically from the elite class. The medical field did not require advanced studies, as it does today. In fact, physicians were likely of a lower social standing and more often associated with barbers. It's hard to reconcile the classical writing of the Gospel with the "beloved physician" of Colossians 4:14 if he were in fact raised in a lower social class and would have been unlikely to be trained in classical Greek education. The best that could be said is that we really don't know the identity of the author of the Gospel of Luke. We only know that he was apparently from a wealthy family that was able to provide him with a rare and expensive education.

As for John's Gospel, if John was, in fact, the author of the fourth Gospel, why does the text never identify him as such? The Gospel does acknowledge "the disciple Jesus loved" as its author (Jn 21:20), but never states that his name is John.

Because those of the apostolic age handed on to us in writing the same message that they preached and named the Gospels by the traditional names of Matthew, Mark, Luke, and John, it remains both convenient and correct to continue to call the authors of these Gospels by those names.

Just because we aren't sure of the identity of those who actually wrote down the Gospels doesn't mean we don't know anything about them. Just as we can tell details of Luke's and Mark's social classes by the way they wrote and the vocabularies they used, we can also tell, by the content of their Gospels, other things about them. For example, we can see by the small ways that Matthew and Luke adapted the Gospel of Mark how their needs, and the needs of their readers, differed from those of Mark's and his readers. These are the types of details to look for as you continue your study of the Gospels and the Acts of the Apostles.

Review

1. Identify the names associated with the traditional authors of the Gospels.

2. Why is it likely that the author of Luke's Gospel had the benefits of a classical Greek education?

Reflect

If someone was looking through your possessions for clues to your identity, which possessions would tell the most about you?

The Gospel of Mark

Mark's Gospel was the first attempt to take all the stories of the life of Jesus and to form them into one narrative—in approximately AD 66–70. Because no indication is given within the Gospel or the ancient tradition that the author was an eyewitness, the author would have had to use a great deal of creativity to form these individual stories into one greater narrative, putting them in a sensible order and then bridging them from one event to the next.

Mark's Gospel is also the shortest of the Gospels. The entire Gospel can be read in one sitting. It has been defined as having two main parts: a long introduction that details Jesus' ministry and travels, followed by the Passion narrative. In both the introduction and the Passion, Mark spent much more time describing what Jesus *did* than what he taught. Where Mark would say that Jesus "taught the crowds," without giving any details, Matthew and Luke, in turn, both expanded Mark's account by adding quite a bit of Jesus' actual teaching.

The author of Mark wrote in Greek, but also used some words and phrases in Aramaic, the language of Jesus. The stories, as they were handed down to the author, retained some of these words and phrases from the earliest historical moments and preaching. Mark also used a number of words from Latin, the language of Rome (e.g., "centurion," "legion," "denarius," etc.). Some suggest that the Latin words indicate that the Gospel was composed in Rome, though these words might have crept into Greek anywhere that Rome governed, which was most of the region around the Mediterranean Sea.

Whom Did Mark Write For?

While the identity of the author of the Gospel is unknown, there are several clues from the Gospel that can help to detect information on his background and the background of the community he wrote for.

Mark's audience was apparently largely Gentile, as they seemed to be un-aware of the customs of the "Pharisees and, in fact, all Jews," which the author took pains to explain. For example:

> Now when the Pharisees with some scribes who had come from Jerusalem gathered around him, they observed that some of the disciples ate their meals with un-clean, that is, unwashed, hands. (For the Pharisees and, in fact, all Jews, do not eat without careful-ly washing their hands, keeping the tradition of the elders. And on coming from the marketplace they do not eat without purifying themselves. And there are many other things that they have tradi-tionally observed, the purification of cups and jugs and kettles [and beds]). (Mk 7:1–4)

That his explanation wasn't entirely accurate (not all Jews did the ritual cleansings described in this pas-sage) suggests to some that Mark might not have been Jewish either, or at least hadn't had a broad experience with the many varieties of Judaism of the first century.

The author wrote with a simple vocabulary and inelegant grammar, scattered with incomplete phrases

AN OUTLINE OF THE GOSPEL OF MARK

Prologue: 1:1-13

Part 1: The Messiah Preaches the Good News: 1:14-8:26

- The beginning of his ministry in Galilee: call of disciples, mighty works, contro-versies (1:14-3:6).
- Jesus in his own territory (3:7-6:6a).
- His teaching on discipleship and miracles meets misunderstanding (6:6b-8:26).

Transition: Who Is Jesus? 8:27-8:33

Part 2: The Way of Discipleship: 8:31-16:8

- The Son of Man is to suffer (8:31-10:52).
- Jesus in Jerusalem (11:1-13:37).
- Jesus' Passion, Death, and Resurrection (14:1-16:8).

Second Ending of Mark: 16:9-20

Read the entire Gospel in one sitting. It will take about an hour. If you want to break your reading into two segments, then first read to Mark 9:1. Read for the big picture. At this point, try not to get bogged down in details.

and redundancies. For example, of the 11,229 words in the Gospel, the Greek word for "and" (*kai*) is used 1,100 times, starting 591 clauses with it. Starting sen-tences or clauses with "and" is as clumsy in Greek as it is in English. This awkwardness of language is unnoticed in today's English Gospel translations be-cause interpreters do not translate the grammar prob-lems or awkward phrases from Greek to English. They do everything they can to *fix* such things, making the

papyrus

A type of paper made from reeds found in the delta of the Nile River and in parts of Italy.

English as clear and readable as possible in the new language.

Overwhelmingly, people living in the first century were illiterate. They were also poor, measured against standards of the developed world today. Since ink, **papyrus**, and the use of a scribe to take dictation were all expensive, most people never learned to read and write. The wealthy and well educated wrote most of what survives from this time period. Very little popular literature, composed by or for the poor majority, endures to this day. However, in the contracts, letters, and a few novels from the period that were created for the lower social classes, the writing style resembles that of Mark's Gospel—simple vocabulary and awkward grammar. In summary, the literary style of Mark's Gospel suggests that it was written from the perspective of the common peasant, living shortly after the time of Jesus.

Mark's Portrayal of Jesus

Mark portrays a very human Jesus who expresses his emotions. For example, in Mark's Gospel, Jesus is angry and "grieved at their hardness of heart" (3:5) and compassionate to the man who wanted to know how to be saved (10:21). Mark also records Jesus being inquisitive, for example, asking questions like "How many loaves do you have?" (6:38), whereas, in Matthew and Luke, Jesus asks few questions—he usually *knows* the answers without

asking (Mt 14:16–17 and Lk 9:13). In general, Matthew and Luke often delete Mark's portrayal of Jesus' emotions (Mt 12:12–13 and Lk 6:9–10; Mt 19:21 and Lk 18:22).

Another difference is that in Mark's Gospel, the evil spirits are sometimes slow to obey Jesus (Mk 5:8), while in Matthew and Luke, Jesus' exorcisms are immediate and complete. In Matthew and Luke, the Holy Spirit "leads" Jesus into the desert, where he was tempted (Mt 4:1 and Lk 4:1), while in Mark's Gospel, the Spirit "drives" Jesus to the desert to be tempted (Mk 1:12).

In Mark, Jesus, though God, understands the most painful moments of human existence: loneliness and alienation from family and betrayal by friends. Jesus becomes despondent because his relatives make offensive judgments and decisions for him (Mk 3:21) and rudely summon him while he is teaching (Mk 3:31). When his disciples fail to understand him, it also leaves him feeling low and even angry (Mk 8:17–21).

 **Reflect**

When was an occasion when Jesus shared your pain?

Parables in Mark

Most people whom Jesus ministered to throughout Galilee were subsistence farmers. This means their lives were difficult; they worked long hours, had few tools, and no machinery to make the work easier, paid heavy taxes to rulers and landlords, and still lived on the edge of hunger. There was little time for an education, apart from learning one's trade. Books, in the shape of scrolls, were rare and prohibitively expensive, so few learned to read. There was little access to the broad philosophical investigations undertaken by the wealthy—who had the luxury of time and the means to pay for a mind-expanding education. In effect, both the people Jesus ministered to and the people Mark wrote for appear to have been very humble people.

Jesus used **parables** to communicate his teachings. The Greek word *ballo*, or "throw," was combined with the preposition *para*, meaning "beside," implying that two things were literally flung together. In that sense, a parable takes simple items from everyday life (seeds, family relationships, lost coins, etc.) and throws them together with concepts or ideas that would otherwise have been difficult for Jesus' disciples to understand (e.g., the Kingdom of God, divine forgiveness, etc.). The relationships between the elements of parables, captivating because they are lively or odd, are usually not immediately clear or even precise. They often provoke further thought as the hearer tries to see precisely how things are both like and *not* like each other. A good parable makes the hearer *think*.

With this in mind, Jesus compared the Word of God to seed sown on varying kinds of soil (Mk 4:3–8, 14–20), the Kingdom of God to a tiny mustard seed

that becomes a big plant (Mk 4:31–32), and the ancient Israelites to a vineyard with wicked tenants looking after it (Mk 12:1–9). He compared the crowds who followed him to sheep without a shepherd (6:34) and invited his disciples to consider God as their heavenly Father (Mk 11:25). Seeds, vineyards, and sheep may give us a romantic impression if we live in urban settings, but they would not have seemed anything of the sort for Jesus' contemporaries or for Mark's audience, either. Seeds and sheep were part of the everyday hard scramble to feed one's family.

Jesus did not invent the use of parables. The Old Testament had many such comparisons:

- The Israelites' relationship with God was compared to that of a cheating wife with her husband (Hos 1:2);
- God was like a shepherd (Ps 22), and yet also defended the people

parables

A typical teaching device Jesus used. They are vivid picture stories drawn from ordinary life that convey religious truth, usually related to some aspect of God's Kingdom. They tease the listener to think and make choices about accepting the Good News of God's reign.

with ferocity like that of a crouching lion (Nm 24:9);

- God's Word was like the rain that fell from Heaven, bringing life wherever it landed (Dt 32:2);

- God's love and commitment for Jerusalem (Mt. Zion) is like a mother for the child of her womb (Is 49:14–15).

Jesus, borrowing some of his images from the Old Testament and inventing some new and very creative ones of his own, invited those who had the ears necessary to hear his parables, and eyes to see the world around them, to understand his parables: "Do you have eyes and not see, ears and not hear? And do you not remember?" (Mk 8:18). An interesting, if not sad, element in Mark's Gospel is that Jesus' disciples are portrayed as mostly not being able to understand his parables any more than they understood his actions. (In Matthew's and Luke's Gospels, the disciples are more attentive.)

 **Reflect**

Which of Jesus' parables gives you the clearest understanding of the Kingdom of God?

Discipleship in Mark

Jesus had foreknowledge of his coming crucifixion—understanding and accepting that he had to go to Jerusalem, where he would suffer and be put to death. He desired that his disciples also understand and appreciate what was going to happen, and so he announced it three times to them: in Mark 8:31–38, 9:31–37, and 10:32–45. Curiously, immediately after each prediction, Jesus' disciples responded in some terribly inappropriate way.

After the first prediction, Peter protested against Jesus' intentions, insisting that Jesus not follow through with what he had described to them. As suffering and dying was a hard future to face, this was attractive advice, but not in accord with the Father's plan. Jesus called Peter "Satan" for having been such a tempter. Jesus taught his followers, in response, that not only did he have to follow through, but that if they were going to be his disciples, they were going to have to pick up their crosses too, and follow him. Unfortunately, they don't seem to have heard or understood.

After the second prediction of his suffering and dying, rather than comforting Jesus, the disciples discussed among themselves who among them was the greatest. While Jesus was asking them to prepare themselves for a hard future, they were trying to position themselves for power and importance. Jesus, in contrast, taught them that if they were going to be "first" in his Kingdom, it could only be as a servant, and that they needed to embrace the powerlessness and dependence like that of a child.

After the third prediction, instead of joining with Jesus in his future struggles, James and John asked if they could be on his right- and left-hand sides when he came into his glory. It is clear again that they didn't understand that they, too, had to pattern their lives on picking up their crosses, suffering, and facing death. This was particularly discouraging, because James and John, along with Simon Peter, were Jesus' frequent companions (Mk 1:16–20, 29; 5:37; 9:2; 13:3; 14:33). In each of these times together, the narrator always listed Peter's name first. What James and John were asking, essentially, was for Jesus to bump Peter from his place of favor. The only positive element in the reaction here comes from the other Apostles, who became "indignant at James and John" (Mk 10:41). At this point, Jesus offered his clearest definition of the meaning of discipleship: "Whoever wishes to be great among you will be your servant; whoever wishes to be first among you will be the slave of all. For the Son of Man did not come to be served but to serve and to give his life as a ransom for many" (Mk 10:43–45).

One of the many hypotheses that have been formed about the Gospel of Mark is that it was written for a community that was suffering, possibly even persecuted by others for their Christian faith. Apparently some in this community, possibly even some of its leaders, needed to be challenged by both the teachings and example of Jesus because of their unwillingness to pull together in this time of great need, to serve one another's needs, and even to be willing to suffer for what was true.

The Passion Narrative

The Passion narrative takes up one-third of Mark's Gospel, even though it only covers a few days. In fact, the chronicle of Jesus' very last day is approximately one-sixth of the entire Gospel. The amount of time dedicated to it suggests its great importance in the mind of the author and his community. The entire event is set in Jerusalem at the time of Passover, a central feast for Jews commemorating the time of Moses, when the angel of death "passed over" the Israelites, striking down the firstborn of the Egyptians.

The Jewish custom on the feast of the Passover was to eat unleavened bread and lamb. The Passion narrative in Mark begins with the disciples asking about the arrangements they should make, "on the first day of the Feast of Unleavened Bread, when they sacrificed the Passover lamb" (Mk 14:2). The sacrifice of an unblemished lamb—like the one whose blood saved the Israelites at the first Passover—is the background for everything that happens in the course of Jesus' Passion.

Mark's version of the Passion is very grim in comparison with the other Gospels. At his Last Supper with his disciples, Jesus makes another prediction about his coming suffering. He mentions that one of the Twelve who was with him would betray him. Not only was it necessary for him to suffer and die, but also that this terrible time would begin with a betrayal by one of his own disciples.

The rest of the Passion narrative is marked by a somber, even heartwrenching sense of abandonment: His disciples repeatedly fall asleep during his agony. He is betrayed by one of them into the hands of his enemies with a kiss. The disciples who had left everything to follow him earlier in the Gospel (Mk 10:28), now abandon everything, including their clothes, to get away from him (Mk 14:51–52). Peter denies that he even *knows* Jesus. In Jesus' trial before the high priests and the Roman procurator, Pontius Pilate, *no one* comes to his defense. Jesus' own people cry out for his crucifixion and beat him (14:65), handing him over to be tortured by the Romans (15:17–20). He is stripped naked. Like the butchered unblemished lamb, Jesus is crucified at a public place where everyone can mock him, while his life leaches out from his broken body. His only sympathetic companions are the women present, but only at a distance: Mary Magdalene, Salome, and the mother of James and Joses, also named Mary (15:40). Notice that in Mark's Gospel, Jesus' own Mother is *not* present.

In the anguish of the moment, Jesus begins to pray Psalm 22, "My God, my God, why have you abandoned me" (Mk 15:34). Human like us in all things (Heb 2:17), except for sin, it is understandable that Jesus could *feel* abandoned, even if he *knew* otherwise. Because crucifixion makes breathing almost impossible, Jesus was unable to finish Psalm 22. To understand what he intended to pray, it would be good to look at the entirety of that psalm, and even to finish it for him. Those who do will discover that it was not a prayer of despair.

Reflect

What do you discover if you finish Psalm 22, Jesus' prayer on the Cross?

Mark's Community

Because of the vivid portrayal of Jesus as the suffering Messiah and the hardships of discipleship, some scholars suggest that Rome was a very likely location for Mark and his community. There was a terrible fire in Rome in AD 64, leading to a great deal of anger against the emperor Nero, whom the populace believed had set the fire. Nero, in turn, tried to pass the blame onto the Christians, whom he used in his "entertainments," according to the Roman historian Tacitus (AD 55–117). Having arrested some who confessed to being Christians, and then using their confessions to arrest an "immense multitude" of other believers, Nero had animal skins tied to them and set dogs on them to kill and devour them. He also crucified them, covered them with pitch, and used them as living torches in his own gardens (*Annals* 15.44.28).

Jesus' very words describe terrible suffering: "Watch out for yourselves. They will hand you over to the courts. You will be beaten in synagogues. You will be arraigned before governors and kings because of me, as a witness before them" (Mk 13:9) and "Brother will hand over brother to death, and the father his child; children will rise up against parents and have them put to death. You will be hated by all because of my name. But the one who perseveres to the end will be saved" (Mk 13:12–13). Some scholars wonder if these words seem to indicate both what would happen in the future to the Church or are a reflection of what had already happened to them as a result of Nero's persecution.

Other scholars prefer to locate Mark's community in Syria. A number of passages seem to indicate that the author was relatively well informed of what was going on in the Jewish rebellion against Rome in AD 66–70. But since his community, and possibly Mark himself, was not Jewish, they were probably not in Judea or Galilee, themselves, where there were largely Jewish populations. The nearest Gentile territory to the war would have been the Roman territory of Syria, across the River Jordan and to the north. Many scholars find this position persuasive. That serious scholars can dispute the location of Mark's community, with reasonably persuasive arguments for either Rome or Syria, suggests that the question really has to remain open.

Most persuasive, though, is the idea that Mark's community itself had difficulty being faithful disciples in the face of their own suffering—a question for

every age and every believer. We all face suffering in our lives and have to confront some terrible evils in the world around us. Mark's Gospel wants its readers to understand how close Jesus is to that suffering. Jesus doesn't understand the human experience from some far-off heavenly throne because of his infinite knowledge and wisdom. He knows our greatest pains of betrayal, abandonment, and bodily anguish, from the inside out, as a human who experienced them himself. At sometime or another in your life, you may well be tempted to cry out, "Where are you, God, in my time of suffering?" The message of Mark's Gospel is that Jesus is right there with you, sharing your pain.

⬤ Review

1. What are the two main parts of Mark's Gospel?

2. Why is it assumed that Mark's audience was largely gentile?

3. How do the evil spirits respond to Jesus in Mark's Gospel?

4. What are the characteristics of a parable?

5. How are Jesus' disciples portrayed in the Gospel of Mark?

6. Name two ways that the Passion narrative in Mark's Gospel is marked by a sense of abandonment.

7. Why are Rome and Syria both suggested as possible locations for Mark and his community?

⬤ Reflect

How do you find it difficult to be a faithful disciple of Jesus in the midst of personal and worldwide suffering?

The Gospel of Matthew

Matthew's Gospel was likely written sometime in the AD 80s. As mentioned, Matthew used 600 of Mark's 660 verses and was, in a general way, faithful to Mark's outline of events. However, Matthew also edited and compacted several of Mark's passages. For example, consider how long it took for Jesus to get on a boat in Mark: "On that day, as evening drew on, he said to them, 'Let us cross to the other side.' Leaving the crowd, they took him with them in the boat just as he was. And other boats were with him" (Mk 4:35–36). Matthew's version says simply, "He got into a boat and his disciples followed him" (Mt 8:23).

After compacting Mark's 11,000 Greek words down to about 9,000, Matthew then added another 9,000 words, ending up with over 18,000 words in his completed work. After the reductions and additions, the end product was roughly half Marcan, and half new. Matthew apparently felt free to reorder events from the first twelve chapters of Mark as he thought

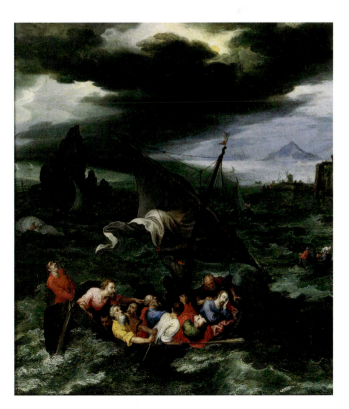

best. We see from this that he did not see Mark's order as either historical or an essential part of the message. He became much more faithful to Mark's chronology from Mark 13 and forward through Jesus' Passion.

Another, more significant change is Matthew's description of Jesus' disciples. In Mark, they did not seem to understand the meaning of discipleship; in Matthew they understand Jesus' instructions more clearly. Whereas in Mark, the disciples are described as having "no faith," in Matthew they are called "you of little faith" (Mt 6:30; 8:26; 14:31; 16:8; 17:20). They made mistakes, but they learned from them. They erred, but they also eventually succeeded in being followers of Christ.

The "Q" Material

In addition to the material Matthew borrowed from Mark's Gospel, Matthew added several more verses that are not found in Mark. A fair portion of this additional material was also found, curiously, in Luke's Gospel, roughly twenty-four passages, or between 220 and 235 verses, depending on whether you counted them from Matthew's or Luke's numbering. Of them, thirteen passages, comprising more than 50 percent of the shared material, were found in the same order between Matthew and Luke.

Most of this common material between Matthew and Luke is made up of sayings and parables, with very few stories or narrative to move the Gospel along. In fact, there are only three narratives of note: the threefold temptation in the desert (Mt 4:1–11 and Lk 4:1–13), the centurion's sick servant (Mt 8:5–13 and Lk 7:1–10; a similar story is told in Jn 4:46–54), and the account of the disciples of John the Baptist coming to Jesus (Mt 11:2–6 and Lk 7:18–23).

The wording in this material common to Matthew and Luke (but not to Mark) is *very* similar, and much of it is found in the same order. Because there was far too much material for it to have corresponded so closely and yet have been oral, most scholars concluded that Matthew and Luke must have each had their own copy of some written source of Jesus' sayings that had been copied and was still circulating in Christian circles. No copy of that written source has ever been found, so it remains hypothetical. This is the source known as "Q," or "Quelle."

There is much we don't know about Q. We really don't know whether Q was written before Mark's Gospel, was Mark's contemporary, or was composed after Mark. We don't even know if Q was only one source, or many. Matthew and Luke may have had two, or even three works common among them that they incorporated into what is now referred to as Q. Even so, the Q hypothesis remains the best explanation for the material shared by both Matthew and Luke, but not found in Mark.

The content of the Q material is strongly **eschatological**, meaning it focuses a good deal of attention on the end of the world, giving the readers warnings and woes, and suggesting that the judgment of the world is imminent. Following the example of the prophets of the Old Testament, Matthew includes several examples of Jesus' announcement of the judgment of the Last Day in his preaching (see, for example, Matthew 3:7–12). Having suffered and died for our Salvation, Christ has the right to determine our eternal destiny based on our acceptance or rejection of his grace and according to our works. We know that at the time of Paul, many Christians seemed to believe that the end of the world was at hand. This suggests that Q might well have been an *early* written source.

Matthew and Luke didn't use Q in exactly the same way. As both Matthew and Luke shaped their Marcan original, as they felt best for their narratives and audiences, we should expect that they did the same with their use of Q.

When the material from the Mark and Q traditions are combined, they still don't make up the entirety of Matthew's Gospel. There are about four hundred extra verses not present in either Mark or Q. This is often called the "M" source. Included in these extra verses are the genealogy of Jesus going back to Abraham, and the birth and infancy stories that focus on Joseph and the Magi (Mt 1–2). Other unique material to Matthew includes the unique and majestic treatment of the key events of Salvation in the Passion and Resurrection narratives, some quotations from the Old Testament, and a large amount of sayings of Jesus, most of which are included in five discourses. While some scholars have proposed that there was a third written source that Matthew drew from, it is more likely that the extra material was drawn from the oral traditions that were still circulating in the early Church.

Whom Did Matthew Write For?

The majority of Christians in the first generation were of Jewish origin, both from Judea and from the Diaspora, that is, the rest of the Mediterranean where Jews had spread for political and economic reasons. By the way Matthew wrote about Jewish concerns, it is discernable that Matthew's intended audience of readers, even as late as the AD 80s, was still comprised of a large number of individuals who saw themselves as both Jewish and Christians. Matthew designed his Gospel to be an aid in his community's debate with Jews who were not Christian. Secondly, Matthew intended that his Gospel would help Jewish Christians to understand the Jewish roots of their faith.

Matthew begins his Gospel with an emphasis on Jewish origins of the community. The genealogy of Jesus begins with Abraham, the father of the Jewish faith. Also in Matthew, Jesus' ministry, which in Mark included Gentiles, was directed entirely to Jews (Mt 10:5–6, 23). Also in the Gospel of Matthew:

- Jesus also strongly *affirmed* Jewish law (5:17–19) and interprets it at length (5:21, 27, 33, 38, 43).

- The Gospel also presumes a number of Jewish religious activities, including participation at the Jewish temple (5:23–24), almsgiving and fasting

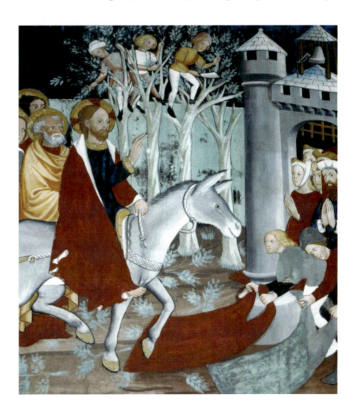

if done secretly (6:1–4, 16–18), cleansings to achieve ritual purity (8:4), paying the temple tax (17:24–27), tithing (23:23), and observance of both the Sabbath and the Passover (24:20; 26:17–20).

- The author also deleted Mark's explanation about Jewish customs (compare Mark 7:3–4 and Matthew 15:1–3). Matthew's audience, with its significant number of Jewish-Christian members, apparently didn't need such explanations because they already understood their own Jewish practices.

Some of the changes Matthew made to Mark's text to restore a more authentically Jewish flavor to Jesus' life are very subtle and easily missed. For example, in Mark's Gospel, a woman who had been bleeding for twelve years reached out and touched Jesus' cloak (Mk 5:27–29), whereas in Matthew 9:20, she touched the "tassel on his cloak." The Torah required observant Jewish men to wear *tzi tzit*, or "tassels," on the four corners of their outer garment (Nm 15:38–39; Dt 22:12; see also Mt 23:5, where scribes and the Pharisees "lengthen their tassels").

In essence, the Gospel of Matthew seems quite aware of and sensitive to Jewish sensibilities, practices, and beliefs. That Jesus was an observant Jew should be obvious, but Matthew's Gospel makes the point more clearly than the others, in great part because the author was almost certainly Jewish, as was a significant proportion of his audience. They understood, appreciated, and identified with Jesus' native culture in ways that Mark's community could not.

Jesus, the New Moses

One of Matthew's considerations was how he could help his largely Jewish-Christian readers understand that Jesus was the Messiah called forth in the Old Testament. One of his starting points was to compare Jesus to Moses, the greatest figure in the history of the Jewish people.

Toward this end, beginning in the stories of Jesus' infancy, we can see certain parallels between Jesus and Moses. Just as Pharaoh attempted to kill all Jewish male babies, including Moses (Ex 1:15–2:9), King Herod desired to kill the infant Jesus and ended up slaying the innocent male children in Bethlehem (Mt 2:3, 7–8, 16–18). Both Moses and Jesus (through Joseph) are sent to Egypt (Ex 4:19; Mt 2:13–15). In bringing the people from Egypt to the land of Israel, Moses became the savior of the Israelites; Jesus, too, left Egypt for Israel, and became the Savior of *all* people (Mt 2:19–21).

Moses was, at least according to ancient tradition, considered to be the human author of the five books of the Pentateuch (see Chapter 1A, "The Pentateuch", pages 30–71). Jesus' teachings (with much of the material taken from "Q") are arranged in Matthew's Gospel into five sermons: the Sermon on the Mount (Mt 5:3–7:27), the Mission Sermon (Mt 10:5–42), the Sermon of Parables (Mt 13:3–52), a sermon on sin, forgiveness, and the Church (Mt 18:1–35), and the Eschatological Sermon (Mt 24:4–25:46). The five sermons in the Gospel of Matthew are thought to parallel the five books of the Pentateuch.

Matthew also notes significant contrasts between Moses and Jesus. From the beginning, the powerful have been at odds with God's plan for the world. There is a new twist, though, on this old story that will hover over the story of Jesus until it is brought home in Jesus' suffering and Death. Moses was threatened by foreigners, but Jesus was threatened, from the beginning, by his own people. Also, while Moses passed on the Law that he received at Mount Sinai, Jesus didn't simply extend the Old Law; he instituted changes to it in his *own* name (for example, by the words "you have heard it said . . . but *I* tell you"). In essence, Matthew taught that Jesus was not simply another Moses, or someone *like* Moses. He was *greater* than Moses, for all things had been handed over to Jesus (Mt 11:27). In this way, the Gospel of Matthew emphasizes the divinity of Jesus.

Matthew also presents Jesus as the founder of the Church. The leaders of the Church should be humble, careful to avoid scandal, forgiving, prayerful, and willing to serve even to the point of suffering. Catholics see in

Matthew's commissioning of Peter as "rock" (Mt 16:18–19) not only Jesus' clear founding of the Church, but also his establishment of a hierarchical leadership headed by Peter and the Apostles and their successors, the pope and the bishops. Christ himself is the source of the apostolic leadership in the Church. After his Resurrection, the Risen Christ gives the eleven remaining Apostles a share in his own mission: "Go, therefore, and makes disciples of all nations, baptizing them in the name of the Father, and of the Son, and of the holy Spirit" (Mt 28:19). From him, they receive the power to act in his name. This is known as the Great Commission.

Review

1. How does Matthew's description of Jesus' disciples differ from Mark's description?

2. What is the "Q" source?

3. Whom did Matthew write his Gospel for?

4. What are the five sermons in the Gospel of Matthew thought to parallel?

5. How did Matthew emphasize the divinity of Jesus?

Reflect

Describe someone you know or are aware of who models humble servant leadership.

The Gospel of Luke

Like the Gospel of Matthew, Luke's Gospel is approximately dated in the 80s AD. This would have given Mark's Gospel time to be hand-copied and circulated by missionaries to communities other than Mark's own.

Luke's own eloquence marked him as well educated, almost certainly from a well-to-do background. There are various theories concerning where Luke wrote, but most are very uncertain. A number of scholars suggest that Luke wrote in Syria, but their evidence is quite slim.

Both of his books, the Gospel of Luke and Acts of the Apostles, are addressed to a "most excellent Theophilus." This form of greeting is used only three other times in the Bible in reference to Festus, the procurator of Judea from AD 52 to 60 (Acts 23:26; 24:3; 26:25). The name "Theophilus" means "friend of God" or "one who loves God." As far back as Church Father Origen, it has been suggested that Luke intended this Gospel for anyone devoted to God, including you. One could also well presume that Luke had a patron of some importance, named Theophilus, for whom he wrote his Gospel.

Differences between Luke and Mark

Luke used roughly 85 percent of the material from Mark's Gospel, about 560 of Mark's 660 verses and roughly forty verses less than Matthew incorporated from Mark. As noted, the author of Luke was a much better educated man than Mark. Luke understood the finer conventions of how to write, had a better vocabulary, and had a desire to put things in a manner he considered "accurate" and "orderly" (Lk 1:3). When placing Mark side by side with Luke, we can see that Luke improved on Mark's grammar, diction, and syntax. He also removed Latin words that had crept into Mark's narrative, such as "census" and "centurion," which proper Greek speakers thought were *vulgar*. He replaced them with the appropriate Greek terms.

Luke also changed some of the chronology of Mark's narrative to a more logical order. For example, in Mark's Gospel, the first time Jesus meets Peter, James, and John is when he calls them to be his followers. They immediately drop their nets and leave their boats to follow him (Mk 1:16–20). Mark then positions the cure of Peter's mother-in-law quickly after the calling of the disciples in Mark 1:30–31. Luke apparently didn't think it was very rational for Peter, James, and John to abandon their livelihood for someone they didn't really know, so he moved the cure of Peter's mother-in-law to a place *before* the call of the three disciples. Luke may have reasoned that Peter, James, and John would have more desire to follow Jesus *after* they had witnessed his amazing ability to cure.

Luke's willingness to change Mark's chronology offers the clear indication that Luke, while valuing the story of Jesus' life that he received from Mark, didn't view it as an orderly, historical presentation that had to be preserved unchanged. Luke was apparently influenced by the need to provide his own well-educated, and probably affluent, Gentile-Greek readers with the kind of orderly and rational narrative that would have appealed to their educated and philosophical worldviews.

Some other differences between Luke and Mark are subtler. For example, Luke didn't feel it was necessary to provide the impression, given by Mark, that Jesus was a peasant. In the story of the healing of the paralyzed man who is lowered through the roof, Mark's version has the men who are carrying the paralytic enter through the roof, as it was apparently a peasant dwelling with mud laid over branches and sticks and regularly painted to keep it from decaying into mud during the rainy season (Mk 2:4). In Luke's version of this same event, the men remove roof tiles, the kind of architectural detail found in the first century in the dwellings and businesses of the affluent (Lk 5:19). In other words, in Luke's Gospel, the miracle takes place in a nicer building.

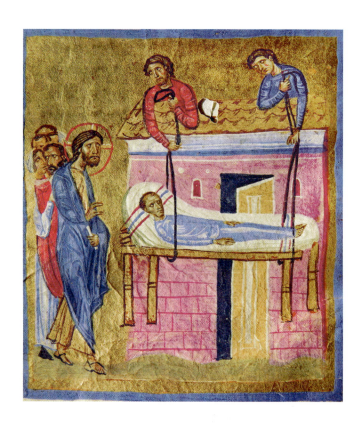

Think about how teachers today have to shape their lessons according to their students' ages, abilities, and cultures. For example, a math teacher can only introduce algebra to students who have been given a foundation in basic math operations. Or, lessons of apartheid in South Africa might be taught differently to children who have heard family stories about the experience of segregation in America versus those who haven't. Likewise, Luke had to shape even the minute details of the Gospel in a way that aided his affluent, Greek-speaking audience to better understand. Luke's audience may have traditionally looked down on peasants and considered them too uneducated to take seriously. Being from this social class, Luke must have been able to work past any of his own prejudices because of the sheer power of the Good News. He wanted to share the heart of the Gospel—that "Jesus is Lord"—with his well-educated contemporaries, but he realized that he had to finesse the narrative to make it more accessible for them. Toward this end, Luke even includes the one incident in the entire New Testament that would communicate to his readers that Jesus himself was literate. Luke 4:16–21 reveals that when Jesus went into the synagogue on the Sabbath, as was his custom, he read from the scroll of Isaiah.

Other differences between Luke's Gospel and Mark's Gospel were necessitated by technical details. The author of Luke had a considerable amount of additional material beyond what was in Mark. As bound books had not yet been invented, he had to live within the realistic limitations of how long a scroll could be without becoming awkward for the reader to manage. With 19,482 Greek words in Luke, and 18,451 in Acts (recall that the author of Luke is also the author of the Acts of the Apostles), these works are the two longest in the New Testament, making up about one-quarter of the whole. As one unrolled one side of the scroll, one had to roll up the other. After a certain length, about the size of the Gospel of Luke, the process became too cumbersome. Today, a scroll of the Torah in contemporary synagogues is very difficult to manage.

With this technicality in mind, Luke had to do some radical editing to Mark's Gospel if he wanted to include his own material or else make other technical adjustments. His choices were to (1) write on a massive scroll too clumsy to use, (2) leave out some of the great teaching material and parables he was aware of, but which weren't in Mark's Gospel (e.g., the Prodigal Son and the Good Samaritan), or (3) simplify and reduce details and repetition in Mark's Gospel. He chose the third option. As a result, he edited Mark in a significant way. For example, the story of the multiplication of the loaves is told twice in Mark (6:34–44; 8:1–9) but only once in Luke (9:12–17).

🜨 Reflect

Share an example of how your ability and culture has impacted the way that you learn.

INFANCY NARRATIVES

Mark's Gospel begins with Jesus already an adult. Mark offers the reader only a little information about Jesus' origins: that he was from Nazareth in Galilee (Mk 1:9), had been a carpenter, was the son of Mary, and was a relative ("brother") of James, Joses, Judas, and Simon (Mk 6:3).

Matthew and Luke, however, both begin with the details leading up to Jesus' birth. They agree on a number of key points:

- The narratives begin when Mary and Joseph were legally engaged or, perhaps, married, but neither living together nor sexually involved with each other (Mt1:18; Lk 1:27, 34).

- Joseph was a descendant of David (Mt 1:16, 20; Lk 1:27, 32; 2:4).

- An angel announces the coming birth of a baby named Jesus (Mt 1:20-23; Lk 1:30-35).

- The baby would be a Savior (Mt 1:21; Lk 2:11).

- Mary conceived, *not* through sexual relations with Joseph, but by the Holy Spirit (Mt 1:18-24; Lk 1:34-35).

- Jesus was born after Mary and Joseph lived together as a family (Mt 1:24-25; Lk 2:5-6) in the town of Bethlehem (Mt 2:1; Lk 2:4-6) while Herod the Great was still king (Mt 2:1; Lk 1:5).

- Jesus grew up in Nazareth (Mt 2:23; Lk 2:39).

The infancy narratives in Matthew and Luke also have some striking differences. For example, in Luke, the Angel Gabriel only speaks to Mary (Lk 1:26-38). In Matthew, an unnamed angel speaks only to Joseph (Mt 1:20, 24; 2:13, 19). In Matthew's Gospel, there is no mention of the angelic choirs and the adoration of the shepherds found in Luke 2:8-18. In Luke's Gospel, there is no visit or gifts from the magi (Mt 2:1-13). The genealogy is also different in Luke's Gospel; unlike in Matthew where the family tree of Jesus extends to Abraham, the father of the Jewish faith, and is placed at the beginning of the Gospel, Luke's geneaolgy begins with Adam, the father of the human race, and is placed near the start of Jesus' public ministry (Lk 3:23-38).

While these differences could be simply omissions on the part of one or the other, some differences are also irreconcilable. For example, in Luke, Joseph's original home is in Nazareth, and Jesus only ended up being born and placed in a manger in Bethlehem (there is no mention of a stable, by the way) because of a census (Lk 2:1-7). In Matthew, however, Joseph appears to live in Bethlehem, itself, and it would seem that Jesus was born at home (no mention of a manger) where magi visit him (Mt 2:9-11). Matthew also adds a story, missing from Luke, in which Joseph takes Mary and Jesus to Egypt to escape Herod's attempt to slay the infant. After Herod's death, they don't return to their "home" in Bethlehem, but go to live in Nazareth because they want to live far from Herod's son, Archelaus (Mt 2:13-23). So, while in both stories Jesus is born in the same town, Bethlehem, and grows up in the same village, Nazareth, the explanations as to how this happened are quite different in each Gospel.

Speaking from a strictly historical perspective, *both* Luke and Matthew cannot be accurate. Joseph's home can't originally have been in Nazareth and Bethlehem at the same time. The Church is content to understand these narratives, but not so much as history, even though they certainly contain historical details. Determining what is historical and what is "creative" has kept biblical scholars busy for centuries now. Rather, it would seem, each Gospel writer, as inspired by the Holy Spirit, took those details known to them about Jesus' early years (perhaps including some of the shared common material as given above), and fleshed them out into creative introductions. They used these forewords, not so much as sources for history, but to lay out for us important themes that would echo throughout Jesus' life and ministry in their distinctive Gospels.

The Needs of the Poor

Throughout Luke's Gospel, Jesus draws the attention of his disciples to the needs of the poor. This focus is indicated, in part, by the way that Luke shapes the traditions he receives. In Matthew's Gospel, Jesus teaches, "Blessed are the poor *in spirit*" (Mt 5:3). In Luke, Jesus says more simply and cuttingly, "Blessed are the poor" (Luke 6:20). In Mark, Jesus tells a rich young man to sell what he has and give it to the poor, not making it clear whether he has to sell some, most, or all of his possessions (Mk 10:21). In Luke there is no doubt: Jesus tells him to sell *all* that he has (Lk 18:22). Also, everyone, bad and good alike, are invited in Jesus' parable of the wedding feast in Matthew 22:9–10. In Luke's version, the servants are specifically instructed to invite "the poor and the crippled, the blind and the lame" (Lk 14:21).

Luke also has a number of passages unique to his Gospel that involve the poor. For example:

- After warning his hearers to avoid greed, Jesus related a parable of a foolish rich man who, thinking that life was about his possessions, lost everything at his death (12:13–21).

- Jesus instructs his hosts to invite the poor when they throw banquets (14:13).

- He tells a parable of a rich man burning in hell while the poor beggar Lazarus rests in the bosom of Abraham in Heaven (16:19–31).

- After Jesus agrees to eat dinner at his house, Zacchaeus offers to give half of his possessions to the poor (19:8).

The key for understanding this focus, perhaps, lies in a unique vignette in Luke in which Jesus, at the beginning of his public ministry, announces that he

has been anointed to "bring glad tiding to the poor," to heal the conditions of blindness and captivity that lead to poverty, and to free the oppressed (Lk 4:18). This teaching, rooted in Isaiah 61:1, is clearly Jesus' "mission statement" in Luke's Gospel. The remainder of the Gospel is a witness to how Jesus lived out this message in his healing and teaching.

It may seem curious that Luke, coming from an affluent family with access to lots of privilege himself, was so clearly focused on the care of the poor and the necessity of setting aside worldly goods and pursuits for the sake of the Gospel. It probably wouldn't have made much sense, though, for Mark, whose intended audience stood a very good chance of being even less educated and poorer than he was, to stress the care of the poor. On the other hand, the affluent and powerful who made up Luke's audience were better able to do something positive about the conditions of those who had little. As a result, Luke had to be more forthright and challenging to his audience while addressing poverty and possessions.

Jesus identified with the poor and lowly. He came into the world humbly. He came to proclaim the Gospel to the poor (Lk 7:22). Generous service of God and others, with compassion for the poor and outcast, are mandatory for all followers of Jesus.

Reflect

"Compassion for the poor and outcast are mandatory for followers of Jesus." How do you plan to keep this command?

Prayer in Luke's Gospel

Another theme that threads its way throughout Luke's Gospel is the importance of prayer. Prayer is mentioned or witnessed in Luke almost as many times as it appears in the three other Gospels combined. The Gospel narrative begins, in fact, with the people gathered for prayer in the Temple in Jerusalem at the hour of incense (Lk 1:10). At that time, the Angel Gabriel appeared to announce to the priest, Zechariah, that his prayer for a child had been heard and would be answered (Lk 1:13).

In Luke, Jesus himself gave firm directives to his followers to pray—even to pray for those who mistreated them (Lk 6:28). When asked, he also offered an example of how to pray in a simple form of the Our Father (Lk 11:1–4). He used parables to encourage his followers to be diligent in prayer (Lk 11:5–13) and to pray without growing weary (Lk 18:1–8).

Jesus practiced what he preached in this regard. He offered an example by praying at important moments throughout his life. In fact, prayer bookends the beginning of his public ministry and the end of his life. Jesus prayed immediately after being baptized (Lk 3:21). His words before dying were words of prayer to the Father commending up his spirit (Lk 23:46). In the midst of his public life, Jesus withdrew away from the crowds to pray by himself (Lk 5:15–16; 6:12; 9:18, 28; 11:1; 22:41). During the Transfiguration Jesus' glory was revealed on the mountaintop while in prayer (Lk 9:28–29). Among his most dramatic acts was his defense of the Temple as a house of prayer against those who "made it a den of thieves" (Lk 19:45–46).

The Holy Spirit is the constant companion to prayer. This is cited in many places in Luke's Gospel: for example, Jesus prays full of power in the Spirit (10:21) and teaches his followers to pray for the Holy Spirit (11:13).

Reflect

When was a key time in your life when you relied on prayer?

Women in Luke's Gospel

Since very few women were allowed formal education in the ancient world, almost all literature that comes to us from those times was written by men, for other men, and about interests and concerns that mattered to men. In this regard, it isn't surprising that Matthew's Gospel framed the entire narrative of Jesus' infancy from Joseph's perspective. So, it is extraordinary that Luke viewed the Annunciation, birth of Jesus, and his infancy through the eyes of Mary (see "Infancy

Narrative," page 216). The first chapter of Luke also contains the words of Mary spoken in a canticle known as the Magnificat (Lk 1:39–56).

Luke's focus on women does not end with Mary. Jesus ministered directly with women, noticing their needs and responding to them. For example, he brought back to life the only son of a desperate widow in the city of Nain (Lk 7:11–15). Again, when a woman broke into the "male only" meal with Simon the Pharisee, Jesus not only affirmed her initiative, flowing as it did from her great love, but also defended her from the unjust judgment of others and forgave her sins (7:36–50).

A careful reading of Luke's text indicates that Jesus had close friends who were women. Martha and Mary shared the kind of friendly intimacy with Jesus that allowed Mary to sit at Jesus' feet in the role of a disciple that was usually reserved for men and Martha to chide Jesus for not encouraging Mary to get up off the ground to help her with the hospitality (Lk 10:38–42).

Luke also had the unique tendency to balance bringing *both* women and men to center stage around some of the most important moments in the Gospel, to the point of providing parallel episodes for this to occur. For example, in the Presentation of Jesus in the Temple, Jesus was greeted and recognized not only by a holy man, Simeon (Lk 2:25–35), but also by the prophetess Anna (2:36–38). When Jesus described how God seeks out the sinner, he told a story for men about a shepherd who went searching for a lost sheep (Lk 15:4–7), immediately followed by the story of a woman seeking a lost coin of some value (15:8–10). In that latter parable, the woman herself was a metaphor for God.

Most significantly, it is women who witness Jesus' Death on the Cross (23:46–49), see the tomb where Jesus is laid (23:55), and discover it empty (24:1). These women were the first to proclaim Jesus' Resurrection to the Eleven and the other disciples, though undoubtedly because of prejudice, they were not believed. Why? Because they were women (Lk 24:8–9). However, by the same token, note how the inclusion of the women's testimony in Luke's Gospel actually strengthens the historical evidence of these events. The fact that Luke records testimony of women who were usually disregarded by their peers offers credibility to the claim of the Resurrection, an essential element of the Christian faith from the beginning.

The Passion Narrative

While Matthew was fairly faithful to Mark's Passion narrative, Luke seems to draw on a unique set of traditions, all the while significantly reordering what he did receive from Mark.

Luke portrays Jesus' disciples in a much more positive light. Whereas Mark's Gospel predicts that the disciples will be scattered and scandalized (Mk 14:27), Luke praises them for standing by Jesus and records Jesus' promise to them that they will sit on twelve thrones, judging "the twelve tribes of Israel" (Lk 22:28–30). Luke also omits two of Mark's scenes, the first in which Peter, James, and John fell asleep three times in the Garden of Gethsemane (Mk 14:37–41), and the second when the disciples fled from Christ at the moment of his arrest (Mk 14:50–52). Mark also presents an extended narrative of Peter's failure to acknowledge his connection to Jesus in the courtyard of the high priest during Jesus' trial there (Mk 14:66–72), On the other hand, Luke frames Peter's denial as Satan's demand, and includes Jesus' prayer that Peter's faith not fail, saying, "once you have turned back again, you must strengthen your brothers" (Lk 22:31–32).

Luke also portrays Jesus' actions differently from the other Synoptic Gospels. Some of Jesus' actions unique to Luke's Gospel are:

- Jesus healing the right ear of the high priest's servant that had been cut off with a sword (22:50–51).

- Jesus negotiating the end of the rift between Herod Antipas, Tetrarch of Galilee, and Pontius Pilate, the Roman governor of Judea (23:6–12).

- Jesus comforting the women of Jerusalem who "mourned and lamented him" (23:27–31).

- Jesus offering Paradise to the good criminal on the cross who recognizes that Jesus was being convicted, though innocent (23:39–43).

- Jesus saying, "Father, forgive them; they know not what they are doing" as he hung on the Cross (23:34).

Also, only in Luke's Gospel did Jesus remind Peter of Jesus' earlier prediction that Peter would deny Jesus (Lk 22:61–62). Also, only in Luke was Jesus sent by Pilate to King Herod where he was mocked but also clothed in "resplendent garb" (23:6–12). Jesus apparently wore these garments all the way to the place where he was crucified. Whereas in Mark's Gospel, Jesus gave out "a loud cry and breathed his last" (Mk 15:37), in Luke, Jesus was in control even until the very end, saying, "Father into your hands I commend my spirit," choosing both the moment and the manner of his own Death, surrendering nothing to his executioners (Lk 23:46). While in Mark's Gospel, all was bleak, and Jesus appeared to die alone, in Luke, the centurion present glorified God, acknowledging that Jesus was truly innocent (Lk 23:47), while "all his acquaintances stood at a distance, including the women" (23:49). The crowds, for their part, repented in Luke, going "home beating their breasts" (Lk 23:48). A Lucan theme is to follow in the footsteps of Jesus as he followed the will of his Father. In these events, the will of God is accomplished. Luke's Gospel also uniquely adds the Resurrection narrative of the Emmaus journey and the disciples recognition of Jesus in the "breaking of the bread" (Lk 24:13–35).

Luke, of course, continues his "second volume" with the Acts of the Apostles (see "Acts of thte Apostles," pages 230–237). In both works, demonstrating concern for historical detail, Luke wrote to show his readers that their faith in the Lord was reliable.

⊙ Review

1. How did Luke make the chronology of his Gospel more logical than Mark's?

2. What evidence from Luke's Gospel is there that Jesus was literate?

3. How does the Church understand the historical differences between the infancy narratives of Matthew and Luke?

4. Why does it make sense that Luke, from an affluent background, would focus on the care of the poor?

5. Name two occasions cited by Luke in Jesus' life when he prayed?

6. Why was it unique that Luke focused much of his Gospel around women?

7. How does Luke portray Jesus being in control of his life to the very end?

The Gospel of John

As mentioned earlier, the Gospel of John is now commonly dated approximately at AD 90. The Gospel of John is unique in the fact that though the author may have shared written or oral traditions with Mark's Gospel and have known certain traditions that appear in Luke's Gospel, the fourth Gospel does not rely on any of the Synoptic Gospels. Rather, his sources are independent traditions preserved in the churches from which they were created.

Though the Gospel of John is expansive of early Christian theology, its outline is relatively simple. After a short and important prologue, only two major sections follow this introduction. The first is called the Book of Signs, which treats Jesus' public ministry. The second major division is the Book of Glory. Beginning with the Last Supper and extending to Jesus' Resurrection, this section of the Gospel includes theologically rooted discourses given by Jesus. An epilogue, probably added later, includes Jesus' appearances in Galilee. The outline of the Gospel of John:

Prologue: "Word made flesh" (1:1-18)

Part 1: Book of Signs (1:19-12:50)

- The wedding at Cana (2:1–11)
- The cure of the royal official's son (4:46–54)
- The cure of the paralytic (5:1–18)
- The multiplication of loaves (6:1–15)
- The walking on water (6:16–21)
- The healing of the man born blind (9:1–41)
- The raising of Lazarus (11:1–44)

Part 2: Book of Glory (13:1-20:31)

- The Last Supper (13–17)
- The Passion and Death of Jesus (18–19)
- The Resurrection (20)

Epilogue: Appearances in Galilee (21)

In John's Gospel, theological insight is often presented in simple, contrasting images (e.g., life and death, light and darkness, flesh and spirit, glory and eternal life) that at the same time convey deep and profound meaning.

The Beloved Disciple

The Gospel of John is popularly attributed to John, called the Evangelist, the brother of James, both sons of Zebedee (Mk 1:19; Jn 21:2). According to this tradition, he was also the author of the Book of Revelation, which clearly indicates its author's name as John (Rv 1:1–4), and also that he had been exiled to the island of Patmos, in the Aegean Sea (Rv 1:9). The Gospel, however, while never mentioning the name of its author, credits its composition to a certain disciple whom Jesus loved: "It is this disciple who testifies to these things and has written them, and we know that his testimony is true" (Jn 21:20–24). Just because the verse says that the disciple "has written them" does

not necessarily mean that he wrote them with his own hand. Similarly, referring to the inscription above Jesus on the Cross, Pilate said, "What I have written, I have written" (Jn 19:22). In that case as well, we can be rather certain that Pilate would not have written the inscription himself. Also, John's community likely omitted his name out of respect for Jesus, but couldn't help referring to him as the disciple whom Jesus loved.

This "beloved disciple" appears in at least four places in the Gospel. He is first identified as such at the Last Supper, where he was reclining on the same couch as, and just in front of, Jesus, as was common in feasts of that time (Jn 13:23–25). His closeness to Jesus indicated a position of high favor, according to the customs of the first century, where up to five people could recline on the same couch to eat.

He next appears at the foot of the Cross at the Crucifixion. He is the only one of Jesus' male disciples with the courage to be present. Jesus' great trust in this disciple was evident in his decision to give the care of his own Mother into the beloved disciple's hands: "Then he said to the disciple [whom he loved], 'Behold, your mother.'" (Jn 19:25–27).

The beloved disciple surfaces seventeen verses later in Peter's company, when Mary of Magdala reports that Jesus' body has been removed from the tomb. Both Peter and this disciple run to the tomb to verify her report. The disciple arrives at the empty tomb first, where he sees the head cloth and believes (Jn 20:1–9).

Finally, in the last of his appearances, Peter asks Jesus what would become of the disciple Jesus loved (21:20–24). Jesus cautions Peter, in response, to focus on following Jesus, and not on the affairs of the disciple. This last passage indicates that the Gospel was later edited to explain the beloved disciple's death for those who believed he would live until the Lord's return.

It should be noted that this beloved disciple is *never* named "John" in any of these passages. Whoever the beloved disciple was, he was clearly both a disciple and eyewitness to Jesus, and also the founder of a community that had taken his message of the Good News to heart. He passed on his memories of Jesus to this community. This disciple probably did not refer to himself as Jesus' "beloved disciple." It seems more likely that the community he had brought to faith by his evangelism referred to him that way, in essence, because *they* loved him. He must have been a very special person. They were convinced that Jesus must have loved their founder with as much enthusiasm as they did. If this is true, he was able to engender this love from others, all the while never making the message center on himself; it was always about Jesus.

 ## Reflect

Why is it important to you to put Jesus first in your life?

Authorship of John's Gospel

Members of this community took the beloved disciple's teachings, and under the inspiration of the Holy Spirit, fashioned them into the cohesive narrative of the Gospel. It wasn't a simple process and clearly required a certain amount of editing, some of which may have been composed while the beloved disciple was still alive, but some of which was clearly written after his death.

There is evidence for new material added to an original draft in several places. For example, in John 14:31, Jesus, after having spoken for almost two full chapters in his final address, says, "Get up, let us go." But they *don't* get up and go. Instead, Jesus continued speaking for another three chapters! Those chapters seem to be important material added at some later point to the original text. Another place where you can see this editing process is at the end of chapter 20:

> Now Jesus did many other signs in the presence of [his] disciples that are not written in this book. But these are written that you may [come to] believe that Jesus is the Messiah, the Son of God, and that through this belief you may have life in his name. (Jn 20:30–31)

These two verses were probably the original formal conclusion of the Gospel. Chapter 21 appears to be an addition, written sometime after the death of the beloved disciple (since John 21:21–23 actually refer to his death!). Chapter 21 provides a rich post-Resurrection account of Jesus and the disciples.

Four other works have also been attributed to "John the Evangelist": The First, Second, and Third Letters of John, and the Revelation to John (Book of Revelation). There is a similar vocabulary, theology, and focus between the Gospel and the three letters, but stylistic differences suggest the same people probably did not write them. The authors seem to be interested, at least in part, in correcting some unfortunate interpretations of the Gospel, perhaps by **Gnostics**.

Gnostics
A generic term to describe adherents to a variety of pre- and early Christian heresies that taught that Salvation rests on secret knowledge (*gnosis* in Greek).

With even greater certainty, experts in Greek style and vocabulary are firm that the authors of "John's" Gospel did not write Revelation. Even a casual skimming of the Gospel and Revelation in English suggests a completely different style of writing and perspective between these two works.

Comparing John's Gospel to the Synoptic Gospels

John's Gospel differs in many ways from the Synoptic Gospels. For example, there are new characters like Nicodemus, Lazarus, a man born blind, and a Samaritan woman. Jesus attends three Passover festivals, not one, and makes several trips to Jerusalem for various festivals. Jesus' teaching usually takes the form of long discourses, not pithy sayings or parables. Even in those occasional instances when John covers similar events that the Synoptic Gospels do (e.g., the multiplication of loaves), there is unique content. Compare, for example, John 6:1–14 and Mark 6:35–46.

In addition, John's Gospel is very poetic, thus presenting a more solemn and holy Jesus. Stylistically, it uses literary techniques like irony (where opponents often say things about Jesus that have deeper meanings than they realize), plays on words, metaphors (implied comparisons), figurative language to help clarify the many misunderstandings people have of him, and other similar techniques.

The content of the Gospel focuses on Jesus as God's Revelation, one who shows us the way to the Father, and it does not stress the Kingdom of God the way the Synoptics do. In John, the term "Kingdom" occurs only twice (Jn 3:3, 5). In Matthew's Gospel, the title "Son of Man" is used thirty times; in Luke it occurs twenty-five times, along with a strong focus on the meaning of discipleship. While John's Gospel does touch on discipleship (Jn 13:13–17), "Son of Man" appears only twelve times.

The framing of time is also different in John. For example, the Synoptic Gospels give an uncertain impression on the length of Jesus' ministry. John's Gospel mentions three Passovers (Jn 1:13; 6:4; 12:1) while only one Passover is included in each of the other Gospels. Thus, according to John's Gospel, Jesus' public ministry was at least three years in length. This time frame seems more plausible, especially since the Synoptic Gospels detail how Jesus captured a certain fame, drew interested crowds from Tyre and Sidon in the north, Jerusalem in the south, and beyond the Jordan River to the east (Mk 3:8; Lk 6:17, and Mt 4:25). A longer public ministry makes it easier to understand how people from such distant places would have heard of Jesus and been willing to journey long distances, almost exclusively by foot, to be with him.

As in the other Gospels, John introduces the public life of Jesus through the ministry of John the Baptist. However, the inclusion of Jesus' baptism is barely alluded to (Jn 1:29–34). There is no mention at all of Jesus' temptation in the desert. Rather, the Gospel moves right to Jesus' call of his disciples. However, unlike in the Synoptics (Mk 1:16–20; Mt 4:18–22; Lk 5:2–11) where Jesus calls Simon Peter to follow him while Simon is with his boat, in John's Gospel Jesus calls Simon's *brother*, Andrew, to follow first. Andrew, in turn, seeks out Simon and brings him to Jesus (Jn 1:35–51). Jesus then gives Simon the new name, "Kephas" or "Peter," on the spot, not waiting for Peter to identify him as the Messiah as in Matthew 16:25–20.

There is a different placement of Jesus' cleansing of the Temple in John's Gospel. In John, this incident occurs early in the Gospel, in John 2:13–25. The Synoptics place the cleansing of the Temple toward the end of their narratives (Mt 21:12–16; Mk 11:15–18; Lk 19:45–48), each recounting how the chief priests were offended by Jesus' actions so much that they would seek his Death within a week of this action. This example points out how the order of the Gospel narratives was determined more by theological concerns than chronological data.

The Last Supper is also placed differently in John's Gospel, where it is described as taking place on the day *before* Passover, the date when the Passover lamb was traditionally slaughtered (Jn 13:1 and Ex 12:1–8). This placement shows that the slaughter of the Passover lamb foreshadowed the Death of Jesus. Both deaths pointed to God's action in the world. Jesus' Death brought about Salvation and Redemption for humankind.

 # Reflect

What part of your life would be difficult to drop altogether in order to follow Jesus?

Unique Elements of John's Gospel

The organization of John's Gospel into two books, the Book of Signs and the Book of Glory, is a distinct feature. The Book of Signs is organized around seven miracles. In contrast to the Synoptic Gospels which describe miracles as "acts of power" (*dynamis* in the Greek), John uses either the word *ergon* (work) or *semeion* (sign) to describe Jesus' miracles. Similarly, the Old Testament referred to the *works* of God that brought Israel out of Egypt at the time of the Exodus and the *signs* of God performed through Moses.

The Book of Glory, the second major part of John's Gospel, consists of two main sections: the Last Supper discourses (Jn 13–17) and Jesus' Death and Resurrection in John 18–20. Jesus is both "lifted up" on the Cross and "lifted up" from the tomb to everlasting glory. In the Last Supper discourses, Jesus offers his priestly prayer that prepares his Apostles for his hour of glory—his Passion—promises them the Holy Spirit, and instructs them how to live after his Resurrection. While the Synoptic Gospels and 1 Corinthians 23–26 all recount the moment on the night before Jesus died when he blessed bread and wine and pronounced the words of consecration of the first Eucharist, John's Gospel does not. John's Gospel does go to much greater depth explaining the significance and purpose of Jesus' Body and Blood being real food and real drink (Jn 6:26–59).

A summary of some of the other main distinct elements in John's Gospel follows.

Teachings on Love

The Gospels of Matthew, Mark, and Luke recognize *love* as the summation of the Law and the prophets, and worth more than all ritual sacrifices (Mt 22:36–40, Mk 12:28–33, Lk 10:25–28). John's Gospel is more concerned with defining love itself, clarifying, for example:

- God's great love for the world (3:16; 16:27; 17:23),
- the Father and the Son's love for each other (3:35; 5:20; 10:17; 14:31; 15:9; 17:24–26),
- our need to love God (21:15–17),
- the Lord's command that we love each other (13:34–35; 15:12, 17),
- Jesus' love for his disciples and friends (11:3, 5, 36; 13:1),
- and how to love according to the Lord's commandments (12:25; 14:15–28; 15:10–13).

John's Gospel teaches that we are to first *accept* love, particularly as it is expressed by Jesus' willingness to die for us (Jn 3:16). Then we are to *commit* to loving one another, even to the point of offering our lives for each other. Being a true disciple of Christ is not for the faint hearted. The Gospel teaches clearly that the true definition of love is to lay down one's life, as Jesus did for us, and as we are to do for one another.

Teaching with Metaphors

In John's Gospel, Jesus teaches using metaphors. This is different from the approach of the Synoptic Gospels, which feature Jesus' parables as a prime method for teaching. Some of the key teaching metaphors are the following:

- "I am the bread of life" (6:35) and "I am the living bread" (6:51)
- "I am the light of the world" (8:12)
- "I am the gate for the sheep" (10:7), "the gate" (10:9), and "the good shepherd" (10:11)
- "I am the resurrection and the life" (11:25)
- "I am the way and the truth and the life" (14:6)
- "I am the true vine, and my Father is the vine grower" (15:1), and "you are the branches" (15:5)

These metaphors help us to come to a better understanding of **Christology**; that is, Jesus' identity as the Second Person of the Trinity and his relationship with his Father.

🌐 Reflect

Which metaphor that Christ uses to describe himself is your favorite?

Nicodemus

The Pharisee Nicodemus, a ruler of the Jews, was a recurring figure in John's Gospel, absent in the Synoptic Gospels.

He surfaces on three occasions, appearing first, somewhat secretly at night—perhaps needing to keep his interest private—and making inquiries into Jesus' identity and teachings (Jn 3:1–10). His understanding of Jesus, at least at first, is not particularly good.

He then appears four chapters later, when Jesus' teachings attract the attention of his fellow Jews. As a result, the chief priests and Pharisees made a failed effort to arrest Jesus (Jn 7:32, 44–49). In the aftermath of this incident, Nicodemus came to Jesus' defense, saying, "Does our law condemn a person before it first hears him and finds out what he is doing?" (Jn 7:50–52). At first courageous, Nicodemus then remained silent when treated contemptuously by his companions.

His third and final appearance occurs at the end of the Gospel, when all the disciples except the beloved disciple and the women were conspicuously

Christology
The branch of theology that studies the meaning of the person of Jesus Christ.

JEWISH PEOPLE ARE NOT RESPONSIBLE FOR THE DEATH OF JESUS

The use of the term "Jews" surrounding the Passion narrative in John's Gospel has at times insinuated that all Jewish people were somehow responsible for the Death of Jesus. This is not true and this belief is a form of **anti-Semitism** and contrary to the love of Christ. The Church teaches that:

> neither all Jews indiscriminately at that time, nor Jews today, can be charged with the crimes committed during the Passion. . . . [T]he Jews should not be spoken of as rejected or accursed as if this followed from holy Scripture. (*Declaration on the Relationship of the Church to Non-Christian Religions*, No. 4, *CCC*, 597)

anti-Semitism
Unfounded prejudice against the Jewish people.

statement of witness for Jesus. This Gospel invites believers, today, to do the same. Being a Christian means more than simply saying we *believe* in Jesus. Being a true disciple of Jesus requires us to *profess* that belief to others, even at great personal cost.

Reflect

How have you been a disciple like Nicodemus—silent or fearful about expressing your commitment to Christ?

Peter and the Beloved Disciple

John's Gospel sets up an interesting contrast between the beloved disciple and Peter. For example at the Last Supper, the beloved disciple is in closer proximity to Jesus than Peter (Jn 13:23); at the empty tomb the beloved disciple came to belief while Peter's faith remained in doubt (Jn 20:8). At the post-Resurrection appearance at the Sea of Tiberias, Peter was questioned three times on his love for Jesus, clearly a chance for him to repent of his three denials of Jesus in the high priest's courtyard (Jn 18:16–18, 25–27). At that same time, Jesus also chided Peter for asking impertinent questions of the beloved disciple (Jn 21:15–23). Also, at the foot of the Cross, when the beloved disciple was given the care of Jesus' Mother, Peter was very conspicuously absent (Jn 19:25–26).

absent. After Joseph of Arimathea arranged with Pilate to obtain Jesus' body in order to bury it, Nicodemus came with a large amount of myrrh and aloes to prepare Jesus' body for its internment (Jn 19:39–42). Though he assisted Jesus in these ways, he was never referred to as a disciple.

Nicodemus seems to represent Christians who were silent or fearful about expressing their commitment to Christ. John's Gospel invited them into a more public

What *is* clear from the mention of Peter in the Gospel in so many key places, including with Jesus after the Resurrection, is that the Johannine community was aware of Peter's primacy in the Church. The contrast of Peter with the beloved disciple also shows how John's community relished the opportunity to portray their own teacher in a positive light. These kinds of subtle differences between the Gospels highlight the rich diversity that has always highlighted

the Church, even as she earnestly pursued unity in belief and practice.

Christology in John's Gospel

Recall that Christology is the study of Jesus Christ, that is, trying to understand who he is. All of the Gospels are interested in Jesus Christ's identity, but the focus of John's Gospel stresses very strongly his heavenly origins, his fundamental identity as the Son of God, and his preexistence as the Word of God.

One of the most profound contributions of John's Gospel has been to clarify Jesus' identity and relationship with God the Father. This relationship is rooted in that profound moment, in the presence of the burning bush out in the desert by Horeb, when Moses had the inspiration to ask for the name of God. In answer, God identified himself as, "'I am who am.' Then he added, 'This is what you shall tell the Israelites: I AM sent me to you'" (Ex 3:1–17).

Jesus echoes these words in John 8:24 by describing himself in the same way: "For if you do not believe that I AM, you will die in your sins." By using these words, Jesus was teaching that he is God. Continuing his teaching, Jesus was asked by his contemporaries how he could speak so authoritatively about Abraham, as though he and Abraham were contemporaries. Jesus responded: "Amen, amen, I say to you, before Abraham came to be, I AM" (Jn 8:58). In essence, Jesus was teaching that not only is he God in the present, but he has always been God, even before he was born as a human, since he has always existed.

In fact, the Prologue to John's Gospel opens with this very teaching in a poem in which Jesus is identified as the "Word," always present with God, and always God:

> In the beginning was the Word,
>   and the Word was with God,
>   and the Word was God.
> He was in the beginning with God.
>   All things came to be through him,
>   and without him nothing came to be.
> What came to be through him was life,
>   and this life was the light of the human race.
>   the light shines in the darkness,
>   and the darkness has not overcome it. (Jn 1:1–5)

This passage speaks of the difference between the way God thinks and the way that humans do. Your thoughts, even when you are remembering someone you know and love very much, are incomplete and sketchy. When God thinks, though, the thoughts are so complete that things come into existence. All God has to do is think, "Let there be light," and, by virtue of him thinking that, "there is light" (Gn 1:3). So, you may ask, what happens when God thinks about himself? God's thoughts are not going to be incomplete or sketchy. That thought he has of himself is so complete, and so perfect, that it is more than a mirror *image* of God. His thought of himself is as complete as the original.

That *thought* is the "Word," in the passage above, or *logos* in Greek—a term that implies much more than the simple term "word" means in English. *Logos* can mean "message," "teaching," "extended speech," or "self-expression." It is in that latter sense that the term *logos* is used here. The "Word" described in the Prologue to John's Gospel is not a *different* God. It is the very same God, complete in every way, including complete enough to be conscious. This complete self-expression of God is called "God the Son."

As God the Father, and his complete and eternal *self*-expression, God the Son, consider each other, they are united in an endless love so great that it takes on an identity all its own, the God the Holy Spirit. As love is essentially *self-love*, it's not something or someone new. God the Son has always existed, since God has always been aware of himself, and has always had a complete understanding of himself. The Spirit has always existed, as God has always loved. This is why Jesus can say, "before Abraham was, *I AM*." As God, he has, in fact, always been. Through him, all other things came to

be as well, as God drew into existence everything else that is in further, but lesser, thoughts.

From the beginning the revealed truth of the **Holy Trinity** has been at the heart of the Church's living faith, principally by the means of Baptism. Drawing on Sacred Scripture and Sacred Tradition, the Church teaches the **dogma** of the Holy Trinity:

- *The Trinity is One.* There are not three Gods, but one God in Three Persons.

- *The Divine Persons are distinct from one another in their origins.* "It is the Father who generates, the Son who is begotten, and the Holy spirit who proceeds" (*CCC*, 255, quoting Lateran Council IV).

- *The Divine Persons relate to one another.* The Three Persons do not divide God's unity; they express their relationship to one another. Just as the Holy Trinity has only one divine nature, so they have only one divine operation. "However each divine person performs the common work according to his unique personal property" (*CCC*, 258). This is especially true in the divine missions of the Son's Incarnation and the gift of the Holy Spirit.

Catholics recognize that Jesus, born a human in time, was God present among us—not a new or different God from the One in Heaven, but one and the very same. This belief is found in the Synoptic Gospels and in the writings of St. Paul, but there is no place where it is stated as boldly or clearly as in John's Gospel.

Holy Trinity
The central mystery of the Christian faith. It teaches that that are Three Persons in one God: Father, Son, and Holy Spirit.

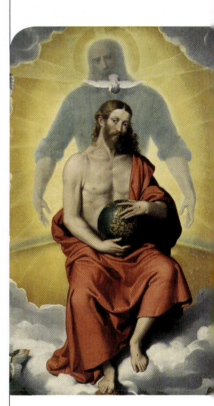

dogma
A central truth of Revelation that Catholics are obliged to believe.

⬤ Review

1. What are the two major sections of John's Gospel?

2. Who is the beloved disciple?

3. Why was the material after John 14:31 when Jesus says "Get up, let us go" likely added to the original?

4. Name some differences between the Gospel of John and the Synoptic Gospels.

5. How does John's Gospel help date the duration of Jesus' public ministry?

6. Who might Nicodemus represent?

7. What is the Christological focus of John's Gospel?

8. What is the meaning of "Word" in the prologue of John's Gospel?

9. How can Jesus say, "before Abraham was, I AM"?

10. What is the dogma of the Holy Trinity?

⬤ Reflect

Explain how you understand God in Three Persons.

Acts of the Apostles

The style, language, and organization of the Acts of the Apostles and the Gospel of Luke are very similar. While Acts is not one of the Gospels, there is a strong proof that the author of Luke's Gospel also authored Acts. Both works are addressed to the same person—Theophilus.

There is also a nice symmetry between Luke and Acts:

Gospel of Luke	Acts of the Apostles
Preface to Theophilus (1:1-4)	Preface to Theophilus (1:1-2)
Birth and Baptism of Jesus—special role of the Holy Spirit and Mary (2:1-12; 3:21-22)	Birth and Baptism of the Church—special role of the Holy Spirit and Mary (1:14; 2:1-4)
Sermons of Jesus (4:18-27; 6:20-49; 8:5-18; etc.)	Sermons of Peter and Paul (2:14-36; 3:12-26; 13:16-41)
Jesus' healings (4:33-41; 7:1-17; 8:26-56; etc.)	Peter and Paul's healings (3:1-9; 5:12-16; 14:8-10)
Jesus' mission to the Jews, openness to Gentiles (4:18-30; 24:47)	Church's mission to the Jews and full openness to Gentiles (1-9; 10-28)
Rejection and Passion of Jesus (22-23)	Paul's rejection and Passion (22-28)

A primary focus of Acts is to provide a chronology of events in the early Church. Two Apostles are primarily featured. Peter, the foundation of the Church as commissioned by Jesus, and his missionary activities are featured in eleven of the first fifteen chapters of Acts. The emphasis then switches to St. Paul, a convert to the faith, and a missionary to the Gentiles. Peter, too, was an excellent missionary and his vision in Acts 10:1–49 helped to inspire the Church's outreach to Gentiles.

Forming a Church

The Gospel of Luke chronicles that Jesus began his public ministry after his baptism with forty days in the desert (Lk 3:21; 4:1–13). Jesus then went to his hometown synagogue where he previewed the meaning and content of his mission by quoting the prophet Isaiah: "The Spirit of the Lord is upon me, because he has anointed me to bring glad tidings to the poor" (Lk 4:18). In a parallel way in Acts, Luke opened the story of the Church by detailing forty days of appearances to the Apostles, preparing them for their baptism in the Holy Spirit (Acts 1:3–8), and outlining their futures:

> But you will receive power when the holy Spirit comes upon you, and you will be my witnesses in Jerusalem, throughout Judea and Samaria, and to the ends of the earth. (Acts 1:8)

Acts then describes the first Church in Jerusalem, consisting of eleven Apostles (prior to the selection of Matthias as a replacement for Judas): "All these devoted themselves with one accord to prayer, together with some women, and Mary the Mother of Jesus, and his brothers" (Acts 1:14). Note here the importance of prayer, the presence of women disciples, and the central role of Mary as a faithful witness to her Son and a source of strength to the Apostles and other disciples. This verse also links Acts with Luke's Gospel because the Apostles could give witness to Jesus' public ministry and to the Risen Lord; the women could attest to his burial and the empty tomb; and Mary, his Mother, could witness to Jesus' birth and the hidden years of his youth.

The Bible began in the Book of Genesis with the Spirit of God hovering over the waters of creation. In Luke's Gospel, the Holy Spirit was present at the time of the announcement to Mary of Jesus' birth. Likewise, in Acts, the Holy Spirit hovers over the beginnings of the Church. The Jewish feast of **Pentecost** (2 Mc 12:32), more frequently called the Feast of Weeks (Ex 34:22), was a harvest festival that Acts notes was the last time the Church was small enough to gather in a single room. On

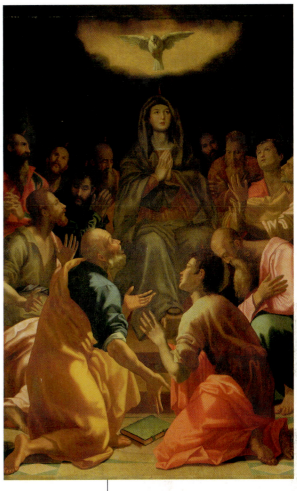

Pentecost
The day when the Holy Spirit descended on the Apostles and gave them the power to preach with conviction the message that Jesus is risen and is Lord of the universe.

that day, the Holy Spirit descended on the entire house as a "strong driving wind" and as "tongues of fire," empowering the Church to speak with such power and clarity that Jews from all over the world, gathered in Jerusalem for the Feast, understood them in their own tongues. Acts 2:14–36 records the first of six discourses that deal with the Resurrection of Jesus and the meaning of his role as Messiah. Five of these sermons were given by Peter, the other by Paul. In his first sermon, Peter connected the outpouring of the Holy Spirit to the fulfillment of the prophet Joel's vision of the end times (Jl 2:28–32). As a result, three thousand witnesses were baptized that day.

For just a brief time after Pentecost there seemed to be an idyllic way of life for the early Church. As Luke summarized it:

> They devoted themselves to the teaching of the apostles and to the communal life, to the breaking of the bread and to the prayers. Awe came upon everyone, and many wonders and signs were done through the apostles. All who believed were together and had all things in common; they would sell their property and possessions and divide them among all according to each one's need. Every day they devoted themselves to meeting together in the temple area and to breaking bread in their homes. They ate their meals with exultation and sincerity of heart, praising God and enjoying favor with all the people. And every day the Lord added to their number those who were being saved. (Acts 2:42–47)

Acts chronicles themes and events in the early Church, many of which paralleled those in the life and ministry of Jesus. For example, as Jesus did, the Church

- healed of the lame and resuscitated the dead (Acts 3:1–11; 9:32–43),

- preached the Good News (Acts 3:12–26),
- opposed the religious leadership of the Temple (Acts 4:1–31), and
- accepted the guidance of the Holy Spirit to lead its ministry and prayer (Acts 4:8, 31).

Remarkably, Peter, who had been such a coward in the courtyard of the high priests (Lk 22:54–62), became courageous in the face of the same leaders, witnessing about Jesus to them repeatedly (Acts 4:7–20; 5:12–42). The numbers of faithful increased, quickly to the same five thousand that once followed Jesus at the multiplication of the loaves (Luke 9:14; Acts 4:4).

There were signs that the Church, then as now, was not a perfect community. Brief stories illuminate how some members, Ananias and Sapphira, lied to the rest of the community (Acts 5:1–11), and how even the religious leaders favored people who spoke their own language—Hebrew (meaning Aramaic)—against Hellenists who spoke Greek as their first language (Acts 6:1–7). Through the guidance of the Holy Spirit and the leadership of the Apostles and their chosen successors, the Church overcame the challenges and continued to grow.

The Church's new outreach was to Gentiles.

 ## Reflect

How does the Church today overcome the imperfections of her members?

Outreach beyond Jerusalem

Luke's Gospel was like a coil winding tighter and tighter, from the moment when Jesus "resolutely determined to journey to Jerusalem" (Lk 9:51). The closer Jesus moved toward Jerusalem, the tighter the coil was wound, building to the events of his Passion and Death in Jerusalem.

The Acts of the Apostle takes that same coil, and unwinds explosively outwards "to all the nations, beginning from Jerusalem" (Lk 24:47). As this coil unwinds, the Church reaches out first to the "devout Jews from every nation," who had come to Jerusalem for the feast of Pentecost. They may have spoken many languages and come from the far corners of the earth, but they heard the Good News, and were astounded at the preaching of Peter and the Apostles. Three thousand joined them at that time (Acts 2:1–41).

The early Church had only a brief time to organize itself until its first great crisis in Jerusalem, the **martyrdom** of Stephen (Acts 6:9 –8:4). In the unwinding of the coil, missionaries spread throughout the Eastern Mediterranean, most going exclusively to preach to Jews in the Diaspora (Acts 11:19). Philip, more likely one of the seven Greek-speaking disciples chosen to assist the Church (Acts 6:5) rather than Philip the Apostle, extends the Church's outreach by witnessing to the people of Samaria (Acts 8:4–8). The Samaritans descended from foreigners who intermarried with the old northern Israelite tribes at the time of Assyria's conquest of the northern kingdom. Jews and Samaritans alike recognized Abraham as their common father. However, Jews viewed the Samaritans as foreigners, perhaps just a notch above the Gentiles.

The coil was then further unwound away from Judaism when the Gospel was shared with those described as "God fearers" (Acts 10:2; 13:16; 13:26) and "God worshipers" (Acts 13:43, 50; 16:14; 17:4, 17). These were terms used by Luke and Josephus (*Ant* 14.110) to describe Gentiles who had found Judaism attractive, admiring it for its monotheism, moral life, sense of historicity, and the fidelity of God for his people. Some affluent God fearers were even financially supportive but didn't take the final step of converting to Judaism. Motives for not taking the ultimate step might have been the dietary restrictions or the need for men to be circumcised.

Philip shared the Gospel with an Ethiopian eunuch and baptized the man on the road out of Jerusalem to Gaza (Acts 8:26–39). Next, Peter preached the Good News to Cornelius, a leader of a hundred men in a Roman army unit, and his family. Acts describes Cornelius as "devout and God-fearing along with his whole household, who used to give alms generously to the Jewish people and pray to God constantly" (Acts 10:2). Because Peter was moved both by a repeated vision in his dreams and by the gift of the Holy Spirit upon Cornelius' household (Acts 10:1–49), he was moved to baptize the entire family without requiring that the men be circumcised. These were the first Christians who were baptized without having come through Judaism (Acts 10:1–49).

The process of welcoming Gentiles *as Gentiles*, and not Jewish converts, wasn't a smooth process. A more conservative faction of Jewish Christians confronted Peter for his actions upon his return to Jerusalem. His explanation seemed to satisfy for the moment (Acts

martyrdom
From a word that means "witness." It describes those who bear witness to the truth of faith, even unto death. St. Stephen is recognized as the first Christian martyr.

11:1–18), but when missionaries to Antioch began to welcome Greeks who weren't even God fearers, Barnabas was sent to investigate. Being a good and perceptive person, Barnabas was able to recognize the grace of God and permit work there to continue (Acts 11:19–24).

Others Jewish Christians from Judea disagreed strongly and actively preached that only those who practiced the Mosaic Law, including circumcision, could be saved. This caused considerable debate and a desire to consult with the leadership in Jerusalem. Christian converts from the Pharisees also made a case for continuing to practice the Jewish Law. Peter, though, argued persuasively that the Holy Spirit had decided the issue by coming upon uncircumcised Gentiles. Between his testimony and that of Barnabas and Paul the assembled leaders in Jerusalem at the Jerusalem Council decided to admit Gentiles, requiring no more than God had of Noah, the father of all humans after the flood (Acts 15:1–29).

With the mission to the Gentiles confirmed, Christianity was set to complete the work set for it by Jesus before he ascended to proclaim "repentance for the forgiveness of sins" to every people (Lk 24:46–48). Christ's transcendent Ascension, a bridge connecting the end of Luke and the beginning of Acts, indicates his entrance into Heaven, where he sits at the right hand of Father, and from where he will come again. The remainder of the Acts of the Apostles details the Church's outreach throughout Asia Minor, Greece, and the islands of the Eastern Mediterranean and, in time, even as far as Rome.

 **Reflect**

How are you able to recognize the grace of God in your life?

Missionary Trips of Paul and Barnabas

Two important missionaries appeared on the scene as the early Church began to spread beyond Jerusalem and Judea. The most well known was Saul, also called Paul, who first showed up as an ardent defender of Judaism against Christianity at the stoning of Stephen, a horrific murder of which Saul approved (Acts 7:58–8:3).

Saul received his comeuppance while on the road to Damascus in a story so key that it was told three times in Acts (9:1–11; 22:3–16; 26:2–18) with curiously different details each time. (Perhaps Luke had received three slightly differing versions, and not knowing which one was most accurate, included all three.) In each of the accounts, Saul saw a bright light, fell to the ground, and heard a voice asking him, "Saul, Saul, why are you persecuting me?" Saul also lost his eyesight in the incident. When he was healed and instructed by a Christian, Ananias of Damascus, Saul became just as ardent of proponent of Christianity as he had been an opponent prior. His preaching became so effective in Damascus that he had to flee for his life from his heretofore compatriots (Acts 9:10–26).

It was at this point that Barnabas, a remarkable and somewhat unsung hero of the New Testament, reappeared. He had quietly entered the narrative earlier, a Jewish convert from the island of Cyprus. A landowner, he must have been affluent, selling property to sustain the early Church. He was so supportive that the Apostles changed his name from Joseph to Barnabas, meaning a "child of encouragement" (Acts 4:36–37). When Saul, having been such a terror to the Christians of Jerusalem before his conversion, returned there, it was hard for the Christians to trust him. Barnabas, being a truly good and courageous man, took a risk, placing Saul under his wing (Acts 9:26–28). Besides offering encouragement to new Christians (Acts 11:20–23), Barnabas took Saul from his home in Tarsus back to Antioch, where they preached (Acts 11:25–26). The evidence suggests that

Barnabas was the key influence in St. Paul's growth as a Christian (also Galatians 2:1–10).

At the direction of the Holy Spirit, Barnabas and Paul were set aside for missionary work by the church of Antioch (Acts 13:1–3). On their first missionary journey, they went to Barnabas's home, in Cyprus, an island south of Turkey and west of Syria. From there they went on to Salamis, Paphos, Perga, Pisidia, Iconium, Lystra, Derbe, Pamphylia, Attalia, and back to Antioch (Acts 13:2–14:26). During those journeys, in Lystra, Barnabas was mistaken for Zeus, the chief of the Greek gods, while Paul was mistaken for Hermes, herald of their gods (Acts 14:12).

Paul, whose name switched from "Saul" to "Paul" without any notice or explanations (see "Why Does Paul Have Two Names?," page 249), began to take a more active role, preaching long homilies (Acts 13:16–41). He was very effective in bringing many Gentiles to the faith but experienced rejection from many Jews (Acts 13:45–52), a pattern that would happen over and over again in Paul's ministry.

 **Reflect**

Who is someone who has influenced your life as a Christian?

To the Ends of the Earth

The final section of the Acts of the Apostles (Acts 15:36–28:31) recounts St. Paul's many efforts to proclaim the Good News to the furthest corners of the earth. Freed by the decision of the Church in Jerusalem to admit Gentiles without the practice of the Jewish Law, Paul traveled north through Syria and his native province of Cilicia. Tarsus, his hometown, was the capital of Cilicia. Traveling on from there, back to Derbe and Lystra, Paul met Timothy, who would become his companion and a co-author of some of his letters (Acts 15:40–16:4). Moved by a vision during his travels, Paul traveled to Macedonia (northern modern Greece). This was the first time Christianity was brought to the continent of Europe, which would be the primary home of the faith for the next two thousand years.

Acts's description of the journey to Macedonia is significant in another way too. It is the first of three passages (Acts 16:10–17; 20:7–12; 21:15–18) where the narration shifted from third person narration (she, he, it, they, her, him, them) to first person, with the use of the plural eyewitnesses perspective, "we" and "us." For example:

> When he had seen the vision, *we* sought passage to Macedonia at once, concluding that God had called *us* to proclaim the good news to them. *We* set sail from Troas, making a straight run for Samothrace, and on the next day to Neapolis, and from there to Philippi, a leading city in that district of Macedonia and a Roman colony. *We* spent some time in that city. (Acts 16:10–12)

It's difficult to know how to interpret the change in tense from third person to first person. It may suggest that the author was an eyewitness to the events recounted in Paul's life. However, if Luke had been a companion of Paul's, it is strange that he doesn't seem to know of Paul's Epistles or some of Paul's main concerns for justification by grace and freedom from the Law. In fact, the lengthy sermons given by Paul in Acts reflect more the theology of Luke's Gospel than Paul's Epistles.

Paul's time in Philippi led to some converts, notably Lydia of Thyatira and a jailer whom Paul met after he was beaten and imprisoned for having disturbed the superstitions of the Greeks by healing a possessed girl. The political leaders released Paul after having been notified that they had beaten a Roman citizen (Acts 16:11–40). This detail of his life—that Paul was a citizen of Rome—is never mentioned in any of his letters. But it surfaces again (Acts 22:22–29) and will be the reason he is eventually sent to Rome.

Paul's journeys from Philippi wound eventually to Corinth, where he remained for some time (Acts 18:1–18). Again having trouble with Jews in the synagogue, Paul grew despondent with his usual practice of going first to preach in them when he entered new cities (Acts 9:20; 13:5, 14:1; 17:1–2; 18:4). He actually continued with the practice, even with some success (Acts 18:19; 18:26; 19:6), but this frustration signals one of the realities of the early Church: it was *much* more successful with Gentiles than it was with Jews.

In Ephesus, Paul encountered poorly instructed converts. For example, a certain gifted speaker by the name of Apollos came to Ephesus and preached with authority, though he had incomplete knowledge of Baptism. Paul's hosts, Priscilla and Aquila, were able to further instruct Apollos, enabling him to more effectively continue his ministry (Acts 18:24–28). Paul, too, encountered poorly instructed Christians in Ephesus who knew nothing of the Holy Spirit or Christian Baptism (Acts 19:1–6). Paul's preaching in Ephesus was so effective that the silversmiths who made the little shrines to the goddess Artemis began to lose business, leading to an almost comical riot in the city (Acts 19:22–40). Feeling an impending sense of trouble ahead, Paul made an impassioned farewell to the **presbyters** of Ephesus, where he had spent so much time.

With a shared sense of impending doom, Paul's companions begged him, to no avail, not to go to Jerusalem. Once in Jerusalem, to appease suspicions, Paul completed the typical purification rites of the Jews. Some of them, angry at what they had heard of his preaching, and suspecting him of bringing Gentiles into the Temple, beat him severely (Acts 21). Being a dedicated teacher, though, he couldn't pass up an opportunity to preach to his persecutors, while under the protection of the leader of the Roman cohort who had come to his assistance. When more violence ensued, the Roman officer was at the point himself of ordering Paul beaten, until Paul confessed, for the second time, that he was born a Roman citizen, once more saving himself (Acts 22:25–29). Given yet another chance to speak to his accusers, he so angered them that the commander had to rescue him yet again.

Fearing a plot on Paul's life, the commander smuggled him out of

presbyters
A term that means "priest." A presbyter is a mediator between God and humans. Jesus is the High Priest *par excellence*. As God-made-man, he bridges both Heaven and earth, bringing God to humanity and humanity to God.

Jerusalem and on to Antonius Felix, the Roman procurator of Judea, who placed Paul on trial (Acts 24:1–23). Felix held Paul in custody for two years, hoping for a bribe, but giving Paul some latitude, including support from his friends. His successor Festus, however, threw Paul in prison (Acts 24:27). Having made the decision to shuffle Paul off to Rome, which Paul declared as his right, Festus did his best to pass on responsibility to the last Herodian king, Agrippa II (Acts 25). To the end, Paul the preacher was true to himself. While defending himself in court, his testimony was a witness to the Good News of Jesus Christ. Though he impressed the king with his preaching and sincerity, the king did not feel free to release Paul until his appeal to the Roman emperor had been heard (Acts 26:1–30).

Paul and his companions were sent off to Rome. The journey by sea was stormy and perilous. Ironically, Paul, still a prisoner, held the crew and his companions together until the ship ended up foundering on the island of Malta. Everyone survived as Paul promised (Acts 27:6–44). While there, not unlike Jesus on the way to his own Death in Luke's Gospel, Paul healed many and continued to preach the Good News. Three months later they continued on to Rome. In Rome, Paul immediately got into contact with the local Jewish community, where he continued his missionary work in chains, waiting for his appeal to Caesar to be heard.

The Acts of the Apostles ends with the ambiguous news that Paul remained in his habitation for two years, proclaiming the reign of God and teaching about Jesus Christ (Acts 28). Tradition holds that Paul was martyred in Rome.

The Acts of the Apostles is a testament to the dedication of the early Church, and Paul in particular, to the spread of the Good News to the Gentiles, Luke's audience. In one **homily** after another, Acts teaches that the saving activity of God, so obvious in the Old Testament, is now available to Gentiles through the merits of Jesus Christ.

Review

1. What are some proofs that Luke and Acts share the same author?

2. What are some themes and events in the early Church that are similar to those in the life and ministry of Jesus?

3. Who were the "God fearers" and "God worshippers" in Acts?

4. What was the decision of the early Church regarding the admission of Gentiles?

5. How did Barnabas help Paul get started in his ministry?

6. Why might the narration in Acts have changed from third person to first person speech?

7. How did Paul call on his Roman citizenship?

8. What did Paul do while he was imprisoned?

homily
A talk that helps the congregation understand more about the Word of God. At Mass, a homily is given by a bishop, priest, or deacon.

Strategies for Reading, Studying, and Praying the Gospels

The Gospels (and Acts) are not history texts or biographies. The different Gospels often present the very same event in slightly and, sometimes, dramatically different ways. These alternations should not be surprising nor cause dismay. The Gospel writers were most interested in telling the truth about Jesus. While they also wanted us to know the key facts about his life, this wasn't always their primary focus.

It is an advantage for Catholics today that the Gospels each portrayed Jesus from different perspectives. All detectives will tell you that they prefer to have many witnesses at crime scenes, not just one or two! The Gospels provide four such witnesses. While there is considerable overlap of the narratives, the differences are enough to provide distinct perspectives on the complex person of Jesus, the Word made flesh. To get the maximum impact from each Gospel, it makes sense to read, study, and pray using just one Gospel at a time in order to learn what is distinctive about it and consider what it has to say to us in our own lives.

Reading and studying are great places to start, but they can't be the end in themselves. The Gospels are not just the story of any man. They are the inspired testimony of the early Church about God made flesh. Jesus taught crowds and drew people into discipleship in Galilee and Judea during his life because they mattered to him. We also matter to him at least as much as did the people he lived with and taught. He would speak to us as well. It is important that as soon as we have sufficient knowledge to understand the worlds of the text that we move beyond reading and studying, to praying the text. Through the Sacred Tradition, the Holy Spirit teaches us to pray. Believing, as we do, that the Holy Spirit is speaking to us in all of Scripture, but most intimately and profoundly in the Gospels that narrate Jesus' life, we need to spend time listening to God's Word.

There is an ancient Catholic practice associated with **lectio divina** (see "Praying with the Bible," page 312) of experiencing the Gospels by entering into the text and trying to picture ourselves in the narrative and to imagine our own response to what happens. It's a slower kind of reading, meaning that there is no need to cover many pages to feel rewarded. In fact, if you do this correctly you might only read a few verses, or even just a few words, as they lead you into a prayerful conversation with Jesus. It's almost more important to listen than to speak at those moments when you are close

to the Lord. The more time you spend on this kind of prayerful reading the better you become at it and, as those who do this frequently will testify, the more rewarding you will find it.

Review

Why is it an advantage for us to have four different perspectives (Gospels) on Jesus Christ?

lectio divina
Literally, "divine reading." This is a prayerful way to read the Bible or other sacred writings.

Research and Report

Choose and complete at least one of the following assignments:

- Listed below are several Old Testament prophecies cited in the Gospel of Matthew that show how Jesus is the Promised One. Read the passages. Write a sentence for each explaining how Jesus fulfills the prophecy.

Mt 1:22-23	Mt 8:17
Mt 2:5-6	Mt 12:16-21
Mt 2:15	Mt 13:35
Mt 2:18	Mt 21:4-5
Mt 2:23	Mt 21:42
Mt 4:14-16	Mt 27:9

- Read the following passages about John, the "beloved disciple": Jn 13:23; Jn 19:26; Jn 20:2-10; Jn 21:7, 20-23. Answer the following questions:

  1. How did Jesus especially favor this disciple?
  2. Describe John in relation to Peter. What does his stepping aside to allow Peter to enter the tomb first signify?

- Read Paul's farewell discourse to the elders from Ephesus in Acts 20:17-38. Then answer the following questions:

  1. How does Paul know that persecution is in store for him?
  2. Who are the savage wolves that might try to devour the new Christians when Paul is gone?
  3. Paul said, "It is more blessed to give than to receive." Share some examples of when you have found this to be true.

SCRIPTURE PRAYER *(from Mark 1:15)*

"This is the time of fulfillment. The kingdom of God is at hand. Repent, and believe in the gospel."

Dear Jesus, help us to accept your holy Word. Open our hearts and minds to the Gospel.
Amen.

2B

THE NEW TESTAMENT LETTERS

Literary Form of Paul's Letters

Paul's letters followed a literary form common among Greco-Roman letters of his time. Unlike modern letters in which senders identify themselves at the conclusion, Greco-Roman letters began with the name of the sender. Any co-senders and their titles were also included at this point. Letters finished as formally as they began. Most formal Greco-Roman letters included a closing personal greeting and wishes for good health, or a prayer for divine favor. Following this style, Paul's letters included four main sections:

1. *Opening Address.* Since the letters were not placed in envelopes, the opening salutation gives the name of the sender, the receiver, and a short greeting.
2. *Thanksgiving.* A short thanksgiving sets the tone of the letter and hints at the letter's contents. Paul's thanksgivings are usually very prayerful and inspiring.
3. *Body of the letter.* The bulk of the letter has two parts to it: *doctrinal teaching* and *encouragement*. Paul elaborates key Christian truths or clarifies misunderstandings his readers are having over points of Church doctrine and applies the doctrinal teaching to Christian living. Today, we look on these sections of Paul's letters for guidance in Christian morality.
4. *Final salutations.* Paul concludes his letters by giving personal news or specific advice to individuals. His final greeting is usually a short blessing like this: "the grace of our Lord Jesus Christ be with you" (1 Thes 5:28).

🌐 Reflect

Name one passage of a letter of St. Paul that you are familiar with and that resonates with you.

Classifying Paul's Letters

Paul's letters are not arranged alphabetically in the New Testament canon, but in a rough approximation of longest to shortest, beginning with Romans and ending with Philemon.

In seven of the letters—Romans, 1 and 2 Corinthians, Galatians, Philippians, 1 Thessalonians, and Philemon—there is a consistency of style, vocabulary, and theological emphasis. For example, these seven letters emphasize a very clear concern about the end of the world, believing that Jesus was returning quickly and unexpectedly:

> For you yourselves know very well that the day of the Lord will come like a thief at night. When people are saying, "Peace and security," then sudden disaster comes upon them, like labor pains upon a pregnant woman, and they will not escape. But you, brothers, are not in darkness, for that day to overtake you like a thief. (1 Thes 5:2–4)

The theme of Jesus' impending return and the end of the world shaped a number of other common themes in these seven letters, including how much effort Paul put into his missionary work in order to bring the message of Salvation to as many people as possible before the end. It was also a springboard to communicate the necessity of casting off sin (Rom 13:11–12) and it even profoundly affected the advice given to married couples (1 Cor 7:29–31).

In the other six letters attributed to St. Paul, the theme of the end of the world is lessened or even ignored. For example, in 2 Thessalonians 2:1–6, the author is preoccupied with convincing his audience that the coming of the Lord is not imminent and in fact they could expect some clear sign of his approach.

Also, in three of these other letters—2 Thessalonians, Colossians, and Ephesians—there are shifts in the use and meaning of some of the chosen vocabulary.

pseudonymous
A work written under a name that is not the name of the person doing the actual writing. It was a common and accepted practice for disciples and admirers of great teachers to write works under their names to extend their legacies.

For example, Paul frequently used the Greek word *ekklesía* (translated as "church" or "assembly") to describe a church in a particular place, for example, the "church in Corinth" (1 Cor 2) or "the churches in Galatia" (Gal 1:2). However, in Ephesians and Colossians, *ekklesía* is used most frequently to refer to the "universal Church" as a whole, and not simply to a local assembly (Eph 1:22–23 and Col 1:18).

Because of the differences in style and speech of this kind, it may be that 2 Thessalonians, Colossians, and Ephesians were penned by close disciples of Paul or by his admirers who wrote them as they thought Paul would have himself, giving him credit because, as they saw it, the teachings were fundamentally his. For example, the Letter to the Ephesians may have been the work of a secretary of Paul's, writing at his instruction, or of a later disciple who sought to develop Paul's ideas for a new time and situation. A name for this form of writing is **pseudonymous**.

Three other letters—1 and 2 Timothy and Titus—may also be pseudonymous works. They seem to have been late additions to Paul's corpus, addressing new issues that had arisen later in the first century. In particular, the more time had passed since the Death and Resurrection of Jesus, the more difficult it was to connect with Paul's teaching that Jesus was going to return quickly. It is possible that the same author, a later follower of Paul, applied what was known of Paul's teachings to new questions that had arisen and authored each of these letters in Paul's name. The First and Second Letters to Timothy and the Letter to Titus are also classified as "Pastoral Letters" because so much of their content is about leadership, ministry, and family life.

You may wonder how it is possible to attribute the writing of text to an author though the author did not manually do the writing. In the ancient world, an author was commonly accepted as the person whose ideas were being used, whether or not the person crafted the exact wording or not. Certainly the practice continues today and often goes by the name "ghostwriting." To be clear, the issue is not whether or not any of the letters attributed to St. Paul are the inspired Word of God. While there are interesting questions to ponder about their exact human authorship, their divine authorship elicits no questions or doubts. As with the other books of the biblical canon, the letters attributed to St. Paul are authentically and historically God's Word, sources of Divine Revelation.

Review

1. How many letters have been attributed to St. Paul?
2. Why might have Paul used scribes in composing his letters?
3. What are the four main sections of Paul's letters?
4. How are Paul's letters arranged in the New Testament cannon?

5. What did Paul teach about the end of the world?

6. How does the topic of the "end of the world" help to clarify authorship of Paul's letters?

7. Why are 1 and 2 Timothy and Titus called "Pastoral Letters"?

 **Reflect**

What are some advantages and disadvantages to ghostwriting as it occurs today?

St. Paul: The Source of the New Testament Letters

Apart from Jesus, there is no person from the New Testament as well known and influential as St. Paul of Tarsus. There are two primary sources for knowing the life of St. Paul: his own letters and the Acts of the Apostles. In his letters, Paul set aside only a small portion of material as autobiographical. However, Luke, the author of Acts, dedicated many chapters to recounting Paul's exploits, beginning with his conversion experience in Acts 9:1–19 and continuing with details of his missionary journeys beginning at Acts 12:25 and extending to the end of Acts. There are many details of the life of Paul that correspond between his letters and the material in Acts. There are also several details that contrast between the two sources. In general, recall that the theology described in Acts is more representative of Luke, its author, than it is of Paul. Pauline theology is more clearly delineated in his letters than in Acts. However, Acts does provide more of the historical details of Paul's life.

Paul's Biography

Paul was born a Jew. Although there is no written account of the date of his birth, he was probably younger than Jesus and hence born between AD 5 and 15. Paul's hometown of Tarsus (Acts 9:11; 11:25; 21:39; 22:3) was a cultured Greek city that was known for its prosperity, intellectual life, and extensive library. It exists on the south coast of Turkey. Though Tarsus would have been primarily made up of Gentiles in what was considered Hellenistic (Greek) territory, it would have also have been home to a fair amount of faithful Jews who had scattered throughout the Mediterranean basin to escape war and famine around Judea and to pursue a variety of economic opportunities.

According to Paul's own words in the Letter to the Philippians, he was "circumcised on the eighth day, of the race of Israel, of the tribe of Benjamin, a Hebrew of Hebrew parentage, in observance of the law of a Pharisee" (Phil 3:5). Paul also admits to being a persecutor of the Church, though according to Jewish law considered himself to be "blameless" (Phil 3:6).

Paul studied at the feet of an esteemed rabbi, Gamaliel (Acts 22:3). The fruits of this education are revealed by his complex use of Greek grammar and vocabulary and the breadth and depth of his knowledge of the Hebrew scriptures. The Roman procurator Festus noted the intensity of Paul's study: "You are mad, Paul; much learning is driving you mad" (Acts 26:24). Certainly a person of great passions, Paul was zealous about everything he did. If he was ardent in his persecution of the Church before his conversion (Phil 3:6), he was even more enthusiastic in building it up after his experience of Jesus. According to the details of his missionary trips, he may have walked anywhere from 6,000 miles to twice that amount from one place to the next in order to spread the Gospel. His emotions often were close to the surface. He was anguished and sorrowful at times (Rom 9:2) while other times being inclined to rejoice (Phil 1:18). Perhaps because he was opposed by Jews, Gentiles, and Christians alike, Paul often felt it necessary to defend his role and authority as an Apostle (Gal 2:6–10; 1 Cor 9:1–6), which he did based on his experience of the Risen Jesus who had commissioned him to the life of ministry (1 Cor 15:3–11).

Acts 18:3 reports that Paul practiced the same trade as a Jewish couple, Aquila and Priscilla, whom he met in Corinth. Their trade was as tentmakers. This might seem to be an oddly menial occupation for one so educated. Certain Stoic and Cynic philosophers of the day also worked to support themselves, especially as gardeners, while propagating their teachings. It was apparently Paul's practice to support himself while doing his missionary work, a point made both in his letters (1 Thes 2:9; 1 Cor 9:14) and in Acts 18:2–3.

Although born a Jew, Paul claimed to also have been a Roman citizen (Acts 22:25–28). There is no indication in the New Testament as to how he received this rare privilege, which served him well on a few occasions (see "To the Ends of the Earth," pages 235–237).

In the first verse of the Letter to the Romans, Paul describes himself as "a slave of Christ Jesus, called to be an apostle and set apart for the gospel of God" (Rom 1:1). It is reasonably assumed that Paul had the same Church authority as the other Apostles. This is verified in the Letter to Titus when Paul gives Titus an apostolic mandate to "appoint priests in every town" (Ti 1:5). Paul could hardly give an authority that he did not himself have.

Reflect

Who is a teacher for you who has approximated the mentoring role of Gamaliel for Paul?

Conversion and Ministry of Paul

Paul is first mentioned in the biblical narrative as a young man actively engaged in the persecution of Christians (Acts 7:58) with the full intent of destroying the Church (Acts 8:1–3). Paul was on his way to Damascus when he had an eyewitness experience of the Risen Jesus. The experience changed him. He became a believer and a dedicated missionary advancing the Gospel throughout the Roman Empire. In the Letter to the Galatians he offered a summary of what happened to him in the years following his conversion:

> When (God) . . . was pleased to reveal his Son to me, so that I might proclaim him to the Gentiles . . . I went into Arabia and then returned to Damascus. Then after three years I

WHY DOES PAUL HAVE TWO NAMES?

There are two names for St. Paul mentioned in Scripture. The other name Paul is referred by is "Saul." There is a common though mistaken theory held by some that Saul was his birth name, and that, at his conversion he was given a new name, "Paul," as when Abram became Abraham (Gn 17:5) and Sarai became Sarah (Gn 17:15). Unfortunately, the Scriptures provide absolutely no evidence that Paul received a new name at his conversion.

It *is* true that in the Acts of the Apostles, the account begins by calling him "Saul," and consistently does so until its first use of "Paul" in Acts 13:9. Paul's conversion experience, though, occurred four chapters earlier in Acts 9. When the shift does happen, it does so without the slightest explanation or any reference back to Acts 9. After this point, in fact, the only times that Acts reverts to using the old name is when the story of the conversion is retold (Acts 22:7, 13; 26:14). The conversion and the name change, then, don't seem to be at all related.

More likely, Paul actually had two names: one, "Saul," from the Hebrew word *sa'ul*, meaning "asked of God," that he used when among Jews; the other, "Paul," a Greco-Roman name, from *paulos*, a Latin word meaning "small" or "little," that he used when among Greeks and Romans. In every one of his letters Paul always refers to himself as "Paul," never "Saul."

The practice of having two names among Jews at this time period seems to have been common. His Hebrew name was particularly appropriate for someone who, like Paul, was from the tribe of Benjamin (Rom 11:1; Phil 3:5), since that was the name of the first king of the Israelites who was also from the same tribe (1 Sm 9:1-2a).

went up to Jerusalem to confer with Kephas and remained with him for fifteen days. But I did not see any other of the apostles, only James the brother of the Lord. . . . Then I went into the regions of Syria and Cilicia. . . . Then after fourteen years I again went up to Jerusalem with Barnabas, taking Titus along also. I went up in accord with a revelation, and I presented to them the gospel that I preach to the Gentiles—but privately to those of repute—so that I might not be running, or have run, in vain. . . . But from those who were reputed to be important . . . made me add nothing. On the contrary, when they saw that I had been entrusted with the gospel to the uncircumcised, just as Peter to the circumcised . . . and when they recognized the grace bestowed upon me, James and Kephas and John, who were reputed to be pillars, gave me and Barnabas their right hands in partnership, that we should go to the Gentiles and they to the circumcised. (Gal 1:15–2:11)

In that ministry to the Gentiles, Paul expended himself for the remaining years of his life, pouring himself out selflessly so that others could come to know and serve the Lord Jesus as he did. He had both successes and defeats, triumphs and great suffering, in this work, as he explained:

> Five times at the hands of the Jews I received forty lashes minus one. Three times I was beaten with rods, once I was stoned, three times I was shipwrecked, I passed a night and a day on the deep; on frequent journeys, in dangers from rivers, dangers from robbers, dangers from my own race, dangers from Gentiles, dangers in the city, dangers in the wilderness, dangers at sea, dangers among false brothers; in toil and hardship, through many sleepless nights, through hunger and thirst, through frequent fastings, through cold and exposure. And apart from these things, there is the daily pressure upon me of my anxiety for all the churches. (2 Cor 11:24–28)

Paul revealed that he was affected by his sufferings: "Therefore, that I might not become too elated, a thorn in the flesh was given to me, an angel of Satan, to beat me, to keep me from being too elated. Three times I begged the Lord about this, that it might leave me" (2 Cor 12:7). What his problem was is never clarified by the text, and it is possible that the thorn was no more than some troublesome person. It's also possible that Paul's thorn was some physical problems. This wouldn't have been unusual, considering the primitive medical care available at the time. He did make the best of this suffering, though, recognizing that the Lord was able to use his suffering for good ends: "[The Lord] said to me, 'My grace is sufficient for you, for power is made perfect in weakness.' I will rather boast most gladly of my weaknesses, in order that the power of Christ may dwell with me" (2 Cor 12:9).

It is amazing to discover a person so completely dedicated to a cause, as Paul was to the spread of the Good News of Jesus Christ. He was convinced he had found something that was so true and so valuable that it couldn't be ignored or kept to himself. As a result, he ventured to one city and town after another, establishing small communities of believers, choosing and laying hands on local leaders to carry on his work after he left for the next town. As new questions, troubles, dissensions, or misunderstandings arose in these churches founded by Paul, they wrote to him or sent him messengers to ask for his continued guidance after he had moved on to the next missionary field. When Paul couldn't return himself, he sent letters supporting, challenging, disciplining, and teaching believers in Corinth, Philippi, Thessalonica, the regions of Galatia, and the city of Rome. Paul's letters are the earliest writings and make up one-quarter of the New Testament.

After recounting many missionary journeys throughout the Eastern Mediterranean, from one town and city to the next, the Acts of the Apostles ends the account of Paul's life with his arrival in Rome. He spent two years there in his lodgings (Rom 28:30). Ancient custom suggests that he died there, in Rome, during the persecutions of Emperor Nero (AD 54–68).

Emperor Nero

🔵 Reflect

How would your life change if you had an eyewitness experience of Jesus?

Theology of Paul

St. Paul is often described as one of the Church's great **theologians**. The difficulty in understanding or labeling Paul's theology is that his study of God was not laid out in a systematic way. He never wrote a textbook. He didn't develop a categorized study of theology, complete with sections and subsections.

However, in Paul's letters he reveals through his missionary work his central focus for explaining the meaning of Salvation History, the role of Jesus, and an understanding of Church and life in the Spirit.

Paul's letters, taken up in more depth in the sections that follow, reveal much of his theology. Before considering the letters individually, consider these main points that serve as a brief summary of Paul's theology:

- Salvation takes place through Jesus Christ, the Lord of the universe (Col 1:15–20).

- The heart of the Gospel is the Death and Resurrection of Jesus Christ (1 Cor 15:1–19).

- Christians will participate in the Resurrection of Jesus Christ. After the Last Judgment, the universe will be renewed. The Kingdom of God will come in fullness. The just will reign with Christ forever. God will then be "all in all" in eternal life (1 Cor 15:20–28).

- Salvation is a free gift from God that demands faith. We cannot earn Salvation on our own merits (Rom 5:1–11).

- Christians are bound together in one Body, the Church, of which Jesus is the head (1 Cor 12:12–30).

- The Holy Spirit is the life of the Church who enables us to call God Abba (Gal 4:1–7).

- The brothers and sisters of Christ should treat others with dignity. We must love one another (Eph 4:17–32).

- Following Jesus means that we must suffer for him gladly (Phil 2:1–18).

⚜ Review

1. What are the two primary sources for discovering the life of St. Paul?

2. What is the greater source of Pauline theology?

3. Describe Tarsus in the first century.

4. What was Paul's occupational trade?

5. How is Paul's Episcopal authority verified?

6. Why does Paul gladly boast of his weakness?

7. Why did Paul begin writing letters to local churches?

8. What is a likely reason for why Paul had two names?

9. According to Paul's theology, what is at the heart of the Gospel?

⚜ Reflect

What is a basic personal and professional study plan for you to discover more about God?

theologians
Theologians are people who study the nature of God and religious truth. Besides St. Paul, two other great Catholic theologians are St. Augustine of Hippo and St. Thomas Aquinas.

The Thirteen New Testament Letters

Under the classification of "New Testament Letters" are the fourteen letters that have traditionally been attributed to St. Paul. One of these letters, the Letter to the Hebrews, has been attached to the group of Pauline letters though it does not make claims to have been authored by Paul.

The other thirteen letters do traditionally list Paul as the author though some of these—Ephesians, Colossians, 2 Thessalonians, and 1 Timothy—may have been written by his disciples.

The New Testament Letters of Paul have been grouped in other ways as well. Recall that the Letters of 1 and 2 Timothy and Titus are known as "Pastoral Letters" because they were written for individuals rather than communities. These letters are addressed to disciples of Paul whom he appointed as bishops for certain churches. They focus on the roles of Timothy and Titus as pastors and are concerned with Church organization and the purity of faith. Also, four of the letters have been grouped as "Captivity Letters" because in each of these the author writes of being in prison.

The thirteen letters that were either written by or attributed to Paul are not arranged in the canon in chronological order. Rather, they are arranged in two groups: letters to communities and letters to individuals. Letters to communities, and probably letters to individuals as well, were read and reflected on by the entire local church. Within each of these groups they appear in the canon from the longest to the shortest.

As mentioned earlier, some of the New Testament Letters may haven been pseudonymous, that is, written by a disciples of Paul. A question to consider is whether or not the original audiences would have understood themselves that Paul may not have been the actual author of these texts. In the case of Ephesians, Colossians, and 2 Thessalonians, these letters may have been intended for the Church at large, simply using these names as a way to remain consistent with the rest of the canon. It *is* accurate to say that most readers throughout history have presumed that Paul was the author of the basic ideas of these letters whether he wrote them or not.

Of much greater importance is the belief of the early Church that these letters were faithful not simply to Paul, but also to the Tradition that had been handed down from the Apostles. This was more important than the identity or *supposed* identity of the authors. There were many other pseudonymous letters and gospels that did *not* meet up to this most important of standards. The early Church judged their content as unfaithful to the true preaching of the Apostles, so they were not included in the New Testament canon.

The next sections examine the background and main themes of the New Testament Letters, addressing them in the order that they appear in the canon.

The Letter to the Romans

The Letter to the Romans is Paul's letter of introduction to the Christians living in Rome. It was written in AD 57–58 from Corinth. Paul had not yet visited Rome, nor did he found the local church there as he had in other places. But he was planning on stopping in Rome on his way to Spain.

The arrival of Christianity in Rome can be dated by the chance meeting in Corinth between Paul and "a Jew named Aquila, a native of Pontus, who had recently come from Italy with his wife Priscilla because Claudius had ordered all the Jews to leave Rome" (Acts 18:2). The expelling of Christians from Rome was also verified by a (non-Christian) Roman historian, Suetonius, who wrote, "Since the Jews constantly made disturbances at the instigation of Chrestus (Christ), [Emperor Claudius] expelled them from Rome." Since it is believed that Paul visited Corinth sometime around AD 50, this would have been about the time when Christians were sent away from Rome and even earlier when a Christian community would have formed there. This is truly remarkable that the Good News had reached Rome from Jerusalem, a distance of over 1,400 miles, less than twenty years after Jesus' Death and Resurrection.

The church in Rome was likely founded directly by missionaries who came from the church in Jerusalem. This actually concerned Paul because he thought that these missionaries with Jewish roots were directing the Gentiles in Rome to keep the Jewish Law. After his conversion, Paul strongly held that legal observance of Jewish Law was no longer necessary for Christians. He often had difficulty in convincing other Jewish Christians that this was true, including Peter (Cephas):

> And when Cephas came to Antioch, I opposed him to his face because he clearly was wrong. For, until some people came from James, he used to eat with the Gentiles; but when they came, he began to draw back and separated himself, because he was afraid of the circumcised. And the rest of the Jews (also) acted hypocritically along with him, with the result that even Barnabas was carried away by their hypocrisy. But when I saw that they were not on the right road in line with the truth of the

> gospel, I said to Kephas in front of all, "If you, though a Jew, are living like a Gentile and not like a Jew, how can you compel the Gentiles to live like Jews?" We, who are Jews by nature and not sinners from among the Gentiles, (yet) who know that a person is not justified by works of the law but through faith in Jesus Christ, even we have believed in Christ Jesus that we may be justified by faith in Christ and not by works of the law, because by works of the law no one will be justified. (Gal 2:11–16)

Paul became well aware how difficult it would be for Jewish Christians to give up a lifetime of practicing Jewish rituals and the Law. He used the Letter to the Romans to expound on the teaching that it is faith in Jesus Christ's Death and Resurrection that reconciles us to God.

The Letter to the Romans is Paul's longest letter besides being his deepest theologically. Even though the language in Rome was Latin, Paul wrote the Letter to the Romans in Greek. This makes sense. Most of the educated Romans spoke Greek. The slaves brought to Rome in the prior centuries during Roman conquests in the Eastern Mediterranean and Egypt were also more likely to speak Greek than Latin. Also, evidence that a majority of the Jewish funeral inscriptions found in Rome were in Greek means that the Jewish community there would also have been better equipped to read his letter in Greek than in Latin.

Themes in Romans

The Letter to the Romans teaches that the sacrificial act of Christ's Paschal Mystery has brought us:

- justification;
- peace with God;
- the gift of the Holy Spirit;
- reconciliation with God;
- Salvation from the wrath of God;
- hope of a share in God's eternal glory;
- God's superabundant love poured out on us.

In Romans, Paul taught that we didn't earn Jesus' intervention in human history, nor could we earn our Salvation by any human means, for "all have sinned and are deprived of the glory of God" (Rom 3:23). This makes Jesus' saving activity all the more remarkable since, as Paul wrote, "God proves his love for us in that while we were still sinners Christ died for us" (Rom 5:8).

So great is this unearned Salvation that it enables us to cooperate with God's saving work, giving us the grace necessary for us to do good. In this sense, even the good we do is to be laid at the feet of God, as it is enabled by God's graces. As a result, the old practices, that Paul referred to as "works of the Law," were no longer necessary. Some interpreters during the Protestant Reformation translated Paul's references to

these works as "good works," but that was not, in fact, Paul's frame of reference, especially since most of the "works" were morally neutral—for example, bathing and sacrifices, which were neither good nor evil, in themselves.

Paul hoped to encourage his readers to understand that we now share in the merits of Christ's Death because we, too, were baptized into his Death. In the ancient rite the baptized were completely submerged in the water, as though they had died to sin and alienation from God. They were then brought up out of the water as though they had been born again to a new relationship with God as Father. As Paul wrote:

> Or are you unaware that we who were baptized into Christ Jesus were baptized into his death? We were indeed buried with him through baptism into death, so that, just as Christ was raised from the dead by the glory of the Father, we too might live in newness of life. For if

we have grown into union with him through a death like his, we shall also be united with him in the resurrection. We know that our old self was crucified with him, so that our sinful body might be done away with, that we might no longer be in slavery to sin. For a dead person has been absolved from sin. If, then, we have died with Christ, we believe that we shall also live with him. (Rom 6:3–8)

Later in Romans Paul expounded that

none of us lives for oneself, and no one dies for oneself. For if we live, we live for the Lord, and if we die we die for the Lord; so than whether we live or die we are the Lord's. (Rom 14:7–8)

Reflect

How does Romans 6:3-8 give you hope?

The First Letter to the Corinthians and the Second Letter to the Corinthians

Corinth was a very prosperous Roman sea colony located near Athens and Greece that was known for every vice imaginable. Slaves made up two-thirds of the population of 600,000 people. The colony itself was located on a very thin isthmus, bridging the southern tip of Greece, called the Peloponnese, with the rest of the country. On one side of the isthmus was the Aegean Sea; on the other was the Ionian. Corinth had two ports, only about four miles from each other, one in each sea.

Because compasses had not yet come into use in navigation, most sailors were reluctant to leave sight of land. As a result, ships followed the shorelines, leading to all too frequent shipwrecks. Rather than ship commerce all the way around the Peloponnesian

Peninsula, a journey of about 250 miles, sailors would land on one of Corinth's two ports, carry their cargo the four miles to the other port, and load it onto ships there that would continue on in their journey. The amount of trade passing through this rollicking two-port city enabled Corinth's financial prosperity.

Because of both its economic and political importance, as the provincial capital of Achaia (modern Greece), it was an obvious place for Paul to visit and spread the Gospel. The Word of the Lord could spread quickly from this important city.

Paul and Corinth

Paul wrote at least two letters to the Corinthian church, which he founded in his missionary work (1 Cor 4:15). At one point, he apparently lived in the city for a year and a half, working to support himself and preaching the Good News (Acts 18:1–18). The church that he founded there seems to have been made up by a mixture of people, from the various different social classes of the city. The very fact that he could say, "Not many of you were wise by human standards, not many were powerful, not many were of noble birth" (1 Cor 1:26), suggests that, while at least a few *were* wise, powerful, and of nobility, most weren't. The church in Corinth was made up of people from a mixture of social classes, education, and influence.

When Paul was in Ephesus during his third journey, he received news that the church in Corinth had broken into rival groups following different leaders. Paul had no desire to compete with anyone, and in fact, spoke very positively about Apollos as a co-worker: "I planted, Apollos watered, but God caused the growth" (1 Cor 3:5–23). Paul also discovered that many members had also fallen back into immoral pagan practices. Paul wrote a letter (referred to in 1 Cor 5:11) to warn the people away from sin and immorality. This letter is now lost to us. When Paul received further news of divisions and challenges to his authority, he wrote another letter, 1 Corinthians, in approximately AD 56. It is a practical but firm letter with good advice for the people of that time and place and

for people today. In AD 57, while in Macedonia, Paul received some good news about the Corinthians from Titus. They were beginning to reject false teachers and respond to Paul's teachings. In response to this happy news, Paul wrote 2 Corinthians, commending the people and trying to make peace with them.

Reflect

When was a time you were misunderstood over an issue of faith?

Themes in 1 Corinthians

The First Letter to the Corinthians has an opening formula (1:1–3) and a prayer of thanksgiving (1:4–7). The conclusion instructs his readers to take up a collection for the needy and his usually personal greetings (16:1–24). Several important themes are included in the letter. Paul explained some of the important details of faith, including things like advice for marriage after the death of a spouse (7:39–40) and an intepretation of the gift of tongues (13:13–19).

For example, Paul encouraged the Corinthians to appreciate their connection with one another and to see themselves as though they were all united into one single body, like a "temple." Because the Holy Spirit was present in that "temple," the whole church of Corinth was holy (1 Cor 3:16–17). Maintaining unity, then, was critical for creating the right environment for the Holy Spirit to work within the Church in Corinth. Paul explained that this unity was established on the foundation of the Apsotles (1 Cor 3:5–23).

Similarly, later in this same letter, Paul described the Church as the Body of Christ, meaning that the members of the Church are as connected to each other in the same way that a foot and an ear are part of a body. They are different, and yet so intimately connected that you can speak of only *one* body. Paul said,

> As a body is one though it has many parts, and all the parts of the body, though many, are one body, so also Christ. For in one Spirit we were all baptized into one body, whether Jews or Greeks, slaves or free persons, and we were all given to drink of one Spirit. (1 Cor 12:12–13)

The responsibility to maintain the connection you have to one another belongs with each believer. The First Letter to the Corinthians challenges believers to recognize that they, in fact, belong to one another. The presence of the Spirit of God not only joins us together with others, but also *wants* us to recognize and preserve our responsibilities to care for one another. This community is in the Church, the Temple of the Holy Spirit, where all parts of the Body of Christ are joined together with Christ as the head.

PROBLEMS WITH PUNCTUATION

As with other letters written in the first century, Paul's letters, including 1 and 2 Corinthians, were written in all capital letters. Also, they had no spaces between words and no punctuation. It would be like trying to read material like the following:

THATSOUNDSLIKEITWOULDBEDIFFICULTTOREADASYOUCANSEETHOUGHYOUAREABLE-TOREADTHESESENTENCESYOUMAYHAVETOREADITALOUDTOKNOWHOWBESTTOPUNC-TUATEIT

(That sounds like it would be difficult to read. As you can see, though, you are able to read these sentences. You may have to read it aloud to know how best to punctuate it.)

The word separations and punctuation that you have now in the books of the New Testament, which were all written in this style, were put there by modern Greek translators. They usually have no more trouble figuring out where one word ends and the next one begins, or the obvious place for putting punctuation than you would in the sentences above. On occasion, though, there are some problems.

Consider how you would translate the following letters into sensible words and phrases in English:

WOMANWITHOUTHERMANISNOTHING

The words are easy to separate, but the resulting sentence(s) can be punctuated in a couple of different ways. For example:

Woman, without her man, is nothing.

Woman! Without her, man is nothing!

The second interpretation makes a completely different point than the first! This kind of problem did happen often in Paul's letters, and in most cases the sense of punctuation was fairly obvious. There are some few places, though, where there has been some confusion. One of the most controversial passages in Paul's writings is found in 1 Corinthians 7:1-2, listed below without any punctuation:

Now in regard to the matters about which you wrote it is a good thing for a man not to touch a woman but because of cases of immorality every man should have his own wife and every woman her own husband.

Without any punctuation the text seems to imply that while marriage was permitted by Paul, it would be better that men and women not touch each other, even in marriage. In the next seven verses (1 Cor 7:3-9) however, Paul seems to make the opposite point, that sexual relations in marriage were good, natural, and the *right* of each spouse. Translators solve this puzzling internal disagreement by providing the following very helpful punctuation:

Now in regard to the matters about which you wrote, "It is a good thing for a man not to touch a woman," but because of cases of immorality every man should have his own wife and every woman her own husband. (1 Cor 7:1-2)

This punctuation makes it clear that Paul encouraged mutuality and a profound spirit of equality. Paul's suggestion that a wife's body belonged to her husband was pretty standard, but the reverse, that the husband's body *belonged* to his wife, was not a common way of thinking at that time. When Paul said "there is no longer male and female" (Gal 3:28) he *really* meant it.

Another prominent theme of the letter involves sexual morality. Greeks in the first century were much more sexually permissive than Jews. In turn, Jesus' teachings called for even *greater* respect for the human body and the most important and intimate relationships, challenging even some aspects of the Jewish culture of the day. Paul had to reprimand a member of the Corinthian church who was living with his father's wife, that is, his own stepmother (1 Cor 5:1–13). He also condemned Christians who went to prostitutes, saying that freedom does not mean a license to do whatever one wants, but means freedom to serve God (1 Cor 6:19–20).

There were other issues involving idolatry and scandal that even spilled over to the ways the Corinthian church conducted itself at Eucharist. Selfishness to the poor, drunkenness among the rich, and quarrels had no place in the **Agape**, the meal shared before Eucharist. The issue involving proper dress of women (especially keeping their head covered) and Eucharist was unique for Paul's time. He advised that women may certainly pray and prophesy in the assemblies, but must dress respectably (1 Cor 11:1–16). In Paul's world, women suggested that they were available for marriage or other less moral activities by not wearing a veil. For a married woman to go out in public unveiled was particularly scandalous. The one place that a married woman could go uncovered was in her own home. This custom of covering women's heads, though not common in North America and most of Europe, is still in place in many Muslim countries today.

The problem for Paul's communities is that the early Church celebrated the Eucharist in homes (Rom 16:5; 1 Cor 16:19; Col 4:15; Phlm 2). The women hosting the local community might have felt free to have their heads uncovered within the confines of her house. In turn, other women might also have felt comfortable removing their veils. If one of them was inclined to lead some element of the prayer and even to prophesy, if the Holy Spirit so moved them, they were no longer acting *privately*, though. They were now *public* and, as Paul saw it according to the custom of the day, needed to have their head covered, even if it was in their own home. Paul even invited the readers to judge this issue for themselves: "Judge for yourselves: is it proper for a woman to pray to God with her head unveiled?" (1 Cor 11:13) .

Paul also addressed the concern that Christians were eating meat that had been sacrificed to pagan gods. For example, most meat in the marketplace at that time would have come from animals sacrificed in pagan religious rites. Jews and Christians of the time had to consider whether it was right to eat the meat from those idolatrous sacrifices. Paul argued that there were no real gods behind the idols (1

Agape

The word *agape* translates to unconditional and thoughtful love. The Agape feasts described in the New Testament refer to meals shared by Christians prior to celebrating the Eucharist.

love. Describing the nature of love (1 Cor 12:31–13:12), Paul offers a number of positive qualities of love (patience, kindness, celebration of the truth, endurance, fidelity, a positive outlook) but didn't describe it as an emotion or a sensual attraction. In fact, he was more inclined to tell of the emotions that didn't combine with love (jealousy, selfishness, quick-temperedness, etc.). In particular, note that Paul taught that "love never fails" (1 Cor 13:8). This is an important criterion for differentiating between real love and infatuation tinged with sexual attraction. While infatuations are fleeting, true love lasts to eternity. Paul later describes the mystery of the Resurrection of the dead when "flesh and blood" have no place. Rather the human body that is sown "corruptible, dishonorable, weak, and natural" will be raised "incorruptible, glorious, powerful, and spiritual." (see 1 Corinthians 15:35–38).

Reflect

- How do you feel connected to the Church as the Body of Christ?
- Explain how you understand the difference between real love and infatuation.

Themes in 2 Corinthians

The Second Letter to the Corinthians is a very personal letter of St. Paul, revealing a great deal about his character and expressing his feelings about his relationship with the Corinthian church. Second Corinthians is a bit disjointed; in fact Chapters 10–13 may be the separate letter Paul wrote to the Corinthians in which he was critical of their abuses. They also make up a defense of Paul's behavior and his ministry. The section is framed by a prologue (2 Cor 10:1–18) and a conclusion (2 Cor 12:19–13:10). The first nine chapters are much more cheerful and positive in tone as Paul tries to make peace with the Corinthians. There

Cor 8:4–5). Since the rituals were meaningless, the meat was just fine for eating. He recognized, though, that new converts might be a little fragile, spiritually, and they might get confused if they saw other Christians eating meat that had be sacrificed to an idol in a pagan temple. He was concerned that no believers do anything to unnecessarily damage another person's faith (1 Cor 8:9–13). This teaching remains important today. When our behavior causes scandal that hurts the faith of others, we are responsible for their anxiety or panic (1 Cor 8:11–13).

Beyond addressing the abuses the occurred at the early celebrations of Eucharist, St. Paul develops the earliest record of the institution of the Lord's Supper in the New Testament (1 Cor 11:23–34), explaining, "For I received from the Lord what I also handed on to you" (vs. 23).

Finally, it is important to mention that one of the most beautiful passages in all of Scripture is Paul's address on the gifts of the Spirit, the greatest gift being

letter and verse 3:1b suggests Paul had written a previous letter, some scholars conclude that Philippians may be the compilation of two or three letters written over a period of time. It is certainly valid to conclude that Philippians is only one letter. There is only one opening address and one concluding formula in Philippians. And the argument can be made that Paul wrote in a "stream-of-consciousness" style while in prison. He may have jumped to, and given advice on, various topics as they came to mind.

 Reflect

Write at least one paragraph about God using the "stream-of-consciousness" technique.

Themes in Philippians

The organization of the Letter to the Philippians follows this outline:

- Salutation and thanksgiving to the Philippians (1:1–11)

- Paul in prison and his attitude toward death (1:12–26)

- Exhortation to follow Christ's example of humility (1:27–2:16)

- Paul and the Philippians and his planned missions (2:17–3:1a)

- Warning against false teachers (3:1b–4:1)

- Instructions to live in unity, joy, and peace (4:2–9)

- Paul's current situation and Philippian generosity (4:10–20)

- Concluding formula, blessing (4:21–23)

Kenotic Hymn

Kenotic is a Greek term that means "emptying." The Kenotic Hymn of Philippians 2:5—11 describes Christ's emptying himself in humility to take on our human nature.

Joy in the Lord for those who live in the Church is a major theme in Philippians. Paul also writes of the need for Christian harmony, peace, and humility, and the necessity to imitate Christ in his sufferings. It was in this spirit that Paul, hoping to encourage them with the example of Jesus' complete self-emptying, recounted the **Kenotic Hymn**, a central focus of the letter. The hymn praises Christ's self-emptying humility in his becoming man and his dying on the Cross to be raised and exalted. These verses reveal the "high Christology" of the early Christians who clearly believed in Christ's divinity:

Have among yourselves the same
attitude that is also yours in
Christ Jesus,

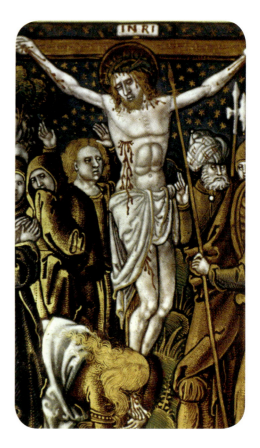

Who, though he was in the form of God,
did not regard equality with God something to
  be grasped.
Rather, he emptied himself,
taking the form of a slave,
coming in human likeness;
and found human in appearance,
he humbled himself,
becoming obedient to death,
even death on a cross.
Because of this, God greatly exalted him
and bestowed on him the name
that is above every other name,
that at the name of Jesus
every knee should bend,
of those in heaven and on earth and under the
  earth,
and every tongue confess that
Jesus Christ is Lord,
to the glory of God the Father. (Phil 2:5–11)

Two of the greatest Christian mysteries are spelled out in this hymn: self-giving affirmation and humility leads to exaltation. This hymn reminds us that there is no true love without the giving of one's self, and that truth, a fundamental principle of humility, is the only foundation for real honor.

The Letter to the Colossians

Colossae was a textile town east of Ephesus. The letter was written to assist a certain Epaphras, the founder of the church there, in counteracting false teachers. They were spreading ideas about the existence of many different spirits, claiming they intervened in human affairs. Belief in intermediate spirits and practices to appease them wooed the Colossians away from belief in the unique saving role of Christ.

The author also specifically requested that this letter be shared with the people of Laodicea, living between ten and eleven miles away in the same Lycus River valley:

Give greetings to the brothers in Laodicea and to Nympha and to the church in her house. And when this letter is read before you, have it read also in the church of the Laodiceans, and you yourselves read the one from Laodicea. (Col 4:15–16)

This manner of circulating letters with neighboring communities indicates one of the primary ways that the faith was able to spread and these books became understood as inspired Scripture by the wider Church. Fed by the zeal of early Christians and their conviction that they were responsible for each other's spiritual relationship and understanding of God, the Word was sent from one community to the next until the entire Mediterranean basin and surrounding lands were brought to faith.

Colossians (written approximately AD 80) is grouped with Philippians, Philemon, and Ephesians as Captivity Letters. While there are few doubts that Paul wrote Philemon and Philippians, scholars today believe that Colossians and Ephesians, closely related letters, were written by Paul's disciples after his death.

Themes in Colossians

The Letter to the Colossians seems to be aware that some incorrect ideas had begun to circulate among some followers of Jesus Christ, which the author felt obliged to correct. After a formal greeting, Colossians opens with a beautiful hymn of creation through Christ, likely sung by the early Church while at prayer, that addressed some of the errors (1:15–20). It clarified that the Christ was the very image (*eikōn*) of God. If you want to *see* God, look at Jesus. Saying that he was firstborn did not mean that he was created, since absolutely *all* things everywhere came to be *through* him. Not only that, but if they continue to exist, it was through his power.

Some of the language used in this hymn, such as "fullness," "principalities," and "powers," is found in the writings of later Gnostics. It is possible that an intention of this letter was to address some false teachings of Gnosticism.

The letter closes with a series of greetings to and from people that seem to have been known to the Colossians, in particular Epaphras (Col 1:7; 4:12). Epaphras was a companion of Paul's while he was imprisoned and wrote his letter to Philemon (Phlm 23). The author of the Letter to the Colossians knew that Paul had not been the founder of the Colossian church (Col 4:8), and yet was moved to write this letter in his name, since his teachings had already spread this far into the Lycus Valley through Epaphras's ministry.

The First Letter to the Thessalonians

The First Letter to the Thessalonians is very likely the earliest New Testament writing, dating in AD 50–51, only twenty years or so after the life of Jesus. In the letter, Paul encourages the Thessalonians, defends his proclamation of the Gospel, shares news about his travel plans, and addresses two pressing issues of his time. First, he encourages the Thessalonians to remain holy, especially avoiding sexual immorality.

Second, he assures them that Christians who have died with Christ will one day rise and live with him forever. He also reminds them of the imminent end of the world.

Thessalonica was a harbor town and prosperous trading post located on the major Egnatia Highway, still a major route through Greece today. The Acts of the Apostles detailed that Paul, and his traveling companions, Silvanus and Timothy, had ministered there, beginning in the local synagogue, but also faced strong opposition (Acts 17:1–10). Later Paul and Silvanus apparently sent Timothy back to the city to "strengthen and encourage" the faithful there (1 Thes 3:1–3). When he returned to Paul and Silvanus, Timothy brought word of the progress that the faithful had made there, but also related some misunderstandings that had crept it.

Paul, Silvanus, and Timothy were actually more than traveling companions. The use of the plural pronouns "we," "us," and "our" ninety-nine times in the letter implies both shared ministry and shared authorship. Paul was apparently the one giving dictation in the letter, breaking into the text in a personal way only three times (1 Thes 2:18; 3:5; 5:27) and in another passage referring to Timothy in the third person: ". . . we decided to remain alone in Athens and sent Timothy, our brother and co-worker for God in the gospel of Christ, to strengthen and encourage you in your faith" (1 Thes 3:1–2).

Themes in 1 Thessalonians

When people do something right, they should be recognized and their successes should be celebrated. The intention of 1 Thessalonians was, in part, to encourage, strengthen, and even applaud the great progress that the Thessalonians had made in the practice of their faith. The Thessalonians had apparently successfully shared the faith they had received throughout their region of Macedonia and down into Greece itself (Achaia, as it was called then; see 1 Thes 1:6–10). Paul felt that the hard work they had done in Thessalonica (1 Thes 2:1–12) had born great fruit in the lives of Thessalonians, and they were grateful (1 Thes 2:13–20).

However, being relatively new converts, Paul surmised that the people needed support and guidance for living a moral life. So, a secondary purpose of this letter was to encourage them to refrain from sexual immorality (1 Thes 4:2–8), to promote their love and concern for one another (1 Thes 4:9–10), and to correct some unnecessary worry. In this last regard, having been taught that Jesus was returning soon, some of the Thessalonians had become worried that their deceased family members and friends would not have a place in the Kingdom of God. The authors wanted to reassure the Thessalonians that, in the resurrection of the dead, all who died in Christ would find a place with God. "Then we who are alive, who are left, will be caught up together (*rapiemur* in Latin) with them in the clouds to meet the Lord in the air. Thus we shall always be with the Lord" (1 Thes 4:13–18). Ironically, the term *rapiemur*, translated as **rapture**, that was originally written to reassure and calm the fears of the Thessalonians, has brought fear and panic among some fundamentalist Christians that some people will be "left behind" at the coming of the Lord and the resurrection of the dead.

Paul clearly wanted his readers to take their faith seriously, and to always be on guard, a message as important today as it was then (1 Thes 5:1–8). You have no idea when the Lord is returning, nor the moment of your own death. Likewise, as you have no control over drunk drivers, earthquakes, tornadoes, and the like, the day to be ready for the Lord is today. However, the motivation for leading a good life should not be fear, since "God did not destine us for wrath, but to gain salvation through our Lord Jesus Christ, who died for us, so that whether we are awake or asleep we may live together with him" (1 Thes 5:9–10).

The closing words of 1 Thessalonians are particularly intended to encourage us in all that is right and good, as we await the coming of the Lord:

> We urge you, brothers, admonish the idle, cheer the fainthearted, support the weak, be patient with all. See that no one returns evil for evil; rather, always seek what is good (both) for each other and for all. Rejoice always. Pray without ceasing. In all circumstances give thanks, for this is the will of God for you in Christ Jesus. Do not quench the Spirit. Do not despise prophetic utterances. Test everything; retain what is good. Refrain from every kind of evil.
>
> May the God of peace himself make you perfectly holy and may you entirely, spirit, soul, and body, be preserved blameless for the coming of our Lord Jesus Christ. (1 Thes 5:14–23)

rapture

In Scripture, the term *rapture* refers to our mystical union with God, or our final sharing in God's eternal life. For many fundamentalist Christians, the rapture signifies a series of events that will occur at the end of time. The Church has no teaching that corresponds to the fundamentalist view.

The Second Letter to the Thessalonians

The traditional views was that Paul wrote 2 Thessalonians shortly after his First Letter to the Thessalonians to address a misunderstanding about his teaching concerning the resurrection of the dead and Christ's Second

Coming, also called the **Parousia**. In their confusion, some of the new Christians thought that Christ was returning any day, so they quit working. This, of course, upset the others who continued to work. The letter notes how hard Paul, himself, had to work to provide for himself without being a burden to others. The readers are encouraged to imitate Paul's behavior (2 Thes 3:6–12).

The current scholarly opinion, however, favors the belief that disciples of Paul wrote 2 Thessalonians around AD 90. There are some noteworthy differences between this letter and those written by Paul that signal that Paul was not the actual author.

For example, considering the issue of Christians who were refusing to work, an interesting point is that the author did not emphasize the imminent Second Coming as had been done in other Pauline letters. In fact, the letter seems to discourage its readers from being misdirected in their concern about the end times:

> We ask you, brothers, with regard to the coming of our Lord Jesus Christ and our assembling with him, not to be shaken out of your minds suddenly, or to be alarmed either by a "spirit," or by an oral statement, or by a letter allegedly from us to the effect that the day of the Lord is at hand. (2 Thes 2:1–2)

Different from 1 Thessalonians where the "day of the Lord" could come at any moment "like a thief" (1 Thes 5:1–8), this passage in 2 Thessalonians points out that there will be clear warning signs for Christ's return.

Additionally, where First Thessalonians was focused on the end of the world (the technical term is "eschatological," meaning pointing to the end times), Second Thessalonians was more alert to the tumult, apostasy, and false leaders that would confront believers before the world's end: "Let no one deceive you in any way" (2 Thes 2:3). This reflects an **apocalyptic** concern, more like the style of the Book of Revelation than the rest of Paul's writing. What could have been the reason for this shift in focus? It seems to indicate that the Pauline communities, in Paul's absence, began to consider how it was that they might live for a more extended period of time, awaiting the coming of the Lord.

Themes in 2 Thessalonians

Related to the apocalyptic themes discussed above, in 2 Thessalonians 2 the readers are told that Jesus will not come again until certain signs take place. Patience and prayer are the weapons Christians need to prepare themselves for this return.

Chapter 3 instructs the Thessalonians what to do with the non-workers. The authors point to Paul's own example—how he worked while preaching among them. The readers are instructed to go to work and earn money for their

Parousia
The Second Coming of Christ, which will usher in the full establishment of God's Kingdom on earth as it is in Heaven.

apocalyptic
From a word meaning "revelation" or "unveiling." Apocalyptic writings, usually written in times of crisis, use highly symbolic language to bolster faith by reassuring believers that the current age, subject to the forces of evil, will end when God intervenes and establishes a divine rule and goodness and peace.

food. Those who ignore this advice should be avoided so in shame they will return to the Church (2 Thes 3:11–15). The purpose of shunning wrongdoers is not to punish but to encourage repentance. Christians are brothers and sisters in the Lord, not enemies. This advice is timeless. Our motive for calling the sinner back must always be love for one another.

Reflect

How can you cultivate patience and prayer in your own life in expectation of Christ's return?

The First and Second Letters to Timothy and the Letter to Titus

With the passage of several decades from the Ascension of the Lord without the awaited Lord's return, the local churches, founded by Paul himself or one of his disciples, recognized that **evangelization** was only part of their mission. They also had to offer ongoing care to the churches already established. It was important to set up leadership, commissioned by an Apostle or one of his representatives, at each Church. The leadership roles were not unlike the care a shepherd gives to a flock of sheep. The word for shepherd in Latin is *pastor*. Because the Letters to Timothy and Titus share this concern for local leadership, they are called the Pastoral Letters.

First and Second Timothy and Titus are arranged in the canon just prior to Philemon, the shortest of all the letters attributed to Paul, from longest to shortest of this group.

The three letters were written approximately AD 100 and were probably the work of the same author, a later follower of Paul. Their style and vocabulary are different from that of Paul, and they reflect a more developed organization of the Church than was present at the time of Paul. They differ from the other Pauline letters in that they are addressed to individuals and give advice on Church leadership. Both Timothy and Titus were fellow missionaries and faithful disciples. Each also shepherded his own local church, Timothy in Ephesus and Titus in Crete.

Themes in 1 Timothy

There are two letters to Timothy. Both are attributed to Paul. Neither letter mentions the other. The First Letter to Timothy is called "first" not because it was written before the other, but because it is slightly longer, and therefore, placed before the "Second Letter," which is shorter in length. In fact, the First Letter to Timothy is very similar in theme to the Letter to Titus.

Timothy worked side by side with Paul and was mentioned by Paul, or those writing in his name, in eleven of the thirteen letters of the Pauline correspondence. Only Ephesians and Galatians from the Pauline letters fail to mention him. The references to Timothy are consistently affectionate and supportive,

evangelization
To bring the Good News of Jesus Christ to others.

referring to Timothy as a "brother" and "coworker" (1 Thes 3:2) or even his "child" (Phil 2:22; 1 Tm 1:2).

This letter begins with careful instruction to Timothy to correct false teachers in the church of Ephesus (1 Tm 1:3–20). It returns to this theme repeatedly, for example, in 1 Timothy 4:1–16 and 6:3–10. Every generation and community seems to need to address the problem of people who invent new and inaccurate ways of understanding the faith. The letter clearly states in 1 Timothy 3:15 that the Church is "the pillar and foundation of truth." The responsibility to refute error, passed onto Timothy in this letter, remains in the hands of the Church in the teaching office of the bishops to the present day.

As in Titus, the public ordering of the community was important, including the relationship of the community to those in authority. The modern-day practice of praying for presidents, governors, mayors, and other civic officials comes from the encouragement in 1 Timothy to pray for "kings and for all in authority" (2:1–4).

While discussing Church order, the author gives some directives regarding women being silent that seem quite repressive by modern standards:

> A woman must receive instruction silently and under complete control. I do not permit a woman to teach or to have authority over a man. She must be quiet. For Adam was formed first, then Eve. Further, Adam was not deceived, but the woman was deceived and transgressed. But she will be saved through motherhood, provided women persevere in faith and love and holiness, with self-control. (1 Tm 2:11–15)

One might dismiss this passage, concluding that the writer was simply expressing the culture of his day, but that can be a slippery slope. Once you begin dismissing passages for being more cultural than scriptural, you can end up dismissing everything that disagrees with your culture's ways of understanding human behavior. You would need to have very good criterion before making any such decision.

Such reasons, in fact, occur in this case where the stated directive of women remaining silent disagrees with Paul, who elsewhere presumed that women would, in fact, pray and prophesy aloud in the gathered community, only directing that they should do so with their heads covered (1 Cor 11:5). Furthermore, while the author of 1 Timothy didn't permit women to instruct men, an *angel*, no less, at the tomb instructed the holy women to proclaim the Good News of the Resurrection to the *Apostles* (Mk 16:5–7; Mt 28:1–7). To further support this evaluation, this particular passage states expressly, "I do not permit," as opposed to "the Lord does not permit," or "the teachings as handed down do not permit." This gives us further confidence that we are not being arbitrary when we recognize the cultural limitations in this particular passage.

The First Letter to Timothy gives directives on the kind of people who should be chosen to hold key positions, giving similar guidelines as found in Titus 1:7–9 about the kind of sober, self-controlled, blameless, hospitable qualities required in men chosen to be bishops, again emphasizing their need to teach others effectively. 1 Timothy is more expansive, requiring an inspection of bishops' management of their own households as indicating the kind of gifts they have to oversee the larger Christian community (1 Tm 3:1–7). The description of the office of bishop as a noble task (1 Tm 3:1), along with the stated fear that some might become conceited (1 Tm 3:6), helps us recognize how important and highly respected the office of bishop was, even in the early Church.

This letter also gives directives about the prerequisite characteristics of deacons, which resemble those given for bishops (1 Tm 3:8–10, 12–13). In a manner that, unlike Titus, distinguishes presbyters from bishops, 1 Timothy also mentions, not only those presbyters who govern well and should be fairly remunerated for their labors, but also how to handle accusations against them (1 Tm 5:17–20). Wherever people are placed in positions of authority there can be a tendency to abuse that responsibility. The fact that a process for fair judgment of cases against presbyters existed before the composition of this letter suggests that the office of priest must have existed from a yet even earlier time. The directive not to lay hands on anyone too quickly (5:22), a seeming reference to ordination of bishops, priests, or deacons, also suggests that the early Church had learned quickly the necessity of doing careful training and observation of people in preparation for religious responsibility. It has often been the case that some have been attracted to ordained ministry for the wrong reason.

Another key group of great concern that made its way into this pastoral instruction was widows. The basic message of 1 Timothy seems to be that if they had family they should continue in their families' care, or if they are young enough to marry, then perhaps they should do so. "True" widows would be those who, through the death of family members, had no outside support or care, and were too old to consider remarriage. These women, who would be otherwise destitute in the ancient economy, were to be cared for by the community (1 Tm 5:3–16).

The First Letter to Timothy closes with sober advice to the rich and those who want to be rich, that is, "the love of money is the root of all evils" (1 Tm 6:10). This remains, to this day, one of the places where true Christianity stands at odds with the publicly proclaimed values of society. A Christian's pursuit is eternal life and the service of the only One who can make that possible, "the King of kings and Lord of lords, who alone has immortality, who dwells in unapproachable light, and whom no human being has seen or can see" (1 Tm 6:15–16).

Reflect

How do people today disregard laws and directions based on only what appeals to them?

Themes in 2 Timothy

It is difficult to fit the narrative details of the Second Letter to Timothy into the actual life of St. Paul unless, as has been suggested, the imprisonment mentioned was his last, in Rome, shortly before his death.

Though included among the Pastoral Letters with Titus and 1 Timothy, 2 Timothy takes a very different approach. For example, it does not include directives for the establishment or maintenance of a hierarchy or any rules for governing the Church as the others do. Instead, it dwells at length on Paul's personal situation, in particular his suffering and reflections, in the midst of his imprisonment. Whether it was written by Paul or not, 2 Timothy offers a very personal reflection of a Christian facing loneliness in the midst of distress, and the near possibility of death, while looking back on his life's efforts with satisfaction and in hope. In some of the most powerful words of Scripture, 2 Timothy quotes Paul as follows:

> I am already being poured out like a libation, and the time of my departure is at hand. I have competed well; I have finished the race; I have kept the faith. From now on the crown of righteousness awaits me, which the Lord, the just judge, will award to me on that day, and not only to me, but to all who have longed for his appearance. (2 Tm 2:6–8)

The author does not see Paul's imprisonment and death as dishonorable, in spite of abandonment (2 Tm 1:15–18) and encourages Timothy to see it in the same way, and to carry on in the proclamation of the Good News, since it was through Jesus Christ's own imprisonment, Passion, and Death that death itself was conquered (2 Tm 1:6–14; 2:1–9):

> If we have died with him,
>   we shall also live with him;
> if we persevere,
>   we shall also reign with him.
> But if we deny him,
>   he will deny us.
> If we are unfaithful,
>   he remains faithful,
>   for he cannot deny himself. (2 Tm 2:11–13)

The author also tells Timothy not to get lost in pointless disputes, or be swayed by false teachings as some in the community apparently have done, but to challenge the wayward gently and persuasively (2 Tm 2:14–26).

Some of Paul's authentic eschatological concerns are in this letter, with dire warnings of the wickedness that will precede the end times (2 Tm 3:1–9). The writer, though, has confidence that if Timothy will remain rooted in the teachings he has received, and the Scriptures that he has known from his youth, he will be "competent, equipped for every good work" (2 Tm 3:10–17).

The letter closes in a very personal way, with a lengthy set of hopes, instructions, and greetings. It seems appropriate, whether this letter was written by Paul or not, that such a faithful and selfless witness to the Gospel of Jesus Christ be memorialized in this way, confidently proclaiming the Good News to the very end: "The Lord will rescue me from every evil threat and will bring me safe to his heavenly kingdom. To him be glory forever and ever. Amen" (2 Tm 4:18).

 **Reflect**

Describe one way that the teachings of your family and Church have left you competent, equipped for good work?

Themes in Titus

Paul's companion, Titus, is mentioned fourteen times in the New Testament, including as a Greek convert and Paul's companion (Gal 2:1, 3), an emissary to the Corinthian community (2 Cor 8:6, 16, 23), and as a missionary to Dalmatia, a peninsula in the Adriatic Sea (2 Tm 4:10).

The Letter to Titus explains that Paul's reason for leaving Titus to minister in Crete, an island in the Eastern Mediterranean, was so that he could "appoint presbyters in every town" (1:5). *Presbyter* is the Greek word for "elder," and is the word from which the modern English word "priest" is derived. It would seem at this very early point in the life of the Church that, at least in some communities, there was a clear connection between a priest (*presbyter*) and a bishop (*episcopos*):

> For this reason I left you in Crete so that you might set right what remains to be done and appoint presbyters in every town, as I directed you, on condition that a man be blameless, married only once, with believing children who are not accused of licentiousness or rebellious. For a bishop as God's steward must be blameless, not arrogant, not irritable, not a drunkard, not aggressive, not greedy for sordid gain, but hospitable, a lover of goodness, temperate, just, holy, and self-controlled, holding fast to the true message as taught so that he will be able both to exhort with sound doctrine and to refute opponents. (Ti 1:5–9)

Notice in this passage that the author switches from talking about presbyters and starts talking about bishops as if they were the same office. In fact, to this day, priests cooperate with their bishops in serving the People of God. They are able to exercise their priestly ministry only by depending on the bishop and being in faithful communion with him.

It is also important to not miss the careful instruction given to bishops, to hold "fast to the true message as taught so that he will be able both to exhort with sound doctrine and to refute opponents" (1:9). From the very earliest times, bishops have been given the particular task of teaching the faith that has been handed down and correcting errors of belief. These bishops being appointed by Titus were not eyewitnesses themselves. They had been taught a Tradition that sprang from the Apostles that was only now being recorded, in letters like this one. The early Church was quite aware of the importance of remaining faithful to the Tradition, *even before there was a New Testament*. To state the obvious, this Tradition, which existed before the writings of Paul and the Gospels, was the source for letters like Titus. Sacred Tradition exists in the beliefs of the Church, both those recorded in the Sacred Scriptures and those that were not.

The need for giving correction was apparently also necessary from the beginning of the Church. The churches in Crete seem to have been beset by some troublesome characters, although it is difficult to discern precisely what was the nature of their problem; perhaps some Jewish Christians were insisting that Gentile converts observe circumcision and the old Jewish customs, rites, and feasts (Ti 1:10–16).

Whereas Colossians 3:18–4:1 and Ephesians 5:2–6:9 gave very clear household rules, Titus gives broader rules for the behavior of differing age groups: older men and women were given one set of instructions, younger women their own, as well as young men. Common to both young men and women was self-control, which becomes so important as they pass out of the control of their parents and begin to make important decisions for themselves (Ti 2:1–10). It is particularly important for young people, considering jobs or a life away at college, to hear this particular encouragement and why they should persist in the Christian life:

> For the grace of God has appeared, saving all and training us to reject godless ways and worldly desires and to live temperately, justly, and devoutly in this age, as we await the blessed hope, the appearance of the glory of the great God and of our savior Jesus Christ, who gave himself for us to deliver us from all lawlessness and to cleanse for himself a people as his own, eager to do what is good. (Ti 2:11–14)

Finally, as in the Letter to the Ephesians, closing words of encouragement are offered for faithfully living the Christian life (Ti 3:1–11).

 Reflect

What are challenges you face in your life to reject godless ways?

The Letter to Philemon

The Letter to Philemon is a very short 335-word letter. It was written during one of Paul's imprisonments, perhaps in Ephesus around AD 55 or from Rome in AD 61–63 It is a personal letter from Paul to Philemon.

Who was Philemon? He seems to have been a convert of Paul's, seeing how he owed Paul his "very self" (v. 19). He was also likely a person with some wealth as he had the capacity to provide hospitality for Paul (v. 22) and was able to host his local church at his house (v. 2). Philemon also owned slaves. Most Greco-Roman households of the time had a number of slaves to cook, clean, care for the children, and manage the family's properties and businesses.

The Letter to Philemon contains many elements of the style Paul used in all of his letters:

- Greeting (vv. 1–3)
- Thanksgiving (vv. 4–7)
- Body (vv. 8–20)
- Closing: Greeting and Blessing (vv. 21–25)

Themes in Philemon

The subject of the letter involves Philemon's runaway slave, Onesimus. There were many slaves during that period, perhaps up to one-half of the population. This was the inevitable result of the recent Roman conquests of the entire Mediterranean basin, in which the Romans enslaved entire cities and nations of people. Slavery would eventually recede in the Roman Empire, but not until nearly three centuries later. In the first century it would have been hard to imagine a society and economy functioning without slaves.

Paul's own response to the question of slavery was complex, and in many ways driven by his perception of how quickly he expected the world to end. Rather than fight a system that was going to fade away at the Lord's return, he suggested that slaves remain as they were, since in the sight of the Lord they were really free (1 Cor 7:20). The Pauline school went on to suggest that, if slaves were to remain in that state, they should be the best slaves possible, and that masters

should remember that they, too, would have to answer to the true Master in Heaven for their treatment of their slaves (Eph 6:5–10).

Inspired as he was, Paul could see that in the eyes of God, the distinction between slaves and their owners did not exist: "There is neither Jew nor Greek, there is neither slave nor free person, there is not male and female; for you are all one in Christ Jesus" (Gal 3:28; see also 1 Cor 12:13; Col 3:11). It was in that spirit that Paul beseeched Philemon not to punish Onesimus; he also hints that he should free him and send him back to Paul (vv. 13–14). Paul tells Philemon that he should at least treat Onesimus as a brother in Christ (vv. 15–17).

🌑 Review

1. What concerned Paul about missionaries with Jewish roots who may have founded the Roman church?

2. Why does it make sense that Paul wrote the Letter to the Romans in Greek?

3. What does the Letter to the Romans teach about the Paschal Mystery?

4. How do Christians share in the merits of Christ's Death?

5. Describe the unique nature of Corinth.

6. What happened to the letter of Paul to the Corinthians referred to in 1 Corinthians 5:11?

7. What were idolatrous and scandalous issues that spilled over from the Agape to the Eucharist in the Corinthian church?

8. How did Paul answer the concern of Christians that they were eating meat sacrificed to pagan gods?

9. Define *apologetic*.

10. What are some main topics addressed in 2 Corinthians?

11. How did the Letter to the Galatians counter the message of the Judaizers?

12. What evidence in writing style indicates that Paul did not write the Letter to the Ephesians?

13. What was the pattern of blessing used in the Letter to the Ephesians that parallels the prayers of ancient Judaism?

14. Why do scholars think that the Letter to the Philippians may combine more than one letter?

15. What are two great mysteries spelled out in the Kenotic Hymn of Philippians?

16. Explain what it means in Colossians to say that Christ is in the very image of God?

17. What was the earliest letter written by Paul?

18. What are two key issues addressed in 1 Thessalonians?

19. Who were Silvanus and Timothy?

20. How did the original intention for describing the rapture differ from how it is often interpreted today?

21. What was the issue related to the disciples ceasing work detailed in 2 Thessalonians?

22. Why did 2 Thessalonians shift to cover apocalyptic concerns over eschatological issues?

23. Why are 1 and 2 Timothy and Titus sometimes called Pastoral Letters?

24. Why did Paul leave Titus to minister in Crete?

25. What evidence is there that the author of 1 Timothy was speaking to the culture of the day, not in God's name, when addressing women being silent in regards to preaching the Gospel?

26. What are some characteristics of bishops described in 1 Timothy (and also Titus)?

27. How does 2 Timothy view Paul's imprisonment and death?

28. Who was Philemon?

29. What was Paul's response to the issue of slavery in the Letter to Philemon?

The Letter to the Hebrews

Traditionally the Letter to the Hebrews was associated with St. Paul. It is placed after the letters attributed to Paul in the New Testament canon. Also, there is a reference to Timothy in Hebrews 13:23. Paul had a companion named Timothy who was mentioned frequently as a co-author of six of the letters (2 Cor 1:1; Phil 1:1; Col 1:1; 1 Thes 1:1; 2 Thes 1:1; Phlm 1:1), as Paul's messenger (1 Cor 4:17; Phil 2:19; 1 Thes 3:2), and as the recipient of the two letters himself (1 and 2 Tm). Unfortunately, the few details in the Letter to the Hebrews leave no way of knowing if this Timothy is Paul's companion or someone else.

It is more accurate to say that the author of Hebrews is anonymous. There is quite a bit of evidence in the text that Paul did *not* write Hebrews. For example, the unnamed author admitted that he depended on the testimony of "those who had heard" for his belief (Heb 2:3). This statement is not typical of Paul, who was proud to have been called by Jesus himself (Gal 1:1). The letter's content and style, as well, were so very different from Paul's that, from as early as the third century, the Church proposed that Paul was not its author. As a result, the Letter to the Hebrews was *not* placed in the sequence according to size (remember that Paul's letters where placed longest to shortest, that is, Romans to Philemon). If arranged by this criteria, Hebrews would be placed between the First and Second Letters to the Corinthians.

Though anonymous, there are several things we can know about the Letter to the Hebrews. The author wrote using excellent Greek grammar, style, and rhetoric, an indication of possessing a classic education. This indicates, in the ancient world, that the author was probably a man, as only men were provided such opportunities. He was almost certainly a Jewish Christian because of his grasp of the Greek version of the Hebrew scriptures, the Septuagint. He quotes from the Hebrew scriptures loosely, probably from memory. In Hebrews 2:6 he begins a citation from Psalm 8:46 by writing "someone has testified somewhere." Again, in Hebrews 4:4, he used that same open-ended kind of reference: "For he has spoken somewhere about the seventh day in this manner, 'And God rested on the seventh day from all his works.'" These types of references also indicate that the community to whom Paul wrote was also apparently made up of many converts from Judaism as he presumed they would understand his passing references to Jewish practices and scriptures without lengthy explanations.

Also, unlike the recipients of Paul's letters, they had been Christians for quite some time and survived a time of terrible suffering:

> Remember the days past when, after you had been enlightened, you endured a great context of suffering. At times you were publicly exposed to abuse and affliction; at other times you associated yourselves with those so treated. You even joined in the sufferings of those in prison and joyfully accepted the confiscation of your property, knowing that you had a better and lasting possession. (Heb 10:32–34)

The time of suffering seems to have passed, though, before the composition of this letter, and the community, once so fervent and willing to gladly embrace those afflictions, had grown slack in its fervor and "sluggish in hearing" (Heb 5:11). It's this very change of heart that provided the author with his motivation to compose this Letter to the Hebrews.

These references to the passage of time place this letter fairly late, perhaps in the last twenty years of the first century. Paul's letters, you will remember, were written considerably earlier in the early to mid AD 50s. At the same time, though, Hebrews had to have been composed before the turn of the first century, because a letter written by Church Father St. Clement to the Corinthians is dated to AD 96 and cites several references to Hebrews.

The Letter to the Hebrews was controversial in the years after its circulation. The Church struggled with its apparent hard-line stance against **apostasy** in Hebrews 6:4–6, attributed to the demands of Christian life and a growing indifference to the faith.

Themes in Hebrews

The Letter to the Hebrews is written as a homily, brilliantly developing the theme of Christ as high priest, the model of our faith. The function of a priest is to offer sacrifices. Jesus willingly offered the sacrifice of his life for us and for our sins. He is the high priest who not only offered the sacrifice on our behalf, but is also himself the sacrifice. In particular, the Letter draws attention to the eternal significance of what God did through Jesus, offering hope for a broken humanity in ways that the yearly repeated sacrifices of the old **Day of Atonement** could not (Lv 23:27–32; Nm 29:7–11). It is truly the Son of God made man who died and was buried on our behalf.

Coming to a new understanding of *sacrifice* would have been very important to Jewish Christians by the time this letter was composed, sometime after the destruction of the Temple in Jerusalem, the only place where the age-old sacrifices of the Jews could be conducted correctly. Jewish Christians needed to consider how their ancient

faith was going to adjust to a world without a place to fulfill the ritual commands found in Torah. The message of this letter is that Jesus' Death on the Cross perfectly achieved, once and for all in the true heavenly Temple where God was present, the reconciliation between humanity and God that the yearly repeated sacrifices in the humanly constructed Jerusalem Temple could not (Heb 9:11–15). This would have been a great comfort to those Jews who had become Christian. In great poetic fashion, the epistle compares the ancient ministry of the Jewish high priest with the ministry of Jesus Christ:

> Every high priest is taken from among men and made their representative before God, to offer gifts and sacrifices for sins. He is able to deal patiently with the ignorant and erring, for he himself is beset by weakness and so, for this reason, must make sin offerings for himself as well as for the people. (Heb 5:1–3)

An amazing difference between the Jewish high priests and Jesus was that Christ is "holy, innocent, undefiled, separated from sinners, higher than the heavens" (Heb 7:26). This purity and divinity of Christ does not alienate us from him in any way; in fact, it allows us to draw nearer to Jesus "because he himself was tested through what he suffered, he is able to help those who are being tested" (Heb 2:18). A powerful

apostasy
The denial of Christ and the repudiation of the Christian faith by a baptized Christian.

Day of Atonement
The Day of Atonement, or Yom Kippur, is the holiest day of the year for Jews. It is a day when Jews ask forgiveness for both communal and personal sins; a person goes directly to the person he or she has offended, if possible, asking forgiveness.

message of the Letter to the Hebrews is that Jesus understands our human problems and trials, not simply because he is the very imprint of an all-knowing God (Heb 1:3), but also from his own participation in our human nature.

Review

1. What is evidence that Paul did not write the Letter to the Hebrews?

2. What evidence is there that the author of the Letter to the Hebrews was a Jewish Christian?

3. What is Jesus' role as high priest?

Reflect

How do you feel knowing that the all-powerful God participated in our human nature?

Research and Report

Choose and complete at least two of the following assignments.

- Read 1 Corinthians 12-15 and record answers to the following questions:

1. What are the gifts Paul lists in the "Body of Christ" passage in 1 Corinthians 12?

2. Study the hymn on love in 1 Corinthians 13. Give examples of each trait listed in verses 4-7.

3. Study 1 Corinthians 15. What is the result for us if Christ has *not* risen from the dead? In your own words, explain Paul's image of what our resurrected bodies will be like (1 Cor 15:35 ff.).

- Read 1 Timothy and write five specific pieces of advice this letter gives. Discuss whether this advice is still applicable for the Church today. Give reasons for each answer.
- Construct a one-page biography of St. Paul based on his own writings. See www.paulonpaul.org.
- The First and Second Letters to the Thessalonians deal with the Second Coming of Christ, also known as the Parousia. Prepare a short report on what the Church teaches about this future event.

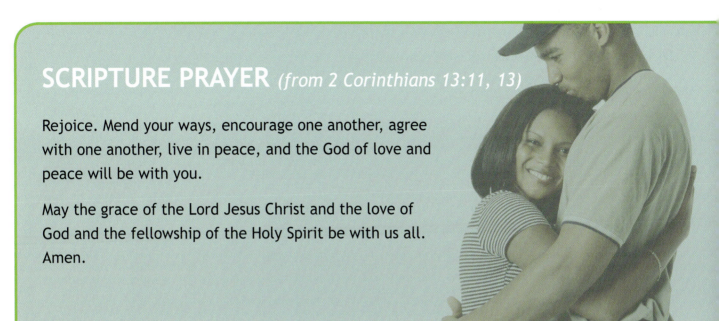

SCRIPTURE PRAYER *(from 2 Corinthians 13:11, 13)*

Rejoice. Mend your ways, encourage one another, agree with one another, live in peace, and the God of love and peace will be with you.

May the grace of the Lord Jesus Christ and the love of God and the fellowship of the Holy Spirit be with us all. Amen.

2c

THE CATHOLIC LETTERS

● Letters to an Entire Church
Seven letters—James, 1 and 2 Peter, 1, 2, and 3 John, and Jude—are classified as catholic or universal letters because they contain general advice helpful to the Church at large.

● The Letter of James
The Letter of James focuses on the response of the believer while offering practical advice on Christian living.

● The First Letter of Peter
A central theme of the First Letter of Peter, written for Christians living in the Diaspora, is that we should imitate the model of Jesus, the Suffering Servant.

● The Letter of Jude and the Second Letter of Peter
The Second Letter of Peter borrows from the Letter of Jude while treating the topic of Christians who were beginning to distort the true teaching they received.

● The First, Second, and Third Letters of John
The three Letters of John come from the same tradition as established by the author of John's Gospel, repeating his important themes and ideas.

● The Revelation to John
The last book of the Bible—also known as the Book of Revelation or the Apocalypse—contains apocalyptic writing while reminding the Church that God controls the events of history.

Letters to an Entire Church

There are seven New Testament documents—James, 1 and 2 Peter, 1, 2, and 3 John, and Jude—that are categorized as Catholic Letters. Catholic means *universal*. The letters are called catholic for three reasons. First, they contain general advice that is helpful to all the churches. Second, they were accepted, even if only gradually, by all the Eastern and Western churches. And third, these letters help us understand better how the catholic, that is, universal or worldwide, Church developed.

Though each of the authors of these letters is identified as an eyewitness of Jesus, like some of the Pauline letters, the Catholic Letters were written by pseudonymous writers, presenting what the named Apostle might well have said in dealing with the situations that developed in the various churches at the end of the first century. The Revelation of John, or Book of Revelation, is also discussed in this chapter. It is written in apocalyptic style to encourage the Church that good will always triumph over evil.

Review

What is meant by the classification "catholic letters?"

The Letter of James

The Letter of James (AD 80s or AD 90s) bears the name of the "brother of the Lord," that is, the pillar of the Jerusalem church who was martyred in AD 62. This James, identified in Mark 6:3, was influential at the Council of Jerusalem (Acts 15:13–21), was known by Paul (Gal 2:9), and remained the leader of the Jerusalem church years later (Acts 21:17–26). In actuality, the author of the letter is unknown. Interestingly, the first verse of the letter does not identify the author as the "brother" or "relative" of the Lord, but as "a slave of God and of the Lord Jesus Christ" (Jas 1:1).

Because the Letter of James lacks the proper greeting, thanksgiving, body, and concluding formulas of the traditional Greek letters, it really resembles an epistle or sermon more than a letter. For example, James 2:1–5:11 is organized to offer moral encouragement to the readers who are identified as "the twelve tribes in the Diaspora" (Jas 1:1). Curiously, the name of Jesus is mentioned only twice in the Letter of James. A focus of this letter is not so much on the role of Christ, but on the response of the believer. It also gives much practical, Christ-inspired advice and encouragement on themes of Christian living, for example, how to handle temptation, how to control the tongue, love of neighbor, the power of prayer, and the anointing of the sick.

Themes in James

The Letter of James begins with a series of wise sayings that invite the believer to an active life, responding both to trials and blessings with faith. The letter calls for us to avoid evil and choose good, while always acknowledging that God, the giver of all goodness and blessing, will both hear and answer our prayer (Jas 1:2–27). The author returns to a number of the themes from this opening chapter later in the letter.

One of the main themes of the letter is God's preferential love for the poor (Jas 2:5) and the need for rich people to care for the poor. As the letter states, the measure of true religion is "to care for orphans and widows in their affliction and to keep oneself unstained by the world" (Jas 2:7). The teachings in the Letter of James coincide with Jesus' special concern for the poor, recognizing that they were blessed (Lk 6:20), and the harder biblical teaching that the rich would be toppled from their place of prestige and affluence (Mt 19:21–24; Lk 1:52–53; 6:24–25). James 2:19 shares a short parable comparing the treatment of a rich, well-dressed man in the synagogue to what might be offered to a poor man.

The comparison of rich to poor is mentioned again in James 5:1–6. The author notes that much wealth is obtained by cheating the poor of their wages. The trouble for those who get rich in this manner is not simply that they can't take their wealth with them when they die, but that their unjustly obtained wealth will cry out in testimony against them: "your gold and silver have corroded, and that corrosion will be a testimony against you; it will devour your flesh like fire" (Jas 5:3). The teachings of this letter make up an important part of the Church's social teaching. The *Catechism of the Catholic Church* teaches:

Those who are oppressed by poverty are the object of a *preferential love* on the part of the Church which, since her origin and in spite of the failings of many of her members, has not ceased to work for their relief, defense, and liberation through numerous works of charity. (*CCC*, 2448)

Related to the care of the poor is another main theme of the Letter of James: the requirement of good works in addition to faith. St. Paul very clearly recognized and taught that a person would be judged according to his or her good works (Rom 2:6–10). He also taught that we didn't *earn* Salvation through those works. Only Jesus, as both God and man, in the events of his Passion, Death, and Resurrection, has earned our Salvation. Faith is the response that is critical to our acceptance of the Salvation that Jesus earned for us. Some misunderstood this teaching, believing that faith meant only some kind of mental assent to God. As a result, they believed they didn't need to do good works "in order to be saved." To draw this conclusion they had to ignore both Paul's own teaching (Rom 2:6–10) and Jesus' teaching as well (see, for example, Mt 25:31–46). Rather, in our personal faith we submit our intellect and wills to God. With our entire being we give assent to God the revealer. The Letter of James points out:

> What good is it, my brothers, if someone says he has faith but does not have works? Can that faith save him? If a brother or sister has nothing to wear and has no food for the day, and one of you says to them, "Go in peace, keep warm, and eat well," but you do not give them the necessities of the body, what good is it? So also faith of itself, if it does not have works, is dead. (Jas 2:14–17)

James also taught that it was useless to wish warmth and food for the cold and hungry while doing nothing about it. Mental activity, without physical action, in this regard, is useless. It is the same with faith in God. As proof, he pointed out that demons believe that God exists, but are most definitely *not* saved. As a summary statement on the issue, he concluded, "For just as a body without a spirit is dead, so also faith without works is dead" (Jas 2:26, a point he also made at 2:17, 20).

Another important instruction of the Letter of James is the clear instruction on how the early Church had carried out the Lord's directive (Mt 10:4; Lk 9:2; 10:9) to cure the sick. James instructs the sick to request presbyters, who would pray, lay hands on them in prayer, and anoint them with oil (Jas 5:14–15), as the Twelve Apostles had done (Mk 6:13). Olive oil was used as a healing agent at the time, and was connected by Jews with cures, especially leprosy

(Lv 14:10–29). This practice, which is part of the rite of the Sacrament of Anointing of the Sick, expresses the confidence of the Church that God hears our prayers, and is able to heal the mind, heart, and even the body, according to his will.

Review

1. Why might the letter of James only mention the name of Jesus twice?

2. What does the Letter of James say will happen to those who cheat to acquire their wealth?

3. How does the Letter of James describe faith without good works?

4. What elements of the Sacrament of the Anointing of the Sick are described in the Letter of James?

Reflect

How do you understand the need for good works to accompany your faith?

The First Letter of Peter

This letter was written in very cultivated Greek, the kind of polished style that seems far beyond what was possible for a humble fisherman, so when, in the very first verse, the author is identified as "Peter, an Apostle," our suspicions about the authorship are rightly raised. The closing verses, interestingly, indicate that Silvanus assisted the author in writing this work. Silvanus was mentioned three times in the Pauline letters (2 Cor 1:19; 1 Thes 1:1; 2 Thes 1:1). It is worth considering whether Peter supplied the content, and Silvanus supplied the elegant writing style and vocabulary. Many ancient authors (modern ones too) used such help to improve their documents. The author also sent greetings from Babylon, an early Christian, cryptic way of implying Rome (Rv 14:8; 17:5–6; 18:2–3), the very place where, the early Church believed, Peter ended his life and ministry as a martyr during Nero's persecution, between AD 64 and 70 (1 Pt 5:12). This might argue in favor of accepting Peter as the actual author of the letter. If so, the letter may have been written between AD 60–65.

Also, the First Letter of Peter expresses a theological approach that is very similar to Paul's. One curious possibility is that, since Paul had encountered Peter in a number of circumstances, and perhaps even studied under him (Gal 2:1–9), what is understood as Paul's theology was actually gleaned from Peter. Perhaps Paul learned from Peter either in Jerusalem or Antioch, where they both lived for a time (Acts 11:25–26; Gal 2:11).

More precisely, however, today's scholarship classifies the First Letter of Peter as pseudonymous, written by a disciple of Peter in Rome to some communities in southern Asia Minor, perhaps sometime between AD 70–90. Because the author curiously quotes the Septuagint, or Greek version, of the Bible

and Peter, a native Aramaic speaker, would have been more familiar with the Hebrew edition than the Greek one, a disciple of Peter, perhaps Silvanus, might be responsible for providing the Greek wording of the texts to which the author referred.

Perhaps the strongest evidence, though, that Peter could *not* be responsible for the content of this letter is that there are references to widespread persecution of Christians, something that didn't happen until the time of the Roman emperor Domitian. Since his reign was AD 81–96, it would have been a *very* late date for Peter to have written, as it is presumed that he died much earlier, as above, in Nero's persecution of Christians by AD 70.

The letter was composed to the chosen in the dispersion, or Diaspora, living in Pontus, Galatia, Cappadocia, Asia, and Bithynia. These are names of Roman provinces in the countries known today as Turkey and Syria. Prior to the conquest of this region in the seventh century by Islamic armies, there were thriving Christian communities throughout the Near East.

Themes in 1 Peter

A central theme in the First Letter of Peter is that Jesus is the **Suffering Servant**, the model in whose footsteps the suffering should walk (1 Pt 2:21). The First Letter of Peter also gives the New Testament's clearest teaching on suffering, especially the suffering of innocents.

It is important for those who have come to expect abundance as normal to be aware that the Scriptures do *not* promise an easy life. In fact, 1 Peter emphasizes that it is precisely through working through the difficulties of life that our faith becomes authentic. With that in mind, 1 Peter returns to the theme of suffering repeatedly, especially comforting readers who were estranged from their Gentile neighbors because of religious differences. True believers at any time in history, who try to live a good and moral life, can find themselves misunderstood and even ridiculed by their neighbors. This letter appeals to anyone enduring mockery at the hands of others, especially when trying to do or be right and good. In that case, the letter counsels the readers to see themselves accompanied by the Suffering Jesus (1 Pt 1:6–13).

The message of 1 Peter is not intended to imply that God prefers that people suffer. However, since suffering is a part of the human condition, the letter encourages us to join our own sufferings with those of Christ for the sake of others. The First Letter of Peter also makes many references to Baptism, reinforcing the belief that it was written for converts. The themes of Christian vocation and suffering for Christ are also connected in the following:

> But rejoice to the extent that you share in the sufferings of Christ, so that when his glory is revealed you may also rejoice exultantly. If you are insulted for the name of Christ, blessed are you, for the Spirit of glory and of God rests upon you. (Gal 4:13–14)

The author of 1 Peter recognized the need for providing households with guidance for living in the world, while awaiting the Lord's return. Everyone was to do good works and to behave well, with the hope that good behavior would save others. This meant obeying just authorities and even honoring them (1 Pt 2:12–17).

Review

1. How does the First Letter of Peter raise the possibility that Paul's theology was actually learned from Peter?

2. What is the strongest evidence that Peter did not write 1 Peter?

3. How does the First Letter of Peter encourage people to respond to suffering?

Reflect

How have you incorporated the message of 1 Peter that faith becomes authentic only through working through life's difficulties?

Suffering Servant

A title for Jesus that was foretold in the Book of Isaiah. By his redemptive Death, Jesus fulfilled Isaiah's prophecy.

The Letter of Jude and the Second Letter of Peter

The Letter of Jude and the Second Letter of Peter are treated together because 2 Peter borrows heavily from Jude 1:4–16.

In a minimal way, the Letter of Jude (AD 90–100) can be considered a letter, as it does seem to be addressed to a particular community. It has some of the Greek elements of a letter, including a closing formula. However, the entire work resembles more an epistle or sermon. The names of "Jude" and "Judas" are identical in the original Greek. The name "Jude" was used in English to distinguish this person from Judas Iscariot who betrayed Jesus. Tradition holds that the Judas mentioned as a relative of Jesus (Mt 13:55 and Mk 6:3) was the author of this letter. However, because of doubts to the identity of Jude, it is really another pseudonymous work. The Letter of Jude is hard-hitting: it speaks out strongly against certain outsiders who have come into the Church and who are upsetting faithful Christians by deviating from the apostolic faith and engaging in various acts of immorality, probably sexual in nature.

The Second Letter of Peter is also a pseudonymous work, penned to a general audience, perhaps from Rome to Christians in Asia Minor. Since it incorporates a majority of the Letter of Jude, most scholars believe that the Second Letter of Peter is the last New Testament work written, dated as late as AD 130. Like Jude, 2 Peter is also concerned with Christians who were beginning to distort the true teaching they received. The author—writing as Peter—tells how he heard God's voice at the Transfiguration. Thus, he speaks with authority against false prophets infiltrating the communities to which the letter is addressed. He assures his readers that God will punish these false teachers.

 Reflect

How can you be sure that your life is an authentic witness to the Gospel?

Themes in Jude

The author of Jude considered faith to be a body of belief, handed down from Jesus Christ and passed on through God's holy ones (Jude 1:3–4). Faith is not subject to change, although some "intruders" and "godless persons" (Jude 1:4) were intent on trying to do so. The letter doesn't say what the false teachings were. That doesn't seem to be the point. The essential message for Christians of every generation is that no one is entitled to tamper with the core and eternal truths of the faith.

Jude points out with three examples that God's response to false belief has been severe punishment: the

inhabitants of Sodom and Gomorrah were punished by fire for their evil ways (Jude 7; Gn 19:1–28); the Israelites who couldn't trust God were fated to die in the desert without entering the Promised Land (Jude 5; from Nm 14:1–38); and even angels who disobeyed God were imprisoned for their offenses (Jude 6; Gn 6:1–4, as interpreted by nonbiblical stories found in 1 Enoch 10–13).

The troublemakers that Jude addressed "defile the flesh," like the people of Sodom and Gomorrah; they "scorn leadership," like the Israelites who rebelled against God's plan for them; and they "revile glorious beings," like the angels who abandoned their heavenly life to take on flesh. In essence, these agitators are worse than the examples because they follow *all* their sins, not just one.

Jude shows why remaining true to the faith of the Apostles is important so as to have an objective standard for Christian faith and Christian living, both of which go hand-in-hand. The verses of the Letter of Jude that best represent its major theme also refer to the Blessed Trinity:

> But you, beloved, build yourselves up in your most holy faith; pray in the holy Spirit. Keep yourselves in the love of God and wait for the mercy of our Lord Jesus Christ that leads to eternal life. (Jude 1:20–21)

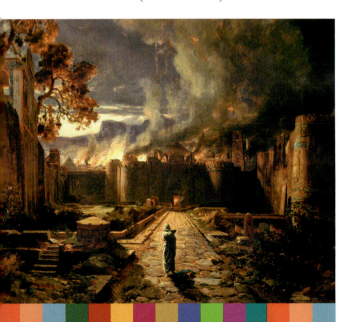

Themes in 2 Peter

The Second Letter of Peter encourages its readers to remain faithful to the true teaching of the Church and to continue to live the Christian life. While advancing in virtue, readers are invited to share in the divine nature of God, through God's glory and power. To do this, we will need to grow in faith, virtue, knowledge, self-control, endurance, devotion, mutual affection and love (2 Pt 1:3–9).

A particular problem, which the author of this letter addresses, are the "scoffers" who, having noted that the Apostles were dying and the Lord had not returned, were beginning to deny the *Parousia*, the return of the Lord, altogether. The letter instructs them that the mercy of God is at work in the delay, giving everyone a chance for repentance:

> But do not ignore this one fact, beloved, that with the Lord one day is like a thousand years and a thousand years like one day. The Lord does not delay his promise, as some regard "delay," but he is patient with you, not wishing that any should perish but that all should come to repentance. (2 Pt 3:8–9)

The homily ends, encouraging readers with a reminder of Paul's teaching, to be ready for the day of the Lord whenever it should come (2 Pt 3:15–18).

◉ Review

1. Why are the Letter of Jude and the Second Letter of Peter often studied and viewed together?

2. What is the essential message of the Letter of Jude?

3. How does 2 Peter address the "scoffers" who had begun to deny the Parousia?

The First, Second, and Third Letters of John

The three Letters of John come from the same tradition established by the author of John's Gospel, repeating his important themes and ideas. All the letters were written sometime after the Gospel of John, perhaps in the late 90s or around the year 100.

The First Letter of John is no doubt the most important of the three letters, though it is missing the elements of a letter, and may be more properly categorized as an epistle. It was written with a sense of urgency to bolster communities threatened by false teachings. The particular brand of Gnosticism that infected the communities for whom the letter was addressed was **Docetism**. In effect, the Docetists denied the Incarnation of Christ. The First Letter of John relentlessly attacks these views throughout the letter. More information about this subject and the themes of all three letters of John follows.

Themes in 1 John

The prologue to the First Letter of John is very similar to the prologue of the Gospel of John, calling to mind the beginning of things and the Logos that comes from the Father. There are also differences between the two prologues. For example, the word "we" is used only twice and "us" only once in the eighteen-verse Gospel prologue.

In the shorter four-verse prologue of 1 John, "we" is used seven times and "us" twice. The focus has clearly shifted slightly off the work of the "Word" to the reception and response of that message by the Johannine community.

A theme common to 1 John and other New Testament writings is that the world is transitory, that is, "passing away," as is evidenced by the presence of **antichrists**. This is a very negative term that occurs only four times in all of Scripture: three times in the First Letter of John, and once in the Second Letter of John. You may have heard the term antichrist used today to describe one person who will rise up against the Church and the world. However, as these four citations attest, there is more than one antichrist: "Who is the liar? Whoever denies that Jesus is the Christ. Whoever denies the Father and the Son, this is the antichrist" (1 Jn 2:22).

The issue surrounding Docetists arose in part from the many Greek philosophical schools that tried to distinguish between what was real and what was illusion. In the ancient world there were many ideas floating around about the need to escape the physical to enter the world of knowledge and ideas. Some early believers went adrift from true Christianity, creating for themselves a fusion between the faith they had received and ideas that encouraged escape from the physical world. Those teaching Docetism claimed to have received special knowledge (in the Greek, *gnosis*) about Jesus and the

Docetism
From the Greek word *dokeo* ("to seem"), it was a heretical belief that Jesus only seemed to be human. In effect, Docetists denied the Incarnation of Jesus.

antichrists
Antichrists are people who deny that Jesus is the Messiah.

Christian life, knowledge they claimed they received from mystical experiences with Christ. If Docetists believed that the body was an illusion, they might conclude either that the only way to be saved was to deny the body, as some apparently did, or that it didn't make any difference what a person did with his or her own body; since it was all an illusion anyway, there could be no sin. For many Docetists, good works done with the body were equally meaningless. This led to a denial of the Incarnation by the Docetists, something that seems to have been addressed very clearly in 1 John:

> Beloved, do not trust every spirit but test the spirits to see whether they belong to God, because many false prophets have gone out into the world. This is how you can know the Spirit of God: every spirit that acknowledges Jesus Christ come in the flesh belongs to God, and every spirit that does not acknowledge Jesus does not belong to God. (1 Jn 4:1–3a)

The First Letter of John relentlessly attacks the Docetist views throughout the letter. God loves us in the midst of our undeserving brokenness and sin, and sent his Son to save us from that condition, motivated only by that love. The desire to embrace his Father's plan for our Salvation inspired Jesus' very life. By his human free will, Christ freely submitted himself to the will of his Father, embracing his Father's redeeming love on our behalf. Anyone who doesn't know or appreciate this side of God can only pretend to actually know God. Likewise, anyone who doesn't, in turn, also love his or her neighbor is not from God (1 Jn 4:1–22). Translated to action, this involves seeing one's neighbor as "another self" (*CCC*, 1931). Further, we are to especially serve those who are disadvantaged for our love of God (Mt 25:4). This was, in no way, a polite suggestion. It was a command from Jesus (Mt 22:39; Mk 12:31; Lv 19:18), which the author of 1 John understood as the key to the whole Law (Rom 13:9; Gal 5:14; Jas 2:8). So 1 John can repeat with assurance, "This is the commandment we have from him: whoever loves God must also love his brother" (4:21).

 Reflect

How have you discovered God's love through loving your neighbor?

Themes in 2 John

The Second Letter of John, a very short work, begins with a traditional opening in the Hellenistic style. It is addressed from the "Presbyter" to "the chosen Lady" and "to her children." The images connect to a particular Christian community with "children" who are its members. Unlike the First Letter of John, this letter addresses a specific problem in the Church and is not intended as a theological sermon. The opening verses of the letter emphasize two themes, truth and love, that were dear to the beloved disciple's teaching (e.g., truth: Jn 1:14; 16:13–17; love: 3:16; 14:21–31) and celebrate that the community (the "Lady's children") walk in that truth (2 John v. 4).

After reminding the recipients to remain rooted in love (vv. 5–6), the same key point of First John, the letter moves to its primary concern. While the Lady's people do not seem to have been influenced, yet, by the troublemaking Gnostics who denied that Jesus had come in the flesh, missionaries representing this false teaching and practice seem to be on their way: (2 Jn 7–9). The Presbyter warns them not to welcome anyone who had gone so far beyond the teachings of Christ that they weren't, in fact, from God at all:

> If anyone comes to you and does not bring this doctrine, do not receive him in your house or even greet him; for whoever greets him shares in his evil works. (2 Jn 10–11)

The letter closes, appropriately, with notice of future contact and greetings.

Themes in 3 John

The Third Letter of John is the shortest letter in the New Testament. It differs from the other two letters of John in that it is addressed to an individual, Gaius, from the Presbyter. The sender has received good news of Gaius's own fidelity (as one of "my children") and Gaius seems to have been one of the Presbyter's converts (vv. 3–4).

The point of the letter is to encourage Gaius to remain helpful to the traveling missionaries. Like Paul (1 Cor 9:14–15), these missionaries were not taking assistance from the Gentiles to whom they preached because it would have made them seem like beggars: "Therefore, we ought to support such persons, so that we may be co-workers in the truth" (3 Jn 8).

The trouble was that another Christian leader, Diotrephes, was behaving poorly, not only failing to respond to letters from the Presbyter and refusing to receive missionaries or help them on their way, but

actually expelling them from the local church. The Presbyter intended to come and expose Diotrephes's bad behavior (3 Jn 9–10).

In the meantime, the Presbyter was sending a fine man, Demetrius to be received by the local church, and was hoping that Gaius would not imitate Diotrephes and would do the right thing by him. As in the Second Letter of John, the author closed with an apology for the short letter and with the hope to see Gaius face to face, sending greetings to the "friends" in the community.

This short letter offers a brief glimpse of the minute details of the early Church, especially how personalities and everyday questions of doctrine and faith played a part in shaping the doctrine and faith of the universal Church both for the current time and for all time.

⊕ Review

1. What are differences between the prologue in the Gospel of John and the prologue in the First Letter of John?

2. How do the First and Second Letters of John define the antichrist?

3. What did the Docetists believe about the body?

4. What does 1 John teach is the key to the entire Law?

5. Who is the Second Letter of John addressed from? Who is it addressed to?

6. What is the specific problem addressed in the Second Letter of John?

7. How is the Third Letter of John different than the other two letters?

⊕ Reflect

What is a question you have about Church life that you have always wanted answered?

The Revelation to John

The Revelation to John (also known as the Book of Revelation or the Apocalypse) is the last book of the biblical canon, written approximately AD 92–96. It is perhaps the least read and most misunderstood, primarily because it is so highly symbolic. While it contains several types of biblical literature, the dominant literary form is apocalyptic writing, which was popular in Jewish circles between 200 BC and AD 200. The Book of Daniel (especially Dn 7–12) is an excellent example of apocalyptic writing from the Old Testament. (The feature "Tracing the Symbols in the Book of Revelation" on pages 296–298 details some of the connections between the Book of Daniel and the Revelation to John.)

The basic message of apocalyptic writing is that God controls history and the outcome of events, not the present evil rulers or the forces of evil. God will usher in a golden age of peace and justice, "a new heaven and a new earth" (Rv 21:1). The glorious outcome is God's pure gift; nothing we do can bring it about. In the meantime, we should patiently endure suffering and live a Christian life.

However, apocalyptic writing couches this simple message in a style that is both highly symbolic and weirdly imaginative, talking about multi-headed dragons and beasts, a Christ-figure with seven horns and seven eyes, and trumpets blasting out plagues on humanity. An ancient scholar said that studying Revelation either finds us crazy or makes us crazy. St. Jerome commented that it contains as many secrets as it does words.

The author of Revelation is a prophet named John. He was exiled to the island of Patmos because he publicly preached the Gospel. John of Patmos is not the same person who wrote the Gospel of John or the letters of John. The author was probably an Aramaic-speaking Jewish Christian who had great command of the Hebrew scriptures, especially the apocalyptic writings. He alludes to the Books of Daniel, Ezekiel, Isaiah, and Zechariah. His Greek is the poorest in the New Testament and, at times, ungrammatical. One theory claims John of Patmos left Palestine at the time of the Jewish revolt of the late 60s and may have settled in Ephesus. His contact with the Ephesus church may have given him some familiarity with the Gospel of John and the Johannine writings.

Themes in the Revelation to John

The prophet John claims that the Lord Jesus sent him visions to unveil what is going to take place in the future—the ultimate victory of God. This unveiling allows us to see things from the heavenly perspective. This message was to be read aloud, most probably in the Sunday liturgies, to reassure those who were suffering

that the Lamb of God has triumphed! Victory is ours. Persevere: "I am coming soon" (Rv 22:20). The first verses of Revelation introduce this theme:

> The revelation of Jesus Christ, which God gave to him, to show his servants what must happen soon. He made it known by sending his angel to his servant John, who gives witness to the word of God and to the testimony of Jesus Christ by reporting what he saw. Blessed is the one who reads aloud and blessed are those who listen to this prophetic message and heed what is written in it, for the appointed time is near. (Rv 1:1–3)

In essence, John pulled back the veil that separated the earth from the very throne room of God in the Heavens, and the presence of Jesus, who had been slain but now lived. While caught up in that experience, he was ordered to write what he experienced and send it on to seven churches (Rv 1:10–20). The Revelation to John is the account of the visions he saw at that time.

Time and again John was summoned back to that throne room to witness the spectacle of the heavenly throng at worship before God in all his glory (Rv 4, 7, 11, 14, 19, 20, 21–22). Seated around God were his servitors, including twenty-four elders, representing the old Israel of the twelve tribes, and the new Israel founded by the Twelve Apostles.

Also there were the four wildly depicted **cherubim** from Ezekiel (Ez 10:22–23). With ecstatic fervor, after the cherubim would sing "Holy, holy holy," the throng before the throne would worship God, crying out:

> Worthy are you, Lord our God,
> to receive glory and honor and
>   power,
> for you created all things;
>   because of your will they came
>   to be and were created." (Rv 4:11)

They also sang of the worthiness of the Lamb who was slain, in essence acknowledging that Jesus, too, was God and worthy of praise (Rv 5:9–14).

Many of the depictions of Heaven seem very liturgical, that is, as intended for public worship. At times they resemble Jewish ritual, with a seven-torch menorah, and other times they are clearly Christian in appearance, with hymn singing (Rv 14:14) and the 144,000 white-robed survivors of the persecution (Rv 14:4–8). The number itself is quite symbolic, since the square of twelve means old Israel and new Israel, the Church, as above. Multiplying that number by one thousand, the final number equates with an all-but-uncountable number of witnesses to the Lamb who was slain. In fact, John saw an innumerable crowd "from every nation, race, people, and tongue" standing before the throne (Rv 7:9). Contrary to

cherubim
Angelic creatures mentioned in the Book of Revelation. They are considered to be a high rank of angels along with seraphim.

some so-called Christian sects who claim otherwise, the number 144,000 represents all God's People and not just a certain number.

All of the elements of John's visions make perfect sense in the world for which he was writing, and the first generation of readers had no trouble figuring out what was meant by them. Various modern commentators who try to suggest modern events and people as the meaning implied by John's visions are severely misguided. John of Patmos wrote the Book of Revelation to wavering Christians of his day to encourage them to remain faithful during times of persecution, false teaching, and complacency. Revelation's second theme for Christians is to remain hopeful. Christ will ultimately vanquish the powers of this world that are persecuting Christians. He has already rescued us from sin and death by his Death and Resurrection. In the coming battle he will conquer for all time the forces of evil: the unholy trinity of Satan (the dragon) and his two minions—the beast of the sea (the emperor) and the beast of the land (the local authority). Rome will fall. Satan will be sent to Hell for all time. And the heavenly city, Jerusalem, will be established for eternity.

That doesn't mean that the Book of Revelation doesn't have meaning for you. You can consider the abuse of power in your own time and recognize that many "Romes," many destructive empires, have risen and fallen since the time of Jesus. The Church has often suffered at their hands. God always triumphs. But that is only part of the message. The messages to the seven churches in Revelation 2–3 are offered with a variety of recognitions, encouragements, and chastisements.

The seven churches were praised for their love and faith, for discerning true Apostles, and for their endurance in not growing weary even when weak or facing martyrdom. They were encouraged not to be afraid of coming suffering, including imprisonment,

and to hold fast in hard times. A few were chastised for not having the love they once had, for tolerating dissenters and tempters among their ranks, and for appearing alive but really being lukewarm in their faith. While persecution did seem to be an occasional problem in some of the churches, only one person, Antipas of Pergamum, had suffered martyrdom (Rv 2:13). A much bigger problem seems to be that not all were as fervent as they once were. Some seem to be more influenced by passions and wealth than by the faith they once had.

This makes sense in light of the social and economic conditions of the Roman Empire. The Romans had cleared the Mediterranean Sea of pirates, opening up sea-going trade. It also built roads, enabling the quick movement of troops to troubled spots in the empire, but *also* enabling the movement of goods and merchandise. With the effective Roman governance,

banditry was reduced and the once frequent wars between the now conquered peoples were almost completely eliminated. Merchants could venture out safely for the very first time in human history to large tracks of the Mediterranean and European regions to carry on their trade. The economy was prosperous. There was a *lot* of money to be made!

People began to speak and write about the *Pax Romana*, the Roman peace, and all the prosperity it brought. It was all very seductive, and, as the letters to the seven churches indicates, some believers were succumbing to worldly ways. It is no surprise that one of the key symbols of the city of Rome, itself, in Revelation is the seductive figure of a person available to engage in sex for hire:

> I saw a woman seated on a scarlet beast that was covered with blasphemous names, with seven heads and ten horns. The woman was wearing purple and scarlet and adorned with gold, precious stones, and pearls. She held in her hand a gold cup that was filled with the abominable and sordid deeds of her harlotry. On her forehead was written a name, which is a mystery, "Babylon the great, the mother of harlots and of the abominations of the earth." I saw that the woman was drunk on the blood of the holy ones and on the blood of the witnesses to Jesus. (Rv 17:3–6)

If the identity of the woman was in doubt to any reader, John clarified that the seven heads represent "the seven hills upon which the woman sat" (Rv 17:9). Rome was known from antiquity as the city of seven hills. Babylon, used by Daniel to represent the abusive rule of Antiochus IV, was now used by John to represent *Rome*, a city of great wealth, hence the gold and precious stones.

One of the most important warnings of the Revelation of John to its readers was for them to not surrender to the allure of wealth. Rome promised much, and carried through for a few who accepted Rome's values and worshipped Roman gods and emperors. But a day of wrath and judgment was coming in which Babylon (Rome) would be judged, convicted, and destroyed. Then what would become of those who had given themselves over to the beast? The prophet John answers:

> The merchants of the earth will weep and mourn for her, because there will be no more markets for their cargo: their cargo of gold, silver, precious stones, and pearls; fine linen, purple silk, and scarlet cloth; fragrant wood of every kind, all articles of ivory and all articles of the most expensive wood, bronze, iron, and marble; cinnamon, spice, incense, myrrh, and frankincense; wine, olive oil, fine flour, and wheat; cattle and sheep, horses and chariots, and slaves, that is, human beings. (Rv 18:11–13)

One of the seeming constants about religion seems to be that the more prosperity there is, the more easily humans convince themselves that they don't really need God. Crises then arise, hearts are broken, and earthquakes, tornadoes, and wildfires destroy. Even for those who escape the above, sickness and old age, and the weakness that accompanies it, set in.

The Book of Revelation would warn you, if you live in affluence, not to forget your God because you have the distractions of things and opportunities in abundance. This world is passing away, and the Lord will come, as taught over and over in the Scriptures, like a thief, unannounced, when you least expect (Rv 3:3; 16:15).

◉ Review

1. Who is the author of the Revelation to John?
2. Who was seated around God in Heaven according to the accounts in Revelation?
3. What does the number 144,000 represent in the Book of Revelation?

TRACING THE SYMBOLS IN THE BOOK OF REVELATION

The style of the Book of Revelation, while fascinating, may seem peculiarly unique to many people. Those who have read the Old Testament extensively, however, know that the book represents an "apocalyptic" genre of literature. In fact, the Book of Revelation (or the Apocalypse) is the most well-known example of this genre. But the origins of apocalyptic writing are much older, finding its roots in the Old Testament Books of Ezekiel and Daniel. (Interestingly, of the 404 verses in the Book of Revelation, 278 allude to Old Testament passages, though there are no direct quotations.) Recall from Chapter 1E that both of those books were written in times of great stress. Ezekiel's prophecies preceded the fall of Judah to Babylon. The Book of Daniel was written while the Jews were experiencing terrible persecution at the hands of the Greek Seleucid kingdom in Syria. Both prophets used very figurative language to communicate to the people of their time.

The original audiences of the Books of Ezekiel and Daniel both understood the meanings of the symbols because they were specifically intended for them. In fact, apocalyptic symbolism only works well when it is read from the perspective of the original writers and readers. For example, the prophet Daniel wisely disguised his appeal to the Jewish people to remain faithful to their religious roots by speaking, not of the Seleucids who were persecuting them at that time, but rather of the captivity in Babylon three hundred years earlier. His readers saw through his clever ruse and knew he wasn't writing about either the past or the future. They easily recognized that he was *really* talking about King Antiochus IV of Syria. It would have been foolish of the author of Daniel to write a scroll that spoke ill of Antiochus and called him by name. In fact, doing so would have meant death for both the writer *and* the possessor. For that reason, Daniel disguised his message in cryptic, hidden language.

Consider the example in Daniel 7 of Daniel having a vision at night of the sea. The sea itself was terrifying to the ancients—chaotic and uncontrollable. Out of the sea in Daniel's vision rose four terrible beasts: "The first was like a lion, but with eagle's wings" (Dn 7:4). The winged lion was an easily identifiable symbol of ancient Babylon. In fact, such beasts were carved with some frequency onto Babylonian architecture. It was safe to use it in Daniel's time because hundreds of years had passed since Babylonian captivity. The next vision was a bear with fierce tusks, a fitting symbol for the rapacious and destructive Median Empire, which gave orders to devour much flesh. Following that came a winged leopard, swiftest of animals, and a suitable representative of the kingdom quickly founded by Cyrus of Persia. These three animals and the ancient kingdoms they represented were not the real point of the vision. It was the next monster, the fourth beast, that really held the key lesson:

> After this, in the visions of the night I saw the fourth beast, different from all the others, terrifying, horrible, and of extraordinary strength; it had great iron teeth with which it devoured and crushed, and what was left it trampled with its feet. I was considering the ten horns it had, when suddenly another, a little horn, sprang out of their midst, and three of the previous horns were torn away to make room for it. This horn had eyes like a man, and a mouth that spoke arrogantly. (Dn 7:7-8)

The ten horns would seemingly be the kings of the Seleucid dynasty, and the little horn was certainly Antiochus the IV (175-163 BC), cleverly disguised.

Daniel's vision, then, shifted its focus to the throne room of God in Heaven, with thousands upon thousands waiting upon the "Ancient One," blazingly glorious on his throne. The fourth beast was condemned, slain, and consigned to the flames, and one like a "son of man" was given authority and power, and an unending kingdom (Dn 7:9-14).

It is important to understand that none of the beasts of Daniel's visions represented future events. The first three all represented events from the past. The fourth beast was a symbol for events that were taking place at present to the composition of the Book of Daniel. Anyone in the age current to the Book of Daniel trying to prophesy future events based on the visions of the lion, bear, leopard, or ten-horned beast would have been misguided in their efforts. The prophecies had *already* come to pass. Daniel's vision was intended to remind his readers that God was really in control, in the Heavens, and that the terrible oppressors would have their own day of judgment. In the meantime, the Jewish people had to remain faithful to their "Ancient One," to their God.

John of Patmos recognized the value of this kind of symbolic writing and borrowed, not only the style of visionary writing, but also the imagery itself from Daniel. Revelation 13 describes a vision in which a horrifying figure comes out of the sea. John's vision contains elements that should be familiar:

> Then I saw a beast come out of the sea with ten horns and seven heads; on its horns were ten diadems, and on its heads blasphemous names. The beast I saw was like a leopard, but it had feet like a bear's, and its mouth was like the mouth of a lion. To it the dragon gave its own power and throne, along with great authority. I saw that one of its heads seemed to have been mortally wounded, but this mortal wound was healed. Fascinated, the whole world followed after the beast. (Rv 13:1-3)

The visionary beast in John's vision was a combination of *all* the beasts of Daniel's vision, incorporating the worst of all of them, and adding new horrifying elements: seven heads, blasphemous names, and mortal wounds.

It doesn't take too much imagination to figure out who this monstrous creature represents, at least if you know the key from the Book of Daniel that the prior beasts all represented oppressive empires of the past. John was writing when the greatest empire of the Western world, Rome, was at the height of its crushing power. Rome had completely swallowed the territories of all the former empires and extended itself into entirely new realms. As far as the people of the Mediterranean world could judge, Rome was the beast that had conquered their known world.

The meaning of the "dragon" as Satan was previously documented in Revelation: "The huge dragon, the ancient serpent, who is called the Devil and Satan, who deceived the whole world, was thrown down to earth, and its angels were throw down with it" (Rv 12:9). The dragon gave its power to the beast—Rome—to wreak his violence upon the world. So if the seven-headed beast represented Rome, the heads themselves almost certainly represented the emperors. It had become fashionable to speak of some of the emperors as divine and even to worship them. Temples in Rome were constructed, priesthoods appointed, and sacrifices were stipulated. Coins were printed with graven images of the emperors and their temples, and words such as *Augustus Divus*—"the divine Augustus." Jews and Christians alike considered these titles blasphemous and the worship of the emperors as idolatrous.

The "mortally wounded" head described in Revelation 13:3 may be a reference to the legend that the Emperor Nero (AD 37-68), a man who had a reputation for terrible violence, having assassinated two wives and his own mother, among others, would come back to life and rule again after his death. Or it could connect to the theory that the Emperor Domitian (AD 81-96) seemed to embody all the cruelty and impiety of Nero and was thus *Nero redivivus* ("Nero reborn")—that is, the head that had been mortally wounded but healed in John's vision. The vision continued with the dragon, Satan, giving his authority to the beast, Rome, for an extended period of time, during which Rome waged war against the holy ones, that is, the early Church

Revelation 13:11-18 describes John's vision of a second beast, a two-horned, lamblike creature with a dragon's voice arising from the earth, mockingly similar to one of the symbols described for Jesus in Revelation 5:6: "a Lamb that seemed to have been slain." This beast forced everyone to be given a stamped image of the beast's name or the number that stood for its name on their hands or foreheads. The number was 666.

The number six, one short of seven, is associated with imperfection. The number 666 is ultimate imperfection, incompleteness, and meaninglessness. Many scholars calculate that it corresponds to Nero. They calculate that when the name Nero(n) Caesar is written in Hebrew letters, its numerical equivalent is 666. The formula for NRWN QSR is 50+200+6+50+100+60+200=666. It was a twice-clever ploy to identify and mock the Roman emperors as a whole in this way because of another connection of the number "7." In the Book of Revelation, there are seven churches receiving the revelation (1:4, 11), seven gold lamp stands (1:12), seven stars (1:16), seven flames representing the seven spirits of God (4:5), and seven seals (5:1, 5; 6:1). There were seven angels bearing seven trumpets before God (6:2, 6), seven thunders that cried out (10:3-4), seven angels with seven plagues, and seven bowls of God's wrath (15:1-16:1; 17:1; 21:9). Most significantly, the Lamb who had been slain, that is, Jesus, had seven horns and seven eyes (5:6). The number seven was clearly identified with God and his servants.

This association didn't go uncontested by the forces of evil, since these many sevens were countered by a seven-headed dragon with seven diadems (12:3; 17:3, 7), and the beast out of the sea with seven heads (13:1), representing the seven hills of Rome and its seven kings (17:9-11). These were the symbols of the emperors, claiming to be gods.

The number *actually* assigned to Caesar Nero, and all his imperial colleagues, though, was 666, the meaning of which is "6" *not* "7," "6" *not* "7," "6" *not* "7." In essence, 666 means "*not* God, *not* God, *not* God." The emperors, with their successes and splendors, may have fooled the world by *appearing* to come close to divinity, but they were simply and absolutely not God!

4. Why did John of Patmos write the Book of Revelation?

5. How did *Pax Romana* lead to a wavering faith among Christians?

6. What does Babylon symbolize in the Book of Revelation?

7. What does the Book of Revelation warn about affluence?

8. How should Revelation 13:1–3 be interpreted?

9. What is the meaning of the mark of the beast, 666?

Reflect

- How have you heard the Book of Revelation incorrectly quoted by someone in modern culture?

- Who are modern "Romes" that bring the Church suffering?

Research and Report

Do one of the following assignments related to the symbols in the Revelation to John:
- Research the origins and meanings of the symbols listed below. Cite other Scripture references and explanations from Jewish, Christian, and other traditions to their meanings.
- Develop an art project around one or more of the symbols in the Book of Revelation. Write a short report to accompany the artwork and share both in a presentation to your classmates.

Symbols in the Book of Revelation

Numbers
- *7* means wholeness or perfection.
- *6*, one short of 7 means, imperfection.
- *3 ½* is half of seven and thus also represents imperfection.
- *12* signifies Israel or the Twelve Apostles.
- *1,000* symbolizes an incalculable amount of eternity.
- *144,000* is a symbol of the new Israel that embraces every nation, race, people, and language.

Colors
- *Black* represents death, unfaithfulness, evil.
- *Red* means violence, killing, the blood of witnesses.
- *White* symbolize purity and victory.

Names and Figures
- *Babylon*, the ancient city that persecuted Jews, stands for the modern persecutor of Christians, Rome.
- A *dragon* represents evil.
- *Four Horses of the Apocalypse*: the white horse symbolizes conquering power, the red horse signifies bloody war, the black horse means famine, and the green horse represents death.
- A *horn* symbolizes power while *eyes* symbolize knowledge. Describing Jesus having seven eyes and seven horns is a symbolic way of saying he is all-powerful and all-knowing.

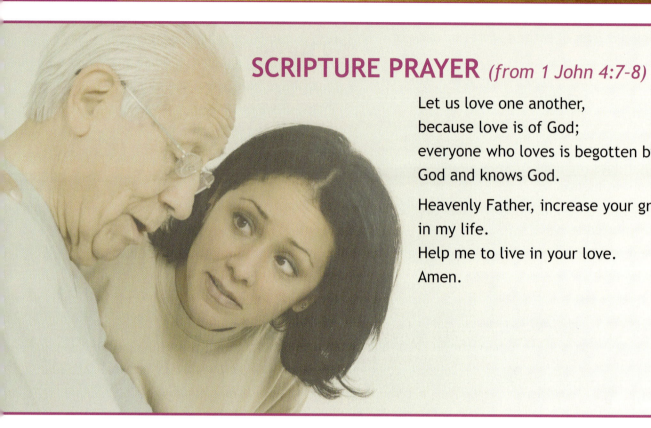

SCRIPTURE PRAYER *(from 1 John 4:7-8)*

Let us love one another,
because love is of God;
everyone who loves is begotten by
God and knows God.

Heavenly Father, increase your grace
in my life.
Help me to live in your love.
Amen.

2D

NEW TESTAMENT
REVIEW

● Final Reflections

The heart of all Scripture is the Gospels, the Good News of Jesus Christ.

● Jesus Is the New Covenant

The New Covenant of Jesus Christ was signed and sealed in the events of his Paschal Mystery.

Final Reflections

The twenty-seven books of the New Testament are divided into three categories the Gospels, the letters written to local Christian communities or individuals, and the letters intended for the entire Church. The interesting Revelation to John, the last book of the Bible, reminds us that the Lord is in control of history and that good will conquer over evil.

The heart of the New Testament, in fact of all Scripture, is the Gospels. The New Testament is central to our knowledge of Jesus Christ. He is the focus of all Scripture.

Jesus Is the New Covenant

Jesus fulfilled the Law of the Old Testament by giving a New Law of love that requires us to look to our interior motives as well as our external behavior. He taught that God's covenant love extends not only to a Chosen People, but to all people everywhere.

Jesus fulfilled the prophets. He was the perfect prophet who spoke for God because he was God's own Son. His words and actions showed that God was actively present in the world: saving, redeeming, and healing people. Jesus proclaimed the coming of God's reign and showed in his words and actions that the Kingdom of God was alive in the world.

Jesus' life and ministry reveal him as the fulfillment of the prophet's hope for a Servant-Messiah. His message of complete trust in God, his healing of the sick, and his compassion toward sinners bring completion to the prophets of the Old Testament.

Finally, Jesus is God's New Covenant. This covenant was signed and sealed in the events of his Paschal Mystery—his saving life, Passion, Death, Resurrection, and glorious Ascension. This Paschal Mystery is the ultimate expression of God's fidelity to the covenant.

The New Testament continues and fulfills the Old Testament; it does not contradict the Old Testament. The New Testament reveals that God has extended his loving-kindness and his Salvation to all people. Jesus is the New Covenant. The books of the New Testament tell his story and what our relationship with him should be like.

🌀 Reflect

Write the names of the twenty-seven books of the New Testament by heart. See if you can group them into the following categories: Gospels, the New Testament Letters, and Catholic Letters.

HOW TO READ AND PRAY WITH THE BIBLE

Defining Bible Scholarship

While it is a worthwhile academic task to gain knowledge about the Bible, the best thing about becoming a "Bible scholar" is simply that you get to meet God in your studies. It is refreshing to think of your studies as a personal "Temple" where you can open yourself to not only new thoughts but also new insights. The goal is to give God the "raw materials" of your careful thoughts and studies in order to allow him to speak through them. Furthermore, no question is off limits. Study is not true to yourself if you avoid hard questions. Often it is the hard questions that most challenge you to think, read, and be open to the guidance of God.

The only rule of asking hard questions is: Don't ask if you aren't prepared to think through the possible responses. A common problem for some students

who study the Bible is that they believe just asking the question is impressive. That is only part of the task, however. Once you ask the question, you must think it through and work toward some kind of response, even if the response ends up with: "I'm not sure, but it was well worth thinking this through!"

It is true that studying the Bible, on the one hand, and using the Bible for personal prayer, on the other hand, may not always be the same thing. It is possible, however, to engage in both tasks without seeing them as conflicting with each other. There are many Catholics and other Christians who believe that serious study of the Bible actually *prevents* them from personal prayer and devotional study with the Bible. This should not be the case because it suggests that Christians can't be allowed to know very much about the Bible or it will disturb their prayers. Perhaps a better point of view is this: The more you know and study the Bible, the more informed are your prayers! As the Pontifical Biblical Commission's study "The Interpretation of the Bible in the Church" begins: "The study of the Bible is . . . the soul of theology." Let's explore some of these ideas further.

One form of Bible study involves private study and prayer. This is what you do on your own—with your Bible and other helpful resources in a private and quiet place where you are free to engage in open thought and contemplation. But this is by no means the *only* form of academic or devotional study of the Bible, though it is definitely *one* form. There are a number of things that can help you in this endeavor.

Review

What is the only rule of asking hard questions for Bible study?

Reflect

What is your reaction to the statement "The more you know and study the Bible, the more informed are your prayers"?

Helps for Private Bible Study

To begin, you need your own Bible. Make sure that you have the latest edition of a good translation—for example, *The New American Bible*, *The New Revised Standard Version*, or *The New Jerusalem Bible*. It is not a bad idea to have more than one edition and to compare the readings between them. Translation, after all, is partly an art as well as a science, and opinions may vary even among biblical scholars on questions of how to best render the meaning of a foreign word or phrase into English. Furthermore, do *not* study with a treasured "Old Family Bible." You need a copy of the Bible that you can write in. In fact, write all over it! Write notes in the margins, at the bottom of the page, everywhere you have questions or have interesting observations. If you have a Bible that is an old heirloom, keep it as an heirloom and not as a Study Bible. A Bible that is heavily written on, pages filled with notes, is a wonderful sight. It is a Bible that is being read and used and studied. Get over the idea that you "shouldn't write" in the Bible. Nonsense. This is a book to be read and studied, not admired from a distance!

However, Bible study is, as you have gathered from working through this book, not a simple matter of reading. Reading the Bible is the beginning, not the end, of serious study of the Bible. Like studying any subject, being serious about Bible study means investing in some assistance. The minimum helps for serious Bible study are:

- A Bible Dictionary
- A One-Volume Bible Commentary
- A Bible Concordance

Bible Dictionary

A Bible Dictionary is a tremendously important resource. In a Bible Dictionary, you can look up names of characters in the Bible, names of cities or villages, and even important events. Most good dictionaries also have sets of maps so that you usually do not need a separate Bible Atlas (although these can be useful if you have a particular interest in geographical issues related to the Bible).

There are some Bible Dictionaries that are actually virtual encyclopedias and are very expensive. The *Anchor Bible Dictionary*, for example, is a six-volume set that sells for over $500. While such a set would be a worthwhile investment and would give you a great deal of critically important information, it is far beyond a mere Bible Dictionary. There are many other dictionaries, such as the *HarperCollins Bible Dictionary* or the *Eerdmans Dictionary of the Bible,* that are single-volume projects.

Bible Commentary

A Bible Commentary is also an important resource to know about. A Bible Commentary is a scholarly work that systematically works through every verse of a book of the Bible. A good commentary can be a very helpful companion. The advantage is that the Bible Commentary is "following you" through the Bible, and you can go from the Bible reading, over to the commentary, and the commentary will be talking about precisely the verse you are working on.

Start with a good one-volume Bible Commentary. Obviously, if you are purchasing a one-volume commentary on the entire Bible, you are not going to get very extensive comments on the verses you are studying, but it will give you some helpful ideas as you read along. Excellent one-volume commentaries are:

- *The New Jerome Bible Commentary* (Prentice Hall)
- *The Oxford Bible Commentary* (Oxford University Press)
- *The International Bible Commentary: A Catholic and Ecumenical Commentary for the Twenty-First Century* (Liturgical Press)
- *The Collegeville Bible Commentary* (Liturgical Press)
- *The Global Bible Commentary* (Abingdon Press)

If you want more extensive discussions of the verses or books of the Bible that you are working with, then you need to move toward multi-volume commentaries that are entire sets of books. They typically feature an individual scholar's works on individual books of the Bible. Some commentaries even feature more than one volume on a single book of the Bible. For example, Professor Claus Westermann wrote three volumes on the Book of Genesis, and Fr. Raymond Brown famously wrote two large volumes on the Gospel of John. Some of the most significant commentary series include:

- *Sacra Pagina* (New Testament; Michael Glazier Publisher)
- *Berit Olam* (Old Testament; Michael Glazier Publisher)
- *The Collegeville Bible Commentary* (Liturgical Press)

- *The Old Testament Library* (Westminster/John Knox Press)
- *The New Interpreter's Bible Commentary* (Abingdon Books)
- *The Anchor Bible Commentary* (Now called *Yale Anchor Bible Commentary*; Yale University Press)
- *The Hermeneia Commentary* (Fortress Press)
- *The Word Bible Commentary* (Word Books)
- *Interpretation* (John Knox Press)

While it is true that whole sets of commentaries may look really nice on your bookshelf, they represent a very serious investment of money, and therefore the average serious Bible student can simply access these books at a public or university library. Catholic high schools, however, may want to seriously consider many of these sets as wise investments to encourage Bible study among advanced high school students.

Review

1. Why should you not study with an "Old Family Bible"?
2. What are the minimum helps for Bible study?

Before Using a Commentary

Before consulting a commentary, however, make sure that you have read through the passage a number of times, and have asked yourself the following kinds of questions:

1. What book is this passage in? Do I have a good sense of when this was written or at least the time period that it is talking about?
2. What kind of literature is this? Is it poetry? Is it a speech? Is it a story?
3. What is the context? What comes before and after, and how does this help me to understand what is happening?
4. Are there any words that I do not understand? Have I looked up any confusing names or words in a Bible Dictionary?

There is lots of debate between scholars, and between students, about whether you should read the Bible itself a few times *before* reading any commentaries, or whether you can go back and forth between the Bible and the commentary. Frankly, either way is appropriate as long as you are comfortable with the biblical passage itself.

One additional message: *Stay off the Internet*. The Internet is *not* a good source of information for Bible study, other than possibly using it as a dictionary for names of cities and definitions of some terms. Why? Because *anybody* can write on the Internet—no matter their lack of qualifications. There is some pretty strange stuff on the Internet. Read it for entertainment if you wish, but not serious study. Nothing takes the place of a good library.

Sometimes the commentaries like those suggested in this section are online in electronic form. That is quite a different matter. If you *know* what the source is, that is fine. If you are just "surfing the Net," then be very careful.

Going Further: Asking the Harder Questions

After you have covered the basics of reading a Bible passage (e.g., What book is it in? What is the immediate context? What kind of writing is this? What difference does it make to answer these first questions?), then move to more probing questions. Ask things like:

- How do I know that this happened this way?

- Would I have said the same kinds of things that the characters in the passage are saying?

- How would I have reacted differently to the situation?

Think about your own life context. In what way does your cultural background suggest other ways of thinking about these issues raised by what you are reading? If your background is from a particular nationality or culture, how might this story be read differently if it was set in a more familiar cultural context—how would you react differently? Or would your reaction be similar? Also ask questions about the setting of this passage.

Even more interesting is to consider questions that probe beyond what was written in the passage. For example:

- Who are we *not* hearing in this passage?

- Are there women in the scene who are not speaking? Why or why not?

- Are there social or economic issues being raised by the text I am reading? For example, have I considered the political context of Jesus speaking to a Roman centurion in Matthew 8 (there was potential danger of speaking to a man of such authority).

Don't forget, Bible study is only as good as the questions we are willing to ask; the more difficult the question, the more we may experience an interesting response that we have not considered before. Do not be afraid to raise questions related to your own background and cultural context. After all, one of the most important things that Church leaders and biblical scholars have come to understand in recent years is that all Bible reading involves an interaction between the words of the Bible and a *reader*! All readers of the Bible have a cultural context—nobody reads the Bible without assumptions, experiences, and backgrounds.

Review

1. Why is the Internet not a good source for Bible study?

2. What does it mean to say that all readers of the Bible come with a cultural context?

Reflect

- Rate and explain your motivation for continuing Bible study.

- When studying the Bible, which do you prefer reading first: the Bible passage or the commentary on the Bible passage? Why?

- What are some "probing" personal questions you have about the Bible?

Tips for Group Prayer and Study

Bible study should never be undertaken completely alone all of the time. In other words, serious Bible study also belongs in the Church as part of our common life together as the People of God. While you could spend many hours in private study, it is also important to share the Bible with others. It is in groups that you have the ability to share your insights, your questions, and your wondering. However, many people are afraid of gathering a group for Bible study if a leader with some experience is not available to help the group. If you do not have someone willing to lead a Bible study, don't be discouraged. There are ways that you can work around this problem and still maintain a workable, rewarding group Bible study.

If you do not have a leader, you should turn to Bible study workbooks and programs to help you. The Catholic Church has a number of such programs available (e.g., *The Little Rock Bible Study* or the *Collegeville Bible Commentary*, both from Liturgical Press). Programs of this kind are for serious groups who want to gather and study the Bible together. There are workbooks, guidebooks, and suggestions for group discussion.

However, you need to be careful here. There are lots of Bible study programs available, but many are of questionable quality and some have a particular religious or even political agenda. Be careful to know the denominational background of any Bible study material you are considering. Is it Catholic or Protestant? A Catholic-based Bible study ought to be familiar with a statement issued by the Pontifical Biblical Commission, titled "The Interpretation of the Bible in the Church" (available in the January 6, 1994, edition of *Origins*). This is a powerful and helpful statement about the serious study of the Bible, and reading it through can be a very helpful exercise for a group wanting to start a serious Bible study. Also, if you have materials that discourage some kinds of questions, or insist that each member of the Bible study agree on certain points, then you should question the appropriateness of the program for you. Bible study should always be open to questions and dialogue.

Review

1. Why is it important to undertake serious Bible study with others?

2. What are some ways to work around not having a leader for Bible study?

Scripture Study Guided by the Church

All Catholics can join in the process of understanding the meaning of Scripture. It is an ongoing exercise of prayerful dialogue and study. Each succeeding generation raises questions about the Scriptures and keeps the dialogue going. In 1943 Pope Pius XII issued his encyclical *Divino afflante Spiritu* ("Inspired by the Divine Spirit") to promote biblical scholarship. Later, the Preface to the Pontifical Biblical Commission document promoted the study of the Bible and stated that it "is never finished; each age must in its own way newly seek to understand the sacred books."

In order for us to interpret Scripture correctly, we must pay attention to both what the human author wanted to say and what the Holy Spirit intended to communicate. To find out the human author's intentions, we must take into account the time and culture, the literary forms of the time, and the manner of speaking and thinking that was current then. Since Scripture is inspired, they "must be read and interpreted in the light by the same Spirit by whom it was written" (*Dei Verbum*, 12 § 3). The Second Vatican Council offered three criteria for interpreting Scripture in the light of the Holy Spirit:

1. Look closely at the content and unity of the whole Scripture.
2. Read the Scripture within "the living Tradition of the whole Church."
3. Be attentive to the analogy of faith. This means the unity of the truths of faith among themselves and within the whole context of God' Revelation.

Our understanding and wisdom of the Scriptures increases over time. And a compassionate God has not abandoned us *only* to the words in the Scriptures. The Holy Spirit continues to lead us through the Church. Recall that the Church teaches that there are two senses of Scripture: the literal and spiritual.

The *literal sense* of Scripture is foundational. It refers to what the actual words directly mean, either in a precise sense (e.g., the narrative of the Passion) or in a figurative sense (e.g., a metaphor or parable).

The *spiritual sense* refers to how the words of Scripture can be signs of something more profound. Understanding the Bible in this way is important for a student of the Old Testament. The spiritual sense has three parts. The allegorical sense helps us understand how some of the events of the Old Testament prefigure Christ; for example, the crossing of the Red Sea symbolizes Christ's victory over death. The moral sense teaches us how to act in a right way; for example, that Abraham's faith obliges us to believe in Christ. The anagogical sense (from a Greek word for "leading") helps us to relate what the events of Scripture have to do with our final destiny—Heaven.

It is the task of those who study the Bible to work according to these rules toward a better understanding and explanation of the Scripture. The Magisterium of the Church is ultimately responsible for "watching over and interpreting the Word of God" (*Dei Verbum*, § 3).

Praying with the Bible

Finally, it is essential to conclude your study of the Bible with a reminder that the Bible is primarily a book of prayer. While acknowledging that Bible study and prayer are not different, let's conclude by examining a traditional way to pray using Scripture (and other spiritual materials) called *lectio divina*, which literally means "divine reading."

You can also think of lectio divina as "prayerful reading." St. Benedict of Nursia in the sixth century left instructions in his Rule of St. Benedict for doing divine reading. His instructions can be divided into three steps:

- The first step, lectio, involves selecting a spiritual reading, in this case Scripture. Once you select a passage, you are to read the passage until a verse or phrase strikes you. At this point you are to stop and begin your meditation.

- The second step, meditatio (meditation), asks you to pause and to let the meaning sink into your mind and heart. Mentally repeat the words over and over again. Let them become part of you. Appreciate what they are saying. After spending some time pondering the meaning of the words, you turn to the prayer.

- The third step, oratio, is from the Latin word for prayer. In this step, you speak to God about the phrase, or simply sit in God's presence and let him speak to you. When you find that you have exhausted your prayer, or when you become distracted, return to the passage again and begin to read until you come to another phrase that seems to be speaking directly to you. Then continue the process as before.

Prayer is the key ingredient to grow in friendship with Jesus. The Bible is the source for prayer. Studying the Scripture is an exercise in knowing God, and adding the element of prayer is helpful for meeting the Lord and knowing him intimately.

Review

What are the three steps of lectio divina?

Report

Choose and complete both of the following assignments:

- Locate an "Old Family Bible." Interview family members to find out its history (how old it is, the occasion for when it was purchased, its place of origin). Also, ask older family members (born before 1960) what they remember learning about the Bible when they were in school or religious education programs. Write up your findings in a short report.
- Purchase a "Study Bible" if you haven't already done so. From information you have gleaned in this course, write at least five new significant margin notes for any of the books of the Old Testament or New Testament.

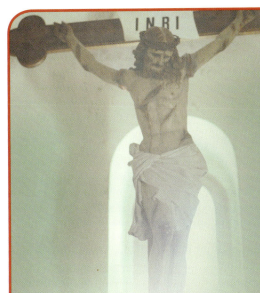

SCRIPTURE PRAYER *(from John 3:16)*

For God so loved the world that he gave his only Son, so that everyone who believes in him might not perish but might have eternal life.

Alleluia!
Alleluia!
Alleluia!
Amen.

CATHOLIC HANDBOOK FOR FAITH

Catechism of the Catholic Church References to Sacred Scripture

Christ—The Unique Word of Sacred Scripture (CCC, 101-104)

- The Scriptures are the Word of God expressed in human language.
- The Scriptures reveal the Word of God, Jesus Christ, who became man and like us in everything but sin. St. Augustine wrote:

  You recall that one and the same Word of God extends throughout Scripture, that it is one and the same Utterance that resounds in the mouths of all the sacred writers, since he who was in the beginning god with God has no need of separate syllables; for he is not subject to time.

- The Church constantly finds her nourishment and strength in Sacred Scripture.

Inspiration and Truth of Sacred Scripture (CCC, 105-108)

- God is the true author of the Sacred Scriptures, both the Old and New Testaments. In other words,

the Holy Spirit inspired the human authors of the Bible. Inspiration, therefore, refers to the Holy Spirit teaching truth through the Bible without destroying the free and personal activity of the human writer. We must read and interpret the Bible inspired by the same Spirit who wrote it:

In composing the sacred books, God chose men and while employed by him they made use of their powers and abilities, so that with him acting in them and through them, they, as true authors, consigned to writing everything and only those things which he wanted. (*Constitution on Divine Revelation*)

The Holy Spirit, Interpreter of Scripture (CCC, 109-114)

- "Sacred Scripture must be read and interpreted in light of the same Spirit by whom it was written" (*Dei Verbum*, 3). How is this done? In reading the Bible special attention must be given to three modes of study:

1. Pay attention to the Bible as a whole, not just individual passages or even books. The entire Scripture presents God's plan, with Christ at the center of it.
2. Read the Bible in light of the living Tradition of the Church. The Scripture is written and remains alive because it is interpreted by

the Holy Spirit through the Church. Scripture must be read from the perspective of the Church rather than individualistically—that is, you must consider what the Church says about its meaning.

3. Be attentive to the analogy of faith. This means the unity and consistency of the truths of faith among themselves and within the whole plan of God's Revelation.

The Senses of Scripture (CCC, 115-119)

*   The Church reminds us that there are two senses of Scripture: the literal and the spiritual (which has three divisions; see *CCC*, 117).

The *literal sense* is foundational. It refers to what the words of Scripture actually mean, using sound rules for interpretation.

The *spiritual sense* refers to how the texts, realities, and events in the Bible can be signs. The *allegorical sense* helps us understand how some event of the Old Testament prefigures Christ, for example, the crossing of the Red Sea symbolizes Christ's victory over death. The *moral sense* refers to how the events in Scripture can help us act justly. The *anagogical sense* (from the Greek word for "leading") helps us see how events lead us to our final destiny—Heaven. For example, the Church on earth is a sign of the heavenly Jerusalem. Given this background on how the Church interprets Scripture, we can turn to uncovering more about the subcategories of the historical-literary method.

The Canon of Scripture (CCC, 120-130)

The Old Testament

The Pentateuch

Genesis	Gn
Exodus	Ex
Leviticus	Lv
Numbers	Nm
Deuteronomy	Dt

The Historical Books

Joshua	Jos
Judges	Jgs
Ruth	Ru
1 Samuel	1 Sm
2 Samuel	2 Sm
1 Kings	1 Kgs
2 Kings	2 Kgs
1 Chronicles	1 Chr
2 Chronicles	2 Chr
Ezra	Ezr
Nehemiah	Neh
Tobit	Tb
Judith	Jdt
Esther	Est
1 Maccabees	1 Mc
2 Maccabees	2 Mc

The Wisdom Books

Job	Jb
Psalms	Ps(s)
Proverbs	Prv
Ecclesiastes	Eccl
Song of Songs	Sg
Wisdom	Wis
Sirach	Sir

The Prophetic Books

Isaiah	Is
Jeremiah	Jer
Lamentations	Lam
Baruch	Bar
Ezekiel	Ez
Daniel	Dn
Hosea	Hos
Joel	Jl
Amos	Am
Obadiah	Ob
Jonah	Jon
Micah	Mi
Nahum	Na
Habakkuk	Hb
Zephaniah	Zep
Haggai	Hg
Zechariah	Zec
Malachi	Mal

The New Testament

The Gospels

Matthew	Mt
Mark	Mk
Luke	Lk
John	Jn
Acts of the Apostles	Acts

The New Testament Letters

Romans	Rom
1 Corinthians	1 Cor
2 Corinthians	2 Cor
Galatians	Gal
Ephesians	Eph
Philippians	Phil
Colossians	Col
1 Thessalonians	1 Thes
2 Thessalonians	2 Thes
1 Timothy	1 Tm
2 Timothy	2 Tm
Titus	Ti
Philemon	Phlm
Hebrews	Heb

The Catholic Letters

James	Jas
1 Peter	1 Pt
2 Peter	2 Pt
1 John	1 Jn
2 John	2 Jn
3 John	3 Jn
Jude	Jude
Revelation	Rv

How to Locate a Scripture Passage

Example: 2 Tm 3:16–17

1. Determine the name of the book.

   The abbreviation "2 Tm" stands for the Second Letter to Timothy.

2. Determine whether the book is in the Old Testament or New Testament.

   The Second Letter to Timothy is one of the New Testament Letters.

3. Locate the chapter where the passage occurs.

   The first number before the colon—"3"—indicates the chapter. Chapters in the Bible are set off by the larger numbers that divide a book.

4. Locate the verses of the passage.

   The numbers after the colon indicate the verses referred to. In this case, verses 16 and 17 of chapter 3.

5. Read the passage.

   For example: "All Scripture is inspired by God and is useful for teaching, for refutation, for correction, and for training in righteousness, so that one who belongs to God may be competent, equipped for every good work."

Relationship between Scripture and Tradition

The Church does not derive the revealed truths of God from the holy Scriptures alone. The Sacred Tradition hands on God's Word, first given to the Apostles by the Lord and the Holy Spirit, to the successors of the Apostles (the bishops and the pope). Enlightened by the Holy Spirit, these successors faithfully preserve, explain, and spread it to the ends of the earth. Pope John Paul II taught that the Holy Spirit is "the principal agent of the whole of the Church's mission" (quoted in *CCC*, 852). As the Church's mission proceeds, it unfolds the mission of Christ. The Second Vatican Council Fathers explained the relationship between Sacred Scripture and Sacred Tradition, and how this task of the Church is completed:

> It is clear therefore that, in the supremely wise arrangement of God, Sacred Tradition, Sacred Scripture, and the Magisterium of the Church are so connected and associated that one of them cannot stand without the others. Working together, each in its own way, under the action of the one Holy Spirit, they all contribute effectively to the salvation of souls. (*Dei Verbum,* 10)

Relevant Church Teaching on Reading and Studying Scripture

If one carefully reads the Scriptures, he will find there the word on the subject of Christ and the prefiguration of the new calling. He is indeed the hidden treasure in the field—the field in fact is the world—but in truth, the hidden treasure in the Scriptures is Christ. Because he is designed by types and words that humanly are not possible to understand before the accomplishment of all things, that is, Christ's second coming.

—St. Irenaeus (second century AD)

[Christ's words] are not only those which he spoke when he became a man and tabernacled in the flesh; for before that time, Christ, the Word of God, was in Moses and the prophets . . . [their words] were filled with the Spirit of Christ.

—Origen (third century AD)

You recall that one and the same Word of God extends throughout Scripture, that it is one and the same Utterance that resounds in the mouths of all the sacred writers, since he who was in the beginning God with God has no need of separate syllables; for he is not subject to time.

The Scriptures are in fact, in any passage you care to choose, singing of Christ, provided we have ears that are capable of picking out the tune. The Lord opened the minds of the Apostles so that they understood the Scriptures. That he will open our minds too is our prayer.

—St. Augustine of Hippo (fifth century AD)

My dear young friends, I urge you to become familiar with the Bible, and to have it at hand so that it can be your compass pointing out the road to follow. By reading it, you will learn to know Christ. Note what St. Jerome said in this regard: "Ignorance of the Scriptures is ignorance of Christ" (PL 24,17; cf *Dei Verbum*, 25). A time-honored way to study and Savior the Word of God is *lectio divina,* which constitutes a real and veritable spiritual journey marked out in stages. After the *lectio*, which consists of reading and rereading a passage from Sacred Scripture and taking in the main elements, we proceed to *meditatio*. This is a moment of interior reflection in which the soul turns to God and tries to understand what his Word is saying to us today. Then comes *oratio* in which we linger to talk with God directly. Finally we come to *contemplatio*. This helps us to keep our hearts attentive to the presence of Christ whose Word is "a lamp shining in a dark place, until the day dawns and the morning star rises in your hearts" (2 Pet 1:19). Reading, study and meditation of the Word should then flow into a life of consistent fidelity to Christ and his teachings.

St. James tells us: "Be doers of the word, and not merely hearers who deceive themselves. For if any are hearers of the word and not doers, they are like those who look at themselves in a mirror; for they look at themselves and, on going away, immediately forget what they were like. But those who look into the perfect law, the law of liberty, and persevere, being not hearers who forget but doers who act—they will be blessed in their doing" (1:22–25). Those who listen to the Word of God and refer to it always, are constructing their existence on solid foundations. "Everyone then who hears these words of mine and acts on them," Jesus said, "will be like a wise man who built his house on rock" (Mt 7:24). It will not collapse when bad weather comes.

To build your life on Christ, to accept the Word with joy and put its teachings into practice: this, young people of the third millennium, should be your program! There is an urgent need for the emergence of a new generation of Apostles anchored firmly in the Word of Christ, capable of responding to the challenges of our times and prepared to spread the Gospel far and wide. It is this that the Lord asks of you, it is to this that the Church invites you, and it is this that the world—even though it may not be aware of it—expects of you! If Jesus calls you, do not be afraid to respond to him with generosity, especially when he asks you to follow him in the consecrated life or in the priesthood. Do not be afraid; trust in him and you will not be disappointed.

—Pope Benedict XVI (twenty-first century AD)

GLOSSARY

Adonai

The name used to replace YHWH by Jews when reading from the Hebrew scriptures. The name simply means "Lord."

Agape

The word *agape* translates to unconditional and thoughtful love. The Agape feasts described in the New Testament refer to meals shared by Christians prior to celebrating the Eucharist.

anthropomorphic

The attribution of human motivation, characteristics, or behavior to inanimate objects, animals, or natural phenomena.

antichrists

Antichrists are people who deny that Jesus is the Messiah.

anti-Semitism

Unfounded prejudice against the Jewish people.

apocalyptic literature

A highly symbolic style of writing in which hidden truths are revealed within a narrative framework. The revelation is often delivered by an angelic or visionary being.

apocalyptic

From a word meaning "revelation" or "unveiling." Apocalyptic writings, usually written in times of crisis, use highly symbolic language to bolster faith by reassuring believers that the current age, subject to the forces of evil, will end when God intervenes and establishes a divine rule and goodness and peace.

apologetic

The term *apologetic* refers to a branch of theology concerned with proving or defending the truth of Church doctrines.

apostasy

The denial of Christ and the repudiation of the Christian faith by a baptized Christian.

apostolic succession

The handing on of the preaching and authority of the Apostles to their successors, the bishops, through the laying on of hands, as a permanent office in the Church.

Ark of the Covenant

The portable shrine built to hold the tablets on which Moses wrote the Law. It was a sign of God's presence to the Israelites. Solomon built the Temple in Jerusalem to house the ark.

Baal

The Canaanite god of fertility, associated with storms and rain. He was the most prominent of the Canaanite gods and the one most often worshipped by the Israelites.

Bet Av

The basic social unit of Israelite society, a patriarchal household of immediate and extended family members.

call narratives

Stories that describe a person's initial awareness that God wanted him or her to do something specific. The calls of the prophet have five common elements: (1) there is something mysterious and holy about the encounter; (2) God acts first; (3) the prophet resists; (4) God reassures; and (5) God sends the prophet on his or her mission.

cherubim

Angelic creatures mentioned in the Book of Revelation. They are considered to be a high rank of angels along with seraphim.

Christology

The branch of theology that studies the meaning of the person of Jesus Christ.

circumcision

The surgical removal of the male foreskin; it was the physical sign of the covenant between God and Abraham.

civil laws

Laws dealing with the day-to-day issues that arise between people living, in the case of the Israelites, in an agrarian community, such as the consequences when one person's animal injures another person, or when borders between properties are disputed.

covenants

Binding and solemn agreements between human beings or between God and people, holding each to a particular course of action.

Day of Atonement

The Day of Atonement, or Yom Kippur, is the holiest day of the year for Jews. It is a day when Jews ask forgiveness for both communal and personal sins; a person goes directly to the person he or she has offended, if possible, asking forgiveness.

Dead Sea Scrolls

Ancient scrolls containing the oldest known manuscripts of the books of the Old Testament in Hebrew. They were discovered in caves near Qumran on the Dead Sea between 1947 and 1953.

deuterocanonical

A term meaning "second canon." Books included in the Catholic Old Testament but not in Hebrew scriptures. These additions are 1 and 2 Maccabees, Judith, Tobit, Baruch, Sirach, Wisdom, and parts of Esther and Daniel.

Diaspora

A group migration or flight away from the homeland into one or more other countries. The word can also refer to people who have maintained their separate identity (often religious, but occasionally ethnic, racial, or cultural) while living in those other countries after migration.

Didache

A Greek word for "teaching," it refers to the teaching directed to Christians who have accepted the Gospel.

Divine Revelation

The way God communicates knowledge of himself to humankind, a self-communication realized by his actions and words over time, most fully by his sending us his divine Son, Jesus Christ.

Docetism

From the Greek word *dokeo* ("to seem"), it was a heretical belief that Jesus only seemed to be human. In effect, Docetists denied the Incarnation of Jesus.

doctrine

The revealed teachings of Christ which are proclaimed by the Church's Magisterium and which Catholics are obliged to believe.

dogma

A central truth of Revelation that Catholics are obliged to believe.

elders

Mature, usually male, members of the Israelite community who met regularly to rule on specific disputes within the community.

Epic of Gilgamesh

Part of a well-circulated Mesopotamian poem discovered to have been in circulation in the ancient world as early as 2000 BC. While there are similarities to this Epic and the Noah flood story, the biblical story is unique because it shows how God reveals himself to humans and hints to humans' eventual destiny.

epistles

The term *epistle* originates from a Greek word that means "to send a message." In the New Testament, epistles are the name for twenty-one formal letters.

eschatological

A term having to do with the end times or the "last things" (death, resurrection, judgment, Heaven, Hell, Purgatory, everlasting life, etc.)

Essenes

A group of Jews whose resistance to foreign influence took them to the extreme position of living in entirely separate communities in the desert around the Dead Sea. Probably, they were the ones who hid the Dead Sea Scrolls, which were not discovered until the middle of the twentieth century.

Establishment religion

A religion that tends to support the power of the ruling class over the common people. In the case of the Israelite monarchy, it joined YHWH worship with the worship of other Canaanite gods.

ethics

A set of principles of right conduct.

evangelization

To bring the Good News of Jesus Christ to others.

exegesis

A word that means "leading out." Exegesis involves critical explanation or analysis, especially of written text.

Feast of Purim

Also called the "Feast of Lots," it celebrates the victory of the Jews over the Persian "prime minister," Haman, in the fifth century BC. "Lots" refers to the lots Haman randomly drew to determine the day on which he would slaughter the Jews.

Gentiles

A term that means "non-Jews."

Gnostics

A generic term to describe adherents to a variety of pre- and early Christian heresies that taught that Salvation rests on secret knowledge (*gnosis* in Greek).

harlotry

In the Old Testament, this term refers not only to a woman's illicit sexual behavior, but perhaps even more commonly to the practice of worshipping Canaanite gods along with YHWH. Jezebel is referred to as a "harlot" in this sense, not because she was ever unfaithful to Ahab.

hasidim

A Hebrew word meaning "loyal ones." It refers to a group who supported the Maccabees in the military effort against Antiochus IV. They also were probably the core members of the later group known as the Essenes.

Hasmonean Dynasty

Descendants of the Maccabees who ruled in Judea after the ousting of the last of the Syrians in 141 BC until the establishment of Roman authority in 63 BC. John Hyrcanus was the first ruler in this dynasty and ruled until 128 BC.

Hellenistic

Relating to the culture, history, or language of Greece after the death of Alexander the Great in 323 BC.

historical Psalms

A Psalm recounting events from the history of Israel such as the covenant with the patriarchs, the Exodus, or the settling of the Promised Land.

historical-critical method

A method the Church uses for understanding biblical texts in their original setting and for discovering the intention of the original author.

Holy Trinity

The central mystery of the Christian faith. It teaches that there are Three Persons in one God: Father, Son, and Holy Spirit.

homily

A talk that helps the congregation understand more about the Word of God. At Mass, a homily is given by a bishop, priest, or deacon.

Hyksos

A group of non-Egyptians who came to power in Egypt between 1650 and 1500 BC.

idolatry

Worshipping something or someone other than the true God. It is a sin against the First Commandment.

Incarnation

The dogma that God's eternal Son assumed a human nature and became man in Jesus Christ to save us from our sins. The term literally means "taking on human flesh."

John Rylands Greek papyrus

A fragment of John's Gospel, found in Egypt and written on Greek papyrus that dates from around 130 BC. It is the earliest fragment from any New Testament book. It is preserved at the John Rylands University Library in Manchester, England.

Jubilee

Every seventh sabbatical year (every forty-ninth year). In a year of Jubilee, all debts were to be forgiven, and land that had been sold to pay a debt was to be returned to the original family. In this way, the wealth of the entire community was to be redistributed among the poor, preventing unrelieved poverty and large gaps between the rich and poor.

Judah

The name of the southern kingdom after the splitting of the monarchy. It included the territory originally belonging to just two of the twelve tribes, Judah and Benjamin.

Judaizers

A group of first-century Jewish Christians who held that circumcision and observance of Mosaic Law were necessary for Salvation. They imposed these criteria on Gentile converts.

judge

In ancient Israel, one who acted as a temporary military leader, as well as arbiter of disputes within and between tribes. Judges were also expected to remind the people of their responsibility to God.

Kenotic Hymn

Kenotic is a Greek term that means "emptying." The Kenotic Hymn of Philippians 2:5–11 describes Christ's emptying himself in humility to take on our human nature.

kerygma

The core teaching about Jesus Christ as Savior and Lord.

laments

Songs or poems that express grief or mourning.

lectio divina

Literally, "divine reading." This is a prayerful way to read the Bible or other sacred writings.

levirate marriage

The marriage of a widow to a near relative of her deceased husband. The first male child of a levirate marriage would be considered the first legal son of the widow's first husband.

liturgy

A name for the official public worship of the Church. The sacraments and Divine Office constitute the Church's liturgy. Mass is the most important liturgical celebration.

Magisterium

The official teaching office of the Church. The Lord bestowed the right and the power to teach in his name to Peter, the other Apostles, and their successors. The Magisterium is the bishops in communion with the successor of Peter, the Bishop of Rome (Pope).

major prophets

Three of the latter prophets—Isaiah, Jeremiah, and Ezekiel—whose books in the Old Testament are quite lengthy.

Marduk

The main state god of the Babylonians during the reign of Nebuchadnezzar. It was to his temple in the city of Babylon that the Temple furnishings and vessels from the Temple of Solomon were carried following the destruction of the Temple in 587 BC.

martyrdom

From a word that means "witness." It describes those who bear witness to the truth of faith, even unto death. St. Stephen is recognized as the first Christian martyr.

messenger formula

The opening words of a prophetic speech, attributing what follows to God, as in "Thus says the LORD . . ." or "The LORD said . . ."

midrash

Commentaries compiled between AD 400 and 1200 by Jewish rabbis on the Hebrew scriptures.

minor prophets

The twelve prophets of the Old Testament whose recorded sayings are much briefer than those of the major prophets: Hosea, Joel, Amos, Obadiah, Jonah, Micah, Nahum, Habakkuk, Zephaniah, Haggai, Zechariah, and Malachai.

monotheistic

Describes religions that believe there is only one God. Christianity, Judaism, and Islam are the three great monotheistic religions of the world.

"murmurings"

The stories in the Book of Exodus about the complaints against Moses and against God.

Neo-Assyrian Empire

A new empire in the Mesopotamian region that eventually conquered the northern kingdom, sending its ruling class into exile in 722 BC.

oracle

A brief, poetic declaration preceded by the messenger formula, "Thus says the LORD," which establishes it reliably as a message from God.

papyrus

A type of paper made from reeds found in the delta of the Nile River and in parts of Italy.

parables

A typical teaching device Jesus used. They are vivid picture stories drawn from ordinary life that convey religious truth, usually related to some aspect of God's Kingdom. They tease the listener to think and make choices about accepting the Good News of God's reign.

parallelism

A characteristic common to Hebrew poetry in which two lines express the same or opposite thoughts, one right after the other.

Parousia

The Second Coming of Christ, which will usher in the full establishment of God's Kingdom on earth as it is in Heaven.

Paschal Mystery

The saving love of God most fully revealed in the life and especially the Passion, Death, Resurrection, and glorious Ascension of his Son, Jesus Christ.

patriarchs

Male rulers, elders, or leaders. The patriarchs of the faith of Israel are Abraham, Isaac, and Jacob.

Pentecost

The day when the Holy Spirit descended on the Apostles and gave them the power to preach with conviction the message that Jesus is risen and is Lord of the universe.

Pharisees

A group of Jews whose response to foreign rule was one of cultural and religious separatism. They valued adherence to the Law, and exhibited great respect for teachers and interpreters of the Torah. They were responsible for the introduction of rabbis and synagogues into the cultural life of the Jews.

presbyters

A term that means "priest." A presbyter is a mediator between God and humans. Jesus is the High Priest *par excellence*. As God-made-man, he bridges both Heaven and earth, bringing God to humanity and humanity to God.

procurator

A person charged by the Roman empire to manage estates and properties, and to govern minor provinces.

pseudonymous

A work written under a name that is not the name of the person doing the actual writing. It was a common and accepted practice for disciples and admirers of great teachers to write works under their names to extend their legacies.

Ptolemies

The dynasty descending from Ptolemy I, a general under Alexander the Great, that ruled Egypt and Palestine from 320 to 200 BC, when they lost control of the land to the Syrian Empire.

punitive justice

Laws which rely on punishment as a deterrent to criminal activity.

"Q"

An abbreviation for *Quelle* (German for "source"), the name given to hypothetical sources, written and oral, thought to be used by both Matthew and Luke in the composition of their Gospels.

rabbi

The local leader of a community's synagogue, respected for his piety and knowledge of the Law. This is a position that came into being with the establishment of the synagogues by the Pharisees.

rapture

In Scripture, the term *rapture* refers to our mystical union with God, or our final sharing in God's eternal life. For many fundamentalist Christians, the rapture signifies a series of events that will occur at the end of time. The Church has no teaching that corresponds to the fundamentalist view.

religious laws

For the Israelites, laws that govern the actions of the priests, the regulations for sacrifice, and the building and maintenance of the Temple.

remnant

The exiles and former exiles who remained faithful to YHWH during the time of captivity and who are expected to restore Jerusalem.

restorative justice

Laws which are concerned primarily with restoring community after an offense has occurred. The goal is to keep the community together, as the survival of the society depended on everyone fulfilling his or her role.

Sacred Tradition

The living transmission of the Church's Gospel message found in the Church's teaching, life, and worship. It is faithfully preserved, handed on, and interpreted by the Church's Magisterium.

Sadducees

Originally an aristocratic group of wealthy Jews in Jerusalem who favored strict adherence to the letter of the Torah and regarded Temple worship as essential to Jewish life. They denied such doctrines as the Resurrection and the existence of angels because those subjects cannot be found in the Torah.

sage

A sage is a person venerated for his or her experience, judgment, and wisdom.

Septuagint

The oldest, complete edition of the Old Testament, it is a Greek translation of earlier Hebrew texts, probably written in Alexandria during the time of Ptolemaic rule over Palestine. The word itself, *Septuagint*, is Latin for "seventy," which refers to the traditional story that seventy scholars from the Promised Land were brought to Alexandria to accomplish this translation.

Servant Songs

Four songs in the Book of Isaiah that describe a messianic figure, known as the "Servant of God," who is described as bringing righteousness to the world. The Servant Songs are connected with the mission of Jesus.

Showbread

The twelve loaves of bread presented on the altar every Sabbath as an offering to God. The priests consumed the bread at the end of every week. (This is also sometimes spelled "shewbread" but the pronunciation does not change.)

stylus

A sharp, pointed instrument that is used for marking, engraving, or writing.

Suffering Servant

A title for Jesus that was foretold in the Book of Isaiah. By his redemptive Death, Jesus fulfilled Isaiah's prophecy.

synagogue

A meeting place for study and prayer introduced by the Pharisees to foster study of the Law and adherence to the Covenant Code.

Synoptic Gospels

The Gospels of Matthew, Mark, and Luke, which because of their similarities, can be "seen together" in parallel columns and mutually compared.

Tetragrammaton

Greek for "four letters," the term refers to the sacred term YHWH as it appeared in the sacred writings of the Jews.

theologians

Theologians are people who study the nature of God and religious truth. Besides St. Paul, two other great Catholic theologians are St. Augustine of Hippo and St. Thomas Aquinas.

Ugarit

An ancient city of the Canaanites which was discovered in 1928. Many texts were found there, from which scholars have learned a great deal about the Canaanite religion.

Vineyard Song

An important passage of the Book of Isaiah depicting the Chosen People as the vine of God. The image recurs in the New Testament in the words of Jesus and the writings of the Apostle Paul.

Zoroastrianism

The official religion of the Persian Empire, which understood the universe to be caught in a constant struggle between light and darkness. Jewish belief in angels and in Satan's influence can be traced to the influence of this foreign religion.

SUBJECT INDEX

SCRIPTURE INDEX

PHOTO CREDITS